THEORIES OF
MOTIVATION

THEORIES OF
MOTIVATION
FROM MECHANISM TO COGNITION

BERNARD WEINER

University of California at Los Angeles

MARKHAM PUBLISHING COMPANY / Chicago

MARKHAM PSYCHOLOGY SERIES
Howard Leventhal, Advisory Editor

Duke and Frankel, *Inside Psychotherapy*
Moscovici, ed., *The Psychosociology of Language*
Moyer, *The Physiology of Hostility*
Sahakian, ed., *Psychology of Learning: Systems, Models, and Theories*
Weiner, *Theories of Motivation: From Mechanism to Cognition*

CREDITS

ACADEMIC PRESS, INC. For the quotation on pages 341–342. From *Personal Causation* by R. de Charms, with permission of publisher and author. Copyright 1968 by Academic Press, Inc.

ADDISON-WESLEY PUBLISHING COMPANY, INC. For the figure on page 292 and the quotations on pages 293 and 294. From Robert B. Zajonc, "Cognitive Theories in Social Psychology," *The Handbook of Social Psychology*, Vol. I, 2nd ed., edited by Gardner Lindzey and Elliot Aronson, 1968, Addison-Wesley, Reading, Mass.

AMERICAN PSYCHOLOGICAL ASSOCIATION. For the table on page 297. From "Effects of Severity of Threat on the Deviation of Forbidden Behavior," *Journal of Abnormal and Social Psychology*, 66 (1963), 584–588. Copyright 1963 by the American Psychological Association, and reproduced by permission of publisher and author.

For the figure on page 207. From "Achievement Motive and Test Anxiety Conceived as Motive to Approach Success and Motive to Avoid Failure," *Journal of Abnormal and Social Psychology*, 60 (1960), 52–63. Copyright 1960 by the American Psychological Association, and reproduced by permission of publisher and author.

For the quotations on pages 90–91. From "Neuropsychological Interpretation of the Effects of Drive and Incentive-Motivation on General Activity and Instrumental Behavior," *Psychological Review*, 75 (1968), 1–22. Copyright 1968 by the American Psychological Association, and reproduced by permission of publisher and author.

39 (1949), 1–14. Copyright 1949 by the American Psychological Association, and reproduced by permission of publisher and author.

For the quotations on pages 155–157 and the figure on page 157. From "Undermanning, Performances, and Students' Subjective Experiences in Behavioral Settings of Large and Small High Schools," *Journal of Personality and Social Psychology,* 10 (1968), 255–261. Copyright 1968 by the American Psychological Association, and reproduced by permission of publisher and author.

AMERICAN SOCIOLOGICAL ASSOCIATION. For the table on page 404. Reprinted from "The Invocation of Moral Obligation," *Sociometry,* 27 (1964), 306, Table 1, by permission of the American Sociological Association.

APPLETON-CENTURY-CROFTS. For the quotations on pages 4 and 93–94. Reprinted from a *History of Experimental Psychology,* second edition, by Edwin G. Boring, by permission of the publishers, Educational Division, Meredith Corporation. Copyright © 1950 by Appleton-Century-Crofts, Inc.

For the figure on page 37. *From Theories of Learning* (3rd edition), by Ernest R. Hilgard and Gordon H. Bower. Copyright © 1966. Reprinted by permission of Appleton-Century-Crofts, Educational Division, Meredith Corporation, and the author.

For the quotations on pages 18, 22, 23–24, 28, 33, and 34. From *Principles of Behavior* by Clark L. Hull. Copyright © 1943, 1967. Reprinted by permission of Appleton-Century-Crofts, Educational Division, Meredith Corporation.

For the quotation on pages 329–330 and for the figure on page 331. From *Punishment and Aversive Behavior,* edited by Byron A. Campbell and Russell M. Church. Copyright © 1969. Reprinted by permission of Appleton-Century-Crofts, Educational Division, Meredith Corporation.

For the quotation on page 178 and the figure on page 190. From *The Achievement Motive,* David G. McClelland, John W. Atkinson, Russell A. Clark, and Edgar L. Lowell. Copyright © 1953 by Appleton-Century-Crofts, Inc. By permission of the publisher, Educational Division, Meredith Corporation.

CLINICAL PSYCHOLOGY PUBLISHING COMPANY. For the quotation on page 250. From *Psychology in the School,* vol. 2. Copyright © 1965 by Clinical Psychology Publishing Company. Reprinted by permission of the publisher.

DUKE UNIVERSITY PRESS. For the figure on page 289. From "The Principle of Short-Circuiting of Threat: Further Evidence," *Journal of Personality,* 33 (1965), 622–635. Reprinted by permission of the author and publisher, Duke University Press.

For the quotations on pages 99–100, 110–111, 115–116, 135, 136, and 137 and the figure on page 122. From *The Conceptual Representation and the Measurement of Psychological Forces* by K. Lewin. Reprinted by permission of the publisher, Duke University Press.

For the quotation on page 415. From "Surveillance and Trust," *Journal of Personality,* 26 (1958), 200–215. Reprinted by permission of the author and publisher, Duke University Press.

HARPER & ROW, PUBLISHERS. For the quotations on pages 14, 84, and 90. Reprinted from *Theory of Motivation* by R. C. Bolles, with permission of publisher and author.

HARVARD UNIVERSITY PRESS. For the figure on page 264. From "Business Drive and National Achievement," *Harvard Business Review,* 40 (1962), 99–112. Reprinted by permission of publisher and author.

HOLT, RINEHART AND WINSTON, INC. For the quotations on pages 174 and 176. From *Personality* by D. C. McClelland. Copyright © 1951 by Holt, Rinehart and Winston, Inc. Used with permission of publisher and author.

UNIVERSITY OF ILLINOIS PRESS. For the figure on page 228. From "The Interactive Effects of Anxiety, Failure, and Intra-Serial Duplication," *American Journal of Psychology,* 65 (1952), 59–66. Reprinted by permission of publisher and author.

IOWA CHILD WELFARE RESEARCH STATION. For the figure on page

108. From "Frustration and Regression: An Experiment with Young Children," *University of Iowa Studies in Child Welfare,* 18, no. 1 (1941), 1–43. Reprinted by permission of the publisher.

For the quotations on pages 103, 131–132, 138–139, 151, 152–153, 193, and 194 and the table on page 141. From *Field Theory in Social Science* (Harper & Row, 1951), originally published as "Formalization and Progress in Psychology," *University of Iowa Studies in Child Welfare,* 16, no. 3 (1940), 9–42. Reprinted by permission of the publisher.

JOSSEY-BASS, INC. For the quotations on pages 275 and 279. From *Cognition, Personality, and Clinical Psychology,* edited by R. Jessor and S. Feshbach, with permission of publisher and author.

THE JOURNAL PRESS. For the figures on pages 188 and 189. From "The Effect of Need for Achievement on Learning and Speed of Performance," *The Journal of Psychology,* 33 (1961), 31–40. Reprinted by permission of the author and The Journal Press.

For the figure on page 337. From "The Growth and Extinction of Expectancies in Chance Controlled and Skilled Tasks," *Journal of Psychology,* 52 (1961), 161–177. Reprinted by permission of the author and The Journal Press.

McGRAW-HILL BOOK COMPANY. For the quotations on pages 33–34. From *Motivation of Behavior* by Judson S. Brown. Copyright 1961 by McGraw-Hill Book Company. Used with permission of McGraw-Hill Book Company.

For the figure on page 114. From "Lewinian Theory as a Contemporary Systematic Framework," by D. Cartwright, in *Psychology: A Study of a Science,* vol. 2, edited by S. Koch. Copyright 1959 by McGraw-Hill Book Company. Used with permission of McGraw-Hill Book Company.

For the quotations on pages 96, 110, 115, 138, 145–146, and 147 and the figure on page 149. Reprinted from *A Dynamic Theory of Personality* by K. Lewin. Copyright 1935 by McGraw-Hill Book Company. Used with permission of McGraw-Hill Book Company.

For the quotations on pages 99–100, 113, 146, and 150 and the figures on pages 105 and 107. From *Principles of Topological Psychology* by K. Lewin. Copyright 1936 by McGraw-Hill Book Company. Used with permission of McGraw-Hill Book Company.

For the figure on page 67 and the quotation on page 69. From "Liberalization of Basic S-R Concepts: Extensions to Conflict Behavior, Motivation, and Social Learning," by N. E. Miller, in *Psychology: A Study of a Science,* vol. 2, edited by S. Koch. Copyright 1959 by McGraw-Hill Book Company. Used with permission of McGraw-Hill Book Company.

For the quotation on pages 170–171. From "Preparations for the Scaffold of a Comprehensive System," by H. A. Murray, in *Psychology: A Study of a Science,* vol. 3, edited by S. Koch. Copyright 1959 by McGraw-Hill Book Company. Used with permission of McGraw-Hill Book Company.

METHUEN & COMPANY, LTD. For the figure on page 311. Reprinted by permission of the publisher from A. Michotte, *The Perception of Causality* (London: Methuen & Co., Ltd., 1946), p. 94.

THE NATIONAL ASSOCIATION FOR MENTAL HEALTH, INC. For the figure on page 221. From "The Effects of Manifest Anxiety on the Academic Achievement," *Mental Hygiene,* 46 (1962), 420–426. Reprinted by permission of the author and the National Association for Mental Health, Inc.

UNIVERSITY OF NEBRASKA PRESS. For the figures on pages 302 and 303 and for the quotation on page 303. From "Motivational Effects of Cognitive Dissonance," by J. W. Brehm, in *Nebraska Symposium on Motivation,* vol. 10, edited by M. R. Jones, by permission of the University of Nebraska Press. Copyright 1962 by the University of Nebraska Press.

For the figure on page 72. From "Stimulus-Response Theory of Drive," by W. K. Estes, in *Nebraska Symposium on Motivation,* vol. 6, edited by M. R. Jones, by permission of the University of Nebraska Press. Copyright 1958 by the University of Nebraska Press.

For the quotations on pages 187 and 258–259. From "Some Social Consequences of Achievement Motivation," by D. C. McClelland, in *Nebraska Symposium on Motivation,* vol. 3, edited by M. R. Jones, by permission of the University of Nebraska Press. Copyright 1955 by the University of Nebraska Press.

For the quotation on pages 41–42 and the figures on pages 42 and 46. From "Behavior Theory and Selective Learning," by K. W. Spence, in *Nebraska Symposium on Motivation,* vol. 6, edited by M. R. Jones, by permission of the University of Nebraska Press. Copyright 1958 by the University of Nebraska Press.

OXFORD UNIVERSITY PRESS. For the quotations on pages 170–171 and 172–173. From *Explorations in Personality* by H. A. Murray. Copyright © 1938 by Oxford University Press. Reproduced by permission of publisher and author.

PSYCHOLOGICAL REPORTS. For the quotation on page 232. Reprinted from "Some Neglected Variables in Contemporary Conceptions of Decision and Performance," *Psychological Reports,* 14 (1964), 575–590, with permission of publisher and author.

THE SOCIETY FOR RESEARCH IN CHILD DEVELOPMENT, INC. For the table on page 344. Reprinted by permission of the publisher from "Children's Beliefs in Their Own Control of Reinforcements in Intellectual-Academic Achievement Situations," *Child Development,* 36 (1965), 91–109. Copyright 1965 by The Society for Research in Child Development, Inc.

STANFORD UNIVERSITY PRESS. For the quotation on pages 297–298 and the table on page 301. Reprinted with permission of the publisher and author from *Conflict, Decision, and Dissonance* by Leon Festinger and others (Stanford: Stanford University Press, 1964), pp. 152, 153, and 155.

For the figure on page 309 and for the table on page 309. Reprinted with permission of the publisher from *Deterrents and Reinforcement: The Psychology of Insufficient Reward* by Douglas H. Lawrence and Leon Festinger (Stanford: Stanford University Press, 1962), pp. 91 and 143.

VAN NOSTRAND REINHOLD COMPANY. For the quotations on pages 83–84, 177, 185–186, 190, 194, 196, 222–223, 227–228, and 233; for the figure on page 160; and for the tables on pages 163, 164, and 165. From *An Introduction to Motivation* by J. W. Atkinson. © 1964 by Litton Educational Publishing, Inc. Reprinted by permission of Van Nostrand Reinhold Company.

For the quotation on page 187. From *Motives in Fantasy, Action, and Society* by J. W. Atkinson. © 1958 by Litton Educational Publishing, Inc. Reprinted by permission of Van Nostrand Reinhold Company.

For the tables on pages 260–261 and 263 and the quotation on page 394. From *The Achieving Society* by D. C. McClelland. © 1961 by Litton Educational Publishing, Inc. Reprinted by permission of Van Nostrand Reinhold Company.

JOHN WILEY & SONS, INC. For the figures on pages 116 and 117. From K. Lewin, "Behavior and Development as a Function of the Total Situation," *Manual of Child Psychology,* edited by L. Carmichael. © 1946 John Wiley & Sons, Inc.

For the quotation on pages 137–138. From *Theories of Personality* by C. S. Hall and G. Lindzey. © 1957 John Wiley & Sons, Inc.

For the quotations on pages 312–313, 314, 316–318, 346, 347, 348–349, and 350. From *The Psychology of Interpersonal Relations* by F. Heider, with permission of publisher and author. © 1958 John Wiley & Sons, Inc.

THE WILLIAMS & WILKINS COMPANY. For the quotation in footnote 1 on page 103. From "The Empirical Basis and Theoretical Structure of Psychology," *Philosophy of Science,* 24 (1957), 97–108. © 1957 by The Williams & Wilkins Co., Baltimore.

YALE UNIVERSITY PRESS. For the quotations on pages 24, 26–27, and 31. Reprinted from *Essentials of Behavior* by Clark L. Hull, with permission of the publisher.

For the figure on page 44. Reprinted from *Behavior Theory and Conditioning* by K. W. Spence, with permission of the publisher.

To Marijana and Mark

Preface

This book is a review of four theories of motivation. The theories and their major contributors are drive theory (Clark Hull, Kenneth Spence), field theory (Kurt Lewin), achievement theory (David McClelland, John Atkinson), and attribution theory (Fritz Heider). Each theory is examined from a historical viewpoint, with the presentation of conceptual developments as new empirical facts and theoretical ideas emerged. Further, extended quotes from original sources are included within the text so the reader has commerce with the writing styles and modes of expression of the leading figures in motivation.

The book progresses along several dimensions. First, there is an ordering according to the historical development of psychology. Drive and field theories of motivation were first formulated in the late 1930s and early 1940s; achievement theory came into prominence during the latter half of the 1950s; and most cognitive theories of motivation first began to reach fruition in the early 1960s. Second, there is a progression from mechanistic to cognitive conceptions of behavior. Drive theorists attempt to explain both human and infrahuman behavior without introducing mediating cognitions (thoughts) that intervene between the perception of the stimulus and the final response. Field and achievement theory do employ cognitive terminology, but the only mediating cognitive structures they consider respectively are the perceived path to the goal and the expectancy of goal attainment. These cognitions pertain to the acquisition of knowledge and the anticipation of the goal. The cognitive theories discussed in Chapters V and VI consider in greater detail the relation between the structure of thought and expressed behavior. In the final chapter, it is argued that a mechanistic conception of motivation is no longer viable.

The order of theories presented in the book also decreasingly captures the influence of the conception on psychological thought. Drive theory dominated the psychology of motivation for more than twenty years (from 1935 to 1955) and remains influential today. Field theory as formulated by Lewin never gained great popularity in America. However, it is perhaps second only to drive theory as a motivational conception familiar to psychologists. Achievement theory is primarily confined to the understanding of achievement-related behaviors and influences only a selected subset of motivational research. Finally, the cognitive study of motivation only recently has offered a clear alternative to the other theories and has, thus far, been least directly influential in generating motivational research.

The factors listed above result in disparities in the manner in which the material in each chapter is treated. Because of its extensive influence in psychology, drive theory is fully discussed in other motivational texts. Therefore, an overview of drive theory is presented here, rather than a detailed examination of the experimental literature. Experiments are selected for discussion because they represent general themes of a vast amount of conducted research. As the book progresses, research studies are examined in greater detail, and more complete experimental surveys are included. Indeed, the final chapters (V and VI) attempt to review many of the relevant studies concerned with cognitive approaches to motivation.

Because the chapters represent a temporal development in psychology, it is possible to present a "looking backwards" view of drive theory. But cognitive theories of motivation are too new to permit such an approach. In addition, the author's own work is more centrally involved in the latter chapters of the book. Thus, criticisms of drive theory give way to suggestions for the cognitive study of motivation, and the broader perspective in which drive theory is examined yields to a more circumscribed discussion of cognitive approaches to motivation.

The four motivational theories examined are guided by different sources of data and do not attempt to explain the same phenomena. Therefore, inequalities in the empirical foundations, breadth and precision of the conceptions, and so forth, are to be expected. This also results in disparities in the manner in which each of the chapters is written. For example, in the discussion of field theory, far less research is reported than in the other chapters of the book; in the cognitive-motivation chapters, there are no formal or mathematical derivations of predictions. However, although the theories greatly differ in origin, focus, and data base, at times they do examine the identical psychological phenomena (conflict and frustration, for instance) and often they confront the same issues (such as how incentives affect behavior, and what role individual differences play in theory construction). Comparisons and contrasts between the theories, therefore, are possible and often are presented.

The audience for this book consists of advanced undergraduates and graduate students. The book may serve as the main text in a motivational course at either the undergraduate or graduate level or as a secondary source in which selected sections are assigned for reading. Although drive and field theories are covered in other books, aspects of these conceptions are examined here that are neglected in other motivational texts. Further, the detailed coverage of both achievement and cognitive theories is not found in any other source book. In addition, whenever feasible, the relevance of the theoretical conceptions to motivation and performance in the classroom is discussed. Selected sections of the book, particularly in the latter chapters, should be of interest to students in education and educational psychology. Of necessity, many of the details of each conception are neglected. References are provided guiding the reader to other sources of information that pursue given problems in greater depth.

Many individuals and agencies have contributed to the final book product. Foremost has been the training provided by John W. Atkinson. Over the years, David Birch, Seymour Feshbach, Norman Garmezy, and Heinz Heckhausen have helped to clarify my thoughts. Edward L. Walker has provided invaluable guidance throughout my career. Andy Kukla was particularly helpful in pointing out faults in an earlier draft of the book. Finally, Nancy Cozier assisted in so many ways; and Penelope Potepan, Carol Price, and Ulrich Kühl aided in the preparation of the manuscript.

For the past six years, my research has been funded by the National Institute of Health, MH 12603. The Office of Early Childhood Education also has been most generous in their financial aid. And above all, I want to thank the Guggenheim Foundation for its support. They are so trusting that one is forced to have a final product, or face a lifetime of guilt! The Guggenheim Fellowship year was spent at the Psychologisches Institut, Ruhr Universität, Bochum, Germany, where Heinz Heckhausen was the perfect host.

Bernard Weiner
Los Angeles, California
August 1972

Contents

I

Mechanistic versus Cognitive Views

INTRODUCTION

Perhaps the most salient controversy in the field of motivation is whether behavior should be conceptualized as "mechanistic" or "cognitive." These two conceptual approaches differ in the extent to which higher mental processes are invoked to account for the initiation, direction, intensity, and persistence of goal-directed behavior.

In general, mechanistic analyses of behavior are characterized as stimulus-response $(S-R)$ theories. According to these conceptions, behavior is instigated by the onset of external or internal stimuli (goads), such as hunger pangs or contact with a hot stove. The direction of behavior is then determined by mechanistic $S-R$ bonds, or habits. The probability of elicitation of the various habits often is thought to be dependent upon prior reinforcement contingencies, so that, for example, in the presence of hunger stimuli the response most likely to be elicited is the one that previously led to the attainment of food. Behavior directed toward the food then persists until the removal of the sustaining stimuli.

Cognitive theories of motivation, on the other hand, conceive of an action sequence as instigated not by stimulation, but by some source of information. External or internal events are encoded, categorized, and transformed into a belief, such as "I am hungry." The direction and persistence of behavior as the organism pursues its goal is a function of the intervening thought processes. This approach may be broadly characterized as stimulus-cognition-response (*S-C-R*). That is, higher mental processes intervene between inputs (antecedent stimuli) and behavioral outputs (consequences); the structure of thought determines action.

Mechanistic versus cognitive approaches implicitly differ in their acceptance of the following distinctions when formulating the laws of motivation: animate versus inanimate behavior, human versus infrahuman behavior, and thought versus action as scientific data.

Animate versus Inanimate Behavior

Simple observation informs us that the behavior of man and animals must be differentiated from the behavior of inanimate objects. Man and animals seem to be capable of *self-induced motion,* whereas inanimate objects appear to be *motionless* until acted upon by some external force.

Mechanistic psychologists generally ignore this fundamental animate-inanimate distinction; that is, in most mechanistic conceptions of behavior, man and infrahuman organisms are also considered to be motionless until acted upon by some set of stimuli. The introduction of a stimulus is believed to *arouse* the organism to action and *cause* the subsequent behavior. The stimulus is considered the source of energy. Following the offset of the stimulating condition, the organism is expected to become motionless again. Mechanists argue further that the organism is automatically carried along the path to the goal; behavior is not undertaken "in order to" reach an end state. This causal analysis implicitly unites man and lower animals with matter (see de Charms, 1968, for a similar analysis).

Cognitive psychologists, on the other hand, are more likely to consider the organism as being in a state of continuous action (see Atkinson and Birch, 1970; Hebb, 1949). The direction of behavior may be altered by transient or stable internal determinants of behavior, such as new intentions (McClelland, 1971). In addition, cognitivists argue that behavior is "purposive"; that is, means can be altered to reach an anticipated end state. A ball rolling down a hill does not have as its "purpose" reaching the bottom of the hill. But end seeking, they argue, does characterize the action of humans and infrahumans. In sum, the cognitivists hold that the laws of behavior must differ for animate and inanimate objects because of the controlling effects of thought on action.

Human Behavior versus Infrahuman Behavior

A second common-sense differentiation is often made between man and lower animals. Man is able to use tools, can act rationally and anticipate ends, and develops the cognitive skills of language and symbolization. Animals are not believed to possess these characteristics, or at least certainly not to the same extent as humans. Infrahumans appear to have less foresight, they act "irrationally," and they are limited in their capacity to communicate and think abstractly. Because these factors are of little importance to the mechanist in the prediction or understanding of behavior, mechanists are not likely to make clear distinctions between man and animals. Experimentation with lower organisms is therefore conducted primarily because of the light it is expected to shed upon human behavior. Needless to say, the Darwinian man-animal continuity postulate serves as the basis for this position. Cognitivists, on the other hand, frequently note the limited mental capacity and limited range of motivations of infrahumans. Clearly, studies of achievement-related behavior are not likely to be conducted with rats as subjects! Thus, the cognitivists are less likely than the mechanists to employ infrahuman subjects to understand human behavior.

While the Darwinian postulate serves the mechanists in their attempt to apply the principles of animal behavior to the understanding of human action, the cognitivists also use the man-animal continuity to promote their view that even infrahuman behavior is guided by cognitive processes. The attempt to explain the behavior of infrahumans by appealing to higher mental processes was most clearly elaborated by the "anecdotal" school of psychology, which came into prominence in the 1880s. Associated primarily with Romanes, who coined the term "comparative psychology," individuals associated with this school gathered stories illustrating the intellectual prowess of animals. In contrast and reaction to this school, Loeb advanced the notion of animal tropisms, and in 1896 C. Lloyd Morgan, designated by Watson as the founder of behaviorism, postulated his famous Canon: "In no case is an animal activity to be interpreted as the outcome of the exercise of a higher psychical faculty, if it can be fairly interpreted as the outcome of an exercise which stands lower on the psychological scale" (p. 59). The essence of the argument between the followers of Romanes and those of Loeb is nicely conveyed in their explanations of why moths fly into fire. While the Romanes group believed that this was an indication of the moth's curiosity, the followers of Loeb argued that the act is innately determined, and the moth has no control over his behavior. One can see that the essence of the argument, and Morgan's Canon, revolve around the cognitive versus mechanistic explanations of infrahuman behavior.

Thought versus Action as Scientific Data

The history of experimental psychology is closely linked with the issue of the inclusion of thought samples versus observed action as the empirical basis for scientific growth. A very brief overview of this history is presented now, for related issues often are raised in the remainder of the book.

Structuralism. The psychological bible states that in the beginning there was Wundt. In 1879 Wundt started what is controversially called the first experimental laboratory in psychology.[1] Wundt championed structuralism, or the science of the contents of the mind. His goal was to obtain a systematic description and explanation of consciousness. Following Leibnitz, he considered the mind a structure; the task of psychology was to define the limits of the mind and to isolate and identify its basic elements. This goal was to be accomplished by using the method of introspection to study pure sensations. Individuals would analyze their sensations and perceptions into the smallest possible components. Wundt hoped that after finding the elements or atoms of sensation he would be able to study their interrelationships and understand more complex feelings.

The work of Wundt was brought to America and continued by Titchener at Cornell University. Titchener made some basic changes in Wundt's methodology, aruging that not every person is a qualified introspectionist. He stressed that training is necessary before expertise can be achieved. Rather than focusing on the stimulus per se, an observer must be able to attend to the basic dimensions included by the stimulus. Titchener also proposed a new classification scheme for the analysis of feelings. However, structuralism, or the science of consciousness, was short-lived in America. Boring (1950) vividly conveys this when describing Titchener's role in American psychology:

Titchener was important in the history of American psychology because he staunchly represented this older conservative tradition against overwhelming numbers. West of the Atlantic in psychology there was "America" and there was Titchener. Names often stand out in history because their owners have opposed something older; movements of thought are always movements away from other thought. However, in Titchener's case the situation was reversed. He has stood out in bold relief because everyone near him moved away from him. If all movement is relative, then Titchener moved—backwards with respect to his advancing frame of reference [p. 419].

The structuralists were opposed by three different movements in psychology. One was the psychoanalytic movement, which argued that

[1] Some historians believe that William James established the first laboratory in 1875, although it is agreed that Wundt first set aside space for a psychological lab. Still others, such as Roback, 1964, contend that G. Stanley Hall founded the first American laboratory in 1881.

man is not aware of his own motivations. Psychoanalysts substituted guided introspection, or free association, in place of the "pure" introspection advocated by Wundt and Titchener. Further, psychoanalysts presented an entirely different conception of man than did the structuralists. A second opposing group was the Gestaltists, led by Wertheimer, Koffka, and Köhler. The Gestaltists convincingly argued that the analysis of elements was not the proper method for psychologists. Rather, they contended that one must study the whole and the relationships between the parts of the whole. We shall return to this position when discussing the Lewinian conception of motivation. Third, structuralism was opposed by the growth of functionalism, and then behaviorism, in America.

Functionalism. The functionalists, led by John Dewey, the eminent psychologist, philosopher, and educator, revolted against the static, descriptive approach of the structuralists. They stressed the adaptive nature of behavior and maintained that one must ask about the causes of events. They wanted to develop a dynamic approach to behavior that would explain the adaptation of the organism to his environment. Functionalists were determined to foster a psychology that would include the concepts of purpose, cause, and capacity. Their orientation was strongly applied— John Dewey founded the program of experimental education at the University of Chicago and later became the first president of the American Teachers' Association. The functionalists accepted introspection, but only as one method of psychological investigation. They also believed in the study of the behavior (movement) of organisms. Thus, the functionalists represent the transition between structuralism and behaviorism.

Behaviorism. Behaviorism received its formal impetus from John Watson in 1913, although its historical antecedents include a long history of associationism, a belief in the analytic approach to science, and the desire to produce an objective study of human behavior. Watson should be considered the chief apostle, rather than the founder, of behaviorism (Kimble, 1961). Watson's behaviorism was a rebellion against both structuralism and functionalism. He argued that introspection is not an adequate methodology of science because the observer is part of the system he is observing. Therefore, the data are not reliable; two investigators cannot agree on the same facts. The apparent fruitlessness of this approach was dramatically revealed in the introspective analysis of the color green. While Titchener maintained, "you can see that green is neither yellowish nor bluish," Holt advocated "on the contrary, it is obvious that a green is that yellow-blue which is exactly as blue as it is yellow" (reported in Osgood, 1953, p. 647). Watson also completely discarded the study of consciousness. He asserted that scientists should not ask questions that cannot be answered scientifically; if only the individual has access to his own mind, then the mind is not a proper subject for psychology. (It is said that psychology first lost its soul, and then its mind!) In place of introspection and consciousness, Watson substituted the study of the movements of organisms. The task of psychology became (1) to predict the response, given the stimulus; (2) to identify the stimulus, given the response; and (3) to predict the change in the stimulus, given a change in the response. Rationalism was indeed completely discarded.

At the heart of Watson's formulation was a thorough commitment to learning. Watson argued, as John Locke did, that the child is a *tabula rasa,* or blank slate, at birth. He asserted,

I wish to draw the conclusion that there is no such thing as an inheritance of *capacity, talent, temperament, mental constitution, and characteristics.* These things again depend on training [1924, pp. 74–75].[2]

The transition between functionalism and behaviorism was not unruffled. Part of a debate between McDougall (a purposive behaviorist and functionalist) and Watson (who originally was a functionalist trained by Angell) is reproduced here to convey some of the aroused feelings and salient issues. In that debate McDougall states,

Lastly, Dr. Watson has the advantage of being in a position that must excite pity for him in the minds of those who understand the situation. And I will frankly confess that I share this feeling. I am sorry for Dr. Watson; and I am sorry about him. For I regard Dr. Watson as a good man gone wrong. . . . Now, though I am sorry for Dr. Watson, I mean to be entirely frank about his position. If he were an ordinary human being, I should feel obliged to exercise a certain reserve, for fear of hurting his feelings. We all know that Dr. Watson has his feelings like the rest of us. But I am at liberty to trample on his feelings in the most ruthless manner; for Dr. Watson has assured us (and it is the very essence of his peculiar doctrine) that he does not care a cent about feelings, whether his own or those of any other person. . . . Dr. Watson and I are, then, engaged in the same enterprise, the endeavor to reform psychology by correcting the traditional tendency to concentrate upon the facts of consciousness to the neglect of the facts of behavior. . . . I, on the other hand, maintain that the two sets of data, the facts ascertainable by introspective observation and the objectively observable facts of behavior, are not data for two distinct sciences, but rather are two classes of data both useful

[2] Earlier, Leibnitz had argued against a *tabula rasa* conception, stating that the existence of the unconscious necessitates that some structural aspect of the mind exist at birth. Wundt was influenced by Leibnitz; a *tabula rasa* conception is antithetical to the position advocated by structuralists.

and both indispensable for the one science of human nature properly called "psychology" [Watson and McDougall, 1929, pp. 47, 48, 57, 58].

The mechanists are guided by the arguments of Watson and other behaviorists and neobehaviorists. They believe that one must observe the *behavior* of organisms to understand motivational processes. They have been especially active in the field of learning. The cognitivists, on the other hand, accept introspection and other thought samples as proper empirical data necessary for the understanding of action. Like the behaviorists, they are often functionalistic in orientation, and ask how adaptation to the environment is mediated and promoted by higher mental processes. But thoughts are believed to be determinants of action, rather than epiphenomena. The cognitive-mechanistic controversy in contemporary psychology must be perceived in the light of the functionalistic and behavioristic reactions to structuralism and introspectionism.

TYPES OF MECHANISTIC AND COGNITIVE THEORIES

Thus far we have contrasted mechanistic with cognitive theories in a rather brief and cavalier manner. Clearly there are types of mechanistic theories, types of cognitive theories, and all shades of grey in between. For the present purposes, two types of mechanistic theories and two types of cognitive conceptions are distinguished. Among the mechanists, some investigators attempt to explain behavior without using hypothetical constructs or intervening variables. They believe that stimuli and responses are sufficient terms in their scientific schema. The approach of B. F. Skinner and his followers is included within this category, although to a lesser extent Guthrie and other associationists may be loosely classified within this camp.

On the other hand, neobehaviorists such as Hull and Spence include many intervening constructs in their theories of behavior. They are still mechanistic theorists, and the intervening constructs do not refer to higher mental processes. However, they recognize that the complexity of behavior necessitates the postulation of complex construct systems.

In Chapter II of this book, the Hull-Spence approach to motivation is examined in detail. In addition, the alternate position offered by "pure" associationists, who do not accept such concepts as drive and incentive, also is presented. Both points of view assume that stimuli are the instigators of behavior, that learning or habits are rigid S-R connections, that infrahumans can be used as experimental subjects to understand human behavior, that behavior is not consciously "end-seeking," and that intervening cognitions should not be employed in the analysis of action. That is, mechanistic principles are sufficient for the formulation of the laws of motivation.

Two types of cognitive theories also must be distinguished. Both approaches accept the necessity of employing intervening constructs in the explanation of action. Indeed, it would be hard to conceive of a cognitive theory that did not accept such a point of view. However, one type of theory limits the range of cognitive constructs. Virtually the only higher mental process included among the determinants of action by these theories is labeled an "expectancy," and connotes that organisms anticipate end states, or goals. The motivational theories of Atkinson (1964), Lewin (1938), Rotter (1954), and Tolman (1955) fall within this category. These conceptions are classified as Expectancy $\times$ Value theories, inasmuch as the direction and intensity of behavior is a function of the expectation that certain actions will lead to the goal, and the incentive value of the goal object. In Chapters III and IV the theories formulated by Lewin and Atkinson respectively are presented. In contrast to the Hull-Spence approach outlined in Chapter II, in these theories stimuli are not conceived as the causes of action, learning is not conceived as rigid S-R couplings, the experimental subjects are primarily humans, organisms are conceived as anticipating future goals, and intervening cognitions are employed in the analysis of action. At the same time, however, these theories are greatly influenced by the mechanistic approach of Hull and Spence. Further, they do not seriously attempt to examine the relationship between thought and action.

A second class of cognitive theories incorporates cognitive concepts and processes in addition to goal anticipations. Information seeking and information assembly, causal attributions, judgments, self-evaluations, social comparison, and so forth, are assumed to be fundamental determinants of action. Further, it is contended that there are two stages in the formulation of behavioral theory. First, there must be laws that relate incoming information to cognitive schemata and belief systems. Second, these belief systems are then related to action. In addition, within this class of cognitive theories cognitions are treated as observables, and they may be manipulated and investigated scientifically. In Chapters V and VI this position is presented in detail, particularly as related to causal attribution systems. The four types of theories differentiated in the above paragraphs are shown in Table 1:1. A third possible category of cognitive theories—the "humanistic" conceptions of Allport, Maslow, Rogers, and so forth—is not discussed in this book.

Finally, Chapter VII of this book summarizes arguments for a cogni-

TABLE 1:1
Summary of Mechanistic and Cognitive Theories

Theory Classification	Theory Structure		Book Chapter
Mechanistic	S-R	Behavior explained in terms of stimulus-response connections. Intervening hypothetical constructs are not employed in the analysis of action. Proponents include Skinner, Watson, other associationists and behaviorists.	II
Mechanistic	S-Construct-R	Behavior explained in terms of stimulus-response connections. Intervening constructs also are employed in the analysis of action, such as drive, incentive, and so forth. Proponents include Spence, Hull, Miller, Brown, and other neobehaviorists.	II
Cognitive	S-Cognition-R	Thoughts intervene between incoming information and the final behavioral response. The main cognitive determinant of action is an "expectancy." Proponents include Atkinson, Lewin, Rotter, and Tolman.	III and IV
Cognitive	S-Cognition-R	Thoughts intervene between incoming information and the final behavioral response. Many cognitive processes determine action, such as information seeking, causal attributions, etc. Proponents include Heider, Festinger, Kelley, and Lazarus.	V and VI

tive approach to motivation. It is contended that the mechanistic position is no longer theoretically viable nor is it supported by recent empirical data.

LEARNING AND MOTIVATION

A word of caution is necessary before beginning the review of specific motivational theories. Frequently one finds the field of motivation conceived as a subset of the field of learning. The main motivational question then raised is how does the level of motivation during acquisition influence the amount learned. For example, is a rat more likely to learn the correct response to a reward of food as hours of deprivation increase? Is learning retarded among highly anxious individuals? However, these are just a small subset of problems relevant to the field of motivation. The goal most motivational theorists have set for themselves is to identify and isolate the immediate determinants of action and to specify the mathematical relationships between these components. For example, one might conceive that the speed of a child running toward a water fountain is a function of his thirst (T), the distance he is from the water fountain (D), the attractiveness of the fountain (A), his fatigue level (F), and so forth. Further, it might be specified that the speed of running is determined by combining these factors additively:

$$\text{Speed} = f[T + D + A + (-F)]$$

Prior experience (learning), which in this example might influence the perceived distance between the boy and the fountain, undoubtedly affects action. But learning is conceived here as only one among a number of determinants of action, with neither greater nor lesser motivational significance than other behavioral determinants.

II

Drive Theory

The most well-known and often-cited motivational conception developed by experimental psychologists is known as drive theory. This conception received its major impetus from Clark Hull, and subsequently was elaborated by Kenneth Spence, Neal Miller, Hobart Mowrer, Judson Brown, and others. It was the first clearly stated motivational conception, has had the greatest influence on the psychology of motivation, and is the most mechanistic of the theoretical approaches outlined in this book. Hull's influence on psychology was so pervasive that in a recent poll psychologists voted him the most important contributor to psychology during the two decades, 1930–50. In addition, Spence and Miller were voted among the five most influential psychologists during the period 1950–60. This poll also revealed that Hull is considered second only to Freud in importance to the field of psychology. (The ten most significant figures in the history of psychology were judged to be: Freud, Hull, Wundt, Pavlov, Watson, Thorndike, James, Wertheimer, Tolman, and Lewin.)

In this chapter the historical antecedents of drive theory are introduced. Then some of the basic concepts used by Hull are examined, his general theory of behavior is discussed, and the extension of his ideas to such diverse areas as frustration and conflict is examined. In addition, the adequacy of the conception is questioned, and alternative interpretations of the data are discussed.

HISTORICAL ANTECEDENTS

The Instinct Doctrine

Darwin's publication of *Descent of Man* (1896) changed the history of Western thought and certainly changed the history of psychology. According to Atkinson (1964), the continuity between man and animal that Darwin postulated had three important implications for psychology. First, it reaffirmed that animals possess intelligence. This immediately led to the extended studies of the intelligence of animals conducted by Thorndike (although Thorndike maintained a mechanistic conception of intelligence), and ultimately resulted in animal learning becoming the foundation of experimental psychology. Clark Hull was part of that tradition, and drive theory grew from the studies of learning and motivation of lower organisms. A second implication of Darwin's theory is that there are individual differences in the capacities and capabilities of organisms. Those organisms best adapted to their environment have the greatest chance of survival. In psychology, individual differences were first investigated extensively by Binet in his studies of school children in France; subsequently, individual differences became one of the core content areas of the functionalist school in America, and individual difference assessment one of the central influences in the study of personality and clinical psychology. Third, the postulated continuity between man and animals justified the argument that man, not just the lower animals, is guided by instincts and is, in part, "irrational."[1]

The concept of an irrational man, lacking control over his own behavior, was a necessary stepping stone for the birth of the psychoanalytic movement. Freud certainly was aware of Darwin's work and was greatly influenced by his findings. This influence is implicit in Freud's genetic approach to personality development and his adoption of the instinct doctrine. Freud (1915) postulated that man is propelled to action by instinctive stimuli "emanating within the organism and penetrating to the mind" (p. 64). Freud vacillated in his taxonomy of instincts, ultimately subscribing to the view that there are two basic instincts: Eros (life) and Thanatos (death). (Psychoanalytic thought is discussed in Chapter V.)

---

[1] It is interesting to note the observation that three great transitions in thought have occurred, and all relegate humans to a lower status level. First, Copernicus took man from the center of the universe; then Darwin proved that man is not unique; finally, Freud demonstrated that man is irrational and not even aware of his own motivations. Perhaps the fourth revolution will find that inanimate objects can be made that are more intelligent than their makers, and we will need a rational conception for the behavior of matter!

Some version of the instinct doctrine was adopted not only by Freud, but by many other prominent psychologists as well. Perhaps the most elaborate instinct theory was proposed by McDougall (1923). McDougall postulated that instincts or propensities propel the organism toward certain end states. Each instinct was believed to have a cognitive, affective, and conative component. For example, the instinct of escape causes the animal to attend to aversive stimuli, exhibit the emotion of fear, and initiate avoidance behavior or flight. This, however, was not a completely mechanistic conception, as was advanced by Watson and Hull. Instincts were believed to be directed toward particular end states; the means to attain these ends could be modified.

The instinct doctrine reached its peak during the early 1900s. Psychologists employed the term as a descriptive and explanatory concept to account for the behavior of animals and man. Osgood (1953) writes,

Holt (1931) has summarized this nonsense neatly . . . [asserting] "If he goes with his fellows, it is the 'herd instinct' which activates him; if he walks alone, it is the 'anti-social instinct'; . . . if he twiddles his thumbs, it is the 'thumb-twiddling instinct'; if he does not twiddle his thumbs, it is the 'thumb-not-twiddling instinct'". Thus everything is explained with the facility of magic—word magic [p. 428].

At the beginning of the 1920s the enthusiasm for the instinct doctrine began to wane, and an anti-instinct revolt ensued. Dunlap (1919) and Kuo (1924) published articles questioning the existence of instincts; they argued that instinct is not a necessary concept in psychology. Bernard (1924), the sociologist and anthropologist, noted that over 2,500 instincts had been postulated. He called attention to the great variability in the patterns of behavior across cultures, and asked how inborn, fixed characteristics could explain the great diversity in observed behavior. (For a more complete discussion of the decline of the instinct concept, see Beach, 1955.)

Thus, the concept of instinct was dying in the 1920s. But, as is so often true in science, a theory does not die—it is replaced. The instinct doctrine (a more accurate designation than instinct theory) was replaced by the concept of drive.

Original Conceptions of Drive

The introduction of the drive concept to experimental psychology is attributed to Woodworth (1918), although the concept of "driving force" was introduced in the eighteenth century as part of the study of ethics, and also was employed by Freud. Woodworth's interests in motivational problems, along with his functionalistic orientation, led him to suggest that physiological deficits, or needs, instigate the organism to undertake behaviors which result in the offset of those needs. Thus drives, the motivational property of need states, result from physiological disequilibria and instigate behaviors that return the organism to equilibrium. This is a homeostatic conception; behavior is directed toward the removal of tissue deficits and reestablishes the original state of the organism.

It is reasonable to ask why "instinct" should be replaced by "drive." Bolles (1967) summarizes the instinct controversy and the reason for the shift to the drive construct:

The only obvious immediate outcome of the Great Instinct Controversy was that the word "instinct" was banished; it virtually disappeared from the psychological literature for the next 15 or 20 years. When it began to reappear (e.g., Lashley, 1938) it was purely as a descriptive term designating unlearned behavior. It had been stripped of its prior connotations of emotion, biological adaptiveness, unconscious impulses, and teleology. These connotations did not perish when the word was banished, however, they merely became attached, with varying degrees of persistence, to the new word "drive."

Drive was an even better compromise concept than instinct had been. It gave the mechanist just the principle of mechanical causation he wanted; and the drives promised to have objective physiological or physical bases, which the instincts lacked. Drives also permitted the vitalist and the mentalist to keep at least a descriptive teleology of the kind Craig and Tolman had proposed. Drives were manifest in behavior, had physiological correlates, and gave rise to man's desires. Thus, they bridged all of the interdisciplinary gaps that instincts were supposed to bridge [p. 100].

In addition to their function as a bridge between mechanism and cognition, drives could be investigated in the laboratory. Drive antecedents could be manipulated systematically and their behavioral effects observed under controlled conditions. This is precisely what occurred during the years 1920–35 (see Marx, 1960).

Early Experimental Work

The general procedure in the first investigations of drive during the 1920s was to deprive animals of a commodity necessary for survival, such as food or water. Then an incentive relevant to the drive—for example, food for a hungry organism, water for a thirsty organism—was placed in a goal chamber. Between the organism and the goal object was an electric shock grid. The animal had to cross the grid and receive shocks to obtain the goal (see Diagram 2:1). Diagram 2:1 illustrates what was known as an obstruction box; it was used extensively by Morgan (1916) and Moss

DIAGRAM 2:1
The Columbia Obstruction Box

Start Box	Electric Grid	Goal Object

(1924). Within a few years additional improvements were made in the construction of this apparatus, and it became known as the Columbia Obstruction Box. The Columbia Obstruction Box is associated with the psychologists Richter, Warden, and Warner.

Let us briefly discuss some of the investigations, findings, and conclusions in these early studies. In 1924 Moss investigated the relationship between the number of hours of food deprivation and the tendency to cross the grid to obtain a reward of food. Animals were deprived of food for 12, 24, 36, 48, or 72 hours. The dependent variable was the percentage of rats crossing the grid within a given time period. The general finding was that there is a monotonic relationship between hours of deprivation and grid crossings. From these data, Moss (1924) concluded, for example, that "if a 72-hour hunger drive is opposed by a 28v. opposing stimulus, or resistance, in eight cases out of ten the hunger drive will overcome the resistance" (p. 183).

We would now perceive this experiment as a prototypical approach-avoidance conflict situation. Moss' basic assumption was that the behavior of animals is the resultant of a drive to action minus the opposing resistances. Hence, the strength of the drive to action could be measured in terms of the resistance it is able to overcome. For example, 72 hours of deprivation is a greater drive to action than 12 hours of deprivation because it is more likely to overcome 28 volts of resistance.

Moss varied the strength of the drive to action, which was considered a function of the hours of deprivation, and the strength of the resistance, which was a function of the magnitude of shock. He also manipulated the type of deprivation and the nature of the aversive stimulus. In addition, Moss investigated what we would now label as avoidance-avoidance conflicts. He placed animals in an electrified compartment and ascertained the magnitude of the shock required before the animals would cross cold water to enter a nonshocked compartment. In still another investigation comparing the aversiveness of stimuli, animals could obtain food by either crossing a shock grid or running through cold water. Thus, Moss attempted to scale the relative values of aversive and appetitive motivations. The relative strengths of behaviors instigated by different sources of motivation remain unknown and relatively ignored in psychology.

Warden (1931) continued the general approach initiated by Moss. He compared the strengths of drives whose source of motivation was the absence of water or food with those drives instigated by maternal or sexual needs. Warden concluded that hunger and thirst are more potent activating stimuli than sexual deprivation, but that maternal needs are the most potent activator of behavior. The rank order of the strengths of the various drives, determined by the resistance the drive could overcome, was: maternal, thirst, hunger, sex, and exploratory drive. The reader is invited to compare this hierarchy, and the method of derivation, with the more famous intuitive need ranking postulated by Maslow (1954): physiological, safety, belongingness, esteem, and self-actualization needs.

It was previously indicated that the primary dependent variable used by Moss was the likelihood of crossing the grid of the obstruction box within a given time period. In the investigations conducted later by Richter (1927), the amount of activity exhibited by animals was employed as the dependent variable. Richter placed rats in a tambour, or mounted cage, and measured the rats' activity while in the cage. Richter found that animals display cyclical variations in behavior, with a period of relative activity followed by a period of quiescence. To demonstrate the relationship between the periods of activity and the hunger drive, Richter added a small "kitchen" to the tambour. Rats were allowed to enter this compartment and eat whenever they desired. Richter found that the period of maximum food intake corresponds to the time of maximum activity in the tambour. He therefore concluded that random or exploratory activity is related to physiological deficits. Here again we see the influence of Darwin and the functionalist tradition. If an animal explores when deprived, it is more likely to find a goal object. This relationship has great survival value; it is an adaptive mechanism.

Attention also was directed to the physiological locus of drives. Cannon and Washburn (1912) demonstrated that there is a correlation between subjective reports of hunger and stomach contractions. They therefore argued for a localized theory of motivation. Thirst, they reasoned, originates from a parched condition in the throat, while hunger is controlled by stomach contractions. In addition, Carlson (1913) reported that stomach contractions are periodical. Richter (1927) noted the relationship between Carlson's findings and his data demonstrating periodic fluctuations in random activity. He reasoned as follows:

Stomach contractions occur periodically (Carlson)
Behavior is periodical (Richter)
. . . Stomach contractions are related to behavior.

To test the relationship between stomach contractions and behavior, Richter inserted distended balloons into the stomachs of rats. He then related the presence or absence of the stomach contractions, detected by the balloons, to the animal's level of activity. As one might anticipate, Richter found a strong positive association between stomach contractions and behavior. He therefore concluded that hunger and thirst are "persisting tormenting stimuli" which "demand ingestion before they cease their goading." (This is very similar to Freud's notions about the persisting internal stimuli "from which there is no flight.")

Summary

The early investigations of drive emphasized the relationship between physiological deficits and (1) the tendency to overcome resistance or (2) random activity. Usually the appetitive drive level was varied, while the aversive restraining stimulus remained constant. The general conclusions from these investigations were that internal stimuli, arising from deprivation states, goad the animal into activity. The instigation of the behavior eventuates in the discovery and ingestion of the goal object. Consummatory behavior results in the offset of the driving, internal stimuli. The animal then becomes quiescent, only to leave the resting state when the internal stimuli again become intense. Recall that mechanistic psychologists frequently conceptualize the behavior of animate and inanimate objects in a similar manner. Stimuli must instigate behavior, and behavior ceases when the stimuli are removed. Higher mental processes do not intervene between the onset of the instigating stimuli and the behavioral event. Thus, one can see why the notion of "drive" became very central in the mechanistic analysis of motivation. We now turn our attention to Clark Hull and his drive theory of motivation.

SCIENTISTS WHO INFLUENCED HULL

A vast amount of data accumulated in the 1920s related level of deprivation (drive) to various behavioral indices. At the same time the psychology of learning was developing, new physiological techniques were being discovered, and the general field of experimental psychology was gathering momentum. The impact of Darwin, the growth of functionalism, the revolt of Watson, the learning psychology of Thorndike, the conditioning procedures of Pavlov, the physiological advances of Richter, the early deprivation experiments reviewed above—these advances, in conjunction with the theoretical style of Newton and Whitehead and Russell, formed the foundation for Hullian theory. Let us briefly examine the manner in which the preceding psychologists, movements, and logicians affected Hullian thought.

Charles Darwin

Darwin's importance is evident in that Hull's system is a model for survival. The organism is conceptualized as having needs that may be reduced with appropriate instrumental acts. Hull (1943) states in his *Principles of Behavior:*

Since the publication by Charles Darwin of the *Origin of the Species,* it has been necessary to think of organisms against a background of organic evolution and to consider both organismic structure and function in terms of *survival.* . . . It is the primary task of a molar science of be-havior . . . to understand why the behavior so mediated is so generally adaptive, i.e., successful in the sense of reducing needs and facilitating sur-vival, and why it is unsuccessful on those occasions when survival is not facilitated [pp. 17, 19].

John B. Watson

Hull was also greatly influenced by the behavioristic arguments of Watson. He states: "Having examined the general nature of scientific theory, we now proceed to the elaboration of an objective theory as applied spe-cifically to the *behavior* (italics mine) of organisms" (Hull, 1943, p. 16). Hull also acknowledged his debt to Watson by naming the unit of measure-ment of a behavioral tendency a "wat." Hull's conception of behavior, like Watson's, is mechanistic; there is no concept of consciousness or discussion of rationalism. There are stimuli and responses. The essential problems for behavior theory are how stimulus-response associations become strengthened and how such connections, or habits, become activated. Hull, however, was a *neobehaviorist*. That is,

While not giving up [objectivity] (and indeed trying to place its pursuit on a more secure footing), neobehaviorism sought to realize and imple-ment objectivism at the level of theory. The idea was to insure that all elements of a system language be "securely anchored" by explicit linkages to antecedent independent and consequent dependent variables, and, in general, to effect a point-for-point correspondence of the logical properties of systematic formulations of psychology with those of psychology's tradi-tional emulation-model, physics [Koch, 1964, p. 10].

Further, they were aware that

there was no one-to-one correspondence between stimulus conditions and response conditions . . . and their theories tend to be replete with references to intervening variables, mediating processes, and implicit stimulus-producing responses, the function of all these devices being to make manageable the conceptual treatment of intricate input-output relations [Berlyne, 1968, pp. 632–33].

In addition to a greater interest in theory construction, neobehaviorists such as Hull also generally attended to motivational, rather than learning, problems.

Edward L. Thorndike

Thorndike's (1911) investigations of the intelligence of animals also substantially affected Hull's position. Hull was quite familiar with Thorndike's work, having previously reviewed one of Thorndike's books for a journal. In a discussion of his own concept of reinforcement and the strengthening of habits, Hull (1943) says, "The term 'law' is here used in much the same loose way that Thorndike has used it in his famous expression, 'law of effect,' to which the above formulation is closely related" (pp. 71–72, footnote).

Thorndike began his investigations of animals in the basement of William James' home in the mid-1870s. His general procedure was to place animals, frequently cats or chicks, in an enclosed box. Outside of the box Thorndike would place food. If the animal made the "correct" response—the one the experimenter had designated as the response which would release the animal from the box—the animal would receive the food. Thorndike observed that initially the animal engages in relatively random (trial and error) behavior, until it accidentally emits the response resulting in its release. When replaced in the box, the animal makes that response sooner and sooner; ultimately, the correct response becomes the most immediate in the animal's hierarchy.

To explain this change in response hierarchies, or learning, Thorndike postulated his well-known Law of Effect. The law states that when a particular stimulus-response bond is followed by a satisfying state of affairs, the strength of that bond increases. Conversely, when a particular stimulus-response bond is followed by an annoying state of affairs, the strength of the bond is weakened. Thus, Thorndike postulated a symmetrical relationship between the behavioral effects of rewards and punishments. This has been called by many psychologists a "hedonism of the past" and is contrasted with Freud's formulation, which is labeled a "hedonism of the future." According to Thorndike, reward or punishment strengthens or weakens the preceding response, while Freud contends that the anticipated pleasure or pain determines future responses.

Thorndike realized that there was some degree of circularity in his formulation of the Law of Effect. One could say a satisfier is something that increases the strength of a connection, and that a connection is strengthened if it is followed by a satisfier. Therefore, Thorndike defined satisfiers and annoyers independent of the learning situation. He asserted that what he meant by a satisfier is something the animal would approach; an annoyer is something the animal would not approach, and would avoid if presented with that stimulus.

Thorndike's conception is indeed mechanistic. No mention is made of higher mental processes. Intelligence is merely an indication of existent associations. Thorndike believed that humans are more intelligent than animals because they have a greater number of associations in their response repertoire (see Bitterman, 1969).

Hull subsequently adopted Thorndike's position, but with an important modification, which we shall discuss in this chapter. (Later in his career Thorndike truncated his Law of Effect and rescinded the position that an annoyer decreases the strength of a connection; see Postman, 1962).

Ivan P. Pavlov

Pavlov, like Hull, was familiar with the work of Darwin, and held Darwin as his personal idol. He believed that through an understanding of the principles of learning he would be able to explain how organisms are able to adapt to their environment. For just as instincts were considered to be "advantageous in the history of the species," habits were believed to be "advantageous in the history of the individual" (Kimble, 1961, p. 18).[2]

[2] There is an interesting anecdote concerning the relationship between Pavlovian conditioning and Darwin's speculations concerning survival of the species. Pavlov initially was a Lamarckian; that is, he believed that acquired characteristics could be inherited. His reason apparently was well documented by data gathered in his laboratory. Pavlov noted that the offspring of the dogs in his laboratory were conditioning faster than their parents, who also had undergone conditioning experiences. Therefore, Pavlov concluded that the offspring must be profiting from the acquired knowledge of their parents. He reasoned that changes as a function of experience could be passed along to subsequent generations. What Pavlov failed to notice was that over time he was becoming a more proficient experimenter. The soundproofing of the laboratory rooms, the manner of stimulus presentation, the restraining of the dogs, and so forth, were being improved. The offspring indeed were conditioning faster, but because of the changes in the experimental

Pavlov's central quest was to determine how an inborn reflex could become modified as a result of experience. For example, he observed that a dog responds with salivation at the sight of bread. Yet this clearly must be a learned reflex, for the sight of bread without prior commerce with it does not evoke this response. Pavlov called the salivation at the sight of the bread a conditional reflex, because "its occurrence was conditional upon a prior association between the food and tasting it" (Miller 1962, p. 182).

To study conditional reflexes systematically, Pavlov tested dogs in a severely restricted environment. He paired a conditional stimulus (a bell) with food (the unconditional stimulus) by sounding the bell immediately before the food was placed in the animal's mouth. Eventually the sound of the bell would elicit salivation (the conditional response) before the food was placed in the animal's mouth.

This experimental procedure, known as classical conditioning, enabled Pavlov to study many phenomena, and to speculate about the neurological functioning of the brain that caused the observed behavior. (Pavlov perceived himself as a physiologist, not a psychologist. Paradoxically, his contributions were extremely important to psychology, while his speculations about the brain have not proved very fruitful for physiology.) Problems of stimulus generalization, discrimination, extinction, spontaneous recovery, and many other issues discussed in most elementary psychological texts were first investigated in Pavlov's laboratory. He also investigated more complex and molar phenomena, such as "neurotic" behavior. In his study of the dynamics of neurosis, Pavlov trained dogs to salivate to a specific tone, and simultaneously trained them not to salivate to a different tone. He then presented a stimulus that was between the two tones—one that did not clearly signal whether to expect or not to expect a food reward. In this situation the animals often exhibit behaviors that might be labeled as neurotic: squealing, urination, and other general indices of fear or anxiety.

Pavlov also examined the consequences of delaying the time interval between the onset of the conditional stimulus and the presentation of food. That is, he analyzed the persisting effects of the stimulus. Since no specifiable stimuli were present during the delay period, it was assumed that any resultant conditioning was caused by the trace of the conditional stimulus. Hull built his entire system around the conception of persisting

---

methodology, rather than because of the changes in genetic constitution. Towards the end of his career Pavlov acknowledged this alternative interpretation of the data, and grew more leery of the Lamarckian hypothesis. However, he never firmly rejected the possibility of transmitting learned behaviors.

neural traces. Hull states: "Indeed, were it not for the presumptive presence of stimulus traces it would be impossible to account for whole sections of well-authenticated molar behavior" (1943, p. 42). The importance of the stimulus trace in the Hullian system will become more evident in the ensuing pages.

As indicated previously, Hull adopted the findings of both Thorndike and Pavlov. He united for the first time the two respective types of learning—instrumental learning and classical conditioning—and contended that they could be explained with identical principles.

Curt P. Richter

Hull was guided by the physiological evidence and conceptions of internal stimuli suggested by Richter. According to Hull (1943):

During recent years physiologists and students of behavior have made important advances in unraveling the more immediate conditions which are associated with the onset of the activities characteristic of the three most complex primary drives—thirst, hunger, and sex. . . . The hunger drive seems to be precipitated, at least in part, by a rhythmic and, in extreme cases, more or less protracted contraction of the stomach . . . [pp. 60–61].

Alfred N. Whitehead and Bertrand Russell

In *Principia Mathematica,* Whitehead and Russell attempt to deduce the bulk of classical mathematics from a small number of explicit definitions and postulates. Guided by this approach and the prior success of Newton, Hull believed that psychological laws also could be derived from a basic postulate system. He included sixteen postulates in his system, and derived theorems and behavioral predictions from these postulates. His theory is labeled *hypothetico-deducto,* for laws are based on the process of deduction, rather than induction. It is evident that Hull also believed that psychology must proceed in a quantitative manner, with precise predictions derived mathematically. Thus, Hull produced a very formal system of motivation based on the premises of mechanism.

Summary and Prospectus

Hull concentrated upon two problems: the formation of habits and the activation of those associations. His thoughts on habit formation were guided by the prior investigations and thought of Thorndike, Pavlov, and

Watson. His conception of activation was based upon Richter's experiments and Darwin's notions of survival. His system was formal and mathematical, modeling the work of Newton and Whitehead and Russell. In the remaining pages of this chapter the question of the formation of associative connections is discussed but not stressed, although it was a central issue for Hull. The issue of habit formation properly belongs in a book on learning processes, rather than motivation. On the other hand, the problem of activation or drive is reviewed in detail, as is Hull's general behavior theory. We begin this discussion with an examination of the basic concepts in his theory, particularly habit, drive, and incentive.

THE BASIC CONCEPTS OF HULL'S THEORY

Hull postulated that at birth the behavior of organisms is the result of inherited, neural connections between receptors and effectors. That is, certain sensory inputs result in the evocation of unlearned response tendencies. These innate or unlearned responses are not merely random. Rather, they are most likely to terminate the needs of the organism. Examples of such unlearned responses include reflexes away from noxious stimulation, urination given a full bladder, and so forth. The unlearned responses are survival relevant; their existence can be analyzed by means of the basic principles set forth by Darwin.

One question Hull attempted to answer was how these unlearned response hierarchies change as a function of experience. That is, how does learning occur? What strengthens some responses while other responses are weakened? An identical question was posed by Pavlov: How are new habits formed that are advantageous to the survival of the organism?

Learning

Hull contended that learning occurs as a consequence of reinforcement. Further, reinforcement is the necessary condition of response acquisition for both instrumental learning (Thorndike) and classical conditioning (Pavlov) paradigms. Specifically, Hull (1943) states,

An inductive comparison of these superficially rather divergent forms of learning shows one common principle running through them all. This we shall call the *law of primary reinforcement*. It is as follows: *Whenever an effector activity occurs in temporal contiguity with the afferent impulse . . . and this conjunction is closely associated in time with the diminution in the receptor discharge characteristic of a need, there will result an increment to the tendency for that stimulus on subsequent occasions to evoke that reaction* [p. 80].

Later Hull (1951) essentially repeated this position:

Whenever an effector activity [response] is closely associated with a stimulus afferent impulse or trace [stimulus] and the conjunction is closely associated with the rapid diminution in the motivational stimulus (S_D or S_G), there will result an increment to a tendency for that stimulus to evoke that response [p. 20].

In summary, Hull believed that if a response to a given stimulus is closely followed in time by a reduction in the stimuli that accompany a drive, learning occurs. Recall that Richter postulated that internal stimuli act as "persisting, tormenting stimuli." The attainment of a goal temporarily eliminates the needs of the organism, and removes these internal stimuli as well. For example, food consumption by a hungry organism reduces the need for food and the stomach cramps that accompany that need; drinking eliminates the need for water and the parched throat accompanying that need; and so forth. The offset of the stimuli associated with the need state (drive stimuli) is rewarding, and the response made to those stimuli will tend to be repeated on subsequent occasions when these stimuli are again present.

Clearly, Hull's conception of learning is very similar to the one proposed earlier by Thorndike. It is, in essence, a restatement of the Law of Effect. However, Hull limited the possible satisfiers to one class of events: those that satisfy a need and reduce the internal stimulation associated with that need.

How does Hull explain the learning of new habits in the simple paradigm used by Thorndike? The response that enables Thorndike's cats or chicks to leave the box and reach food is observed to grow in strength over trials. Hull reasons that food consumption is rewarding because it reduces the internal stimuli associated with a state of food deprivation. Hence, on trials subsequent to the reward the cues or stimuli in the cage are more likely to evoke the response that was followed by the offset of the need. Hull labeled the acquisition of learned acts "habits" (*sHr*). The *s* and *r* indicate stimulus and response, and the *H* indicates that there is some mechanistic bond between the two, such that on the representation of the *s* there is a reasonable probability of the *r* recurring.

The *s* in *sHr* is not a simple construct; it is composed of many sources of stimuli. For example, in the Thorndikian box, or in a straight-runway apparatus, there are stimuli arising from the need itself, or *internal drive*

DIAGRAM 2:2
Stimuli in a Straight-Runway Situation

Start
Box

Goal
Box

S_D S_D S_D S_D S_D

S_{1E} S_{2E} S_{3E} S_{4E} S_{5E} $\longrightarrow$ $R_G \longrightarrow S_G$

$r_1\text{-}s_1$ $r_2\text{-}s_2$ $r_3\text{-}s_3$ $r_4\text{-}s_4$ $r_5\text{-}s_5$

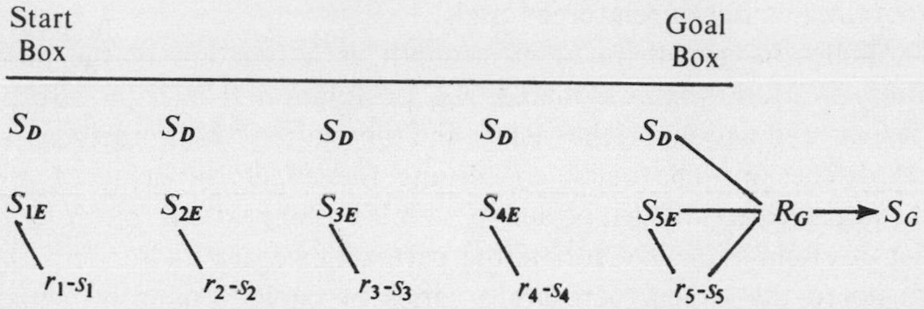

stimuli (S_D); there are stimuli whose source is the cues in the apparatus, or *external* stimuli (S_E); and there are the stimuli produced by the animal's response, or *response-produced* stimuli $(r\text{-}s)$. The latter stimuli represent internal, proprioceptive feedback generated by the musculature of the organism. The stimuli in a straight-runway situation may therefore be represented as in Diagram 2:2.

Diagram 2:2 indicates that the three sources of stimuli become associated with the goal response (R_G), and that the goal response also produces its own stimulation (S_G), or proprioceptive feedback associated with the eating response. Although all the sources of stimuli are associated with the response at the goal, the *S-R* connections are strengthened in differential degrees. The environmental stimuli close to the goal (S_{4E}) are believed to be more like the stimuli at the goal than are the stimuli at the start box (S_{1E}). Hence, the stimuli near the start box are not connected with the response to as great an extent as are the stimuli near the goal box. Perhaps an analysis of classical conditioning procedures makes this point clearer. Assume that an animal is trained to salivate to a tone of 500 cycles. It will then salivate more to a 600-cycle tone than to a 700- or 800-cycle tone. This observation calls attention to the phenomenon of *stimulus generalization:* the greater the similarity between the originally conditional stimulus and the testing stimulus, the more the likelihood of response evocation. Similarly, in an instrumental learning paradigm, the greater the similarity between the stimuli present at the time of the reward and the stimuli located at other points in the alley, the stronger is the association between those stimuli and the response.

The Determinants of Habit Strength. According to Hull, the necessary condition for the growth of a stimulus-response bond is *reinforcement* (drive stimulus reduction). Yet many other factors were postulated to influence the magnitude of the growth of a habit. Specifically, Hull (1943) postulated that the greater the quantity and quality of the reinforcing agent, and the more immediate the reinforcement following the response, the greater the growth of the habit. In addition, habit strength grows as a function of the number of reinforced trials.

While the growth in habit strength as a function of the number of rewards is intuitively reasonable, the postulation that habit strength also varies as a function of the delay and amount of reinforcement requires some discussion. The belief concerning the effects of delay of reinforcement was apparently supported by Hull's observations of the backward order of elimination of errors in the performance of rats in complex mazes. Hull noted that when there are a series of choice points in a maze, rats eliminate errors that occur near the goal sooner than errors that are far from the goal. The delay of reward in such maze situations is in one-to-one correspondence with the distance from the goal. Hull therefore reasoned that the habit to approach the goal, which is reflected in the error rates, is strengthened more at points near the goal because the correct response at those choice points is more immediately followed by the food reward. The discovery of a backward order of elimination of incorrect responses, and Hull's explanation of this observation, is known as the goal-gradient hypothesis; that is, there is a gradient in the efficacy of a reward as a function of distance (delay) from the goal region.

In addition, it was noted that the performance of organisms is a function of the amount and quality of the reward. Hull therefore concluded that the increment in the strength of stimulus-response bonds is a function of the amount of need reduction.

Secondary Reinforcement.   It is evident that a great deal of learning occurs when responses are not followed by primary reinforcers of food, water and the like. Consequently, Hull introduced the concept of secondary reinforcement into his theoretical system. The conception of secondary reinforcement was guided by a phenomenon also first observed by Pavlov. In the Pavlovian conditioning procedure a neutral stimulus (bell) presented in contiguity with an unconditional stimulus (food) comes to evoke a response similar to that evoked by the unconditional stimulus (salivation). By then pairing a different neutral stimulus with the bell, Pavlov was able to condition salivation to this new stimulus. That is, the bell itself was able to function as an unconditional stimulus and promote new learning. This phenomenon is called higher-order conditioning.

Hull borrowed from this conception in his analysis of secondary reinforcement:

A neutral receptor impulse (stimulus) which occurs repeatedly and consistently in close conjunction with a reinforcing state of affairs, whether primary or secondary, will itself acquire the power of acting as a reinforcing agent [1951, p. 28].

That is, a stimulus object that itself is not a primary reinforcer can acquire the properties of a reinforcer if it has been associated with a reinforcing state of affairs. The originally neutral stimulus is then labeled a secondary reinforcer.

Examination of experimental work to support the notion of a secondary reinforcement will make this concept somewhat clearer. In one early study, Bugelski (1938) trained rats to press a bar for food. He then extinguished the response by no longer having the reward follow the activity. In one group the depression of the bar that led to food was accompanied by the customary click of the food-releasing mechanism. In a second group the click did not accompany the bar press during the extinction period. Bugelski found that the click-extinction group executed 30 percent more bar pushing before they ceased responding than the nonclick group. This apparently indicated that the click, which always had been paired with the primary reinforcement of food, had acquired qualities of a secondary reinforcer. The presence of the secondary reinforcer during extinction helped to sustain the instrumental response. But because the click was no longer followed by the primary reinforcer, its secondary reinforcing properties also extinguished, and the bar-pressing response ultimately was not exhibited.

Another classic study is often cited to exemplify the phenomenon of secondary reinforcement. Cowles (1937) trained monkeys to insert tokens into a vending machine to obtain a primary reward of food. Following this training the monkeys would work for, and even hoard, the tokens. They would also learn new responses to obtain the tokens. Hence, the tokens must have had reinforcement value—that is, must have become secondary reinforcers—because of their prior association with the primary reward of food. (See Kimble, 1961, for a discussion of the many complex issues regarding primary and secondary reinforcers.)

Drive

Habit is the associative or learning construct in Hull's theory. A habit hierarchy specifies the direction behavior will take in given stimulus situations. Habit, however, is not isomorphic with the concept of behavior. It is a necessary but not sufficient construct to explain a behavioral event. For the organism to act, or to exhibit its learned responses, Hull states that there also must be some unsatisfied needs. It is debilitating for an organism to search for food if it is satiated, and adaptive for behavior to occur only when a need exists that is not satisfied. Hull (1943) states:

Since a need, either actual or potential, usually precedes and accompanies the action of an organism, the need is often said to motivate or drive the associated activity. Because of this motivational characteristic of needs they are regarded as producing primary animal *drives.* . . . The major primary needs . . . include the need for foods of various sorts (hunger), the need for water (thirst), the need for air, the need to avoid tissue injury (pain), the need to maintain an optimal temperature, the need to defecate, the need to micturate, the need for rest (after protracted exertion), the need for sleep (after protracted wakefulness), and the need for activity (after protracted inaction) [pp. 57, 59–60].

Hull's conception of the relationship between need and drive was:

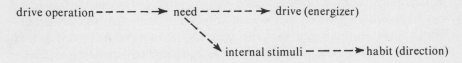

That is, antecedent conditions such as hours of food or water deprivation create a state of need. This need state has consequences for both the direction and the magnitude of behavior. Associated with each drive state is an internal stimulus (S_D), or proprioceptive feedback from the drive state, which direct the organism to the appropriate goal object (see Diagram 2:2). In addition, the state of need has drive characteristics, and drive provides the motor that energizes or activates behavior.

Acquired or Learned Drive.   The issue of secondary motivation, or learned drives, is of fundamental importance in Hullian theory. Osgood (1953) succinctly summarizes the reasons as follows:

It has been clear to psychologists for a long time that primary energizers, like hunger, thirst, and sex, are not the immediate determinants of human behavior. The graduate student slaves long hours over his books and papers, not because he is hungry nor because he relieves physical pain by these endeavors—then why? . . . If we conceive of motivation as an energizing process having roots in organismic physiology and conceive of reinforcement as a reduction in the intensity of this energizing process, we run full tilt into a puzzle: How can dollar bills, the praise of others, or saying "I'm good" modulate the dynamic energy systems of the organism? [p. 428]

The similarity between the concepts of secondary reinforcement and secondary drive should be evident. Organisms learn when a response is not followed by a primary reinforcer. Therefore, the Hullian conception had to be extended to include the possibility of secondary reinforcers; that is, stimuli that have rewarding properties yet are not drive reducing. Similarly, as Osgood indicates, behaviors occur when primary drives are absent. Therefore, Hull's conception had to be extended to include the possibility of secondary drives—stimuli that have drive properties yet are not bodily needs.

Fear as a learned drive was the focus of the initial work on acquired drives. The basic procedure in the investigation of fear as an acquired drive (Miller, 1948; summarized in Miller, 1951, and Mowrer, 1960) is probably familiar to most readers. Rats are placed in a two-compartment shuttle box. One of the compartments is painted white; the other is black. The two compartments are separated by a door. When placed in the white compartment, the animals receive an electric shock. The construction of the apparatus permits the animals to escape from the shock by running through the door into the black compartment. Initially the animals make this escape response with a relatively long latency and, when receiving the shock, exhibit signs of fear and pain such as urination, defecation, squealing, and so forth. Upon subsequent placements in the white compartment, the escape response rises in the animal's response hierarchy, and the response latency becomes shorter and shorter. After a number of trials, the animals run into the black compartment before the shock actually is on. That is, they *avoid* rather than *escape* the shock.

The experimental procedure then is slightly modified. The door between the black and white sides remains closed when the animals attempt to escape. The animals are required to learn a new response, such as turning a wheel that opens the door, to escape from the white compartment. Further, the shock in the white compartment is not turned on. In this situation the animals again initially exhibit behavioral indicators of fear when they discover that their previous avenue of escape is no longer available. They then engage in what appears to be a number of random activities; eventually a proportion of the animals discovers the response that enables them to escape. Again, over trials, this response is made with a shorter and shorter latency. The experimental sequence of events is portrayed in Figure 2:1.

The experimental investigation conducted by Miller became one of the most important demonstration experiments in psychology. Despite the relative simplicity of the experimental design, or perhaps because of it, the experimental results were responsible for a number of theoretical revisions in psychology. The study illustrated clearly the distinction between escape responses, which are made with the aversive stimulus present, and

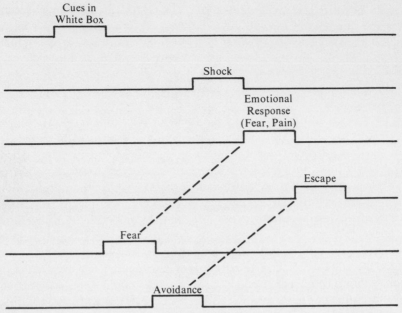

FIGURE 2:1.   Schematic representation of the temporal sequence in the fear-as-an-acquired-drive paradigm. The fear response, which initially follows shock, moves forward in the temporal sequence and is elicited by cues in the white box prior to the onset of the shock. Similarly, the instrumental escape response, which removes the organism from the aversive situation, is emitted prior to the onset of shock, thus becoming an avoidance response.

avoidance responses, which occur before the onset of the aversive stimulus. Secondly, the experiment apparently combines into one situation two types of learning—*instrumental learning* and *classical conditioning*. Thorndikian instrumental learning requires the selection of one response from a number of possible alternatives; it is the learning of responses. Pavlovian conditioning refers to the associative shifting of a response to a different stimulus; it is a stimulus substitution, or "*S-S* learning." In the fear-as-an-acquired-drive paradigm, both forms of learning are exhibited. Further, they appear in a temporal sequence. As indicated in Figure 2:1, fear is elicited by the stimuli in the white compartment prior to the onset of shock. This is the shifting of a response to a different stimulus. The laws regulating this learning apparently are based on Pavlovian contiguity principles. In addition, the animals learn to escape and avoid the shock in the white box. This is the selection and learning of new responses. Thus, two types of learning are exhibited in this experimental paradigm, and accordingly, two-factor theories of learning were postulated by Miller and Mowrer. (This position has since been revised by Mowrer, who now believes that all learning involves the conditioning of emotions. Further, Miller also has greatly revised his thinking about learning. These stories, however, would take us too far afield; the reader is directed to Mowrer, 1960, and Miller, 1963, for further details.)

For our purposes, the tremendous impact of the Miller procedure on learning theory is of secondary importance. Of prime consideration is the influence of his experiment on the conception of drive. Recall that according to Hull a tissue need acts as a drive and goads the organism into activity. Given no deficits, he argued, it would be maladaptive for the organism to continue to expend energy. He further maintained that drive reduction is a necessary condition for the acquisition of new responses. Let us see if the principles originally set forth by Hull can account for the observations of Miller. In the second phase of Miller's experiment, animals learn a new response when the shock is not on. In that condition, what motivates the organism or energizes the behavior? There is no damage to any body tissue before the onset of shock. In addition, why is the response learned and maintained? What drive is being reduced? Within the framework of Hull's 1943 conception of behavior it is impossible to explain the activation and the learning of avoidance responses.

Hull corrected this deficit in his 1951 book, *Essentials of Behavior,* in which he distinguishes between primary and secondary sources of drive. Hull (1951) states:

It is a matter of common observation that situations which are associated with drives themselves become conditioners. . . . Such acquired associative connections not only have motivational powers, but their diminution or cessation will now possess the power of reinforcement [pp. 21–22].

Generalizing on the above considerations [he continues], we arrive at the following corollary:

When neutral stimuli are repeatedly and consistently associated with the evocation of a primary or secondary drive and this drive stimulus undergoes an abrupt diminution, the hitherto neutral stimuli acquire the capacity to bring about the drive stimuli (SD) *which thereby becomes the condition* (CD) *of a secondary drive or motivation* [p. 25].

Let us see how this reasoning applies in the Miller paradigm. In this investigation, the cues in the white compartment are contiguously associated with the onset and offset of a drive. Therefore, the cues acquire the character of the drive itself. That is, they become secondary drives, or secondary motivators of behavior. Miller and Mowrer label this secondary drive fear, or anxiety. Anxiety or fear ". . . is a learned emotional reaction . . . acquired in accordance with the associative laws of classical conditioning" (Brown, 1961, p. 144). According to Miller (1951):

Fear is called *learnable* because it can be learned as a response to previously neutral cues; it is called a *drive* because it can motivate the learning and performance of new responses in the same way as hunger, thirst, or other drives [p. 436].

Miller states that the cues in the white compartment come to elicit the response of fear. Fear is conceptualized as a response that produces strong internal stimuli. These stimuli fall under the rubric of drive stimuli; therefore, responses associated with the reduction of these stimuli are reinforced. These principles were used to explain the instigation and the persistence of the avoidance response. The avoidance response is assumed to be activated by the learned drive of fear and acquired because it preceded the offset of the fear or anxiety stimuli (also see Mowrer, 1939).

In summary, in the Miller experiment on fear as an acquired drive, the alleged sequence of events is as follows: The cues in the white compartment become associated with shock because the cues and shock are presented contiguously. These cues then elicit fear. Fear produces strong stimuli; these stimuli energize behavior and persist until the correct response is discovered. This correct (escape) response leads to the offset of the anxiety stimuli and eventually becomes the prepotent response in the organism's hierarchy.[3]

Other secondary drives have been studied. In theory, secondary drives need not be limited to fear or anxiety. Any neutral stimulus paired with the onset and offset of a drive could become a secondary drive, according to the Hullian conception. However, the pairing is not a sufficient condition; Hull stated that there must be a rapid diminution of the primary drive stimuli. It might prove difficult for stimuli paired with appetitional drives to become secondary drives because the onset of hunger and thirst are relatively slow processes. For many years investigators have been unable to establish definitively a learned hunger drive (e.g., Siegel, 1943). Recently, however, some successful attempts to condition hunger have been reported (e.g., Wright, 1965).

An Alteration in the Conception of Action.   The investigations concerned with acquired drives changed the 1943 Hullian conception of drive.

[3] The reader should be aware that there are alternate conceptions of avoidance behavior that do not use a drive concept; see Schoenfeld, 1950.

Sources of drive were no longer limited to tissue deficits. Any internal stimulus could acquire drive properties, if it were of sufficient intensity. That is, strong internal stimuli motivate behavior, direct behavior, and their offset theoretically leads to new learning. The conception of drive advocated by Hull in 1951 is:

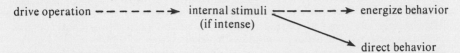

The Nondirective Conception of Drive. We have until now neglected an important aspect of the Hullian conception of drive. According to Hull, drive is a nonspecific energizer of behavior. All drives pool into one, and this pooled drive energizes all associative bonds or habits. Hull (1943) states:

The drive concept, for example, is proposed as a common denominator of all primary motivations, whether due to food privation, water privation, thermal deviations from the optimum, tissue injury, the action of sex hormones, or other causes. . . . This implies to a certain extent the undifferentiated nature of drive in general, contained in Freud's concept of the "libido." However, it definitely does not presuppose the special dominance of any one drive, such as sex, over the other drives [pp. 239, 241].

The conception of a nonspecific drive has been championed by Judson Brown, one of the most articulate spokesmen for and defenders of the drive concept. Brown (1961) asserts:

In current discussions of motivation it is commonplace to encounter the word 'drives.' For certain writers, this term apparently conveys the idea of multiple directedness. The hunger drive is said to be directed or to direct behavior toward food, the thirst drive toward water, and so on. But this terminology is confusing if, as we have argued, it is desirable to limit the function of a drive to that of an activator or motivator. If this latter position is adopted, drive can never be directed toward any specific goal, nor can it selectively activate one type of associative tendency to the exclusion of others, since this would indirectly involve a directive function. To speak of "drives" implies that the constructs so designated are alike, yet different. If they are exactly alike when *functioning as motivators,* then identical processes must be involved in all cases, and all drives, as activators, become one. If they are not alike as motivators, then each must be motivating, but in a unique way. Just what these different yet comparable ways might be is difficult for one to imagine. One might suppose, of course, that drives are all alike save that each is the result of its own distinctive motivational variable. But if this is the case, then we no longer have different drives as behavior determinants, but only *different sources of drive*. It is this line of reasoning that led us to entitle this chapter "Primary Sources of Drive" rather than "Primary Drives" [p. 60].

Brown continues:

As a further step toward terminological clarity, it was proposed that the use of the plural word 'drives' be dropped in favor of the singular form. This suggestion was supported primarily by the contention that the so-called drives can be differentiated with respect to their individual antecedent variables, but not in terms of their postulated effects upon behavior. The phrase 'multiple sources of drive' is proposed in place of the word drives [p. 94].

The Integration of Habit and Drive

Thus far we have outlined the determinants of habit strength and have presented a general conception of drive. A postulated mathematical relationship between drive and habit strength forms the heart of Hull's theory of motivation: Hull (1943, p. 242) states:

Physiological conditions of need, through their sensitizing action on the neural mediating structures lying between the receptors and the effectors (sHr), appear to combine with the latter to evoke reactions according to a multiplicative principle, i.e., reaction-evocation potentiality is the product of a function of habit strength multiplied by a function of the strength of drive: $sEr = f(sHr) \times f(D)$.

That is, behavior is emitted that previously was reinforced in the immediate stimulus situation, if there also exists a state of deprivation. Note that the organism does not "consider" what action to undertake, "anticipate" the goal, or the like. The mechanistic principles of drive and $S\text{-}R$ bonds are sufficient to explain action.

In summary, Hull's 1943 conception of the determinants of behavior specifies that motivation is a function of Drive $\times$ Habit. Habit strength, in turn, is a function of the number, amount, and delay of reinforcement. Drive is conceived as a pooled energy source comprised of all physiological disturbances, and is generally operationally defined as hours of deprivation of commodities necessary for survival.

The Emergence of Incentives

By 1951, in addition to changing his conception of drive, Hull altered his conception of the motivational role of incentives. He declared that the quality and the quantity of reinforcement affect behavior independent of their influence on habit. That is, incentive was conceived as a determinant of performance, rather than a determinant of response acquisition. Hull's conception of behavior in 1951 was altered from Drive × Habit to:

$$sEr = f(\text{Drive} \times \text{Habit} \times \text{Incentive}), \text{ or } sEr = f(D \times H \times K)$$

Incentive is generally symbolized with the letter "K", which supposedly stands for Kenneth Spence, because Spence was most responsible for the alteration in Hull's thinking.

Two questions that immediately come to mind are: Why did Hull alter his theory in this manner? What new evidence forced the conceptual change? To answer these questions the concept of "latent learning" must be examined.

Latent Learning. The psychologists employing the Columbia Obstruction Box in their search for the laws of behavior rarely manipulated the quality or quantity of the incentive in the goal box. When they did vary incentives it was because they believed that the goal object must be appropriate to the drive being manipulated; for example, food when animals are hungry, water when thirsty, and so forth. While studies manipulating drive level were being conducted by Warden, Warner, and Moss, Tolman and his colleagues concentrated their investigations upon the role of incentives in learning and performance. These investigators were especially concerned with the behavioral consequences of a change in incentives during the course of learning.

The classic experiment involving an incentive change was conducted by Blodgett (1929). In that investigation three groups of rats were trained in a multiple T-maze to approach a reward of food. One group of animals received food at the goal box on every trial. A second group was given nothing for two trials, and then food was introduced at the goal box. The third group of rats was given no apparent reward for six trials, with food then given on subsequent trials. The error scores of the three experimental groups revealed the pattern of results shown in Figure 2:2. It is clear from the figure that an immediate and disproportionately large gain occurs in the performance of the two groups first receiving rewards on the third and seventh trials.

A replication of this experiment was conducted by Tolman and Honzig (1930). These investigators also employed three groups of animals and a T-maze paradigm. One group of animals received a reward of food on every trial; a second experimental group never received food in the goal box; and for the third group of hungry rats reward was introduced on the eleventh trial. The findings of this study are shown in Figure 2:3.

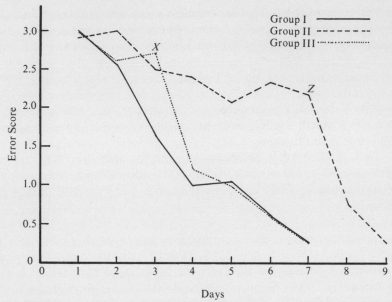

FIGURE 2:2.   The latent learning phenomenon. Group I was given a food reward on every trial. In Group II, the food reward was not introduced until the seventh day (at point Z). In Group III, the food reward was introduced the third day (at point X). Both Group II and Group III show a substantial decrease in errors after the first rewarded trial (from Blodgett, 1929, p. 120).

Again there is a disproportionate increment in performance as a consequence of the introduction of the food incentive.

The results of the Blodgett (1929) and Tolman and Honzig (1930) studies had important implications for Hull's conception of behavior. Recall that Hull first specified that the incentive value of a goal influences habit strength. But in the Blodgett and Tolman and Honzig experiments the changes in the level of performance occur suddenly and dramatically, immediately following the introduction of the reward. Therefore, it follows that incentive does not influence habit (or at least not *only* habit). For if incentives affect only response acquisition, then the performance level should not shift suddenly following the introduction of the reward. Habits are structures and do not vary abruptly, but grow in an incremental fashion. Hence, the demonstrations by Blodgett and Tolman and Honzig posed a difficult problem for Hullian theory.

An experiment by Crespi (1942), also altering the incentive value of the goal, further focused attention upon the issue discussed above. Instead of changing the incentive value from zero to a large amount, Crespi shifted the relative magnitude of reward during the course of his experiment. One group of animals, after receiving a relatively large reward, found a smaller reward at the goal. On the other hand, a group of rats receiving a small reward was shifted to a larger reward.

The data of this investigation again revealed abrupt shifts in the performance levels of the groups. The large-to-small reward group exhibited immediate decrements in performance level, while the small-to-large group displayed marked performance increments. Within the Hullian framework it is impossible to account for the performance decrements exhibited when the reward is shifted downwards. Drive level was not changed, and habit strength theoretically did not decrease, for the response was still being rewarded.

To account for the findings of Crespi, Blodgett, and Tolman and Honzig, Hull (1951) made incentive a determinant of performance, rather than a determinant of learning. As indicated, his new conception of behavior specified that performance is a function of Drive × Habit × Incentive. Learning was a function only of the number of rewarded trials. It was postulated that any reward of sufficient magnitude results in an increment in a stimulus-response bond. The amount of the reward was not believed to influence the degree of learning.

The change in Hull's conception enabled the theory to incorporate

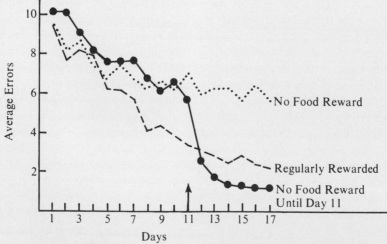

FIGURE 2:3. Evidence for latent learning in the maze. With no food reward there is some reduction in errors, but not as great a reduction as with regular food reward. Despite the higher scores prior to the introduction of food, the group rewarded only from the eleventh trial immediately begins to do as well as the group that had been regularly rewarded. The interpretation is that some learning went on within the first 10 trials that did not show in performance until the food incentive activated it (after Tolman & Honzig, 1930, from Hilgard & Bower, 1966, p. 200).

the results reported by Crespi and some of the data from the latent learning studies. Consider first the findings reported by Crespi. Changing the magnitude of the incentive alters the incentive (K) component of the determinants of behavior. If the magnitude of K increases or decreases, then reaction potential or the strength of motivation immediately is theoretically augmented or lessened. Thus, the basic data reported by Crespi may be considered evidence in support of Hull's (1951) conception.

The same general explanation can be applied to the latent learning investigations. However, the latent learning findings pose other difficulties for Hullian theory. The disproportionate drop in error scores for groups suddenly given reward indicates that the animals possessed the requisite instrumental habits prior to the rewarded trial. Thus, they must have been learning on the unrewarded trials. However, this learning was "latent,"—not exhibited in behavior—until there was a "reason" to perform. The learning-performance distinction clarified by Tolman is one of the essential stepping stones in the growth of motivational psychology, and its separation from the field of learning.

In summary, latent learning and incentive shift studies resulted in the incentive value of the goal being conceived as a determinant of performance, with behavior expected to vary directly with the magnitude of the incentive properties of the goal object. Habit strength was no longer postulated to be a function of the amount of reward. However, whether learning could occur without *any* reward remained a point of theoretical contention. Hullians argued that some reward must have been received on all trials in the latent learning experiments, even though the experimenter had not purposely introduced that reward. For example, perhaps the handling of the animals or the smell of the goal box served as secondary reinforcers. The latent latent learning studies thus clarified the role of incentives in a theory of action, while raising questions that remained unanswered about the conceptualization of the acquisition of knowledge.

Kenneth Spence and the Conceptual Analysis of Incentives.   Spence contends that in instrumental learning paradigms the events within the goal box are of central importance in the determination of subsequent performance. He argues that these events, or goal responses (R_G), become conditioned to the cues in the goal box. Further, the goal responses produce their own pattern of stimulus feedback (S_G). The goal responses, which include chewing, salivating, and so forth, theoretically will then be emitted earlier in the runway, prior to the entrance into the goal region, for the stimuli in the alleyway are similar to those at the goal. However, the identical responses are not emitted in the goal and in the runway, for the stimuli are not identical in these locations. Further, goal responses cannot be emitted at all points in the runway; there is no environmental sup-

DIAGRAM 2:3
Stimulus Situation in a Straight Runway According to Spence

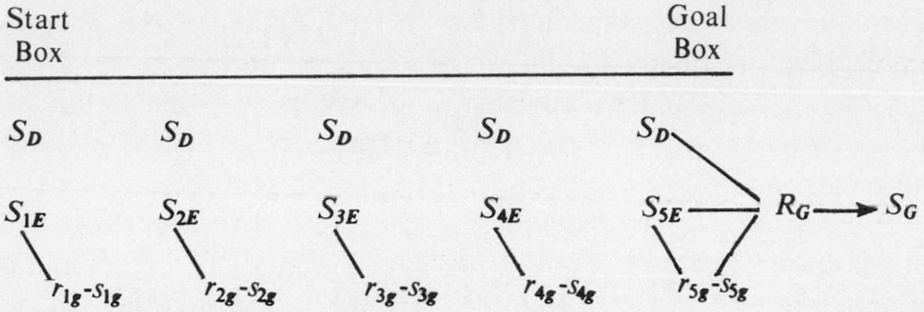

Start
Box

Goal
Box

$$S_D \qquad S_D \qquad S_D \qquad S_D \qquad S_D$$

$$S_{1E} \qquad S_{2E} \qquad S_{3E} \qquad S_{4E} \qquad S_{5E} \longrightarrow R_G \longrightarrow S_G$$

$$r_{1g}\text{-}s_{1g} \qquad r_{2g}\text{-}s_{2g} \qquad r_{3g}\text{-}s_{3g} \qquad r_{4g}\text{-}s_{4g} \qquad r_{5g}\text{-}s_{5g}$$

port for an eating response when food is not available. Thus, only part of the goal response can generalize back from the goal to the prior sections in the alleyway. The runway responses, which are similar to the goal responses, are labeled by Spence as *fractional anticipatory goal responses* (r_g) They are "fractional" because the entire goal response is not emitted. And they are "anticipatory" because the animals appear to be expecting a reward. They lick their lips, salivate, make chewing motions, and the like.[4] Hence, one might infer that the animals are acting in a purposive manner and have foresight of the goal, although Spence would argue such an anlaysis is incorrect. Diagram 2:3 shows the conception of the stimulus situation in a runway.

Diagram 2:3 is very similar to Hull's prior formulation (see Diagram 2:2). However, Hull generally ignored the importance of response produced feedback in his theoretical anlyses, while Spence makes them the heart of his theory.

Spence states that the anticipatory goal response (r_g-s_g) is the mechanism that underlies the construct of incentive. He argues that incentives, like drive, motivate the organism. The goal responses, by producing their own stimulation, increase the total amount of internal stimuli acting upon the organism. Miller's studies of fear as a learned drive resulted in the belief that any strong stimulus could act as a drive. Therefore, because incentives result in an increment in the internal stimulus situation, they have drive properties. Rather than accepting Hull's statement that drive multiplies incentive, Spence postulates that drive and incentive are additive, and together multiply habit to determine effective reaction potential:

$$sEr = f(\text{Drive} + \text{Incentive}) \times \text{Habit}$$

In this conception incentive and drive have the same energizing function. Thus, the existence of either a drive state (push) or an incentive (pull) is sufficient to activate behavior. However, the antecedents of drive and

---

[4] See Bindra, 1969, for contradictory evidence regarding behavior at different points in a runway.

incentive vary. Drive is operationally defined as the number of hours of deprivation, strength of an aversive stimulus, and the like, while the incentive value of a goal is assumed to be a function of the properties of the goal object, such as amount or quality, and the number of rewarded trials. The latter antecedent indicates that incentives, as habits, are learned. Thus, incentive may be considered a structural as well as a dynamic variable.

EMPIRICAL SUPPORT FOR DRIVE THEORY

The basic concepts in the Hull-Spence theory of motivation—habit, drive, and incentive—have been introduced. In addition, the evolution of the conceptual meaning of these constructs has been examined. We now turn to some of the data generated by the drive theory conception of behavior. Three questions will be raised: (1) What empirical support is there for the conception of drive as an energizer of behavior? (2) What data support the postulation that drive and habit are related multiplicatively, while incentive and drive are related additively? (3) Is drive a pooled energy source? Following a brief review of relevant supporting investigations, successful extensions of the theory to the areas of frustration and conflict are examined.

Investigations with Infrahuman Subjects

An early study conducted by Perin (1942), combined with data from an investigation by Williams (1938), is prototypical of experiments cited in support of the Hullian conception of motivation. These investigators trained rats to make a simple bar-press response to receive food. The animals learned this response while under 23 hours of food deprivation, and received from 5 to 90 reinforced trials. The groups were then subdivided, and extinction trials were administered when the animals had been deprived for either 3 or 22 hours. Figure 2:4 shows the results of these experiments. The figure shows that both the number of reinforced trials (habit strength) and the amount of deprivation (drive) influence resistance to extinction. As anticipated, the greater the magnitude of drive during the extinction trials, and the greater the number of reinforced trials during original learning, the stronger the tendency to emit the previously learned response. The curves representing the two deprivation groups also diverge. This indicates that the relationship between habit and drive is multiplicative, as specified by Hull. If the two determinants were related additively, the curves would be parallel, rather than divergent. The general pattern of results found by Perin and Williams has been replicated many times

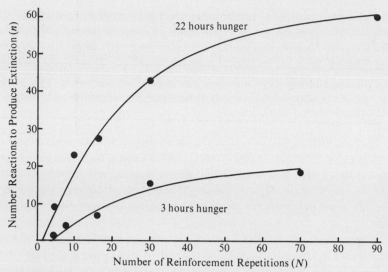

FIGURE 2:4. Graphic representation of smooth learning curves showing the combined effects of two levels of drive (hours of deprivation) and habit (number of reinforced trials) on resistance to extinction (adapted from Perin, 1942, p. 101).

with somewhat different experimental procedures and various dependent variables (see reviews in Bolles, 1967; and Brown, 1961).

A number of investigations conducted by Spence and his students also are representative of the work supporting the Drive $\times$ Habit theory of behavior. The hypotheses guiding these investigations are simple yet precise derivations from the Hullian postulate system. Therefore, they nicely illustrate the capability of the theory to make specific predictions. Consider, for example, the following prediction by Spence (1958b):

The first test of this theoretical schema that we shall consider involves a further implication with regard to instrumental conditioning. As we have seen, the theory, as formulated, derives the established fact that level of performance in instrumental reward conditioning is a positive function of the deprivation period (T_d). The further prediction may be made that generalization curves of performance for groups trained to respond to the same stimulus under different drive levels will converge. The derivation of this implication is as follows:

$$E_s = H \times D_s$$
$$E_w = H \times D_w$$
$$E_s - E_w = H(D_s - D_w)$$

in which E_s represents the response potential of a strong-drive group and E_w that for a weak-drive group. As may be seen from the third equation, the magnitude of $(E_s - E_w)$, the difference between the excitatory potentials of the two groups, is a multiplicative function of H and $(D_s - D_w)$, the difference between the drive levels of the two groups. Since habit strength decreases as a function of the distance of the generalized stimulus from the original training stimulus, it may be predicted that the difference between the excitatory strengths of the two drive level groups will decrease as the distance along the generalization dimension increases. Or, in other words, generalization curves for performance measures linearly related to E will exhibit convergence [p. 83].

That is, Spence predicts that the difference between response tendencies of groups differing in drive level will decrease as the habit strength of the response also decreases. This follows because drive multiplies habit. Taken to its extreme, if habit strength were equal to zero, there would be no difference between the response tendencies of strong and weak drive groups.

Spence reports evidence from an experiment by Newman (1955) that confirms this hypothesis. Rats were trained to run toward a circle of food when under $23\frac{1}{2}$ hours food deprivation. After training, half the animals were shifted toward a higher level of deprivation, and half were shifted downward. The groups were further subdivided and the animals given generalization test trials by varying the diameter of the training circle. The results of this investigation are shown in Figure 2:5. As the Drive $\times$ Habit

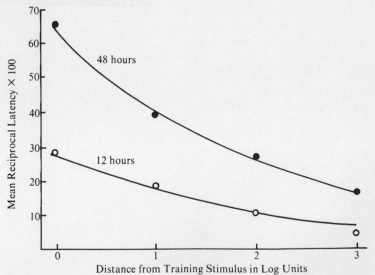

FIGURE 2:5. Data from Newman (1955) showing the joint effects of hours of deprivation and habit strength on response latency. Habit strength was varied by manipulating the similarity of the stimuli during the training and testing periods (from Spence, 1958b, p. 84).

conception predicted, the curves tend to converge as habit strength, which in this situation is a function of the similarity of the training-testing circles, decreases.

More Complex Theoretical Derivations. Spence is a two-factor learning theorist, as opposed to Hull, who believed that the principles of classical conditioning and instrumental learning are identical. Spence suggests that in instrumental learning situations habit strength is a function of the number of trials, or the amount of response experience. He asserts that drive reduction is not a determinant of response acquisition in instrumental learning. When considered in conjunction with his postulation that drive and incentive are additive, a number of interesting hypotheses are derived from the drive theoretical position.

Consider a straight runway apparatus in which animals under different degrees of food deprivation learn to approach the food cup in the goal box. The excitatory potential (strength of motivation) at short (E_s) and long (E_l) distances from the goal box is conceptualized as:

$$E_s = H(D + K_s)$$
$$E_l = H(D + K_l).$$

Inasmuch as incentives are learned reaction to specific stimuli, it is assumed that the magnitude of K varies as a function of the distance from the goal box. K_s symbolizes the incentive value at short distances from the goal, and K_l the value at longer distances.

Multiplying this equation and subtracting yields:

$$E_s = HD + HK_s$$
$$E_l = HD + HK_l$$
$$E_s - E_l = HD + HK_s - (HD + HK_l) = H(K_s - K_l).$$

The final equation indicates that the difference in the excitatory potential at the long and short distances from the goal is independent of the level of drive. Spence (1956) reports data that confirm this prediction. The differences between the speed of running for food of animals 3 or 9 feet from the goal are identical when the animals are under deprivation of 3 or 22 hours duration (see Hilgard, 1956, p. 420).

A similar prediction was derived by Spence in a discrimination experiment in which the number of responses to the reinforced and nonreinforced stimuli are equated. In the choice paradigm employed by Spence, animals were allowed to make a free response at a choice point on two successive trials. Both the positive (E+) and negative (E-) stimuli—that is, the stimuli paired or not paired with the reward—were available. On the next two trials the selected alternative was unavailable (a barrier was placed in the path), and the animal was forced to respond to the previously unchosen stimulus. Following Hilgard (1956), the difference between the strengths of the excitatory potentials toward the correct and incorrect stimuli is, in part, conceptualized as:

$$E+ = (H+)(D + K)$$
$$E- = (H-)D$$
$$(E+) - (E-) = (DH+) + (KH+) - (DH-)$$
$$(E+) - (E-) = KH+$$

(where $H+$, the correct habit, and $H-$, the incorrect habit, are equal because of the forced response procedure). The equation indicates that the difference between the strengths of the excitatory tendencies is independent of the level of drive. This prediction also has been confirmed by Spence (1956): discrimination performance in this situation is not related to the time of deprivation. That is, differences in the tendencies to respond to the correct or incorrect stimuli are not affected by the level of drive when exposure to the two stimuli are forced to be equal.

As the above equation indicates, the tendency to respond to the positive stimulus $(E+)$ exceeds the tendency to respond to the negative or

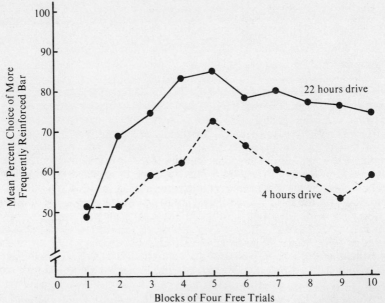

FIGURE 2:6.   Data from Ramond (1954) showing percentage choice of the more frequently reinforced bar for two groups differing in drive level. Ramond utilized a double-bar Skinner-type box in this free choice situation. One of the bars $(E+)$ was reinforced twice as frequently as the other bar $(E-)$ (from Spence, 1956, p. 210).

unrewarded stimulus $(E-)$. This is due to the added K factor given the correct response. In a free-, as opposed to forced-response situation, the number of choices of the two stimuli will therefore differ. The strengths of the correct and incorrect habits $(H+$ and $H-)$ will therefore diverge over trials. In a free-response situation, the conceptualization of the excitatory potentials is:

$$E+ = (H+)(D + K)$$
$$E- = (H-)D$$
$$(E+) - (E-) = (DH+) + (KH+) - (DH-)$$
$$(E+) - (E-) = D[(H+) - (H-)] + (KH+).$$

The difference in excitatory potentials when responses are not equated is therefore expected to be a function of the level of drive during the testing period. Ramond (1954) reports evidence that supports this complex derivation (see Figure 2:6).

Investigations of Human Behavior

Spence also presents evidence in support of the Drive $\times$ Habit conception from studies of classical aversive conditioning and verbal learning. To explain data in these areas Spence utilizes additional intervening variables incorporated within the drive theoretical framework. Spence (1958a) states:

The theory takes its start from Hull's basic assumption that the excitatory potential, E, determining the strength of a response is a multiplicative function of a learning factor, H, and a generalized drive factor, D, i.e., $E = H \times D$. We have assumed, further, that the drive level, D, in the case of aversive situations at least, is a function of the magnitude or strength of a hypothetical response mechanism—a persisting emotional response in the organism, designated as r_e, that is aroused by any form of aversive stimulation. That is, aversive, stressful stimulation is assumed to arouse activity under the control of the autonomic nervous system, which, according to some neurophysiological evidence, may act as an energizer of cortical mechanisms. Those of you who are familiar with the theoretical writings of Miller and Mowrer will recognize that this mechanism is similar to one these writers have postulated in connection with their investigations of acquired motivation. Thus they assumed that aversive stimuli arouse a hypothetical pain (emotional) response which, when conditioned to previously neutral stimulus events, provides the basis for an acquired drive of fear.

On the basis of an analogy with overt reflexes to noxious stimulation, there were a number of properties that could be assigned to our hypothetical response mechanism. Three, in particular, will be discussed here. The first and most obvious is based on our knowledge that the magnitude or strength of observable reflexes to noxious stimulation (e.g., the corneal reflex to an air puff, the GSR to an electric shock) varies directly with the intensity or degree of noxiousness of the stimulus. Assuming our hypothetical emotional response, r_e, would exhibit the same property, it followed that the level of drive, D, present in classical defense conditioning would be a positive function of the intensity of the US. From the remaining portion of the theory, it could be deduced that the performance level, e.g., frequency of CR's, would vary positively with the intensity of the US employed [p. 132].

To summarize, Spence is stating that emotional responses are the mechanisms that mediate drives in classical aversive settings. Further, these emotional responses directly vary as the function of the intensity of an unconditioned stimulus. Hence, performance in a classical aversive setting is expected to be a function of the level of unconditioned stimulus, such as the strength of shock or intensity of an aversive air puff.

Spence reports a number of studies that demonstrate that the probability of a conditioned eyelid response is a function of the intensity of the UCS, which is operationally defined as the strength of an air puff to the eye (see Figure 2:7). Summarizing Figure 2:7, Spence (1958b) states, "it is clearly evident that the curves exhibit an increasing divergence with

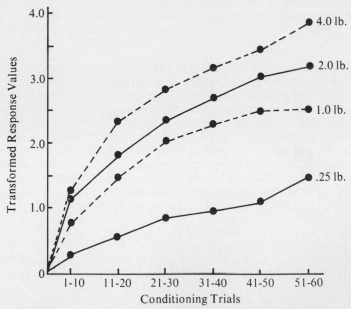

FIGURE 2:7.   Performance during acquisition of eyelid conditioned responses as a function of the intensity of the UCS (units in lbs.) (adapted from Spence, 1958b, p. 78).

conditioning trials, thus corroborating the multiplicative law found in the case of appetitional motivation" (p. 78).

Spence (1958a) carries his analysis of r_e mechanism still further, when he states,

[Another] implication of our theoretical mechanism was based on the well-known fact or observation that individuals differ in the magnitude of their reflex responses to a given intensity of stimulation. By analogy, again, we were led to assume that individuals would differ characteristically in the magnitude of this response, r_e, to the same intensity of stressful stimulation. If now there were available some means of assessing differences in this emotional responsiveness of individuals, our theoretical schema would lead to the prediction that highly emotional subjects, as assessed by the measuring device, would exhibit a higher level of performance in aversive forms of conditioning than subjects who scored low on the device [p. 132].

That is, given the same magnitude of the *UCS,* some individuals act "as if" it were more intense than others do. If these individuals could be identified, then it would be predicted that they will condition faster than individuals reacting less emotionally to the shock. Note that the operations of setting two levels of shock, or setting only one level but identifying two levels of reactivity, are logically equivalent.

Individual Differences and Aversive Conditioning. To measure the tendency to respond emotionally to an aversive stimulus, Janet Taylor (1953) developed the Manifest Anxiety (MA) scale. The MA scale consists of fifty keyed items taken from the Minnesota Multiphasic Personality Inventory and a number of buffer or unkeyed items. The keyed items were agreed upon by four out of five clinicians as being manifestations of high anxiety.[5] Typical items and their scaling keys are:

I cry easily	<u>T</u>	F
I work under a great deal of tension	<u>T</u>	F

Spence and his colleagues have conducted a number of studies comparing the performance of subjects classified as high or low in anxiety (drive) in eyelid conditioning situations. A representative experimental result obtained by Spence and Taylor (1951) is shown in Figure 2:8. In the Spence and Taylor (1951) experiment, air puffs at two levels of intensity are combined with two levels of emotionality. Examination of the

---

[5] Kimble and Posnick, 1967, report very high correlations between the MA scale and other scales comprised of items unrelated to anxiety per se, but containing items pertaining to unique reactions or responses at variance with the behaviors of others. An example of such an item is: I laugh easily.

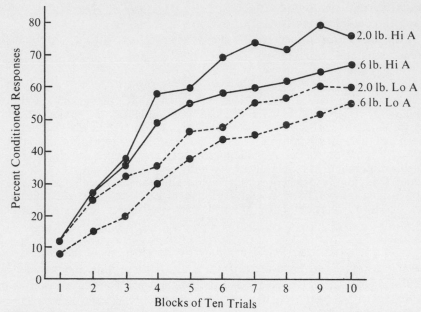

FIGURE 2:8.   Data from Spence and Taylor (1951) showing performance in eyelid conditioning as a function of level of anxiety and intensity of the *UCS* (adapted from Spence, 1958a, p. 134).

figure reveals that within each of the levels of puff intensity, subjects classified as high in anxiety (HA) exhibit more conditioned eyelid responses than subjects low in anxiety (LA). In addition, the higher intensity *UCS* produces faster conditioning than the lower intensity *UCS,* as was indicated in the previous discussion. The divergence of the curves again indicates a multiplicative relationship between drive and habit.

Spence (1964) summarized his research relating eyelid conditioning performance to score on the MA scale (see Table 2:1). He concludes:

Looking at the findings of the studies included in Table [2:1], a number of characteristics may be noted. First, the proportion of instances in which the conditioning performance of the HA group was higher than that of the LA group is much greater than one would expect by chance. Thus, the results of 21 of 25 comparisons were in this direction. If there actually were no relation between the MA scale and conditioning performance, the probability of obtaining such a percentage of differences (84 percent) in the same direction by chance is less than .01 [p. 133].

Not all the data, however, support the Spence-Taylor predictions. For example, in an experiment reported by Bindra, Patterson, and Strzelecki (1955), subjects classified as high or low in anxiety were com-

TABLE 2:1
Iowa Studies of Conditioning Performance of Preselected HA and LA Scale Ss
(from Spence, 1964, p. 130)

Iowa Experiments	Number of Trials	Ready Signal	UCS (psi)	Number of Ss	Percent Conditioned Response		Difference (H–L)	P
					HA	LA		
1. Taylor (1951)	80	Yes	1.6	60	59.6	27.9	21.7	.001
2. Spence-Taylor (1951)	100	Yes	.6	50	48.2	33.8	14.4	.05[a]
	100	Yes	2.0	50	55.0	41.7	13.3	.05
3. Spence-Farber (1953)	60	Yes	1.0	64	48.8	34.1	14.7	.05
4. Spence-Beecroft (1954)	50	Yes	1.0	45	56.5	36.3	20.2	.02
5. Spence-Weyant (1960)	100	No	.25	36	41.8	28.6	13.2	.10[b]
	100	No	2.0	36	65.4	53.2	12.2	.10
6. Spence (unpublished)	80	Yes	.25	60	36.5	21.6	14.9	.02[c]
	80	Yes	1.50	60	48.0	38.8	9.2	.02

[a] The F value based on all groups provided a p value < .01.
[b] The F value based on all groups provided a p value < .05.
[c] The F value based on all groups provided a p value < .01.

pared in a salivary conditioning paradigm. The investigators report that there are no differences in conditioning as a function of individual differences in score on the MA scale. Salivary conditioning procedures however, do not employ an aversive stimulus. According to Spence (1958a):

So far as the usual type of human learning experiment is concerned, the question as to whether High A subjects would be more emotional than Low A subjects, and hence have a higher D level, is a moot one. In this connection two alternative sub-hypotheses have been proposed: (a) the chronic hypothesis: that High A subjects react emotionally in a chronic manner to all situations, whether stressful or not; and (b) the emotional reactivity hypothesis: that High A subjects have a lower threshold of emotional responsiveness and react with a stronger emotional response than Low A subjects to situations containing some degree of stress. As may be seen, according to the first of these hypotheses, mild nonthreatening situations would produce a differential drive (D) level in subjects scoring at extremes of the scale; whereas according to the second, there would not be a difference [p. 137].

The experiment by Bindra et al. suggests that the emotional reactivity conception outlined by Spence is the better one. In a salivary conditioning experiment stress is not aroused. If the score on the MA scale were representative of a disposition to react emotionally in stressful situations, then no differences in behavior would be expected between the groups in the Bindra et al. experiment.

Paired-Associates Learning.   Spence and his colleagues also have applied the Drive × Habit conception in the learning of simple and complex paired-associates. Spence reasons that a simple list of paired-associates, or any easy task, is one in which the correct response is dominant in the person's response hierarchy. That is, the response paired with the stimulus is the most probable response the individual will give upon presentation of the stimulus. Spence contends that in this situation an increase in the level of drive will augment performance; that is, result in faster learning, fewer errors, and so forth.

The derivation of this hypothesis requires that an increment in drive level increase the absolute difference between the tendencies to emit the correct and incorrect response to a stimulus. Assume, for example, that a stimulus elicits two responses—one correct (C), the other incorrect (I). Further, assume that the strength of the C habit equals 2, while the strength of the I habit equals 1. For a low drive group (D = 1), the difference in the excitatory potentials of the two responses (EC and EI) is:

$$EC = 1 \times 2 = 2$$
$$EI = 1 \times 1 = 1$$
$$EC - EI = 2 - 1 = 1$$

However, for a high drive group $(D = 2)$, the difference in the excitatory potentials of the two responses is:

$$EC = 2 \times 2 = 4$$
$$EI = 2 \times 1 = 2$$
$$EC - EI = 4 - 2 = 2$$

Thus, the difference in the excitatory potentials between the C and I responses is higher among high drive than low drive persons. Subjects classified as high in anxiety (drive) therefore are expected to perform relatively better on simple tasks than subjects classified as low in drive.

The analysis of a complex task is more difficult and involves the use of other concepts in deriving predictions from the Hull-Spence theory. Spence reasons that a number of competing responses are aroused by the stimuli of a difficult (complex) task. The excitatory potentials of some of these responses are below the threshold level. The threshold refers to a limen of response strength that must be reached before the response can be expressed in overt action. According to Hull (1943), the term threshold "implies in general a quantum of resistance or inertia which must be overcome by an opposing force before the latter can pass over into action" (p. 343).

Let us analyze a complex task and discover how the threshold, in part, determines the hypothesized speed of learning. Assume a task in which the magnitude of the correct (C) habit is again 2. In addition, assume that there are two competing habits. The magnitudes of these two incorrect (I) habits are 2 and 1. Further, assume that the threshold level is 2; that is, two units of excitatory potential are necessary for the response to be overtly expressed. For a weak drive group $(D = 1)$, this situation may be conceptualized as:

$$EC = 1 \times 2 = 2$$
$$EI_1 = 1 \times 2 = 2$$
$$EI_2 = 1 \times 1 = 1$$

$$\text{Probability } EC = \frac{EC}{EC + EI_1} = \frac{2}{2 + 2} = .50[6]$$

The strength of the incorrect tendency equals that of the correct response tendency, and has an equal chance of being elicited. EI_2 is not included among the determinants of behavior, for it is below the threshold level by one unit.

---

[6] For ease of illustration, derivations here are shown as probabilities or ratios, rather than as differences. Predictions of difference versus ratio models are not necessarily equivalent.

For a strong drive group $(D = 2)$, this situation is conceptualized as:

$$EC = 2 \times 2 = 4$$
$$EI_1 = 2 \times 2 = 4$$
$$EI_2 = 2 \times 1 = 2$$

$$\text{Probability } EC = \frac{EC}{EC + EI_1 + EI_2} = \frac{4}{4 + 4 + 2} = .40$$

The combined strength of the I tendencies exceeds that of the C tendency by two units, for both EI_1 and EI_2 are above threshold, and have some probability of competing with the correct response.

In sum, in a strong drive group the probability of the correct response (.40) is less than the probability of a correct response among subjects in a weak drive group (.50). In a complex task, subjects low in drive should perform better than subjects high in drive.

An interaction is therefore expected between drive level and performance at easy and complex tasks. Given an easy task, individuals high in drive are expected to perform better than those low in drive. Conversely, given a difficult (complex) task, persons high in drive are expected to perform worse than those in a low drive group.

Spence and his associates (Spence, Farber, & McFann, 1956; Spence, Taylor, & Ketchel, 1956; Taylor & Chapman, 1955) believe that they have established the experimental conditions necessary to test the above hypotheses. They employ paired-associates tasks and create easy (noncompetitive) and difficult (competitive) lists by varying the degree of pre-experimental associations between the stimulus-response pairs in the list. In the easy list, the stimulus words tend to elicit the responses prior to list learning. Examples of the pairs in the list are:

Roving–Nomad
Tranquil–Quiet
Pious–Devout

Because the response members of the pairs are synonyms of the stimulus members, they are high in the repertoire of response associates to the stimulus words. Heightened drive should therefore increase the differences between the excitatory potentials of the correct and incorrect responses and facilitate learning.

The experiments testing this hypothesis are straightforward. Subjects scoring in the upper and lower extremes on the MA scale form high and low drive groups. They then are presented the stimulus-response pairs, and must correctly anticipate the response members in the list. The results of

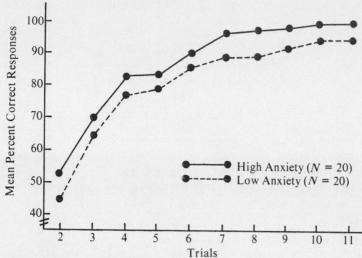

FIGURE 2:9. Paired-associates learning as a function of anxiety under conditions of minimal interpair competition and high initial stimulus-response associative strength (from Spence, Farber, & McFann, 1956, p. 300).

these investigations confirm the hypothesis that subjects scoring high on the MA scale learn the easy list faster than subjects scoring low on the scale. Figure 2:9 portrays the results of one pertinent study conducted by Spence, Farber, and McFann (1956).

To create a difficult or competitive list of paired-associates, the response members of the pairs are selected from those low in the subject's response hierarchy before he starts the task. In addition, incorrect responses to the stimuli that are high in the subject's hierarchy are included among other responses in the list. Examples of pairs used to establish competitive lists are:

Tranquil–Placid
Quiet–Double
Serene–Headstrong

The stimulus words in this example are synonyms, and all tend to elicit the response of placid. Thus, two pairings are created in which an incorrect response has a reasonable probability of elicitation. Figure 2:10 shows that the speed of learning of words with high interpair competition is faster among subjects low than high in anxiety (Spence, Farber, & McFann, 1956).

In sum, the hypothesized interaction between task difficulty and drive

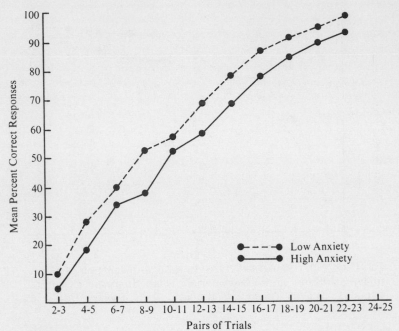

FIGURE 2:10.   Paired-associates learning as a function of anxiety under conditions of high interpair competition. The graph shows only word pairs of low initial stimulus-response associative value (adapted from Spence, Farber, & McFann, 1956, p. 301).

level has been confirmed in verbal learning investigations. Substantiation of the predictions provides evidence for the conception of drive as an energizer of behavior, for the hypothesized multiplicative relationship between drive and habit, and for the belief that the MA scale is a measure of drive.

Summary of Empirical Evidence.   There are a great deal of data supporting the Hull-Spence conception of behavior. One source of evidence is investigations in which the performance of organisms under varying degrees of deprivation is compared. The general finding in these studies of appetitive behavior is that performance (speed of running, resistance to extinction, latency of the response, and so forth) is positively related to the amount of deprivation during the testing period. Another series of animal investigations supporting the Drive × Habit conception utilizes discrimination learning paradigms, with predictions derived from the modifications of drive theory proposed by Spence. Spence is able to predict correctly whether the response will or will not be influenced by time of deprivation, as a function of the free- versus forced-response procedure. Finally, studies of human behavior in classical aversive conditioning paradigms and verbal learning situations, often using the MA scale to infer drive level, also provide confirmatory evidence for the Hull-Spence conception of motivation. It thus appears that a wide variety of infrahuman and human behavior may be predicted without appealing to mentalistic concepts. (More detailed reviews of supporting empirical evidence are presented by Bolles, 1967; Brown, 1961; and Cofer & Appley, 1964).

Evidence for Drive as a Pooled Source of Energy

The conception of drive as a pooled energy source has been tested with two experimental procedures. In one paradigm attempts are made to demonstrate that responses acquired under one deprivation condition (the "relevant" drive) can be energized by a different biological deficit (the "irrelevant" drive). The prototypical experiment utilizing this methodology was conducted by Webb (1949). Webb trained rats to make a simple instrumental response to attain food while the animals were under 22 hours of food deprivation. The animals then were tested under varying degrees of water deprivation while satiated with food. Table 2:2 shows that resistance to extinction of the response instrumental to the attainment of food is a function of the amount of water deprivation during testing (Groups I–IV), although extinction is slowest when nonreward is introduced given the conditions present during initial learning (Group V).

A similar experiment by Kendler (1945) yields corresponding findings. In Kendler's experiment animals were trained and tested under 22 hours of food deprivation. During the test trials they also were deprived of water for varying numbers of hours. Again the data reveal that a source of drive apparently uninfluential during original learning facilitates a previ-

TABLE 2:2
Measures Obtained During Extinction
(adapted from Webb, 1949, p. 10)

| Group | N | Motivating Condition (Hours of Deprivation) | | Mean Number of Responses to Extinction |
		Hunger	Thirst	
I	18	0	0	2.8
II	18	0	3	5.2
III	18	0	12	5.1
IV	18	0	22	7.2
V	16	22	0	14.2

ously learned response. Resistance to extinction was positively related to the amount of water deprivation during the testing period.

The second experimental procedure used to demonstrate that drive is an aggregate of various sources of motivation employs fear or shock in conjunction with a deprivation condition. This general procedure is illustrated in an experiment conducted by Meryman (1952). Meryman investigated whether food deprivation would influence the sound-induced startle response, and whether hunger and conditioned fear together produce greater augmentation of startle than either of these motivators acting alone. Meryman's animals were given fear conditioning and startle trials during the training period. Then fearful (conditioned) and nonfearful (unconditioned) animals were deprived of food for either 1 hour or 46 hours. The amplitude of the startle response for the groups (2 levels of fear $\times$ 2 levels of hunger) was tested. The results are presented in Figure 2:11. Figure 2:11 shows that the group both fearful and hungry exhibit the greatest amplitude of startle, while the nonhungry, nonfearful group manifest the least intensity of response. This is in accordance with the conceptualization of drive as a pooled energy source that multiplies all habits aroused in a stimulus situation.

A number of other investigators have demonstrated response facilitation when shock is combined with a biological deficit. For example, Amsel

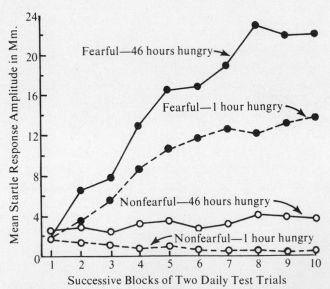

FIGURE 2:11. Investigation by Meryman (1952) examining startle-response amplitude as a function of fear, no fear, intense hunger, weak hunger, and their combinations.

and Maltzman (1950) trained animals to drink ten minutes a day in their home cage. They found that during this time period the animals drink more following the reception of a shock in a different compartment. These investigators conclude that the persisting effect of shock energizes the habit of drinking. In a similar manner, Braun, Wedekind, and Smudski (1957) established that hungry rats escape faster from water and other aversive stimuli than do nonhungry rats, even when the escape response is not instrumental to the attainment of food.

In summary, the general pattern of results indicates that two sources of drive can combine to facilitate behavior. The two sources may be established by need deprivation (food and water, as in Webb or Kendler), a deprivation condition combined with an unconditioned response to pain (as in Amsel & Maltzman, Braun et al.), or a biological need in conjunction with the learned drive of fear (as in Meryman). The investigations apparently provide strong evidence that drive is an aggregate of disparate motivational sources.

THEORETICAL EXTENSIONS

Frustration

Frustration has a diversity of meanings in psychology (see Lawson & Marx, 1958; Lawson, 1965). Frustration may refer to an independent variable, or experimental manipulation. Often this involves blocking the attainment of a goal, inducing failure, or delivering a personal insult. Performance of the "frustrated" group is then compared to the performance of a "nonfrustrated" group to assess the effects of the independent manipulation. Frustration also may refer to a dependent variable; investigators attempt to measure the amount of frustrated behavior. For example, one might ask whether highly anxious subjects exhibit more frustrated behavior than subjects low in anxiety. Finally, frustration frequently refers to an intervening variable, or a complex process that is inferred from certain observable responses; for example, on the basis of his aggressive behavior, one might conclude that subject X is frustrated.

It also is important to distinguish frustration as a *product* from frustration as a *process*. An analogy to the field of learning makes this distinction clearer. Learning is a product; it refers to a change in the organism as a result of experience. But learning also is a process. It is an ongoing activity with dynamic qualities. Similarly, frustration is a product, or a result of an event. But it also is a process, referring to a change or dynamic state within the organism.

Many response indicators of frustration (an intervening process) have been observed in laboratory situations. These responses include aggression, apathy, fixation, regression, deteriorated performance, and withdrawal. A variety of theoretical viewpoints evolved to explain these behaviors. Maier (1949), for example, postulates that frustrated behavior is qualitatively different than goal-oriented behavior. In Maier's conception there is a frustration threshold; any excess of frustration beyond the threshold point results in fixation. Animals exhibiting fixated behavior do not respond to reward, and punishment merely intensifies the degree of fixation.

In contrast, Dollard, Doob, and their co-workers (1939) relate frustration to the general principles of learning. They hypothesize a causal relationship between aggressive actions and prior frustration. This so-called frustration-aggression hypothesis has generated a great deal of debate and research, perhaps because it was one of the first attempts to extend *S-R* psychology to personality and social psychology.

Brown-Farber Theory of Frustration.   Two theories of frustration have been derived from the Hull-Spence motivational approach. One theory was formulated by Brown and Farber (1951), while the second is primarily the work of Amsel (1958). Brown and Farber assume that frustration results from interference with an ongoing behavioral sequence. The source of the interference may be either a competing habit or something that delays response completion, such as a barrier in the world. Brown and Farber postulate that frustration has drive (energizing) and stimulus (directional) properties. The energizing function of frustration is assumed to be nondirectional; the drive generated by goal thwarting multiplies all the habits aroused in the particular stimulus situation. The stimuli associated with frustration have directional properties and influence habit formation.

The formal aspects of this conception are shown in Diagram 2:4. In the illustrated situation two incompatible habits (A and B) are competing for expression. Drive multiplies the two competing habits to yield effective reaction potential (E), or the strength of motivation. Because competing habits are activated that impede goal-directed behavior, frustration (F) is aroused. Frustration is assumed to have drive properties; it therefore adds to the total drive already present (ΔD indicates an increment in drive). The increase drive level augments the reaction potential associated with all the habits aroused in the situation. Further, inasmuch as frustration is conceptualized as a drive, it produces its own internal stimuli (S_F). The frustration stimuli can become conditioned to other responses; that is, they provide the potentiality for the formation of new habits (Habits C and D).

In one study guided by this conception, Haner and Brown (1955)

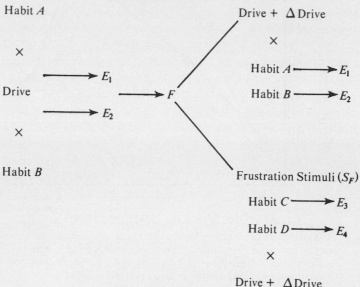

DIAGRAM 2:4
The Brown-Farber Theory of Frustration

hypothesized that the amount of frustration produced following goal interference is a function of the strength of the ongoing behavioral tendency.
The strength of this tendency, following Hull-Spence, is conceived to be
a function of Drive $\times$ Habit. Thus, the amount of frustration was expected to be positively related to both the magnitude of the drive during
thwarting, and the habit strength of the response.

Haner and Brown manipulated habit strength by employing a task
that required subjects to place marbles in holes. Thirty-six holes had to
be filled within a given time to complete the activity. The experimenters interrupted the subjects (children) after they had filled 25 percent, 50 percent, 75 percent, 89 percent, or all of the holes. In Hull's initial conception
of motivation, habit strength was postulated to vary as a function of distance of the response from the goal. Haner and Brown, guided by the
goal-gradient hypothesis, assume that the strength of the instrumental response varies as a function of the "distance" from task completion.

Interruption was signaled by the onset of a buzzer, followed by the
marbles falling to the bottom of the apparatus. A plunger could be pushed
that turned off the buzzer and allowed the initiation of the next trial. The
dependent variable in the experiment, or index of frustration, was the pressure the subject exerted when pushing the plunger.

The results of the study are shown in Figure 2:12. The data reveal

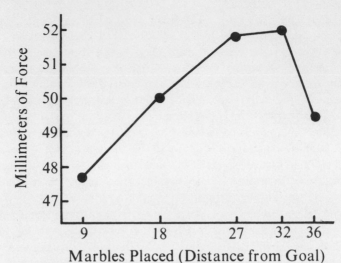

Marbles Placed (Distance from Goal)

FIGURE 2:12. The effects of frustration related to five degrees of goal proximity. The dependent variable was the millimeters of force exerted following the interruption of the task (adapted from Haner & Brown, 1955, p. 205).

that the intensity of the push response is a function of the distance from the goal at the time of thwarting. Thus, the hypothesis of Haner and Brown is supported. The results apparently demonstrate the nondirective energizing function of a frustration drive.

Amsel's Theory of Frustration. The most systematic theoretical analyses and investigations of frustration have been conducted by Amsel and his colleagues (Amsel, 1958, 1967; Amsel & Ward, 1954, 1965). These investigators relate frustration to nondirective drive and build upon the model of Brown and Farber. Amsel and Roussel (1952) define frustration as a state resulting from the nonreinforcement of an instrumental response that previously has been consistently reinforced. That is, if a habit and an expectancy of reward (r_g-s_g) are established, and the instrumentality of the response is altered so that it no longer results in a reward, then frustration is experienced. The amount of the frustration is postulated to be directly proportional to the expectancy of the reward. Frustration is conceived as having both drive and cue properties, as Brown and Farber previously had specified. In addition, Amsel postulates that frustration is aversive, and the cues similar to those present when frustration is experienced also generate some degree of frustration.

The third property of frustration is the central contribution of Amsel's formulation. This feature of the theory becomes clearer when reconsidering

Spence's analysis of the r_g-s_g mechanism. According to Spence, originally neutral cues elicit the "expectation" of a reward because these cues are either present or similar to cues appearing during the time of reward. In a similar manner, according to Amsel, originally neutral cues paired with frustration become aversive. And cues similar to those in which frustration is experienced also become aversive. Therefore, following nonattainment of an expected reward in a straight-runway situation, the greatest amount of frustration is experienced at the goal, and the least frustration at the start box. Because frustration is assumed to generalize back in the runway, Amsel labels the frustration experienced before entering the goal chamber as "anticipatory frustration." And because the frustration in the runway is not as great as that occurring in the goal box, it is labeled as "fractional anticipatory frustration" (r_f). Again guided by Spence, Amsel postulates that frustration responses produce their own pattern of stimulus feedback (s_f). The increased internal stimulation accounts for the drive properties of frustration; the stimuli associated with this drive then can also lead to new learning.

An early demonstration of the motivational (drive) properties of non-reward is reported by Amsel and Roussel (1952). These investigators employed a double-runway apparatus in which two runways were joined (see Diagram 2:5). The goal box in the first runway served as the starting box for the second runway. During the training period of the experiment the animals were fed in both the first and second goal boxes; in the testing phase food was withheld in the first goal box. Amsel and Roussel report that following nonreward in the first goal box the vigor of performance in the second runway increases above the previous asymptotic level. They contend that this performance increment demonstrates the drive effects of frustration. The immediately augmented response strength following non-attainment of an expected reward is termed the Frustration Effect.

Subsequent studies isolated some of the determinants of the Frustra-

DIAGRAM 2:5
Apparatus for the Demonstration of the Frustration Effect
(from Amsel & Roussel, 1952)

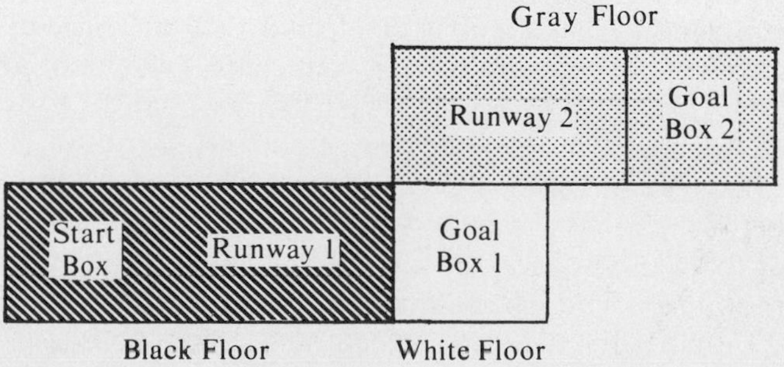

Gray Floor

Runway 2   Goal Box 2

Start Box   Runway 1   Goal Box 1

Black Floor   White Floor

tion Effect. For example, the energizing effects of frustration increase as a function of the number of rewarded trials (Marzocco, 1951). This logically follows from Amsel's theory, for the greater the number of reinforced trials, the greater the anticipation of food, and the greater the amount of experienced frustration when reward does not follow the instrumental response.

In more recent studies (see Amsel & Ward, 1965), the cue and affect properties of frustration have been examined. For example, the notion of frustration generalization is employed to explain experimental extinction. Amsel and Ward argue that the tendency to run toward the reward in the goal box, supported by the r_g-s_g component, is opposed by a stronger force "not to run," guided by the r_f-s_f feedback. The stimuli associated with the anticipatory frustration become conditioned to responses antagonistic to running. Hence, the positive tendency to approach the goal is not diminished. Rather, an antagonistic response has developed (also see Chapter VII).

Conflict

One of the foremost problems in psychology is the conceptualization of conflict. Each motivational model discussed in this book explicitly deals with conflict. The conflict may be between a right-turning and a left-turning response (drive theory), between a driving and a restraining force (field theory), between a hope of success and a fear of failure (achievement theory), between self versus other perception of responsibility (attribution theory), or between instinctual desires and the demands of society (psychoanalytic theory).

As an aid in the understanding of conflict, different taxonomic schemes have been proposed. Brown (1957) suggests that there are three types of conflict: spatial, temporal, and discriminative. *Spatial conflict* involves physical distances. For example, a child who runs toward water to reach a toy and away from it when the waves come in is exhibiting spatial conflict. *Temporal conflict* involves a time dimension, or a temporal distance from a goal. Many stories are told about the bride and groom who become more and more doubtful as the date of their marriage approaches. *Discriminative conflict* refers to the classical conflict situation first demonstrated by Pavlov. As previously indicated, Pavlov trained dogs to salivate to food in response to one tone while the animals also learned that food would not be given following a different tone. A tone was then presented that was between the two training tones. Hence, a discriminative conflict (is this the "food" or "no food" tone?) was established.

A second taxonomic scheme for conflict situations has been proposed by Lewin. Lewin delineates three types of conflict: approach-approach,

approach-avoidance, and avoidance-avoidance. In an *approach-approach* conflict the organism is confronted with two attractive but mutually exclusive alternatives. Many of us face such a conflict when passing the pastry section in the cafeteria. *Avoidance-avoidance* conflicts occur when an individual must make a choice between two equally unattractive alternatives. One might tell his child either to wash the dishes or do his homework. *Approach-avoidance* conflicts arise when positive and negative tendencies are simultaneously elicited by one or more alternatives. For example, we like to buy nice clothes, but they are expensive; we want a candy bar, but it is fattening.

Miller's Conflict Model. Applying only principles derived from the Drive × Habit conception, Neal Miller (1944, 1959) was able to describe systematically and predict behavior in approach-avoidance conflicts. His conflict model, among the most cited works in the study of motivation and personality, illustrates how mechanistic principles derived from the study of infrahumans can aid in the explanation of human action. Six postulates are included in Miller's analysis of approach-avoidance conflicts. The postulates, and derivations from the Drive × Habit formula, are:

Postulate 1. The tendency to approach a goal is stronger the nearer the subject is to it.

Derivation: To understand this postulate it is again helpful to consider the paradigm of a hungry rat running down a straight alleyway to receive a food reward. As the animal traverses the runway his drive level, defined operationally as the number of hours of food deprivation, remains relatively constant. That is, he is equally hungry when ten feet or one foot from the goal. However, because of the lesser delay in reinforcement as the goal is approached, and because of the greater similarity between the goal and alley stimuli as the animal nears the food, habit strength varies as a function of distance from the goal. In Diagram 2:6, values are assigned to the drive and habit determinants of behavior to illustrate the

DIAGRAM 2:6
Strength of the Tendency to Approach
a Goal in a Runway

	Start Box			Goal	
Hunger Drive	2	2	2	2	2
Approach Habit	1	2	3	4	5
Drive × Habit	2	4	6	8	10

strength of the motivational tendency as the goal box is approached. Drive level is given a value of 2, while habit strength varies from 1 to 5. The diagram indicates that reaction potential, or the approach tendency, increases as the animal traverses the alleyway. This indicates that the animal will run faster, pull harder, and so forth, as it nears the goal.

Postulate 2. The tendency to avoid a feared stimulus is stronger the nearer the subject is to it.

Derivation: The reasoning is virtually identical to that already given for Postulate 1.

Postulate 3. The strength of the avoidance tendency increases more rapidly with nearness to the goal than does the strength of the approach tendency (see Figure 2:13).

Derivation: This is the key postulate in the conflict model, and follows from principles of Drive × Habit theory and the conception of fear as an

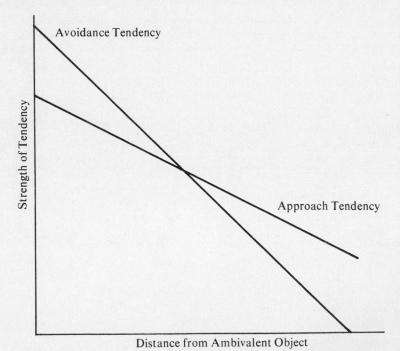

FIGURE 2:13.   Graphic representation of an approach-avoidance conflict situation. The individual has tendencies to approach and withdraw from an object. The point at which the gradients cross indicates the place of maximal conflict.

acquired or learned drive. In an appetitive situation, the level of a drive such as hunger is operationally defined in terms of hours of deprivation. The changes in an animal's appetitive drive during the time it takes to traverse a runway are minimal. In an aversive situation, the drive, labeled fear or anxiety, is learned. The degree of fear varies as a function of the similarity between the immediate stimulus situation and the stimuli present at the time the aversive stimulation was received.

In a runway it is assumed that the cues in the start box are least similar to the cues in the goal box. Thus, if an animal receives shock at the goal, his fear increases as the goal box is approached. In addition, the habit strength of avoiding shock also increases as the goal is approached (see Solomon, 1964, for discussion of this point). The avoidance tendency therefore is conceptualized as in Diagram 2:7.

When compared with Diagram 2:6, Diagram 2:7 indicates that the avoidance tendency is steeper than the approach tendency (see Figure 2:13). That is, the change in the strength of the tendencies as a function of the distance from the goal, or the slope of the functions, is greater for the avoidance than the approach tendency. This is because both drive and habit vary with distance in the avoidance situation, while in the approach tendency only habit strength is affected by distance from the goal.

The above analysis suggests that in certain situations the gradient of approach may be steeper than that of avoidance. This should occur if the approach drive is learned and aroused by external stimuli, while the avoidance drive is based upon internal stimuli that do not vary as a function of distance from the goal. For example, if sexual avoidance behavior is influenced by a strong and fixed superego, while sexual approach drives are aroused by cognitions, such as the sight of an attractive partner, then the steepness of the approach and avoidance gradients might be reversed.

Postulate 4. The strength of the tendencies to approach or avoid the goal varies directly with the strength of the drive on which they are based.
Derivation: This follows because the gradient is determined by drive

DIAGRAM 2:7
Strength of the Tendency to
Avoid a Goal in a Runway

	Start Box				Goal
Fear Drive	1	2	3	4	5
Avoidance Habit	1	2	3	4	5
Drive × Habit	1	4	9	16	25

level multiplying habit strength. Hence, increasing drive, or habit, increases the strength of the tendencies.

Postulate 5. Below the level of asymptote of learning, increasing the number of reinforced trials increases the strength of the response tendency that is reinforced.
Derivation: Identical with Postulate 4.

Postulate 6. When two incompatible response tendencies are in conflict, the stronger one will be expressed.
Derivation: A simple additive model is assumed in which the probability of the approach or avoidance response is determined by the absolute difference in the strength of the opposing tendencies. Other models for conflict resolution are possible. For example, the probability of the response may be determined by the ratio of the two tendencies. This assumption may lead to predictions different from those made by Miller.

Tests of the Model.   Miller, Brown, and others have conducted a number of experiments to test Miller's conflict model. In one of the original investigations, Brown (1948) developed a technique to measure the strength of the approach and avoidance tendencies in rats. The rats were fitted with a harness device allowing the experimenter to assess how hard they pulled. Animals that had been trained in separate goal boxes either to approach food or to avoid a shock were placed at various distances from the food or shock. As hypothesized, the strength of pull varied directly as a function of distance from the goal. In addition, the intensity of the pull away from shock was more affected by the distance from the shock compartment than the strength of the pull to approach food was influenced by distance from the reward compartment.

In a subsequent study, animals were trained to receive both food and a shock in the identical goal box. Hours of deprivation and the level of shock were varied in a factorial design. The maximum degree of approach to the goal was the dependent variable. The results of this investigation are illustrated in Figure 2:14. The data indicate that for any given level of shock intensity, as hours of deprivation increase, the animals approach closer to the goal (zero point in Figure 2:14). On the other hand, when hours of deprivation are held constant, approach toward the goal decreases as shock intensity increases.

In another investigation, Murray and Berkun (1955) trained rats to approach food located at the end of a straight runway. They then shocked the animals while eating until they would no longer enter the goal compartment. This approach-avoidance conflict was aroused in a distinctive stimu-

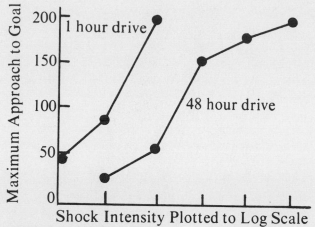

FIGURE 2:14.   The joint effects of strength of shock and hunger on the distance animals will traverse toward a goal in a conflict situation. The lower numbers on the graph indicate that the animal approached closer to the goal. Thus, as shock increases and hunger decreases, the animal does not approach as close to the goal (from Miller, 1959, p. 212).

lus situation (a black runway). Following conflict training the apparatus was altered and the runway attached to two other runways (see Figure 2:15). The three runways were connected and it was possible for the animals to pass from one to the other by going through any of the openings located at various places throughout the alleyway. The stimuli in the runways formed a stimulus generalization continuum; they were ordered from black to gray to white.

After the initial training period Murray and Berkun expected the animals to approach the food somewhat when replaced in the black alley. At the hypothetical point where the avoidance gradient is stronger than that of the approach gradient, the animals were expected to vacillate and not approach further. It was hypothesized that the animals would then enter the gray alleyway and would progress farther toward the food. This prediction was based on the assumption that the alteration in the stimulus situation changes the avoidance (fear) drive, but not the drive for food. That is, changing the stimuli, like varying the physical distance from the goal, has more of an effect on the avoidance than the approach tendency. Similarly, the animals were again expected to reach a point of equilibrium in the gray alley, and then shift to the white alley. There it was predicted that they would proceed still closer to the goal region. This pattern of behavior was observed by Murray and Berkun.

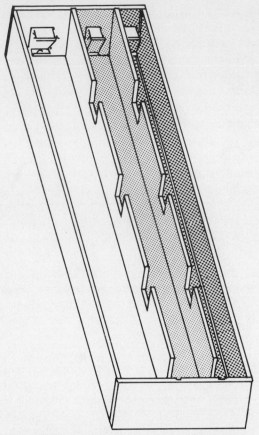

FIGURE 2:15. White, gray, and black runways, ordered on the basis of stimulus generalization, employed in the study of displacement. Windows in the dividing walls
permit the animals to change runways (from
Murray & Berkun, 1955, p. 50).

Miller's Conflict Model and Displacement.   Displacement refers to
the observation that objects of behavior change although the desire to attain the original goal has not subsided. Freud contends that there are
"vicissitudes of the instincts"; that is, a variety of goals may serve to satisfy
an underlying wish. The most frequently cited example of such displacement activity is in the study of aggression. It is often pointed out that the
worker in the family cannot express anger at the boss, and therefore comes
home to "take it out" on his or her unsuspecting mate. In one primitive
society displacement activities are institutionalized. Outside every hut is

a dog; when the male of the household is angry he may punish this unfortunate animal.

Displacement activity, or the shifting of goal objects, has been incorporated into Miller's conflict model. Consider the employee angry at the boss, but not directly expressing this hostility. Miller reasons that the aggressive tendency directed toward the supervisor is inhibited by a stronger avoidance tendency. Thus, the person will respond aggressively only to someone similar to the boss. Aggression is expressed "farther" from the goal, because the change in the stimulus situation reduces the avoidance more than the approach drive. This analysis assumes that one's mate, for example, is similar, along some psychological dimension, to the boss. The scaling of such stimulus generalization gradients is a difficult psychological problem.

Miller has derived a number of postulates concerning displacement activity from his conflict model. A few of these postulates, along with illustrative examples, are listed here.

1. When the direct response to the original stimulus is prevented by the absence of that stimulus, displaced responses will occur to other similar stimuli, and the strongest displaced response will occur to the most similar stimulus present.

For example, a girl who is prevented from marrying her sweetheart by his death, and who is completely recovered from her grief and other possibly negative factors, will be expected to prefer the suitor who is most similar to him.

2. When the direct response to the original stimulus is prevented by conflict, the strongest displaced response will occur to stimuli which have an intermediate degree of similarity to the original one.

Thus a girl who is prevented from marrying her sweetheart by a violent quarrel would be expected to prefer someone not completely similar, but not completely different.

3. If the relative strength of the inhibitory response is increased, the point of strongest displacement, and hence object choice, will shift in the direction of stimuli which are less similar to the original one eliciting the direct response.

In other words, the more unhappy the girl's experience with her previous sweetheart, the less similar should be her choice of a second love object [Miller, 1959, pp. 218–19].

ASSOCIATIONISM WITHOUT A DRIVE CONSTRUCT

The growth and influence of drive theory has not been without opposition. The arguments do not necessarily concern the empirical evidence per se. For the sake of theoretical exposition, the data reviewed in the prior pages are considered facts. However, empirical evidence may be interpreted with different conceptual schemes. One conceptual point of view used to interpret much of the data reviewed here, labeled "pure" associationism, includes only stimulus and response among its theoretical terms (see Table 1:1). A drive concept is not included among the determinants of behavior. Rather, drive stimuli produced by the drive state are believed to be sufficient to explain the facilitating effects of deprivation.

Drive Stimuli

The drive operation produces at least two consequences. One hypothesized consequence is an energizing effect; the second is a change in the pattern and intensity of internal stimulation. Postman (1953) views the postulation of drive stimuli as a critical issue for drive theorists.

A distinction between the functions of drive and habit leads to operational and conceptual difficulties. The operational differentiation of drives *qua* stimuli and drives *qua* energizers presents a problem. The antecedent conditions for producing both of these conditions are the same. [p. 56].

Some psychologists, notably Estes (1958), have attempted to account for the results of the experiments discussed in the previous pages by invoking only the conception of drive stimuli. The conception of drives *qua* energizers is ignored. Postman (1953) states the rationale for this approach:

It seems equally possible, however, and perhaps more parsimonious, to seek the source of such variations and/or constancies (of behavior) in changing patterns and intensities of drive stimuli (recall that whatever conditions produce changes in drive probably affect the drive stimuli as well). In short, it may be that a nondirective drive which is indifferent with respect to goals, is expendable. Drive stimuli can carry the burden [p. 57].

The conception championed by the associationistic camp (Postman, Estes) is a truncation of the one formulated by drive theorists:

drive operation ⟶ internal stimuli ⟶ response selection

Associationists appeal to a set of reference experiments to support their position. One experiment, conducted by Campbell and Sheffield (1953), demonstrated that the random activity of rats is unrelated to their degree of hunger. However, animals deprived of food increase their activity level when the environment is altered. Campbell and Sheffield argue that drives do not energize behavior, but increase the sensitivity of the animal to its environment. The conception of drive lowering a stimulus threshold is an associationistic position.

An interesting study by Cotton (1953) also is cited as supporting the associationist position. Cotton related speed of running down a straight alley for food to hours of deprivation. He found the monotonic relationship believed to support the drive conception (see Figure 2:16). However, he noted that as an animal proceeds down the alley, it emits responses other than running, such as grooming, exploring, and the like. Cotton measured the amount of time the animals spent at these various activities and subtracted that time from the total time taken to traverse the alley. He found that the relationship between deprivation and response intensity vanishes when the irrelevant task responses, or competing responses, are eliminated from the data. The results therefore suggest that drive does not energize behavior but that the drive operation affects stimulus elements that determine the response elicited in the animal's hierarchy. (Other investigations, however, using somewhat different procedure, do find some absolute re-

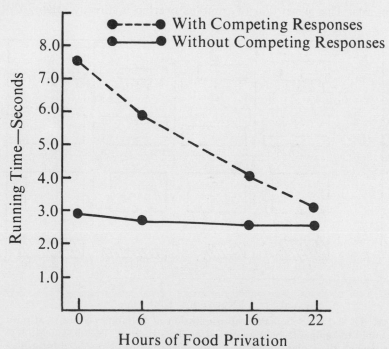

FIGURE 2:16.   Response strength as a function of the number of hours of food deprivation. The curves represent running speed with and without the elimination of competing responses (from Cotton, 1953, p. 194).

sponse facilitation after competing responses are excluded; see King, 1959).

Estes's Associative Model.   Estes (1958) has attempted to explain the data reported by Campbell and Sheffield and Cotton, as well as evidence considered as supporting the Drive $\times$ Habit conception, without employing an energizing concept. Estes assumes that there are four sources of stimuli in experimental situations manipulating hunger or thirst: *satiation, deprivation, experimentally controlled signals,* and *extraneous stimuli* (see Figure 2:17). In Figure 2:17 the horizontal dimension represents the number of stimuli in that set, the vertical dimension gives the sampling probability of these stimuli, and the area represents the weighting of the stimulus set. Some of the sources of stimuli change as a function of the amount of deprivation. Figure 2:17 indicates that as deprivation increases, the number of satiation cues decrease and the number of deprivation cues increase, while the controlled signals (*CS*) remain constant, and the extraneous cues fluctuate randomly.

The numbers under the rectangles in Figure 2:17 represent individual cues. The satiation and deprivation cues are represented as partially overlapping sets. The proportion of stimulus overlap is directly related to the

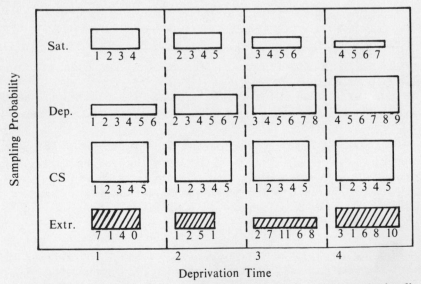

FIGURE 2:17. Schematic representation of the four classes of stimuli assumed to be operative in an experimental situation. The classification is based on the relationship between deprivation time and stimulus sampling probabilities. Cross-hatched rectangles for the extraneous stimuli indicate that they cannot be conditioned to the correct response (from Estes, 1958, p. 44).

differences in deprivation time periods. For example, the overlap in deprivation cues at Time One and Time Two (cues 2, 3, 4, 5, and 6) is greater than the overlap in cues between Time One and Time Four (cues 4, 5, and 6).

Estes assumes that the probability (and latency) of a response is equal to the weight of the conditioned cues divided by the weight of the total number of cues present during the time of testing. In Figure 2:17 the white spaces represent conditioned cues and cross-hatched areas represent unconditioned cues. For example, assume an organism is trained to press a lever for food while under 3 hours of food deprivation. After training is completed, the deprivation cues associated with 3 hours of deprivation, the 3-hour satiation cues, and the controlled cues are all conditioned to the bar-pressing response. It is assumed that the extraneous cues randomly vary and do not become conditioned to the response under investigation.

Estes also assumes that as deprivation lengthens, the increase in the weight of the deprivation stimuli is greater than the decrease in the weight of the satiation stimuli. A numerical example will perhaps clarify this point. Assume the following values for the four sources of stimulation at two levels of deprivation:

	Low Deprivation	*High Deprivation*
Controlled signals	5	5
Deprivation cues	5	8
Satiation cues	5	4
Extraneous cues	2	2

Note that the increase in the relative weight of the deprivation cues (5 to 8) is greater than the decrease in the weight of the satiation cues (5 to 4).

On the basis of Estes's formula for response probability in the above numerical example, the probability of elicitation of a well-learned response acquired and tested in the low deprivation condition is:

$$\frac{15 \text{ (Total number of conditioned cues)}}{17 \text{ (Total number of cues)}}$$

But in the high deprivation condition, the probability of emitting the learned response is 17/19. The latter value, 17/19, is greater than 15/17; the probability of the response is greater in the high drive than in the low drive condition. Estes, therefore, is able to account for data indicating that amount of deprivation is related to level of performance. These data are part of the empirical foundation of drive theory, yet Estes explains the data without including a drive component in his analysis.

There is a further extension of the analysis presented above. Note what happens when the extraneous stimuli are omitted. These are stimuli which elicit the competing responses of grooming and exploring that were observed by Cotton. In the low and high drive conditions, eliminating these stimuli results in a ratio of 1 (15/15 and 17/17) in both conditions (assuming identical conditions in training and testing). Therefore, the probability of the response under consideration is unrelated to the level of deprivation. Cotton's data empirically support this derivation.

Let us briefly examine some other implications of Estes' model. One derivation from his assumptions is that there should not be any systematic relationship between random activity and level of deprivation, as Campbell and Sheffield report. Given no reinforcement, none of the stimulus cues can be conditioned to the "correct" response. The level of deprivation, therefore, should be unrelated to the behavior; responses elicited in the various deprivation conditions should be relatively random.

Estes also attempts to account for the studies by Webb (1949) and Kendler (1945) that allegedly demonstrate the energizing effect of an irrelevant drive. Estes assumes that hunger and thirst have some overlapping stimuli. Therefore, when training occurs under conditions of hunger (or thirst), the reinforced response becomes conditioned to some cues associated with both hunger and thirst. During the testing phase the introduction of an "irrelevant" drive then increases the probability of the previously learned response, for some of the stimuli associated with that deprivation state have already been conditioned to the instrumental response.

The striking aspect of Estes' analysis is the apparent ease with which he accounts for data that have in general been the province of drive theorists. One can only speculate how much more powerful this conception would be if the time devoted to it equaled that spent on the great number of studies supporting the conception of drive as an energizer.

Arguments that Drive Stimuli Are Not Sufficient.   The purely associative position is able to explain a great deal of data incorporated by drive theorists. However, some experimental results cannot readily be translated into the associative framework. The associative position holds that *"behavior occurs when stimuli appropriate for its elicitation are present and does not occur when they are absent."* (Brown, 1961, p. 112). But data (Loess, 1952; Deese & Carpenter, 1951) indicate that animals trained under low drive exhibit increments in performance level when tested under high drive. Loess, for example, found that animals trained under three hours of deprivation exhibit greater intensity of performance when tested under 22 as opposed to 3 hours of deprivation. The associative position would predict decrements in performance as a result of any shift in conditions between the training and testing periods. The obtained behavioral increments, in spite of the shifting level of deprivation between training and testing, and the better performance of groups tested under high than low drive when trained under low drive, provides strong evidence against a pure associative position (see Brown, 1961).

A second class of experiments is also difficult for pure associationists to interpret. These experiments demonstrate a facilitating effect of fear on appetitive behavior or an intensifying effect of deprivation on avoidance behavior (for example, Amsel & Maltzman, 1950; Braun et al., 1957). To account for these findings the associative theorists would posit an overlap between the stimulus sets generated by the two motivational conditions being manipulated. Yet this explanation seems unlikely. Few psychologists would argue that hunger and thirst do not have common cues. But equally few would contend that food deprivation and an aversive stimulus (shock) have common cues.

An example related to Meryman's experiment clarifies this point. Assume that a noise is unconditionally associated with a startle response, and that extraneous stimuli in the situation elicit competing responses.

S_1, S_3, S_5 (noise) $-------------- R_1$ (startle)

S_2, S_4, S_6 (extraneous stimuli) $------- R_2$ (competing responses)

The probability of the startle response, given that each stimulus is assigned a weight of one, is 3/6 or 1/2. Three of the stimuli are conditioned to the startle response and three are not. If an animal is hungry at the time of the noise, the stimulus situation might be portrayed as follows:

$$S_1, S_3, S_5 \text{ (noise)}$$

$$S_2, S_4, S_6 \text{ (extraneous stimuli)}$$

$$S_X, S_X, S_9 \text{ (hunger)}$$

If S_x is the equivalent of S_1 or S_3, then food deprivation would facilitate the startle response. The probability of the startle would equal 5/9, which is greater than 1/2. However, there is only the *post hoc* evidence provided by Amsel and Maltzman, Braun et al., Meryman, and others to indicate that hunger and unconditioned or conditioned fear have common cues. If S_x, S_x, and S_9 have been conditioned to food related responses, perhaps incompatible with startle, then, according to association theory, the probability of a startle response would decrease, given a hungry organism. The probability of the startle to noise would be 3/9, which is less than 1/2. This reasoning seems more consistent with the associative position than a *post hoc* explanation that there is an overlap of the stimulus sets of the motivating conditions. To explain the assumed behavioral increments in this "irrelevant" drive example, and in the Amsel and Maltzman, Braun et al., and Meryman studies, it appears that the employment of a drive construct is necessary.

SOME SHORTCOMINGS OF DRIVE THEORY

We have now examined the drive conception, supporting empirical evidence, and the alternate position of the associationists. Now let us turn to some criticisms of drive theory not raised by associationists. Three issues have been selected for discussion:

1. The inability of the drive conception to predict the learning of easy and complex tasks, and the challenge of a cognitive position.
2. Problems in the conceptual analysis of incentive, and the place of both "push" and "pull" in a theory of motivation.
3. The nondirective conception of drive, and some experimental confounding.

In addition, we will raise questions concerning the basic empirical and conceptual foundation of drive theory and will reexamine the conceptualization of frustration and conflict.

Problems in Predicting Speed of Verbal Learning

The interpretation of the paired-associate experiments conducted by Spence and his colleagues is subject to a number of conceptual difficulties. Recall that Spence hypothesizes that on an easy task subjects high in drive will perform better than subjects low in drive. Given an easy task, the multiplicative relation between drive and habit specifies that the difference between the correct and incorrect response tendencies will increase as drive increases. This decreases the probability that incorrect responses will be elicited. Conversely, on a difficult task subjects high in drive are expected to perform worse than subjects low in drive. The additional response strength resulting from the increased drive level theoretically brings other competing responses above the response threshold. This increases the probability of responding with an incorrect associate.

While these explanations seem to follow logically from the theory presented by Spence, the exactness of the predictions is more apparent than real. Opposite predictions can be derived from the theory without great difficulty. For example, assume the following numerical values for the constructs employed by Spence:

$$\text{Habit } C = 5 \qquad \text{Low drive} = 1$$
$$\text{Habit } I = 1 \qquad \text{High drive} = 2$$
$$\text{Threshold} = 2$$

The habit hierarchy is representative of an "easy" task. The strength of the dominant correct response is five times greater than the strength of the subordinate incorrect response. In the low drive condition, the excitatory potential associated with each habit is:

$$E \text{ (Habit } C) = 5 \times 1 = 5$$
$$E \text{ (Habit } I) = 1 \times 1 = 1$$

$$Pr \ C = \frac{5}{5} = 1$$

The probability of Habit C being elicited among subjects low in drive is one, since Habit I is below the response strength needed for evocation.

Among subjects high in drive the excitatory potentials of the responses are:

$$E \text{ (Habit } C) = 5 \times 2 = 10$$
$$E \text{ (Habit } I) = 1 \times 2 = 2$$

$$Pr \ C = \frac{10}{10 + 2} = .83$$

Habit I is now at the threshold level and has some finite probability of being elicited. (Note that a ratio model is used to represent the probability level.) Therefore, the probability of the response of Habit C is less than one. Given the hypothetical conditions outlined above, subjects low in drive should perform better than subjects high in drive.

It also is a simple matter to derive the opposite predictions from those made by Spence, given a difficult task. For example, subjects high in drive would perform better than subjects low in drive at a difficult task if the correct response were below the threshold for the low drive group, but above threshold for the high drive group. It is easily possible to create other hypothetical conditions in which heightened drive will facilitate performance at a difficult task.

The main point of the above discussion is that it is impossible to predict accurately the relative level of performance between high and low drive groups without a complete and exact specification of all the potential responses and their numerical strengths, a specification of the threshold level and oscillating response functions (the moment-to-moment random shifts in response strength), and a conflict model specifying how conflicts between competing tendencies are resolved.

Spence (1958a) is not unaware of these many problems. In a footnote in his *American Psychologist* paper, he states:

As discussed in my Silliman Lectures, there are a number of other considerations that need to be taken into account in extending the theory to such competing response situations. Thus the particular composition rule (law) assumed in these lectures to describe the manner in which the competing responses interacted with each other led to the implication that the percentage of occurrence of the competing responses is a function, not only of the magnitude of the difference between the competing Es, but also of their absolute level above the threshold L. As a consequence in the low range of E values, there may actually be an inverse relation between performance level (percent choice of the response with stronger E) and the level of drive. Still other considerations involve whether habit strength (H) in learning situations is or is not assumed to be dependent on the reinforcer and whether drive strength (D) determines the inhibitory factor (I_n). Different combinations of these alternative assumptions, including even other possible composition rules, lead to different behavior consequences. Critical evaluation of the different conceivable theoretical models will require considerably more empirical data obtained under a wide variety of experimental conditions than is now available [p. 138].

Cognitive Processes in Verbal Learning.   In addition to the above criticisms of the drive conception, there are data indicating that the interpretation of the observed Anxiety $\times$ Complexity interaction is incorrect (Weiner, 1966b; Weiner & Schneider, 1971). In the Weiner (1966b) paper it is stated that:

The theoretical position of Spence et al. ignores the cognitive and affective processes which occur as the subject attempts to learn these easy and difficult lists. It is likely that the rapid learning of the easy list indicates to the subject that he is succeeding. That is, on the basis of the frequent number of correct responses he may evaluate his performance positively. On the difficult list the subject may perceive his performance as a failure. That is, because of the many incorrect responses he may evaluate his performance negatively. Previous studies (Child & Whiting, 1950; Katchmar, Ross, & Andrews, 1958; Lucas, 1952; Mandler & Sarason, 1952; Sarason, 1957; Weiner, 1965a) have shown that highly anxious subjects exhibit relative increments in level of performance following success. Conversly, failure depresses the subsequent performance of these subjects. For subjects low in anxiety, failure has been demonstrated to enhance subsequent performance, while success produces later performance decrements. Thus the findings of Spence et al. can be included among the research which has demonstrated interactions between individual differences in level of anxiety and the effects of success and failure on subsequent performance [p. 340].

A study was then conducted to determine which of the two plausible interpretations, drive theory or success-failure effects, could best account for the obtained Anxiety $\times$ Task Difficulty interaction. Weiner (1966b) continues:

This experiment was undertaken to determine whether the findings from the paired-associates studies cited above are really to be attributed to the differential reactions which high- and low-anxious individuals exhibit to success and failure experiences. To ascertain this, the inherent relation between the easy task-success experience and difficult task-failure experience was experimentally severed. Subjects learning an easy list of paired associates were told that they were performing poorly relative to others. In this manner the easy task was paired with a failure experience. Subjects learning a difficult paired associates task were told that they were doing well relative to others, thus pairing the difficult task with a success experience. If the differential reactions to success and failure experiences are the essential determinants of behavior in this situation, then on the easy task highly anxious subjects experiencing failure should perform *worse* than subjects low in anxiety experiencing failure. On the difficult task, highly anxious subjects experiencing success should perform *better* than subjects low in anxiety experiencing success. The experimental design consequently provides a definitive test of the alternative explanation of the Spence et al. data [p. 340].

Weiner employed the verbal learning tasks used by Spence. Subjects were classified into high and low anxiety groups according to their scores on the Mandler-Sarason Test Anxiety Questionnaire (TAQ) (Mandler & Sarason, 1952, see Chapter IV). The TAQ is a self-report measure of situationally aroused anxiety. Sample questions are:

1. If you know that you are going to take a group intelligence test, how do you feel *beforehand?*
2. *While* taking an individual intelligence test to what extent do you (or would you) perspire?

The items are answered on a Likert-type scale that is anchored at both extremes. For example, item one above would have "very confident" at one end of a line and "very nervous" at the other end. Subjects respond by checking any point on the line that represents their feeling.

During the experiment subjects receiving the difficult task were given

TABLE 2:3
Mean Number of Trials to Criterion Among Subjects Scoring in
the Upper and Lower 25th Percentile in Anxiety Level
(from Weiner, 1966b, p. 341)

	Condition					
	Easy List (Failure)			Difficult List (Success)		
Anxiety	N	M	SD	N	M	SD
High	9	9.55	3.78	12	14.85	6.57
Low	12	7.08	1.85	10	20.10	7.35

false norms indicating that they were succeeding. Subjects learning the easy list received false norms that indicated failure. Hence, an easy task was paired with a failure, and the difficult task with a success.

The mean number of trials required to master the lists is shown in Table 2:3. The table indicates that subjects classified as low in anxiety perform better than subjects high in anxiety on the easy list, but perform worse than subjects high in anxiety on the difficult list. This is opposite to the findings of Spence, but consistent with the position stressing the differential reactions to success and failure among subjects differing in level of anxiety. The results led Weiner (1966b) to the conclusion that

it is erroneous to cite prior research in this area as validating evidence for drive theory. The important determinants of behavior in this situation are the cognitive and motivational consequences resulting from success or failure at the task, rather than the individual's drive level interacting with the structure of the task *per se* [p. 342].

A replication and extension of these findings, using a serial learning rather than paired-associates task, is reported by Weiner and Schneider (1971).

In sum, it appears that cognitive processes cannot be ignored in the explanation of the observed Anxiety × Task Difficulty interaction. Investigations reviewed later in this book demonstrate the role of cognitive processes in behavior instigated by biological deficits of food and water deprivation. The general issue raised in the Weiner (1966b) and the Weiner and Schneider (1971) investigations is whether a mechanistic conception is adequate to explain behavior.

Problems in the Conceptual Analysis of Incentives

The Independence of Drive and Incentive. According to Spence, as we have indicated, incentive and drive are additive. Hence, organisms theoretically may be activated in situations where the value of drive is zero. However, it is probable that the incentive value of a goal is, in part, determined by drive level. An animal that is satiated is not likely to respond to a goal object. In addition, at very low levels of drive the consummatory activity is not very vigorous, thus theoretically decreasing the amount of conditioning at the goal box between the cues in that environment and the eating response. This, in turn, decreases the magnitude of the bond between the stimuli and the anticipatory goal response. It thus appears that K is not independent of D (see Black, 1965).

Incentive Motivation and Reinforcement.   It has been argued that reinforcement effects are confounded with incentive mechanisms (Bindra, 1969; Walker, 1969). All reinforcing events involve incentive manipulations. That is, a reward, by definition, is an incentive. Thus, the increment in the probability of a response following a reward may be due to the increase in the habit strength of the response, or due to the instigating effects of the incentive when the organism is replaced in the rewarding stimulus situation. Bindra (1969) notes that both the "backward-working" reinforcement effect and the "forward-working" incentive effect are inferred from subsequent behavior. Thus, "the comparisons that define the two effects are the same" (p. 2). Reinforcement and incentive effects are operationally inseparable.

Incentives as Energizers.   Investigators have attempted to account for data presented earlier in this chapter by focusing upon the incentive variable, or r_g-s_g mechanism, while ignoring the drive concept. For example, Birch, Burnstein, and Clark (1958) argue that conditional fractional anticipatory goal responses are the source of drive. This contrasts with the position of Hull and Brown, who anchor drive to antecedent deprivation conditions.

Birch et al. reason that drive stimuli vary discriminately as a function of time of deprivation, and that these drive stimuli become associated with anticipatory goal reactions. Therefore, if animals are fed after a certain period of deprivation throughout their lives, then the stimuli associated with that period of deprivation should come to elicit r_gs, for these internal deprivation stimuli have been repeatedly associated with the goal reaction (R_G). Birch et al. further reason that the r_gs elicited by stimuli not associated with reward extinguish, for they are not followed by the goal reaction. Therefore, a gradient of response strength throughout the range of internal stimuli (S_D) is expected. Response strength is predicted to be at a maximum at, or slightly beyond, the time of deprivation at which the animal has been fed. At prior deprivation points and with continued deprivation the probability of food-related responses is expected to decrease.

In summary, Birch et al. assume that drive is a function of the strength of r_g. The postulated mechanisms of drive are:

$$\text{deprivation} \longrightarrow S_D \longrightarrow r_g \longrightarrow \text{drive}$$

Recall that the r_g-s_g mechanism is responsible for the functioning of K. Birch et al. therefore could substitute K for D in their postulated determinants of activation, and eliminate the drive construct.

Birch et al. created the conditions necessary to test their conception. Three weeks after birth, rats were enclosed in a controlled environment and put on a constant maintenance schedule. They were fed for two hours each day, following 22 hours of deprivation. The food was placed in a food trough. During the testing period, Birch et al. measured the frequency of the food trough depressions when food was not provided. They found that the frequency of these responses rose to a maximum near feeding time, and then fell as deprivation increased beyond the feeding time (see Figure 2:18). Birch et al. also substantiate their predictions using speed of running a straight alley for food as the dependent variable. Running speed is maximized when animals are fed and then tested under 22 hours of deprivation.

The results shown in Figure 2:18 indicate that response strength is not monotonically related to the time of food deprivation. On the contrary, response strength seems to be determined by the prior learned association between the pattern of internal stimulation and the food reward. Birch et al. conclude, therefore, that drive is a function of the strength of the anticipatory goal reaction. Other investigators also have reported that instrumental behavior does not increase monotonically with time of deprivation (see Bolles, 1967).

Drive theorists such as Brown have responded to the Birch et al. investigation and have presented a strong defense for the theoretical conception of drive. Brown and Belloni (1963) point out some experimental problems inadvertently overlooked by Birch et al. In the experiment by Brown and Belloni, the Birch study was modified in two crucial respects. First, the trough containing the food reward was present only during the time the feeding occurred. In addition, Brown and Belloni employed five groups of animals, deprived of food for different periods of time. These procedural changes stem from the conceptual distinction between drive and habit emphasized by Brown. Continued deprivation, which theoretically increases the strength of drive, would not result in performance increments

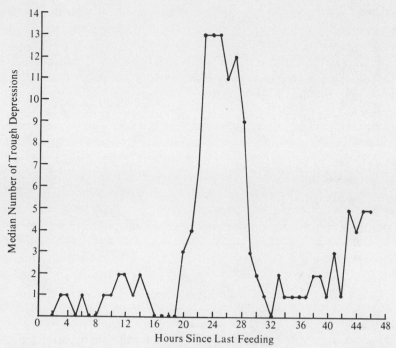

FIGURE 2:18. Median number of trough depression responses per hour as a function of hours since last feeding. Animals were fed during training after 22 hours of deprivation (adapted from Birch, Burnstein, & Clark, 1958, p. 351).

if the response under consideration had undergone diminution because of continued nonreinforcement.

The results of two studies conducted by Brown and Belloni are portrayed in Figure 2:19. The figure indicates that response frequency increases from the 2-hour to the 35-hour deprivation groups. In contrast to the findings of Birch et al., performance does not decline when the time of deprivation during testing exceeds the time during training. Further, response speed in a straight runway is not maximized among the animals tested under 22 hours of deprivation. The data indicate that time of deprivation contributes as a source of drive, as Brown has consistently maintained.

Clearly, the conception of incentive as the only source of activation has not completely dethroned the drive concept. As Atkinson (1964) writes:

The current questioning of the need for the separate drive concept, as Hull originally conceived it, is based mainly on a desire for parsimony. The

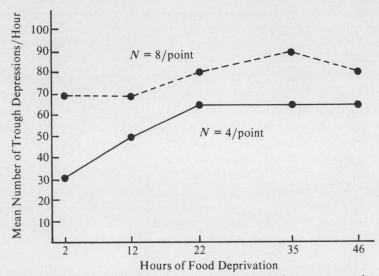

FIGURE 2:19.   Mean number of trough depression responses obtained during a 1-hour test period from five differentially deprived groups of rats in two studies (from Brown & Belloni, 1963, p. 107).

S-R conceptual scheme contains a number of different interrelated variables all of which can produce general performance-enhancing effects. It is posited that drive (D) and r_g (K) are nonspecific exciters. But, according to the principle of stimulus generalization (which no one suggests should be discarded), both S_D and the usually ignored s_g produced by r_g are also capable of eliciting responses that were never immediately associated with them in training. The issues are perplexing and will require substantial future experimental and conceptual analysis [p. 200].

Bolles (1967) at one point suggests that perhaps both drive and incentive are necessary determinants of behavior, for,

Just as the concept of drive arises from the notion that there are conditions which impel an organism to some sort of action, so the concept of incentive arises from the notion that there are objects in the environment to which the organism is attracted. Drives push and incentives pull; the two complement each other in providing a motivational explanation of behavior. The question is how much of motivation is push and how much is pull [p. 332].

The Nondirective Conception of Drive and Some Experimental Confounding

Evidence supporting the nondirective pooling property of drives was presented earlier in this chapter. The studies conducted by Webb and Kendler, which employed two appetitive sources of motivation, have been subject to much criticism. Hunger and thirst are not independent need states. Thirsty rats do not eat as much as nonthirsty rats (Verplanck & Hayes, 1953), and many investigators have substantiated that hungry rats do not drink as much as satiated rats. Therefore, it is likely that during the testing period in the experiments conducted by Webb and others the rats on water deprivation also are hungry. It cannot be said with surety that the drive whose source is water deprivation per se energized the response learned while the animal was deprived of food.

To demonstrate the effects of this confounding, Grice and Davis (1957) repeated the Webb experiment using an additional control group. Animals learned a motor response while under food deprivation and were tested under one of four conditions. During testing one group remained deprived of food, a second group was deprived of water, and a third group was satiated with food and water. Animals in a fourth group, the crucial control, were deprived of water prior to the test phase, but were allowed to drink immediately prior to the testing. If water deprivation increases hunger, then this control group should behave like the animals provided with water but deprived of food.

Grice and Davis found that thirst apparently inhibits food consumption and increases hunger. During the test phase of the experiment, the group deprived of water but allowed to drink prior to testing behaved similarly to the group that was deprived of food but water sated. It is therefore likely that in the investigations by Webb and others, the drive generated by hunger at least in part energized the response during testing.

Drive theorists would probably agree that studies of the nondirective properties of drive combining biological needs of hunger and thirst may be misleading. However, this does not necessarily characterize investigations that demonstrate, for example, that shock enhances consummatory behavior, or that hungry rats escape an aversive stimulus faster than satiated rats. That is, some studies demonstrating the existence of a nondirective drive seem free of experimental error. It is imperative that in these investigations the response not be conditioned to both sources of drive being manipulated.

Secondary Drive and Secondary Reinforcement

The concepts of secondary drive and secondary reinforcement were introduced into drive theory to broaden the domain of data the theory is able to incorporate. Yet many behaviors are undertaken that apparently have not been linked contiguously with the onset or offset of a primary drive state (see the quotation from Osgood on p. 28). Brown (1961) attempts to account for these "everyday" behaviors by suggesting that anxiety is a mediator of a wide variety of human behavior. For example, he reasons that we work because obtaining money reduces the anxiety experienced when money is absent. This view implies that at some time in the individual's life the absence of money has been paired with a primary drive state, such as food deprivation, and with the fear associated with the state of hunger. However, this falls short of a reasonable explanation. It is unlikely that many readers of this book have experienced any prolonged absence of food, while most have held jobs! The drive conception is quite limited in the extensity of the behavior that is amenable to explanation.

There also is a confusion between the Hullian conception of secondary drive and secondary reinforcement. A neutral stimulus associated with the offset of a drive is assumed to become a secondary reinforcer, while a neutral stimulus associated with the onset and offset of a drive becomes a secondary drive. Thus, a secondary drive also functions as a secondary reinforcer; the same stimulus both activates and depresses behavior. For example, assuming that food is a primary reinforcer, the scent of food should acquire secondary reinforcing properties. That is, one should be able to learn new responses with the scent of food as the reward. But if that scent is associated with the onset of a drive, which is aroused by the sight of food, then the smell also acquires drive properties. In sum, the identical originally neutral stimulus arouses the organism, and reduces its needs. Conceptually, a secondary drive, such as fear, is distinguishable from a secondary reinforcer, such as the tokens hoarded by the chimps in the investigation by Cowles. But within drive theory there is no statement to indicate clearly when cues evoke internal stimulation, and when they reduce that stimulation.

Conceptualization of Frustration and Conflict

Frustration.   Amsel and his associates predicted and found an increment in response vigor following the nonattainment of an expected reward. But it is not possible to predict from the Amsel conception when this response increment will be observed, and when extinction will begin to be displayed. For example, assume a situation in which there is a 100 percent reinforcement schedule and a single-alley runway. After the rewarded trials extinction procedures are initiated. On the subsequent trials during which the expected reward is withheld, drive is expected to increase because of the frustration experienced. This should energize behavior. But the aversive properties of frustration theoretically cause a decrement in the resultant habit (approach response minus avoidance response) to locomote toward the goal. It is not possible to specify under what conditions this decrement in the relative habit strength to approach the goal is greater than the increment in drive strength. That is, one cannot predict whether the Frustration Effect will be exhibited, how long it will be displayed, and when response extinction will begin to be observed. This merely exemplifies a pervasive problem in the drive conception. As Postman (1953) indicates, drive and habit are affected by the same operation. Thus, if the Frustration Effect is observed, then the increment in drive is, by definition, greater than the decrement in the resultant approach habit. On the other hand, if the Frustration Effect is not observed, or is dissipated, then the decrement in the resultant approach habit is greater than the increment in drive. But these inferences must be *post-hoc*.

Conflict.   Miller's fourth postulate in his analysis of conflict specifies that "The strength of the tendencies to approach or avoid varies directly with the strength of the drive upon which they are based" (1959, p. 205). But this postulate suggests that drive is not nondirective, but selective; only the relevant habit is energized by an increment in drive. Note the implications for Miller's conflict model if drive multiplies habits both relevant and irrelevant to the specific source of drive, as the Drive × Habit conception specifies. As hunger increases, the strength of the approach tendency also increases. However, if the hunger drive also multiplies the avoidance habit, then the strength of the avoidance tendency also will increase. It would then be impossible to derive that animals approach closer to a goal given increased hours of food deprivation. This is illustrated in Figure 2:20. In Figure 2:20 both the approach and avoidance tendencies are enhanced; there is no change in the distance traversed toward the goal in this particular situation.

Brown and his colleagues have recognized this difficulty with the conflict model. They state:

The basic supposition, that a source of drive relevant to a particular reactive tendency affects that tendency alone, will be described hereafter as the selective-drive assumption. While this somewhat *ad hoc* notion fits the available data, the expectations it yields differ from those provided by Hull's (1943) multiplicative drive ($D \times H$) assumption and from the predictions of driveless theories (Brown, 1961; Estes, 1958) that rely upon associative and generalized tendencies between one or both responses and the internal stimuli produced by the operations of feeding and fasting.

For instance, Hull's view generates the conclusion that a deprivation-induced increase in general drive (D), subsequent to the acquisition of approach and avoidance reaction tendencies, increase both tendencies equally through its nonselective multiplicative effect. Therefore, the locus of conflict, where the two gradients cross and are of equal strength, would not

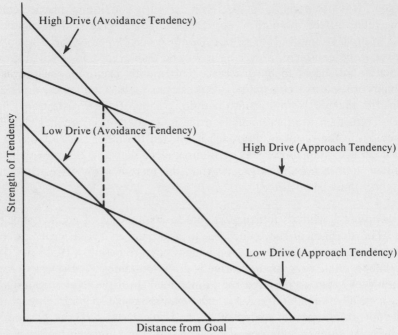

FIGURE 2:20. Graphic representation of an approach-avoidance conflict situation in which the drive generated by food deprivation also energizes the avoidance habit. The animal does not approach closer to the goal although food deprivation has increased (low-low versus high-high) intersection.

be shifted toward the goal, and closer approach to the goal would not be predicted [Brown, Anderson, & Brown, 1966, pp. 390–91].

The statement is illustrated in Figure 2:20. There the nondirective, or nonselective, drive equally increased the approach and avoidance tendencies.

In a complex study to assess the adequacy of various conflict models, Brown et al. varied hours of deprivation during approach and avoidance training, as well as during the testing period. The dependent variable was how far from the bivalent goal the animal would stop during training. To account for their experimental results, which need not be reviewed here, Brown et al. (1966) conclude:

To facilitate the exposition of the foregoing interpretation it has been assumed that changes in hunger-produced drive do not change the strength of the avoidance response. This selective-drive notion is probably an oversimplification, however, since hunger is known to affect the acquisition of fear-motivated behavior, rate of cortical self-stimulation, and other non-hunger related reactions (Brown, 1961). Moreover, Hull's *multiplicative-drive* conception which holds that each and every habit strength is multiplied by the same numerical value of *D*, regardless of the source of drive, is doubtless also only a rough approximation. Perhaps it is time to reject both these views and propose a third, namely, a *graduated-drive* theory. This conception embodies the assumption that all habits are multiplied by the drive arising from any source, but *the numerical value of the multiplier is graduated according to the relevance of the response to the motivational variable*. Specifically, a habit is described as highly relevant to a particular source of drive if the response has led to the diminution or elimination of the drive source. The greater the relevance of response to drive source, the larger the multiplier provided by a given motivational variable. Thus, as in our experiment, responses of approaching a given region for food that have been reinforced should be intensified substantially (multiplied by large values of *D*) by increased food deprivation. But reactions of avoiding that region, even though evoked in the presence of the same internal deprivation stimuli and external cues, should only be slightly augmented by increased time of deprivation [p. 400].

Brown is, therefore, attempting to hold to a nondirective drive, while at the same time suggesting a modification of the Hullian conception that drives equally multiply all habits. He offers instead that drives multiply all habits, but unequally, or selectively.

GENERAL SUMMARY

In this chapter the Hullian conception of the determinants of behavior has been presented. The growth and changes in drive theory have been stressed. The concept of drive has undergone constant modification: from drive as a tissue deficit, to drive as an intense internal stimulus, and finally to the possibility that drive is an anticipatory goal reaction. In a similar manner, the number of the determinants of performance, and their mathematical relationships, also has changed over time: from Drive $\times$ Habit, to Drive $\times$ Incentive $\times$ Habit, and then to the Spencian formula of (Drive $+$ Incentive) $\times$ Habit. In addition, the growth of the theory to include secondary reinforcers, secondary drive, and individual differences has been examined.

Evidence both supporting the conception and challenging the theory has been discussed. Investigations manipulating hours of deprivation and the number of reinforced trials (Perin & Williams), studies of discrimination learning with free- and forced-trials (Spence and his colleagues), experiments combining various sources of drive (Meryman, Webb), and studies of aversive conditioning and paired-associates learning (Spence and his associates) are included among the studies cited in support of the drive conception. Conversely, studies of latent learning and incentive shift (Blodgett, Tolman & Honzig, Crespi), investigations of the motivational effects of success and failure (Weiner), experiments controlling feeding schedules (Birch et al.), and studies demonstrating the interacting effects of biological needs (Grice & Davis) are cited in opposition to drive theory.

Extensions of the Drive $\times$ Habit conception to explain frustration (Farber & Brown, Amsel) and conflict (Miller) also have been examined. Experiments supporting the extensions of the conception (Haner & Brown, Amsel & Roussel, Murray & Berkun), and analyses calling into question these theoretical extrapolations, have been presented.

Finally, alternative conceptions that reject a drive concept have been outlined. These include "pure" associative positions (Estes, Postman) and a conception that stresses the role of incentives as a drive (Birch et al.). Arguments against the adequacy of these alternative theories, and data in support of these arguments, has been inspected (Loess, Brown & Belloni).

If the reader has retained all these points he will have some understanding of the evolution of drive theory and the controversies associated with the conception. However, many relevant theoretical issues and experimental investigations were not discussed in this chapter, and other sources must be sought (such as Bolles, 1967; Brown, 1961).

Despite the diversity of changes and disputes, or perhaps because of them, the theoretical conception proposed by Hull and Spence remains an integral part of contemporary psychology and current motivational theory. The necessity of a drive construct, for example, is a central controversy in motivational theory (see Atkinson, 1961). To convey the extent of this controversy, and its implications for drive theory, compare the following quotes from two contemporary experts on the psychology of motivation:

The drive concept is like an old man that has had a long, active, and yes, even useful life. It has produced a notable amount of conceptual and empirical work; it has, perhaps indirectly, made a great contribution to our understanding of behavior. But the fruitful days are nearly gone. The time has come when younger, more vigorous, more capable concepts must take over. So, as sentimental as we may feel about our old friend, we should not despair at his passing [Bolles, 1967, pp. 329–30].

As much as on any other point, psychologists seem agreed that behavior is determined by the joint operation of two relatively independent factors, habit and motivation. Habit is characterized as the response choice factor, and is linked to training variables (e.g., prior stimulus-response pairings, reinforcement) that determine which response is likely to be made under a given set of stimulus conditions. Motivation is characterized as an action-instigational factor, and is linked to organismic variables (e.g., states created by food deprivation, fatigue, hormones, or drugs) that determine the probability and vigor of response occurrence. When habit variables are held constant, and motivational variables are varied, the resulting changes in response characteristics are described as motivational effects [Bindra, 1968, p. 1].

Certain drive states, if not all, are individually, each in itself, sufficient to raise the level of general activity. They are also, in the absence of incentive-motivational stimuli, sufficient to facilitate the occurrence of relevant consummatory acts in the presence of appropriate consummatory objects [Bindra, 1968, p. 17].

The main contribution of drive theory has been the systematic and precise exploration of motivational phenomena from an entirely mechanistic position. Drive theorists provided the first model for the scientific study of motivation. While accepting the methodological advances of drive theorists, the remaining chapters raise doubts about the adequacy of drive theory. The main issues raised are whether a mechanistic conception of motivation can adequately explain the relatively simple behaviors instigated by food and water deprivation, whether the theory is sufficient to incorporate the richness and complexity of human behavior, and whether the influence of thought upon action can be ignored in motivational theory.

III

Field Theory

Drive and field theory were roughly contemporaneous developments in the psychology of motivation. Lewin's systematic treatise of motivation in his 1938 monograph *The Conceptual Representation and the Measurement of Psychological Forces* preceded Hull's *Principles of Behavior* (1943) by five years. Field theory offered a more cognitive approach to the study of behavior than drive theory, as well as a completely different language for the understanding of motivational phenomena. However, field theory is not, strictly speaking, a "pure" cognitive theory. Lewin was not devoted to the study of cognitive processes per se, nor did he attempt to relate thought to action systematically. Further, he was greatly influenced by physicalistic conceptions in science, and borrowed many of the concepts of physics. However, Lewin, like Tolman, did contend that behavior is guided by a knowledge of the path to the goal; that is, the encoding of past experience was described mentalistically, rather than with the logic of *S-R* bonds. In addition, the general approach of Lewin—his experimental methods, use of human subjects, acceptance of introspective reports, selection of areas for investigation, embracement of phenomenology, and so forth—is clearly that of a cognitivist.

In this chapter Lewin's conceptual system is discussed and data supporting his theory are examined. Further, the field conception is often compared and contrasted with drive theory. An asymmetry between the Hullian and Lewinian systems is highlighted: Lewin attempted to incorporate and account for the data gathered by drive theorists, but it is not possible for Hull, Spence, or others to consider the empirical research of

Lewin within the drive theoretical position. It falls beyond the boundary conditions of their conception. However, we will see that the breadth of Lewin's conception is achieved at the cost of precision.

HISTORICAL EVOLUTION

It was noted previously that structuralism was rejected by three different movements in psychology. The American functionalist-behaviorist approach was one of these movements. This position was presented in Chapter II. The Freudian psychoanalytic movement, which was alluded to briefly in that chapter, also is incompatible with the position of the structuralists. Man, psychoanalysts argue, is not completely aware of his motivations; psychological understanding is not possible without a detailed analysis of the unconscious sources of motivation. Psychoanalysts contend that the usual introspective method cannot tap the deeper, underlying motives. Structuralists ignore these "dynamic" aspects of psychology. Finally, Gestalt psychologists also opposed the approach advocated by Wundt and Titchener. Gestaltists did not accept the position that an analysis of the basic elements of feeling can lead to an understanding of more complex emotions. They challenged the notion that the whole is merely the sum of its parts.

Gestalt Psychology

The founding of Gestalt psychology generally is attributed to Max Wertheimer. In 1912 he published his paper on the phi phenomenon. This phenomenon refers to the apparent movement of physically proximal lights when their onset is temporally contiguous. Wertheimer challenged the structuralists by contending that an analysis of this phenomenon into separate sensations or elements could not explain the perceived movement. Movement depends upon a relationship between the incoming sources of stimulation. Wertheimer argued that perceived movement is not merely a sensation, but a phenomenon.

Boring (1950) introduces Gestalt psychology and its influences in America in the following manner:

Functionalism, . . . the fundamental American trend, leads directly into behaviorism and the whole behavioristic development in America . . . behaviorists ultimately absorbed functionalism, but first we must examine the nature and the origin of Gestalt psychology. Often the two movements—Gestalt psychology and behaviorism—are said to be contemporaneous. That is because the starting point for modern Gestalt psychology is Wertheimer's paper on seen movement, published in June 1912, and the starting point for behaviorism is Watson's paper on "psychology as the behaviorist views it," published in March 1913. Both of the movements, however, have their roots in antiquity. Each is a symptom of a *"Zeitgeist,"* but they are different symptoms of different *"zeitgeister."* Each is a protest against the "new" German psychology of the late nineteenth century, the psychology of Wundt, G. E. Müller and Titchener, but the two are different protests. Gestalt psychology primarily protested against the analysis of consciousness into elements and the exclusion of values from the data of consciousness, whereas behaviorism mostly protested against the inclusion of the data of consciousness in psychology.

As a protest, behaviorism may be said to have been farther along in 1913 than was Gestalt psychology in 1912, for behaviorism was the second phase of the American protest against the Wundtian tradition. The first was functionalism. Gestalt psychology, however, was but the first phase of the German protest against the Wundtian tradition. That is why, when the Gestalt psychologists brought their protest to America in the 1920's, many American psychologists did not understand them, for they were protesting against something that was no longer important in America. America had already moved further away from conscious elementism than had Europe. The reasons are the reasons for American functionalism [p. 587].

Following Wertheimer's discoveries, Koffka completed his treatise on the *Growth of the Mind* (1924), and Köhler wrote *The Mentality of Apes* (1925). These books discuss in detail the position of Gestalt psychologists. As indicated previously, the main contention of the Gestaltists was a protest against an analysis of psychological phenomena into elements. Gestaltists dealt with wholes, and the whole was considered more than the sum of its parts. In discussing the total situation, the Gestaltists made use of field conceptions originated by physicists. In a given physical field, alteration of any part of that field affects the other parts. A field is organized by all the forces acting upon all the objects in that field.

The Gestaltists applied the notion of fields in their analysis of psychological processes. The process that they most thoroughly investigated was perception. The perception of an object, they characteristically argued, is determined by the total context in which the object is embedded. This was dramatically illustrated in their demonstration of perceptual illusions, such as the Müller-Lyer illusion (see Figure 3.1). In the Müller-Lyer illusion two lines of equal length are perceived as being unequal. According to the Gestaltists, this is caused by the differing fields of forces around the judged lines.

Gestalt psychologists conducted investigations in numerous areas within perception. They attempted to discover how field forces interact with one another and what distribution of forces leads to a state of equilibrium. They formulated many laws of perceptual organization, such as

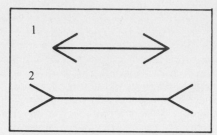

FIGURE 3:1.   The Müller-Lyer illusion. Both lines are about one inch
in length. However, Line 2 appears
longer than Line 1.

the Laws of Similarity, Proximity, Closure, and Good Continuation. These
are factors that influence the perception of objects as units. (Adaptation
of these ideas to explain social phenomena is discussed in Chapter V.)

The Gestaltists also expressed an interest in learning, but the type
of learning they investigated can be considered a subset of the field of
perception. In Köhler's book, *The Mentality of Apes* (1925), experiments
are reported that demonstrate insight learning in animals. The general procedure in these studies is to place a stick in one corner of an ape's cage,
and food outside the cage at an opposite corner. The animal can reach
the food only if he uses the stick as a tool. Köhler reports dramatic changes
in the ape's behavior that seem to occur in an all-or-none fashion. The
animal suddenly perceives the correct solution to the problem and reaches
the food with the aid of the stick. Köhler contrasts this insight learning with
the blind trial and error learning exhibited by Thorndike's cats and chicks.

In Köhler's experiments, learning apparently involves perceptual processes. Although the path to the stick is physically opposite to the path
toward food, it must be perceived as being in the path toward the goal.
The discovery of the correct response in this situation depends upon the
way in which the animal organizes his field; the solution requires the correct perception of the relationship between the parts in the field. Insight
learning is a perceptual reorganization.

As Boring (1950) states, "There is much more to be understood
about Gestalt psychology than that it deals with wholes and phenomena"
(p. 593). The theories postulated by Gestaltists were applied to retention,
meaning, and other psychological processes. Our concern here, however,
is only with their immediate influence on Kurt Lewin.

The language used by the early Gestaltists became incorporated into
Lewinian field theory. Terms such as structure of the field, relation between the parts, subjective perception, reorganization of the field, force,

energy, and attraction are prevalent in all of Lewin's writings. Lewin (1935) states:

Fortunately I experienced Max Wertheimer's teaching in Berlin and collaborated for over a decade with Wolfgang Köhler. I need not emphasize my debts to these outstanding personalities. The fundamental ideas of Gestalt theory are the foundation of all our investigations in the field of the will, of affection, and of the personality. In the few articles in which the problems of general Gestalt theory are not explicitly discussed, this is solely because they have become the self-evident foundation of experimental practice [p. 240].

Lewin-Ach Controversy

Lewin broke away from the Gestalt emphasis on perception and initiated a systematic analysis of motivation. His theoretical position was revealed early in his career when he presented a theoretical argument against the position of Ach, another German psychologist. These arguments and Ach's replies became known as the Lewin-Ach Controversy.

Lewin (1935) stated that most psychologists postulate pure association as the sole principle of psychological causation. Contiguity was considered to be the sufficient principle of learning and performance. He describes the associative position:

The relations to which theory has heretofore looked in experimental psychology, when seeking the causes of a psychical event, belong almost exclusively to one quite specific type of relation. This is a real connection which one may designate as *adhesion* of any sort of object or collection of objects or processes. The fact that certain single objects are connected with each other, or that a whole event sticks together in the sense of adhesion, is given as the cause of a psychical event.

The most pronounced case of such a type of connection is presented by the association between two psychical objects in the sense of the old association theory. The objects *a* and *b* have entered into an association by reason of earlier contiguity. And this association phenomenon is claimed to be the cause of the fact that on the occurrence of experience *a*, experience *b* results. . . .

In psychology these couplings were conceived for the most part as mechanically rigid connections in the sense of an association of individual stimulations with established reactions [pp. 43–44].

Ach's Modification of Association Theory.   Ach was a member of the Würzburg school in psychology. This group wanted to supplement the concept of association with more dynamic constructs. These dynamic constructs included will, set, and the determining tendency. To provide empirical support for this theoretical position, Ach (1910) attempted to demonstrate the existence and to measure the strength of a determining tendency. In a paired-associates task, subjects learned to reproduce nonsense syllables according to certain specified principles. Some lists were composed of all rhyming pairs (dak-tak), while other lists included pairs in which the stimuli and responses were mirror images (mep-pem). After the subjects initially learned the lists, Ach introduced a determining tendency by providing a new experimental instruction. The instruction was designed either to hinder or facilitate performance, depending on the relationship between the new instruction and the previously learned task. For example, after initially learning a list of rhyming paired-associates, the subjects were told to respond to a new list of stimuli by repeating these stimuli backwards as fast as possible. Alternately, after learning a paired-associates list composed of mirror image stimulus-response terms, subjects were told to respond to a new list of stimuli with a rhyme. In both experimental conditions some of the second list stimuli had been included as stimuli during first-list learning. Ach's dependent variable was the latency of the subject's response during the performance of the second task. The existence and strength of the determining tendency, or will, was inferred from the response latency. Ach predicted, and found, that the shortest latencies are exhibited when the second-list instructions are congruent with the associations strengthened during first-list learning. The longest latencies are exhibited when the "force of the will" is set in opposition to the prior associations; for example, when one has to respond with a rhyme to a syllable previously associated with a mirror image. Ach argued that the differences in latencies indicate that there are two causal determinants of behavior: will and associative strength. Behavior was considered overdetermined; knowledge of the strength of both determinants was believed necessary for accurate predictions.

Lewin's reaction to Ach was somewhat similar to Watson's feelings toward functionalism (although the affect and vociferousness differed tremendously). Ach was proceeding in the right direction, according to Lewin, but he failed to carry his analysis to its logical conclusion. He did not distinguish a need habit (determining tendency) from an executive habit (prior association), although the two are conceptually distinct constructs. If there is a need, Lewin argued, then a tension exists that demands satisfaction. An executive habit, however, is not itself a source of action, and is not expressed in behavior unless accompanied by a need habit. Lewin contended that an association is merely a link in a chain; it does not possess any force toward change. On the other hand, a need represents a tendency toward change.

Stated somewhat differently, Lewin contended that couplings created by repetition or association do not provide the motor, or energy, for behavior. A habit of execution (a link from A to B) cannot be a cause (a directed force from A to B). The laws of association do not include directed forces and, therefore, err by omitting dynamic or motivational constructs. This argument is similar to Brown's plea for a conceptual distinction between drive and habit, and to Brown's arguments against associative theory. Lewin is making an identical appeal, but from a very different theoretical position.

Lewin, therefore, concluded that Ach's analysis was incorrect. Ach conceptualized association as a force that could act in opposition to, or in the same direction as, the force instigated by the new instruction. Ach had coordinated intention with an association. Lewin's position was that in Ach's experiment there must have been a force or need habit acting in conjunction with the prior association. Lewin reasoned that in the Ach experiment the prior learning functioned as an internalized command. That is, following initial learning the subject covertly self-instructs: "When the stimulus occurs, respond with a rhyme (or say it backward)." The new experimental instruction then acts as a second command that can conflict with the already internalized command. The conflict created is not between an association and a determining tendency; the conflict is between two determining tendencies.

Evidence in Support of Lewin's View. Lewin cites common sense examples and everyday observations in support of his view that associations are not causes of actions. For example, a subject might repeat any stimulus-response coupling, such as mep-pem, thousands of times. Yet if the subject is then told to respond to the syllable "mep" with his own name, the probability that he will respond with "pem" is virtually zero. Lewin argues that an extremely large number of repetitions do not interfere with a new directed tendency.

Lewin also believed that the consequences of a delay between the occurrence of the stimulus and the final action, or consummatory response, support his position concerning causes. Assume a situation in which a simple motor response, such as bar-pressing, has been followed by the reception of food and a reduction in hunger. The bar is then introduced to the animal but retracted before the response can be completed. According to a strictly associative view, there should be no long-lasting after effects (only that of the stimulus trace) attributed to the initiation of the response sequence. However, Lewin believes that the tendency to engage in and complete the initiated activity may persist indefinitely in the absence of the instigating, external stimulus. A determining tendency or need habit is not stimulus bound.

Lewin offers one further argument against the associative principle of cause. He notes that the occurrence of the stimulus has no effect on the intended action once the act has been completed. Lewin cites the familiar act of mailing a letter to illustrate his point. Assume that an individual opens a mailbox and drops in a letter. When passing the next mailbox, there is no tendency for the box to "call out" the "opening" response. According to the laws of association, there should be some tendency for the mailbox to elicit this response. Lewin states that if the intent to mail a letter has been fulfilled, then the onset or occurrence of the stimulus will not initiate a new activity. One might contend that the absence of the letter has changed the stimulus situation. However, many of the identical cues remain. Therefore, association theory would specify that there is some probability of the mailbox eliciting the prior mailing response.

The arguments against the pure associative position form an integral part of Lewin's more formal conception of behavior and his subsequent ideas concerning tension system and energy. The Lewin-Ach controversy had a pervasive influence throughout Lewin's career.

THEORETICAL ORIENTATION

The Use of Concepts

Let us now consider the more formal aspects of Lewin's later theorizing. Lewin's orientation toward scientific theory can be characterized by a few strongly held points of view. He was very disturbed by the collection of data not guided by theoretical analyses, and by a reliance upon statistical analysis rather than conceptual understanding. In his *Principles of Topological Psychology* (1936), he states that

investigators are coming to feel that a mere piling up of facts can only lead to a chaotic and unproductive situation. The simple collecting of facts is indispensable at certain stages of a science; it is a wholesome reaction against a philosophical and speculative building of theories. But it cannot give a satisfactory answer to questions about causes and conditions of events. Only with the help of theories can one determine causal interrelationships. A science without theory is blind because it lacks that element which alone is able to organize facts and to give direction to research. Even from a practical point of view the mere gathering of facts has very limited value. It cannot give an answer to the question that is most important for practical purposes—namely, what must one do to obtain a desired effect in given concrete cases? To answer this question it is necessary to have a theory, but a theory which is empirical and not speculative. This means that theory and facts must be closely related to each other.

Psychology needs concepts which can be applied not merely to the facts of a single field like child psychology, animal psychology, or psychopathology, but which are equally applicable to all of them. One should be able to use the same concepts for problems of emotional life as for problems of behavior; or for problems concerning the infant, the adolescent, and the aged; the healthy and the sick; animals and human beings; the personality and the environment. Does this mean that we are to return to the making of speculative "systems?" Yes and no. Yes, in so far as we should not content ourselves with a blind collecting that splits the field of psychology into a number of unrelated branches. No, in so far as we must not try to derive all psychological facts neatly from one single concept such as association, reflex, instinct, or totality [pp. 4–5].

Lewin's interest in theory did not result in a neglect of empirical evidence. His theoretical advancements guided and were guided by his data. Yet he believed that the very essence of science lay in the building of theories. In his classic monograph, *The Conceptual Representation and the Measurement of Psychological Forces* (1938), he states, "The danger of speculation lies not in the introduction of constructs, because they are unavoidable, but in the way they are introduced" (p. 12). On the very next page of that monograph he again cautions against the neglect of theory-building in psychology:

The recently growing interest in "operational" definitions in psychology (Stevens, 1935) has helped to emphasize the necessity of introducing concepts (constructs) beyond the level of directly observable phenomena, and has helped emphasize the necessity of linking these constructs in a definite way to concrete manipulations. Unfortunately, however, the emphasis on operational definitions seems to have led in some cases to a somewhat dangerous disregard of the conceptual side of constructs. Some workers seem to be satisfied with coordinating a conceptual "something" with some empirical operation even if the conceptual properties of this something are left so vague and unclear that one could hardly speak of it as a "concept."

The concept of intelligence, for instance, is today one of the best defined constructs as far as its coordinating definition to empirical operations is concerned. At least, this is the case if one accepts the widely used definition: "Intelligence is what is measured by intelligence tests." The operations which then define intelligence are most exactly and elaborately determined. If one accepts coordination with empirical operations as the criterion of a scientific construct, one would have to say, therefore, that the concept "intelligence" is probably as good and as exact a concept as can be had in psychology for quite a while to come.

On the other hand, one might well hold the position that the concept thus defined is entirely inexact, unclear, and vague. Because, there is nothing within this concept which permits any statement about its dynamical nature, except maybe that intelligence is not an energy or need (not something which can be treated as a source of action), and that it is merely an "ability" (leaving it rather open as to what logically is meant by "ability"). In other words, the conceptual side of the construct "intelligence" is so vague that it is hard to see how one could use such a concept within a frame of scientific derivations, if one understands by scientific derivations a strictly logical sequence of sentences [pp. 13–14].

Field Theory

The conceptual framework advocated by Lewin is called field theory. When asked what field theory is, Lewin (1951) replied that it is a "method of analyzing causal relations and of building scientific constructs" (p. 45). Field theory is a set of beliefs about a way to build theory; it is a metatheory.

Ahistorical Analysis. Field theory starts with the position that behavior is a function of the field as it exists at a moment in time. The approach is ahistorical; causation is contemporary. Lewin, of course, believed that both the past and the future influence behavior. However, their effects must be manifested in the present. To clarify any misunderstandings about his position, Lewin (1938) writes:

I have been accused of "ahistorical" thinking. It is true that I try to distinguish more sharply than is usually done between historical and ahistorical problems in psychology. However, that does not imply at all a neglect of the historical categories. As a matter of fact, anyone who defines stimuli in psychological rather than physical terms, and does not forget about the social side of psychological phenomena, cannot possibly omit the historical aspect of every psychological datum [p. 2].

Lewin contrasts the ahistorical approach with a genetic or historical analysis. Assume, for example, that an individual has a compulsion to wash his hands every ten minutes. To explain this behavior, a geneticist such as Freud might investigate the individual's past history, that is, the pattern of child-rearing, the events that occurred during the stages of development, and so on. It could then be ascertained how these historical antecedents influence present behavior. Lewin, on the other hand, would determine the forces acting on the person in the immediate present. He might represent the individual as avoiding dirt or the soap as having a positive attraction. The antecedent historical conditions, or reasons why the individual perceives the present situation as he does, would be important. However, in predicting behavior one must specify the contemporary determinants of behavior. The past is incorporated into the present.

Representation of the Entire Field. A second fundamental position of the field theorists is that an analysis of behavior must consider the whole situation. As the Gestalt psychologists prior to Lewin had emphasized, one must represent the entire field of forces. Each part within a field interacts with other parts; there are relationships between the elements. Lewin depicts this position by contrasting the Aristotelian and Galilean approaches to science. Aristotle, Lewin contends, reasoned that the explanation of behavior resides within the particular object under consideration. The cause was the very essence of the object; for example, fire rises because of its nature. One might paraphrase Aristotle by saying that fire rises because of an inherited disposition. One of Galileo's important contributions to science was changing this conception of cause. Galileo believed that causal explanations do not reside entirely within an object. Rather, the determinants of behavior (motion) depend on the totality of the situation—the relation between the objects in the physical field.

There are a number of other essential distinctions between the Aristotelian and Galilean approaches. According to Lewin, the Aristotelian approach can be characterized as a method of abstraction. Observations are made, and frequently and mutually occurring events are identified. Laws are derived from these mutual occurrences. For example, if balloons A and B rise, while nonballoon C does not rise, and so on, then it could be postulated that all balloons and no other objects rise. This Baconian approach to science establishes laws or generalizations by observing empirical relationships.

Lewin objects to this procedure for two reasons. First, the method of abstraction ignores unique events; unique events are not considered lawful. On the other hand, Lewin wants to explain the behavior of a concrete individual in a concrete situation. Unique events, he argues, are lawful. Lewin also objects to the method of abstraction because the formulated laws are direct observations. That is, explanation is presented by nature; man must merely find the regularities that actually occur. However, phenomenologists such as Lewin argue that all knowledge begins with experience. Thus, the elements of construction of a theory do not actually appear in the behavior. The elements are ideas, or constructs: laws are made by man, not by nature. The elements of construction are then used symbolically to represent a concrete situation and the individual case.

Appropriate Areas of Psychological Investigation

Lewin also believed that psychologists should study all aspects of human behavior, even though certain behaviors are not amenable to exact scientific measurement. He contended that it was premature to expect rigor at all levels of psychological investigation. However, the lack of rigor should not hinder the study of the phenomena. The existing problems, rather than the availability of "proper" methodology, should determine which experiments are conducted. The purpose of psychology, he argued, is to explain reality; to explain the events one observes in everyday life. His feelings about quantitative exactness rather than theoretical advances are conveyed in his comments concerning the Zeigarnik Effect (the greater recall of incompleted than of completed tasks):

Take, on the other hand, such questions as whether the effect of an intention is that of a link (association) or the creation of a quasi-need (equivalent to a tension system). If the latter theory is correct, one should expect a fair number of resumptions after interruption. The study of about one hundred interruptions by Ovsiankina shows indeed 80% of resumption. There is some merit in trying another group of one hundred interruptions. If, however, this group again shows about 80% of resumption, one can follow two lines. Either one tries to determine the actual percentage of resumption as accurately as possible, or one is mainly interested in the question whether the effect of an intention can be adequately understood as the creation of a tension system. For the latter question it is at present of minor importance whether the percentage of resumption is 75, 80, or 85, because any of these figures would be in line with the general assumption. To prove or disprove the theory of tension systems, it seems much more important to find a variety of derivations from this theory which should be as different as possible from each other, and to test as many as possible of these derivations, even if this test should be rather crude quantitatively at the beginning [Lewin, 1951, pp 8–9].[1]

Mathematical Language. To explain the diverse behaviors observed in nature, Lewin employed a mathematical logic. His attempts at theory

[1] Lewin's desire to study the complex phenomena occurring in nature is contrary to the position of many of the proponents of drive theory. Spence (1957), for example, states:

Now, undoubtedly . . . [the] statement quoted earlier implies, [that] it is easier for psychologists whose research interests have been concerned with such relatively simple phenomena as animal learning and simple conditioning, or even the acquisition of motor and verbal skills in human subjects, to hold to the criteria that such a methodological behaviorism demands. Unquestionably, the more rapid progress that has been made in the study of these simpler events, as compared with the more complex aspects of human personality, is due, in part, to the fact that the simpler phenomena have readily lent themselves to study by acceptable operations, whereas such methods have not been so available in the case of complex phenomena.

One must also agree . . . that we objectivists have tended to concentrate our efforts in these simpler areas; not, however . . . because we have any special aversion to the problems of personality and certainly not because we have a preference . . . "for externals rather than internals, for elements rather than patterns, for geneticism, and for a passive or reactive organism rather than for one that is spontaneous and active." The explanation of our interests is, I think, much simpler. . . . We have chosen to investigate simpler phenomena first because we are of the belief that progress in the formulation of psychological laws and theories will be more rapid in this area than in the case of more complex behavior. We also believe that many of the variables and laws isolated in the study of simpler forms of behavior will be operative in more complex instances, interacting presumably with the additional factors introduced into these more complex situations. If such is the case it would appear to be more efficient in the long run to investigate the simpler phenomena first [pp. 102–3].

building were represented in topological or, more correctly, hodological space. (The Greek stem "hodos" means path.) This nonquantitative use of mathematics does not require certain assumptions about distance. Lewin felt that hodological language makes it possible to take seriously the idea of a psychological space. For example, in hodological space the distance from A to B is not necessarily equal to the distance from B to A. The distance between one's home and school psychologically might be greater or less than the perceived distance between school and home. Other differences between physical and psychological movement also necessitate a hodological conception of space. Passing an examination or getting married involves psychological movement, although there may be no physical change in location. In addition, psychological distance may at times be opposite to physical distance. For example, one may have to run through a burning room to escape a fire. In that situation the psychological direction is away from the fire although the physical direction is toward it.

Lewin states that hodological space also makes it possible to represent dynamic laws. Laws of behavioral dynamics are needed because small differences in observed behavior might represent great dynamic differences. A distinction must be made between a "phenotype" and a "genotype." That is, the behavior exhibited in action must be differentiated from the underlying causes of that behavior. For example, individual A might act as aggressively toward an authority figure as individual B. However, A may be mildly resentful toward the object of attack, while B might be extremely hostile yet somewhat inhibited in his actions because of the fear of retaliation. In Miller's approach-avoidance conflict terminology, individual A has a moderate approach tendency, while individual B has both strong approach and strong avoidance tendencies. Hence, the genotypic representation of the two individuals markedly differs, although their observed behaviors are similar. The phenotype-genotype distinction is perhaps more easily conveyed by an example in the field of biology, from which it originated. Two individuals with identical hair color (phenotype) could have offspring with different hair colors, thus revealing an unobserved genotypic difference. Again the arguments put forth by Lewin are similar to those later subscribed to by drive theorists such as Brown. Brown states that motivational (dynamic) constructs are necessary because the same response may be elicited in different stimulus situations (1961, p. 3). For example, in situations involving either High Drive $\times$ Weak Habit or Low Drive $\times$ Strong Habit, the identical excitatory reactions might be exhibited. Although the observed responses in the different stimulus situations are identical, the mathematical specification of the behavioral determinants would reveal genotypic differences.

FORMAL THEORY

The Life Space

It is convenient to dichotomize Lewin's conceptual scheme into two categories: person constructs and environmental constructs (Heider, 1960). Lewin's basic and well-known programmatic statement is that behavior is a function of the person and the environment: $B = f(P, E)$. The person and the environment comprise the life space. The life space represents psychological reality; it depicts the totality of facts that determine behavior at a moment in time. The life space is represented as a finitely structured space (see Figure 3:2).

Within the life space the person and the environment are mutually dependent. The life space consists of the environment as it is perceived by the person. The psychological field is not isomorphic with the physical environment. A mouse in the corner of a room, if it is not perceived, will not cause anxiety. That is, to have any behavioral effects the mouse must be part of the psychological environment or field. To illustrate this point somewhat more dramatically, Lewin related the oft-cited illustration of the horseback rider lost in a snowstorm. The rider saw a light in the distance and rode directly toward it. Upon arrival at his destination he was told that he had just crossed a barely frozen lake. The rider's behavior certainly would have been different if the danger involved in crossing the lake had been a psychological, as well as a physical, reality.

The pyschological environment is "influenced" by the person. Numerous investigations demonstrate that needs, values, attitudes, motives, and the like, affect the perception of environmental objects and events. Similarly, the environment influences the person. The sudden appearance of

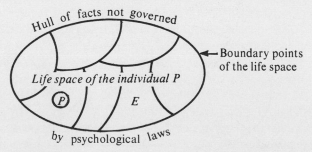

FIGURE 3:2. Representation of a life space. E represents the psychological environment (from Lewin, 1936, p. 73).

an attractive female may change the needs or tensions of a male. To understand behavior, the person and the environment must be considered a constellation. According to Lewin, the task of explaining behavior is to find a scientific representation of the life space and then to determine the functions that link behavior to the life space. The functions that link behavior to the life space are called "laws."

Concepts Related to the Person

Structural Constructs. The person is conceptualized both as a point in the life space and as a region. In Figure 3:2 the person is depicted as an undifferentiated point. In many instances one is concerned primarily with the person's position in the life space, and in these cases it is convenient not to differentiate the person into subparts. In other situations, however, it is necessary to conceptualize the person as a region. When the person (*P*) is conceptualized as a region, it has the same structural properties as the regions in the psychological environment: subregions, boundaries, and adjacencies (see Figure 3:3). (In the present context subregion and region generally are used interchangeably.)

The regions within the person are "containers"; they represent "vessels with walls." The walls or boundaries of the vessels differ in their permeability; some allow more "leakage" than others. The regions at times may be thought of as symbolizing potential needs. Adjacent regions would then represent similar needs, and proximity between regions would capture a stimulus generalization gradient. The structure of the person, or innerpersonal regions, is important because it determines the fate of the tension that is contained within the regions.

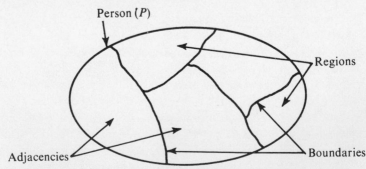

FIGURE 3:3. Representation of the structural properties of the person. The regions are separated by boundaries which differ in their permeability. Adjacent regions border one another.

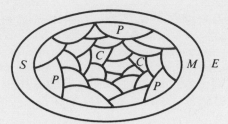

FIGURE 3:4. Further topology of
the person. *S-M* represents the perceptual (sensorium)-motor region; *C*, the
central regions; and *P*, the peripheral
regions. Central regions are bordered
by more regions than are peripheral
regions. In this diagram the peripheral
regions have greater access to the perceptual-motor system than do the
central regions. Thus, the peripheral
regions are "outer," while the central
regions are "inner" (adapted from
Lewin, 1936, p. 177).

Other structural properties are associated with the person, but they
play a less important role in Lewin's theory than the constructs discussed
above. Lewin distinguishes between central (*C*) and peripheral (*P*) regions (Figure 3:4), and between inner and outer regions. The centrality
of a region refers to its distance from other regions. The more central the
region, the more regions to which it is immediately connected and the
greater its influence on behavior. Therefore, central regions are more likely
to be affected by changes in other regions; they are ". . . sensitive to the
state of the whole" (Lewin, 1951, p. 123). In other theoretical languages,
such as Koffka's, these central regions might represent the self, or the "ego
system."

The inner-outer distinction refers to the access which the region has
to the motor system. Contents of inner regions are less likely to be expressed overtly. Americans and Germans differ, Lewin (1948) states, in
their willingness to reveal important aspects of their selves. Americans
maintain a sharper distinction (stronger boundaries) between inner and
outer regions than do Germans.

Central regions are generally inner regions, but this need not be the
case (see Figure 3:5). Further, personal regions are not permanently fixed
as central or inner. Events may lead to structural change. Thus, central
regions may become peripheral as a function of new experiences, and vice
versa.

In the following passage, Kounin (1964) summarizes some potential

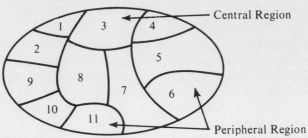

FIGURE 3:5.   Example in which both central and peripheral regions are outer. Region 3 is bordered by six other regions, while region 6 is adjacent to only two other regions. In this diagram, region 8 is an inner region (adapted from Barker, Dembo, & Lewin, 1941, p. 57).

behavioral differences affected by the central-peripheral and inner-outer distinctions proposed by Lewin:

From the degree of centrality of a need one can logically derive such consequences as: (a) the number of other needs affected by it, (b) the degree of effect upon the person-as-a-whole, (c) the variety of expressions (though not necessarily substitute-satisfactions), (d) the resistance to change and tendency to longer lastingness (since it is connected with more other needs and hence involves changing more other systems of the person as well).

From the degree to which a need has a position in the outer-inner dimension one can derive such consequences as: (a) the degree to which it is private or public, (b) the degree to which the behavioral expression has a one-to-one relationship with the content of the need as compared to a "disguised" or indirect relationship with the content of the need, (c) the degree to which it may be diagnosed, (d) the degree to which it is influenced by events emanating from outside the person [pp. 151–152].

Individuals may differ in the number (degree of differentiation) and arrangement of the inner-personal regions and in the strength of the boundaries between regions. Lewin (1951) states that differentiation "refers to the numbers of relatively separated or distinguishable parts contained in a definite whole" (p. 116). The degree of differentiation is assumed to increase with developmental age and increasing knowledge. Lewin indicates that the rate of differentiation depends on the environmental conditions and the native propensities of the person. His solution to the nature-nurture controversy in the development of cognitions corresponds to the presently accepted position; both are important contributors.

Individuals also vary in the relative differentiation of regions. A psychology student might have a number of subregions within the "psychologi-cal-region," while a nonpsychology major might only have one region representing psychology. In addition, the strength of the boundaries be-tween the regions differs between individuals. A psychology major with weak boundaries between the regions may see psychology as an unitary field (as does Lewin), while one with strong boundaries between the re-gions may perceive many different and distinct areas in psychology.

There also may be dedifferentiation or integration of the regions. In strong emotional states, separate entities may seem like one; stimulus differentiation (discrimination) breaks down. Also, with increasing knowl-edge previously distinct facts may appear unified, resulting in a decrease in the number of regions.[2]

Another structural component associated with the person is the per-ceptual (sensorium)-motor (*S-M*) region. This region is at the boundary zone between the inner-personal regions and the distal stimulus, or "for-eign hull" (see Figure 3:4). Lewin, (I assume with tongue in cheek) labeled distal stimuli as part of the foreign hull, implying that Clark Hull and his colleagues were studying factors removed from the real determi-nants of behavior. The perceptual-motor region is the closest region to the environment because the person affects, and is affected by, the environ-ment through sensory input and bodily expression. Again, there are possi-ble individual differences in the firmness of the boundaries and unity of the perceptual-motor system. If the boundaries around the "motorium" are weak, then tension may spread from the inner-personal regions to the motorium. Lewin believes that the inability to act when affected by great needs (freezing) is one example of need affecting the motoric system. In children, the motor and personal regions are more of a unit; children are more likely than are adults to express nonspecific and noninstrumental be-haviors given unsatisfied needs.

In the Lewinian system, the inner-personal regions are arranged hier-archically. The dominant, or personal, system uses the subordinate, or motor, system as a tool. Lewin contended that changes in the motoric sys-tem cannot be entirely accounted for by postulating that tension spreads into it from the personal system. If this were the case, then with increasing tension there necessarily would be increasing speed of behavior. However, an individual might be involved and concerned with his work, and yet pro-ceed very slowly, as a watchmaker or glassblower. Therefore, Lewin postu-lates an organizational independence (relative to tension) between the motor and personal regions. Lewin describes this as a "head-to-tool" rela-

[2] In these examples a region represents more than a construct that influences the state of tension. The regions depict factual discriminations made by the person. Regions often have much surplus meaning in the Lewinian system.

tionship; one in which the personal system uses the motoric system to aid in the attainment of its needs.

Dynamic Constructs.   The dynamic inner-personal construct is tension. Tension refers to a particular state of a region. (When dealing with the state of a region, the region generally is called a system. Here region and system are used interchangeably.) The concept of tension is related to that of need; a need is represented as a system in a state of tension. For ease of understanding, it is often helpful to think of tension as a fluid contained in the inner-personal regions.

Lewin, like Hull, was guided by the then dominant theme of homeostasis. Lewin believed that psychological processes could be derived from the organism's tendency to strive for equilibrium. He states,

The transition from a state of rest to a process, as well as change in a stationary process, may be derived from the fact that the equilibrium at certain points has been disturbed and that then a process in the direction of a new state of equilibrium sets in [Lewin, 1935, p. 58].

In the Lewinian system the concept of equilibrium refers to the totality of systems, rather than to any particular system. Given specified conditions, systems can reach equilibrium although they are in a state of tension. For this to occur all the regions must be in the same tense state.

The magnitude of tension varies as a function of the strength of the physiological or psychological need (intention). Lewin (1938) explains the coordinating definition of tension as follows:

Whenever a psychological need exists, a system in a state of tension exists within the individual. This hypothesis includes also "quasi needs" resulting from intentions [p. 99].

Tension also is given explicit conceptual properties:

(a) It is a state of a system S which tries to change itself in such a way that it becomes equal to the state of its surrounding systems S^1, S^2, . . .
(b) It involves forces at the boundary of the systems in tension [p. 98].

The two conceptual properties of tension indicate that if the magnitude of the tension in two neighboring regions is unequal, then there is a tendency for them to become equal. More formally, Lewin (1938, p. 98) states:

If $t(S) \neq t(S^1)$ and $b_S \cdot b_{S}{}^1 \neq 0$, a tendency exists to change t so that $t(S) = t(S^1)$.

In the previous passage, $b_S \cdot b_{S^1} \neq 0$ symbolizes that systems S and S^1 have a common boundary, and $t(S)$ symbolizes tension in system S. Similarly:

If $t(S) > t(S^1)$ and $b_S \cdot b_{S^1} \neq 0$, there exist forces f_{b_s}, $S^1 > 0$ [Lewin, 1938, p. 99].

(The term f_{b_s}, $S^1 > 0$ indicates a force working on the boundary (b) of S in the direction of the neighboring system S^1.)

In the discussion concerning the structural properties of the person, it was stated that boundaries between regions differ in their degree of permeability. The spread of tension between regions is a function of both time and the firmness of the boundaries between the regions. If the boundary between two regions is not completely permeable, then some minimal difference in the degree of tension between two regions will be maintained. If the regions have a common permeable boundary (adjacent regions in Figure 3:3) or are in dynamic communication (tension from one can flow into the other via an intermediate region), then, over time, a need corresponding to one system will become a need in another system. Recall that in Estes' model responses conditioned to hunger also are conditioned to thirst because of an overlap in the stimulus sets associated with these two needs. Lewin is stating that because of an "overlap" or communication between need systems, the desire to see movie X may also result in a desire to see movie Y. Lewin's notions concerning the spread of tension also resemble Brown's conception of semi-specific drive.

There is an unspecified number of inner-personal regions that correspond to different needs or intentions. Lewin has a pluralistic conception of need, as opposed to the Hull-Spence-Brown conception of a nondirective or pooled source of drive. Drive theorists do consider multiple origins of drive, but the various sources combine to multiply all habits. In the Lewinian system different systems in tension do not combine to influence all behaviors. Each tense state is associated with a particular class of goal objects.

Realization of a goal reduces the level of tension within a system. Goal attainment need not involve the consumption of the desired object. Thinking, remembering, going to a movie, and so on may reduce the level of tension within a system. Note again the difference between the Lewinian conception of goal attainment, and that of Hull-Spence. It is difficult to condition goal responses, such as salivation, if the goal is not consumed!

Summary. A need or intention creates a system in a state of tension. The inequilibrium in tense states initiates a force at the boundary between regions, causing the tension to flow from one region to another. The amount of interchange of tension depends on the firmness of the boundaries between the systems and the amount of time in which the system is in tension. If the boundaries are not completely permeable, then a system can remain in a relatively fixed tense state. Tension is postulated to dissipate following goal attainment, and equilibrium is reestablished.

Concepts Related to the Environment

Structural Constructs. The structural concepts applied to the environment are identical to those of the person: regions, barriers, and adjacencies. However, the conceptual and coordinating definitions of the environment and person constructs differ. Again it is necessary to emphasize that the environment under consideration is the psychological environment. The psychological world is composed of "what has effects" (Lewin, 1936, p. 19). It differs in many respects from the physical world. For example, wishes exist in the psychological world. In addition, there may be many psychological worlds, but there is only one physical world. Further, the life space conceived by Lewin is an open system. It is influenced by forces originating from outside the psychological world.

For each psychological distinction or differentiation in the life space there is a separate region. Regions are coordinated to (1) activities, such as going to a movie; (2) passive states, such as being in a movie; and (3) social entities, such as being a chaperone at a movie. In the present context the coordination with activities is of fundamental importance. For example, if individual P wishes to attend a movie, he may have to get money from his father, start the car, drive to the movie, and so on (see Figure 3:6). When the regions represent activities they appear to be instrumental acts. Yet the regions also represent spaces through which one loco-

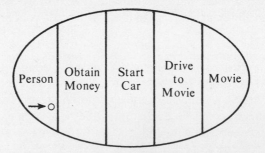

FIGURE 3:6. Representation of an environment. Regions represent instrumental activities and a path through which P locomotes to reach the goal.

motes to get to the goal. For this reason some psychologists (for example, Heider, 1960) consider the life space a medium.

The number of regions at any time is determined by the number of extant psychological facts. These may change from moment to moment. For example, if the car needed to reach the movie fails to start, then new regions (such as calling for help) are manifested in the life space. Lewin states that the number of regions in the life space may be inferred from the behavior of the individual and from the physical qualities of the environment.[3]

Regions are surrounded by boundaries that may act as barriers or impediments to locomotion. The regions and boundaries determine the space of free movement. Lewin (1936) defines the space of free movement as:

Regions accessible to the person from his present position. . . . Its limits are determined mainly by (1) what is forbidden to a person, (2) what is beyond his abilities [p. 217].

In a prison, for example, the space of free movement is confined to rather narrow limits. Yet in some situations the space of free movement is virtually unlimited, although the individual does not have access to one certain region. For example, the individual is not admitted to the school of his choice but can go to all other schools; or he can date any girl except the one girl that he likes; and so on.

Regarding the interaction between physical and psychological environments, Lewin outlined three areas of environmental change that could be of interest to scientists:

1. Changes in the life space.
2. Changes in the boundary zone around the life space in which the physical world does have some effect on the life space (the foreign hull).

---

[3] Two criticisms leveled against Lewin are relevant here. One criticism is that he oftens confuses the physical and psychological environments, invoking whichever is more convenient at the time. Inferring the psychological environment from the ecology of the physical environment is an example of such a confusion. Allport (1955), for example, asks how a person can "leave the field," which is a postulated method of conflict resolution discussed in this chapter, when the field is psychological. For further discussion of this point, see Allport (1955) and Leeper (1943). A second criticism is that Lewin's analysis is *post hoc;* that is, he infers the number of regions in the life space after, rather than prior to, the behavior. This criticism also has validity. Lewin, however, felt that post-diction is an important part of a theory, provided that the post-diction employs the constructs in the theory in a logical and consistent manner. Both Freud and Darwin also were post-dictive, in that they investigated how the individual or the species came to be in its present state.

3. Changes in the physical and social world that do not affect the life space (alien factors).

The boundary zone or foreign hull includes factors not in the individual's immediate consciousness that have a physical specification or locus. Such factors may include the climate, the size of one's high school, or the number of workers in a factory. The study of nonpsychological factors that influence the life-space Lewin labeled "psychological ecology." Ecology is derived from the Greek "oikos," or house; it connotes the natural surroundings of an event. Psychological ecology has been most thoroughly investigated by Roger Barker and his colleagues (Barker, 1960, 1963, 1965; Barker & Wright, 1955). Later in this chapter the work on ecology is examined in detail.

One problem Lewin attempted to resolve that prompted his interest in ecology was how to capture the determinants of behavior that reside in the "real" world. Lewin also had to cope with the problem of getting the person to interact with and act upon the real world. (Brunswik (1943) accused Lewin of being "pre-motor and post perceptual." That is, the life space is conceptualized after perception but before any action.) In an attempt to clarify the vagueness in Lewin's system concerning the relationship between the real and psychological worlds, Cartwright (1959) suggested a conceptual scheme of the person (P) and the environment (E), as shown in Figure 3:7. In Figure 3:7, A denotes those "alien factors" of the physical world that do not influence the life space. The name of the reader's mother has no influence on this writer's life space, although the name, in fact, exists. H represents the "foreign hull," which, as was indicated, contains factors not subject to psychological laws that affect behavior. The study of ecology pertains to this region. S and M refer to the sen-

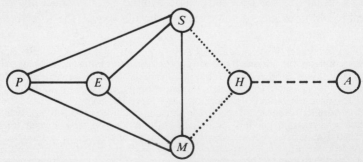

FIGURE 3:7. Schematic diagram of the facts and relations involved in the life space, boundary zone, and the physical and social world. For a detailed explanation of the symbols, see text (from Cartwright, 1959, p. 71).

sorium and motorium, which were briefly mentioned previously. They link the person to the hull and represent processes through which the person interacts with the real world. The sensorium receives information, while the motorium acts on the real world. The adequacy of the sensorium and motorium clearly can influence behavior. For example, an individual may be foiled in his attempt to reach a goal because of inadequacies in his sensorium (insensitivity) or motorium (lack of skill). In addition, factors in the foreign hull can impede goal satisfaction (for example, lack of rain ruins the crops; a foreigner cannot become President).

Cartwright employs this system to point out differences between the Lewinian and Hullian approaches. According to the Hullian position, behavior is initiated when an external stimulus impinges upon the organism. Responses are then elicited, and these eventually modify the environment. The sequence of events is represented in Cartwright's system as *H-S-M-H*. That is, a stimulus in the foreign hull is perceived by the sensorium. This elicits a response that changes the foreign hull. In the Lewinian system, however, behavior must begin with the person (*P*). The person's perceptions determine the psychological environment and cause the person to act on that environment, using the motorium as a tool. This action alters the foreign hull and sensory inputs, and changes the person and his perceived environment. The sequence of events is represented as: *P-E-M-H-S-P-E*.

Dynamic Constructs.   There is a relationship between the dynamic properties of the individual and the dynamic properties of the environment. When an inner-personal region is in a state of tension, an appropriate environmental region (object) acquires a valence. Lewin (1935) wrote:

The valence of an object usually derives from the fact that the object is a means to the satisfaction of a need, or has indirectly something to do with the satisfaction of a need. The kind (sign) and the strength of the valence of an object or event thus depends directly upon the momentary condition of the needs of the individual concerned; the valence of environmental objects and the needs of the individual are correlative [p. 78].

In *Conceptual Representation of Psychological Forces,* Lewin (1938, pp. 106–7) expands this relationship into a more formal statement:

There exists a relation between certain tensions of the inner-personal regions of the person and certain valences in the environment: with a state of hunger the strength of the valence will change $Va\ (G) = F(t)$. However, the existence and the strength of the valence does not depend only upon the tension of the person but also upon certain nonpsychological "alien" factors. . . . Whether within the environment food exists, what type of food, and at what place is not a result, or at least not alone the result, of psychological factors. More specifically, the valence $Va\ (G)$ which an object of activity G possesses for a person at a given time depends upon the character and state of the person P, and upon the perceived nature of the object or activity G: $Va\ (G) = F(t, G)$.

Although valence, which may be positive or negative in character, is coordinated to a need, needs are independent of valence. If a food object has a positive valence, then there must be a corresponding "hunger" system in a state of tension. However, given a hunger need, there may not be any corresponding region of positive valence. The person must be in an environment that provides support for his needs. There will not be any region of positive valence if there are no perceived edible objects in the environment. As the individual becomes hungrier and tension increases, there is a tendency for the tension to spread to more remote regions. Eventually there may be an object coordinated with these more remote regions that has the necessary properties to acquire a positive valence. Shoes become edible, that is, have positive valence, in situations of great deprivation.

Valence therefore varies quantitatively as a function of the intensity of the need and the properties of the goal object. As hunger increases, so does the positive valence of food; similarly, steak has a greater positive valence than shoes for a hungry person. Valence, however, is not a force; it is not directly coordinated to movement or to locomotion. A region with a positive or negative valence becomes the center of a force field (see Figures 3:8 and 3:9). A force field specifies the magnitude and direction of behavior for all points in the life space. At a given moment in time the

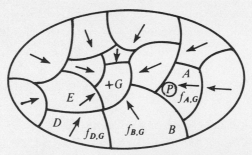

FIGURE 3:8. A positive central field of forces corresponding to a positive valence. The force has magnitude, represented by the length of the vector, and direction. The point of application is on P in the direction of the goal G (after Lewin, from Carmichael, 1946, p. 806).

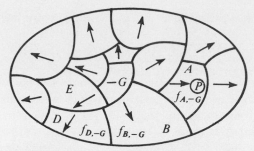

FIGURE 3:9. A negative central field of
forces corresponding to a negative valence.
The forces are away from the goal G (after
Lewin, from Carmichael, 1946, p. 806).

person is in one of the regions and has a specified force acting on him.
Lewin states that if $Va\ (G) > 0$, then the force acting on the person
toward the goal $[(f)(P, G)]$ is > 0.

Force is conceptualized as a vector; it has magnitude and direction.
In addition, force has a point of application. The point of application is
that region in which the force is operative. Since the individual is located
in this region, the point of application is the person.

The strength of force is in part a function of the valence of the goal.
As indicated, valence is a function of needs of the person (t), and properties of the goal object (G). In addition, the strength of force is dependent
upon the relative·position of the person and the goal. Lewin states that
force increases as the psychological distance between the person and the
goal object decreases. This is not an invariant relationship; Lewin acknowl-
edges that at times increased distance increases the force toward the goal.
For example, countries a great distance away are attractive, as are potential mates who play hard to get. In most instances, however, the determinants of the force on the person toward the goal are conceptualized as:

$$\text{force} = f\left[\frac{Va\ (G)}{e}\right] = \frac{(t,\ G)}{e}$$

(Where e symbolizes psychological distance between the person and the
goal. The e represents the German *entlang,* or distance.)

It is instructive to note the similarity between the Lewinian statement
for the determinants of action, and the formulae of Hull and Spence. Both
the Lewinian and Hull-Spence positions include similar components in
their models: needs of the person (drive (D) or tension (t)), properties
of the goal object $(K$ or $G)$, and a learning variable (habit (H) or psychological distance (e)). However, Lewin's t is not nondirectional, G is

dependent on the existence of t, and e is a cognitive representation of the environment.

Given Lewin's formula, it is possible to determine the resultant force at every region in the life space. When the resultant of psychological forces acting on a person is greater than zero, there is locomotion in the life space. The psychological force acts on the person, and the person in turn utilizes the motoric system to reach his goals. Hence, the person is not mechanically carried to the goal, as in the Hullian system. Further, locomotion is not derived solely from the level of tension within the person. Tension is related to valence, and valence is related to force and locomotion. Needs are linked to the environment, rather than to the motorium. Therefore, a need does not necessarily result in physical locomotion. Needs can be satisfied by thinking, remembering, and the like. Lewin believed that this virtue was not built into the Hullian system.

A goal is a region in the life space. When the goal is attained or realized, the tension within the tense system dissipates. This reduces the valence of the environmental object and results in a decrement in the force acting upon the individual. The inner-personal regions are now in a state of equilibrium, and there is a cessation of behavior.

Further Discussion of Hodological Space

While the conceptual and operational definitions concerning tension and valence have been discussed, very little has been said concerning the conceptual properties of psychological distance. To understand psychological distance, the geometrical conceptualization of space must be examined. Both distance and direction will emerge as interdependent constructs that can be represented in hodological space, or the space of paths.

Distance and Direction of Behavior.   Distance and direction in hodological space are based primarily upon three factors: (1) the "distinguished path"; (2) the characteristics of this path, such as its wholeness or segmentation; and (3) the characteristics of the life space, such as the degree of differentiation within it.

Direction in the life space connotes a relationship between two regions. For example, assume that an individual located in region A has a force acting upon him in the direction of region B. The behavior of the individual in A therefore would be in the direction of B ($d_{A, B}$). The various linkages between regions A and B are considered to be "paths." There might be many paths between any two regions. Figure 3:10 indicates that one path uniting A with B is X, Y, Z; a second path is R, S, T; still a

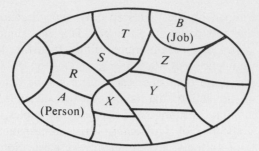

FIGURE 3:10. Representation of a life
space with various paths from *A* to *B*.

third path might be *X, R, S, T*; and so on. Recall again that the regions
in the life space often represent instrumental acts, as well as a medium
through which one locomotes to reach the goal. Hence, Figure 3:10
might indicate that the individual in (doing) *A* wants to obtain a new
job (B). To obtain this position he might either go to school (*X, Y, Z*),
or become an apprentice for this job (*R, S, T*). Either of these two paths
will lead to the desired end state.

One of the paths or connections is designated by Lewin as the "distinguished path." This connotes the path selected when locomoting towards
the goal. Direction always refers to a characteristic of this particular path,
and distance is defined as the number of regions contained within this path.

Lewin did not clearly specify why one path is chosen rather than another. He did indicate that the preferred path might be the "shortest";
that is, contain the fewest number of intermediate regions. However, the
distinguished path could also be psychologically easiest. For example,
perhaps going to school would take longer or require more instrumental
activities than becoming an apprentice, yet it is perceived as the more
comfortable route. Lewin did specify that the intermediate links in the
distinguished path would have the greatest relative attractiveness to the
individual. However, the determinants of attraction are unspecified, and
therefore the problem of the particular characteristics of the distinguished
path remains unsolved.

In summary, the psychological distance (*e*) between a person and
a goal is a function of the number of regions comprised within the distinguished path. And the distinguished path includes those regions between
the person and the goal which are most attractive to the individual.

The direction of the distinguished path is defined as the "first step"
in the path. For example, if the path selected in Figure 3:10 is *A, X,
Y, Z, B*, then the direction is characterized as from *A* to *X* ($d_{A,x}$). Because

direction is determined by the first step only, two directions are equal if the initial steps in their paths are identical. This is assumed even though the termination points of the paths might differ. It further logically follows that direction is influenced by the "segmentation" of the path. A path is segmented if it has more than one step, where step is defined as an individual subpart of an action that is not further divisible. Lewin, in his usual manner, examines a number of everyday examples to illustrate the psychological significance of segmented versus nonsegmented paths. He cites the example of an individual about to take a vacation, which we will specify as in Europe. Further, assume another person at the same point of origin is taking a journey to Africa. They are on different airplanes, but both planes must stop in New York. If neither individual perceives New York as a distinct part of the flight, then, according to Lewin, they are locomoting in different directions. Each traveler is locomoting along an unsegmented path, one from home to Europe $(d_{H,E})$, the other from home to Africa $(d_{H,A})$. On the other hand, if both individuals consider New York as part of the trip, then they are going in the same direction along segmented paths. The respective distinguished paths would be: $(d_{H,NY,E})$ and $(d_{H,NY,A})$. Both paths then have the identical first step. Direction, therefore, depends on the manner in which the life space is structured, and upon the segmentation of the distinguished path.

Taxonomy of Direction. Lewin provided a relatively simple and useful taxonomy of direction (see Table 3:1). Directions are represented as "toward" or "away from," and as including or excluding a region other than the one in which the force originates. The combination of these two dimensions yields four different classes of direction. The "toward" direction may be from a given region (A) toward a second region (B), as discussed already, or from A in the direction of A $(d_{A,A})$. The latter classification attempts to portray situations in which the individual is in a region of positive valence and wants to remain there. In this situation forces are assumed to act at the boundary of the region in opposition to forces directed away from the region. For example, a child might actively resist a parental command to stop playing and come home for dinner. The force

TABLE 3:1
Lewinian Taxonomy of the Direction of Behavior

Number of Regions	Direction of Behavior	
	Toward	*Away From*
One	(A, A) Consummatory behavior	$(A, -A)$ Escape behavior
Two	(A, B) Instrumental behavior	$(B, -A)$ Avoidance behavior

originating from the parents' command is resisted by the forces to remain in the play region.

Forces characterized as "away from" also may or may not have an alternative region specified. A force can be categorized as in A directed away from A $(d_{A,-A})$. For example, administering shock in a given setting will cause the animal to seek safety, with any nonshocked region being an acceptable alternative. Finally, the fourth type of direction refers to a force originating in one region, but away from a different region. For illustrative purposes, consider a criminal who committed a crime in New York. He is now in Chicago, going toward Los Angeles. His direction can be considered $(d_{C,-NY})$, or $(d_{C,LA})$. That is, his direction is characterized as either away from New York, or towards Los Angeles, with both forces originating in his present location of Chicago. The former designation of direction may more accurately depict the dynamics of this situation.

Many of the behaviors discussed in the prior chapter can be readily subsumed within this classification scheme. Instrumental approach behavior is generally directed toward a goal $(d_{A,B})$; consummatory behavior theoretically reflects a situation in which there are forces acting to remain in the goal region $(d_{A,A})$; escape behavior is away from a region $(d_{A,-A})$; and active avoidance behavior can be depicted as a series of actions leading away from an aversive state, with many of the activities occurring when the individual physically is no longer in the shocked region $(d_{B,-A})$.

DRIVE THEORY REINTERPRETED

Studies Employing the Columbia Obstruction Box

The Columbia Obstruction Box discussed in Chapter II was a classic device employed in the investigation of motivational phenomena. The results of the studies using the obstruction box often are cited in support of the position espousing drive as an energizer of behavior.

To recapitulate briefly, in the experimental paradigm employing the obstruction box, the animal initially is placed in the start box. At the far end of the box is an appropriate incentive. Between the animal and the goal there is an obstacle, such as an electrified grid (see Diagram 2:1). In a series of systematic studies, Moss (1924) and other investigators related the amount and type of deprivation to the tendency of the animal to cross the grid.

Lewin believed that the obstruction box aids in the measurement of psychological forces. A force to reach the goal (C) is opposed by a force not to enter the shocked region (B). The animal is expected to locomote

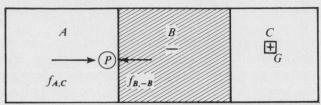

FIGURE 3:11. Schematic representation of the physical properties of the obstruction box, and the corresponding forces. P, the animal, is located in A; G, the goal, is located in region C; B is the electrified compartment separating A from C. There is a force on P acting in the direction from A to C ($f_{A,C}$), and a force acting on P in the direction of not entering B ($f_{B,-B}$) (from Lewin, 1938, p. 72).

toward the goal when the force in the start box (A) toward C is greater than the force at B not to enter ($-B$). That is, locomotion will occur when $f(A, C) > f(B, -B)$.[4]

If there is a force from A to C, then the region C must be the center of a field of forces. That is, region C has a positive valence. The animal, therefore, must have a system in a state of tension and be aware that an appropriate goal object exists in the environment. To establish this valence, animals are deprived of food (or some other necessary commodity) and are given training (exposure) so that they will discover that food exists in region C.

For one to measure the relative strengths of the approach and avoidance forces, the forces have to be opposed to one another. If the animal could circumvent region B, then a conflict would not be established. The physical environment in which the animals are placed insures that the forces will act in opposition to one another. Barriers (walls) are placed around the regions or runway, which limit the space of free movement. The only available path to region C is through region B.

Frequently, the measure of the strength of the resultant force in the early studies conducted by Moss was the frequency of grid crossings per unit of time. If the number of crossings (the inverse of response latency) is greater in a specified condition (Condition Two) than in a different condition (Condition One), then the force from A to C in Condition Two must be greater than the force from A to C in Condition One (given that the force of opposition is a constant).

[4] The force B, $-B$ indicates that the force opposing the force toward C does not act on the animal when it is in region A. It is only operative when the animal is at the boundary of region B. This "restraining force" is characterized as a restrictive force field; the force does not reach beyond the boundaries of region B. The organism is not actively avoiding B; it will, however, attempt to escape from that region.

Lewin believed that the frequency of crossings per unit of time generally is not a good dependent variable. If the animal crosses the grid to reach the goal, then the approach force must be greater than the force of avoidance. Why, then, doesn't the animal immediately cross the grid when replaced in the start box? If the animal remains in the start box, then there has been a change in the constellation of forces between the two trials. Lewin says that this "historical" change may have been caused by any one of a number of factors such as chance variation, loss of energy, or increased aversion of *B* after the initial shock. Because the frequency measure necessitates a changing constellation of forces, Lewin did not fully accept this motivational index.

A number of predictions derivable from Lewin's conception of the determinants of force are confirmed in the studies by Moss, Warden, Warner, and others. Lewin postulates that force is a function of the magnitude of the need or intention. Animals are expected to run with greater vigor (shorter latency) as the amount of hunger increases. The empirical evidence supporting this prediction, given in Chapter II, is cited as validating evidence for the drive theoretical conception. However, the data also are consistent with the predictions of Lewin's field theory. Similarly, greater strength of response is expected as the properties of the goal object increase in attractiveness. The studies by Tolman, Crespi and others, which varied the incentive value of the goal, confirm this prediction.

The Speed of Consumption

Brown (1961) summarizes evidence from studies with lower animals which indicate that the speed of a consummatory response (licking, eating) increases as deprivation increases. He cites this evidence in support of the Drive $\times$ Habit conception. On the other hand, Lewin specifies that the relationship between the strength of a need and the speed of consumption is not invariant. In Lewin's system needs are not directly linked with the motorium. The intensity of the need and the intensity of the response, therefore, are not necessarily related. For example, the speed of a dance, which can be a goal response in the Lewinian system, may be unrelated to the desire to dance. Similarly, "A child might eat dessert particularly slowly for the purpose of staying as long as possible within the region of the pleasant consumption" (Lewin, 1938, p. 145). Lewin argues that in most animal studies eating is the result of a negative or aversive state of hunger. For humans, however, eating often is pleasurable and an end in itself. Food may be eaten slowly and enjoyed; the state of hunger alone does not determine the speed of eating.

The Goal Gradient

Hull initially postulated that habit strength is inversely related to distance from the goal (delay in reinforcement) to account for the backward order of elimination of errors in complex maze performance (see p. 26). Subsequently, Hull made delay of reinforcement a determinant of performance, rather than a determinant of learning, paralleling the history of the incentive construct. The relative increment in various indices of performance as the goal is approached also can be easily incorporated within the Spencian as well as the Hullian framework. It has been suggested that as an animal traverses a maze the stimulus similarity dimension generates differential amounts of anticipatory excitement, and hence disparate amounts of incentive-produced drive to locomote toward the goal.

Lewin also can account for differential performance as a function of distance from the goal by utilizing the construct of psychological distance. As the goal is approached, the e in the denominator of his formula decreases, thus increasing the force to approach the goal. Lewin also noted a "goal gradient" in his naturalistic observations of children. He reports that as children locomote toward a movie theater, they increase their speed of approach.

Secondary Reinforcement

Secondary reinforcement plays an essential role within Hullian theory. Without this concept, it would be impossible for drive theory to account for the persistence of behaviors occurring in the absence of a commodity that reduces a tissue deficit. Apparently, very little human behavior in our society is directed toward the immediate offset of primary needs.

Lewin argues against the notion of secondary reinforcement; he contends that means can never become ends. Consider, Lewin asks, what would be the consequences if the stimuli in a straight alleyway actually become secondary reinforcers by virtue of their contiguous association with a food reward. The animal in the start box then locomotes toward the goal region because of the forces originating throughout the maze, some from the goal itself and some from the stimuli in the maze associated with goal attainment. Both these sources of force are acting on the organism in the direction of the goal. But as the animal traverses the maze, there should be an increasing quantity of force acting *in opposition* to the goal-directed behavior. More and more of the secondary reinforcers are actually behind the animal as it approached the goal. Lewin contends, perhaps rhetorically, that if the maze were of sufficient length, at a certain point the animal would reach equilibrium in terms of the strength of the

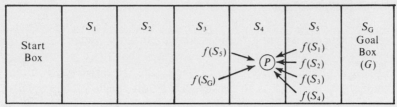

FIGURE 3:12. Hypothetical illustration of an animal in an approach-approach conflict in a straight alley. The positive forces generated by "secondary reinforcement" are assumed to be equal in strength to the approach forces generated, in part, by the primary reinforcing agent.

forces toward and away from the goal. At that point the animal would stop running and might actually turn around and run back toward the start box (see Figure 3:12). This would indicate that the forces generated by the secondary reinforcers located throughout the maze are greater than the force generated by the primary reinforcement in the goal box. However, such oscillation or "about-face" behavior has not been reported in this situation (and probably never will be). These observations, or perhaps the lack of such observations, in part, led Lewin to conclude that neutral stimuli do not actually acquire reinforcement value. Rather, they might function as signals indicating that reward is forthcoming, and thus influence the psychological distance from the goal or the expectancy of the food reward.

FURTHER EXTENSIONS OF THE THEORY

In the previous chapter we noted that drive theory has made important contributions in the study of conflict and frustration. This is also true of Lewinian theory. Indeed, Miller's analysis of approach-avoidance conflict extends the earlier insights of Lewin. Lewin had included the approach-avoidance paradigm within his taxonomic scheme of conflict, and even had specified that the gradient of avoidance is steeper than that of approach. In the following pages the field theoretical approach to conflict and frustration is examined in some detail. We start with a discussion of conflict, because this work is more closely linked with Lewin's formal theory.

Conflict

It has been specified that the strength of force acting upon a person is directly related to the needs of the individual (t) and the valence of the goal object (G), while indirectly or inversely related to the psychological distance from the goal (e). At any one moment in time, it is likely that many forces are acting upon the individual, and he is impelled in different directions by competing forces. This indicates that there are overlapping force fields in the life space. For example, the reader might want to go to a movie, but also wishes to finish reading this thrilling chapter; a child might want to go out and play, but his parents have told him to clean his room. Lewin provided a taxonomy of the situations in which more than one force is acting upon the person at a given moment in time. In all such conflict situations Lewin specified that the person will locomote in the direction of the greatest force. His model of conflict resolution, like that of Spence and Miller, specifies that the strongest force "wins." In contrast to physical models, a conflict of forces does not result in a net force in a third direction, which makes little psychological sense. Lewin defined three types of conflict: approach-approach; approach-avoidance; and avoidance-avoidance.

Approach-Approach.   In an approach-approach conflict the person is included in more than one positive field. For example, a person considers two movies worth seeing; at a restaurant both fish and steak are good; a child must choose between spending his allowance on candy or a comic book. Lewin believed that approach-approach conflicts are easily resolvable, and hence labeled them unstable situations.

The instability of approach-approach conflicts becomes evident when some simple numerical values are introduced into his model for the determinants of force. Assume, for example, that you are in a cafeteria line. You perceive two pies: apple on the left, and cherry on the right. Both pies are equally attractive in terms of physical properties such as size ($G = 4$), and you are fairly hungry ($t = 3$). Further, to reach both pies requires the identical number of psychological steps. The apple pie requires a left turn and then an arm movement, while the cherry pie requires a right turn and reaching movement ($e = 2$). The strength of the forces involved in this approach-approach conflict are identical:

$$\text{Apple pie (left)} \qquad\qquad \text{Cherry pie (right)}$$
$$\text{Force} = \frac{4 \times 3}{2} = 6 \qquad\qquad \text{Force} = \frac{4 \times 3}{2} = 6$$

Hence, the outcome of the action is indeterminate; a momentary equilibrium is established.

Now suddenly someone in the line behind you becomes rather impatient with the delay and gives you a slight shove. It happens that the shove is toward the right, and you find yourself confronted with the cherry pie. Now the psychological distance from the cherry pie shifts downward, say from 2 to 1, and the psychological distance from the apple pie increases from 2 to 3. The strengths of the forces are conceptualized as:

Apple pie (left)   Cherry pie (right)

$$\text{Force} = \frac{4 \times 3}{3} = 4 \qquad\qquad \text{Force} = \frac{4 \times 3}{1} = 12$$

The strength of the force toward the cherry pie now is greater than the force toward the apple pie. Hence, you will locomote in the direction of the red calories. The conflict is resolved; that is, the conflict equilibrium was only momentary, or unstable.

The example just presented includes only one source of tension and two valences of equal strength. Approach-approach conflicts need not be limited to such situations. Consider the conflict generated when a child has a small amount of money and is deciding whether to purchase candy or a comic book. Assume, for illustrative purposes, that his candy "need" is 10 units, and the jelly beans he plans on buying have a value of 3. Further, he must perform 6 psychologically distinct acts to obtain the candy (dress for the walk, walk three blocks, ask for help to cross the street, and so on). The force acting on the child toward the candy has the value of 5 units $[(10 \times 3) \div 6 = 5]$. On the other hand, assume his "need" for the comic book has 2 units of strength, the book has 5 units of valence, and his psychological distance from the book has a value of 2. Hence, the forces acting upon him in the direction of the book would also have a value of 5 $[(2 \times 5) \div 2 = 5]$. Equilibrium thus is established; the strength of the forces acting on the child are equal.

How can this conflict be resolved? Any cognition that changes the relative attractiveness of the two goal objects would create unequal forces. Perhaps seeing a certain TV show now makes the comic book more attractive. Perhaps just vacillating in his decision makes him more hungry, and now the tension caused by food deprivation increases, thus making the force toward the candy greater than the force toward the comic book. Once the forces become unequal, the individual locomotes in the direction of the greater force. This reduces the psychological distance from the object he is approaching, while it increases the psychological distance from the unselected alternative. The differential shifting of psychological distance further increases the differences in the strength of forces.

In sum, approach-approach conflicts represent situations in which the person is located in more than one field of forces generated by positive valued goals. Resolution of the conflict can be achieved if any of the determinants of force (tension, valence, or psychological distance) change. This can occur because of a new cognition, changes in tension, or any number of other factors. Once an imbalance is created, the individual locomotes toward the goal associated with the greater force. This locomotion further increases the inequality in the magnitude of the forces, because the psychological distance from the chosen alternative decreases, while the distance from the unchosen alternative increases.

Avoidance-Avoidance. When a person is in overlapping fields of forces generated by objects with a negative valence, avoidance-avoidance conflicts are aroused. For example, a child is told he must mow the lawn or do his homework, or the town marshal has two gunmen pursuing him from the left and two from the right. Lewin specified that avoidance-avoidance conflicts are stable; that is, the opposing forces tend to remain in a state of equilibrium.

Again a simple mathematical exercise reveals why avoidance-avoidance conflicts tend to remain in a stable state. Consider for a moment the town marshal caught between two pairs of gunmen he wishes to avoid. Let us assume that his need for safety is 5 units, and that each pair of gunmen is equally despicable ($G = -3$). If the marshal perceives himself as equidistant from the gunmen as they come stalking toward him ($e = 2$), then the forces are as follows:

Gunmen on left   Gunmen on right

$$\text{Force} = \frac{5(-3)}{2} = -7.5 \qquad \text{Force} = \frac{5(-3)}{2} = -7.5$$

Thus, there are equal and opposite forces to flee both to the left and the right.

Now assume that the marshal suddenly remembers that the gunmen on the left are poor shots or cowards. The new field of forces then might be:

Gunmen on left   Gunmen on right

$$\text{Force} = \frac{5(-2)}{2} = -5 \qquad \text{Force} = \frac{5(-3)}{2} = -7.5$$

Because the negative valence is now greater away from the right, the marshal proceeds toward the left. In so doing, the psychological distances are altered; the forces might change as follows:

Gunmen on left   Gunmen on right

$$\text{Force} = \frac{5(-2)}{1} = -10 \qquad \text{Force} = \frac{5(-3)}{3} = -5$$

Now the force to avoid the left gunmen is greater than that away from the right gunmen. Even though the killers on the left do not appear as aversive, the decrease in psychological distance increased the force to avoid the confrontation. This indicates that the marshal will again shift his direction, this time to the right. In theory, the marshal will continue to oscillate between the two negative alternatives.

Does this signify that it is always impossible to solve avoidance-avoidance conflicts? This clearly could not be the case, for humans indeed are placed in many such situations, and usually cease their vacillation. Any cognitive change might alter the strength of the avoidance forces, and help to resolve the conflict. Needs can change, valences can shift in magnitude and even in direction, and psychological distance can be altered. Lewin also indicates that such conflicts are often solved by "leaving the field." This means that frequently the person in such a conflict will follow a path that increases the psychological distance from both alternatives. If the marshal ascended in a helium balloon just before the gunmen arrived, his conflict would be resolved. However, leaving the field can be employed as a method of conflict resolution only if the boundaries around the conflict situation are sufficiently permeable. For example, if a child is told to mow the lawn or do his homework, he apparently is placed in a difficult avoidance-avoidance situation. But if he knows he can escape either task by appealing to his mother or hiding in the attic, the conflict is readily (if only temporarily) resolved. Lewin indicates that one consequent of establishing behaviors through the use of punishment and negative sanctions is that strong barriers must be erected that keep the person in the situation. And energy must be expended to ensure that these barriers persist.

In sum, avoidance-avoidance conflicts are determined by needs, valence, and psychological distance. The conflict generated by multiple regions of negative valence is not readily resolvable. As one approaches the aversive region, the tendency to avoid that region becomes even stronger. Hence, ambivalent behavior is exhibited; the person vacillates between the various alternatives. For such conflicts to have any degree of permanence strong boundaries must exist to prevent the person from leaving the field; that is, from avoiding all the alternatives.

Approach-Avoidance. The third classification of conflicts, approach-avoidance, is discussed in detail in the previous chapter. In such conflicts the same region acquires both positive and negative valence, thus establishing both positive and negative fields of forces. For example, the reader might want to go to a movie, but does not want to spend that much money; he might want to stop reading, but knows that a test is forthcoming. As in all conflict situations, the exhibited behavior is postulated to be determined by needs, valences, and psychological distance. In this situation the relative steepness of the approach and avoidance slopes is also an important determinant of action.

Approach-avoidance conflicts also are relatively stable. The person is expected to approach the goal, but then avoid it because of the differential change in the strength of the approach and avoidance tendencies (see the previous chapter). Again, a number of factors can lead to conflict resolution; for example, the positive aspects of the goal may gain in attractiveness, or the person may experience a reduction in the amount of fear.

Empirical Studies of Conflict.   Surprisingly few studies have been generated by the Lewinian conflict taxonomy. Probably the most investigated aspect of his classification scheme concerns the relative stability and instability of the various types of conflict. In one prototypical experiment, Arkoff (1957) asked students to decide which of two positive qualities they would rather possess (Would you rather be more intelligent or more attractive?) and which of two negative alternatives they would rather not possess (Would you rather be less intelligent or less attractive?). He then measured the latencies of their responses, or the time necessary to resolve the conflict. Arkoff found, as Lewin had presumed, that the approach-approach conflict situation is less stable, or more easy to resolve, than the avoidance-avoidance type. In this study the average time taken to choose an alternative in the positive conflict situation was approximately 2 minutes, while the latency of the responses in the avoidance-avoidance situation was over 2.5 minutes. Further, the subjects judged the approach-approach conflict to be easier to resolve than the avoidance-avoidance situation.

Frustration

One interesting scientific game is to compare how various theorists study identical topics. Because the behavior under investigation generally is conceptualized quite differently by the theorists, the experiments conducted and conclusions reached often are surprisingly unrelated.

A simple examination of the learning theories introduced in this book illustrates this point. Thorndike believed that reward and punishment are essential for response acquisition. Therefore, his reference experiment involved responses instrumental to the attainment of a food reward. On the other hand, Pavlov believed contiguity to be the necessary and sufficient condition for learning. Hence, in his experimental paradigm two stimuli were presented in close temporal contiguity. Finally, the Gestaltists contend that organization is an essential characteristic of the learning process. Their experiments on insight learning created situations in which perceptual reorganization apparently is necessary to reach the correct solution.

In sum, each theoretical position employed a particular experimental procedure, or reference experiment, that could demonstrate each theorist's own bias. And, quite naturally, the conclusions reached were indeed disparate.

The study of frustration exemplifies this point. Brown, Farber, and Amsel were trained within the *S-R* theoretical framework. Therefore, in their studies frustration generally has been operationalized by withholding food from a previously rewarded animal. Further, it is not unreasonable to expect that the construct of frustration would be related to drive and habits and would be used to explain phenomena such as resistance to extinction and discrimination learning. After all, these were the problems with which Hull, Spence, and their cohorts struggled. On the other hand, Lewin was a field theorist with strong interests in child development. His investigations of frustration were directed toward the understanding of psychological forces, and to provide insights into the dynamics of development. In sum, the reader should not be startled by the great disparity between the experiments conducted by Lewinians as opposed to *S-R* theorists. Nor should he be stunned that the inferences the theorists draw often are unrelated to one another.

Frustration and Development. In *Field Theory in the Social Sciences* (1951), Lewin writes:

One of the standard criticisms made by *S-R* theory has been that field theory is not sticking to a physical definition of the conditions. The term "expectation" for instance, has been taboo, as much as terms like "degree of acceptance," or "feeling of belonging." Even today some veterans of *S-R* theory seem to hold to the idea that scientific psychology means definition in terms of physics. The study of frustration and aggression, on the other hand, seemed to be a clear departure from this position. Most of the terms, like frustration or cooperation, are defined in psychological terms. . . .

There seems to be no difference [between field theory and *S-R* theory] in regard to the tendency toward a quantitative approach to frustration. There is, of course, no difference in regard to problems of reliability or similar methodological questions of a technical nature. There is no difference of opinion in regard to the necessity of an operational definition of psychological concepts nor a difference of opinion in regard to the desirability of strict theories and derivations.

An important difference seems to lie in the following direction: In *S-R* theory "frustration" is treated as a "concept," as an "element of construction." The attempt is made to define this concept operationally and to proceed from there to a quantitative theory, for instance, about the relation between frustration and aggression. When the psychologist who follows field-theoretical lines speaks about frustration, learning, hope, friendship, aggression he is conscious of the fact that he is using "popular terms." These terms are quite helpful, even necessary, in the beginning. However, they are not considered, within field theory, as psychological concepts in the sense of scientific "elements of construction." The reason for this is that a term like "frustration" (a) lacks a conceptual definition through coordination to mathematical concepts, (b) refers in a vague way to a multitude of different settings rather than to *one* conceptually definable type of situation.

If this is correct, it would be scientifically meaningless to attempt, for instance, to link the intensity of frustration lawfully with any specific effect (such as aggression); for one would have to know the type of frustration and the detailed setting in order to make any definitive derivations. Indeed, the experiments show that it is as correct to say "frustration leads to increased friendship and nonaggression," as it is to say "frustration leads to aggression." It is as correct to say that frustration leads to increased as well as to decreased productivity, that it leads to new efforts as well as to passivity [pp. 33–35].

This extended quote is repeated here because it is often incorrectly inferred that Lewin believed frustration inevitably leads to regression. As Lewin's quotation indicates, this interpretation is incorrect. It is true, however, that Lewin did investigate the relationship between frustration and regression.

Lewin was greatly influenced by Freud, and was one of the first investigators to test rigorously some of Freud's fundamental concepts, such as persisting goal tendencies, substitution, and regression. Regression refers to a return to an earlier mode of behavior. Freud specified that during the genetic stages of development the individual selects certain "problem solutions" to cope with conflict and stress. These behaviors tend to reduce the amount of the aversive, incoming stimulation. During times of later stress Freud postulated that there is a tendency for the person to repeat these earlier modes of behavior, although they might be inadequate or maladaptive given the present situation. A mild regression might be "running home to mother" in difficult times, while a more extreme form of such behavior might involve thumbsucking all day, as could be exhibited in a severely psychotic state.

Barker, Dembo, and Lewin (1943) consider regression a form of "negative development" (p. 441). Hence, they contend that understanding the laws of development would shed light upon regressive behavior, and vice versa. These investigators reason that development can be conceptualized as an increase in the degree of inner-personal differentiation, a growth in the separation of fantasy from reality, and an increment in the organization between the subparts within the person. Therefore, any state that results in a dedifferentiation of regions, a breakdown in the degree of organization, or a decrease in the separation of reality from irreality, is regressive.

Barker, Dembo, and Lewin further contend that increasing the level of innerpersonal tension could lead to a regressive state. Lewin previously suggested that strong emotional states and large increases in tension levels lead to a lessening in the number of discriminations which an individual can make. That is, increasing tension may result in a weakening of the boundaries between regions, or dedifferentiation. Further, with great increases in the level of tension the motorium is more likely to be directly affected by strong needs. That is, the head-to-tool or hierarchical organization between the person and his motor expressions may be temporarily disrupted.

One manner of increasing tension is to prevent the attainment of a desirable goal. The reader will recall from Chapter II that goal-thwarting frequently is considered to be the operational manipulation that produces frustration (see p. 58). Frustration, or goal-thwarting, is employed by Barker et al. to increase the level of tension, and, in turn, to examine the nature of regression.

The experiment conducted by Barker et al. to examine regression was relatively straightforward. Children were brought into an experimental room and allowed to play with attractive toys. Then they were separated from the toys by a partition. The children still could see the toys, but were prevented from handling them by the barrier. That is, there was a limitation in their space of free movement. During the separation period the children could play with other objects located in the room. Throughout the "prefrustration" and "frustration" periods the experimenters measured the "constructiveness of play." Unconstructive play is described as "primitive, simple, and with little structure" (for example, examining toys superficially), while constructive play is described as "imaginative and highly developed" (for example, using toys as part of an elaborate story).

Constructiveness of play does increase as a function of mental age. Further, it was reasoned that continued differentiation increases the variety of possible behaviors and the amount of planned play activities. Elaborate play activities also indicate future time perspective, which Lewin believed to be characteristic of later development. Thus, both experimental evidence and a logical analysis of play suggested that an index of constructiveness would reflect regressive tendencies.

The results of the Barker, Dembo, and Lewin study reveal that the constructiveness of play activities do decrease from the prefrustration to the frustration period. During the time of frustration the observations of the children suggest that their play is more primitive, less elaborate, and so forth. Hence, the investigators conclude that frustration, or tension increment, can lead to regression (dedifferentiation of regions, decrements in future time perspective, and so forth.) (The reader is directed to Lawson, 1965, and Yates, 1962, for further discussion of this research and some methodological criticisms. The main research criticism has been that this study did not include a "no-frustration" control group. Thus, the "regressive" behaviors might be due to fatigue, boredom, or similar factors.)

Frustration and the Measurement of Psychological Forces.   The experimental design employing the Columbia Obstruction Box allowed Lewin to speculate about the measurement and properties of psychological forces. Similarly, the study of frustration also provided Lewin an opportunity to investigate the nature of forces.

Lewin's (1935, 1938) theoretical analyses of the forces operative in frustration situations is based upon data collected and interpreted by Fajans (1933). Fajans offered young infants and five-year-old children an opportunity to obtain an attractive toy. However, the toy was placed beyond their reach. Fajans varied the actual distance between the child and the toy, with some children being frustrated nearer to the goal than others. She then measured the amount of time the subjects spent in activities directed toward attaining the toy, such as hand stretching, asking the experimenter for help, looking for tools, and so on.

The results of the study revealed that all children ultimately withdrew from attempts to reach the toy, with younger and older children spending relatively equal amounts of time in pursuit of the goal. In addition, for both infants and older children persistence at the activity was greater when they were frustrated nearer to the goal. Finally, Fajans also observed that the younger infants display more emotional behavior when thwarted closer to the goal, while the older children display relatively equal amounts of emotionality at the varying distances from the goal object.

Lewin concluded from these data that the conceptual representation of the behavior of the older children and infants differs. The younger children, Lewin contends, discontinue the activity because the barrier separating them from the goal became aversive. However, for the older children an additional factor was operative. Lewin believed that the older children no longer sought the reward because they also underwent a cognitive change. That is, they realized that their activities were not in the path toward the goal (not instrumental to object attainment).

Lewin's rather surprising conclusions from these data were derived from an analysis of the psychological forces in this situation. His reasoning is complex, and indicates Lewin's sophistication when inferring the relationship between behavioral observations (phenotypic behavior) and the underlying behavioral dynamics (genotypic representation).

Because the subjects in the experiment initially attempt to secure the toy, Lewin reasons that there must have been a force acting at their present region (A) in the direction of the goal (G). That is, there exists a force from A in the direction of G $(d_{A,G}) > 0$. However, the children find that they are unable to enter the goal region. Therefore, there must also exist an opposing force that is equal in magnitude to the force toward the goal (force B, $-B$). This would then result in a state of equilibrium. Lewin labels this opposing force a "restraining force." A restraining force "corresponds to a barrier or obstacle to locomotion and is effective only when some driving force opposes it" (Cartwright, 1959, p. 26). This is in distinction to a "driving force," such as the force from A to G, which is "coordinated to a tendency to change, usually to a locomotion of the person" (Cartwright, 1959, p. 26). The representation of the forces in Fajans' experiment is:

$$\text{force } (A, G) = \text{force } (B, -B)$$

where B represents the psychological region separating the subjects from the desired toy (see again Figure 3:11).

Eventually, however, the children quit in their efforts to reach the goal. They withdraw from the activity to engage in other actions. This apparently indicates that the resultant force away from the goal has become stronger than the force toward the goal:

$$\text{force } (A, G) < \text{force } (A, -B)$$

Notice that the opposing force is now conceptualized as acting on the individual while he is in region A, rather than merely acting at the boundary of region B. This signifies that the opposing force originating at B is no longer considered merely a restraining force. If this were the case, the subjects would not withdraw; they would remain in this state of equilibrium. A restraining force or barrier does not act beyond the boundaries of the region in which it originates. Lewin (1938) concludes:

The condition for this change, which terminates one period of action toward the goal, is a change in the character of region . . . B. This region which previously has been an obstacle [a restraining force] acquires a negative valence, of which the corresponding force field must be sufficiently strong and must spread at least into the region [A] [p. 129].

To review the analysis thus far, the approach behavior first displayed by the subjects indicates that there is a force on them in the direction of the goal. According to Lewin, because the goal cannot be attained, a force of equal magnitude is acting in the opposite direction. The force derived from the obstacle initially is not itself aversive. It is merely a restraint, and not the center of a negative force field. However, inasmuch as the subjects do locomote away from the goal, it must follow that the barrier itself becomes a region of negative valence and establishes a force field of greater magnitude than that of the positive force. Further, to quote Lewin (1938):

Just as in the case of the obstruction box, the duration of the action toward or away from the goal G depends upon a "historical" process involving a change in the character of the situation [p. 130].

Lewin and Fajans also conclude that the older children withdraw because of an additional cognitive change that does not characterize the infant subjects. This conclusion was reached with the following reasoning. The data reveal that both younger and older age groups persist for a longer time when physically closer to the goal. However, only the younger children display differential emotional tension as a function of the physical distance. For the younger infants emotionality varied inversely with the distance from the toy, while older children display the same intensity of emotions when blocked at relatively large or small distances from the toy.

In prior studies Lewin and his colleagues had demonstrated that emotional tension is related to the degree of conflict. Greater conflict gives rise to heightened emotionality. Thus, it was inferred that the younger but not older children were in greater conflict when closer to the goal. Further, because the degree of conflict is determined by the magnitude of the driving or approach force, the forces acting on the infants must vary with the physical distance from the goal. That is, children are more emotional when close to the goal in this situation because the driving force, and hence degree of conflict, increases with decreasing physical distance. On the other hand, older children are assumed to have equal magnitude of forces acting at various physical distances from the goal.

Why was psychological distance unrelated to physical distance for the older children? Lewin suggests that perhaps these children recognized the social character of the situation, and realized that the true barrier was the experimenter, rather than the physical distance from the toy. Further, older children might perceive distances of a few inches or feet as identical, while for infants such distances might be psychologically great.

A question still remains unanswered: Why do the older children, as well as the younger children, exhibit greater persistence at the short than long distances from the goal? Lewin contends that at greater distances from the toy the older children more immediately perceive that their actions, such as reaching and tool seeking, are not instrumental to goal attainment. That is, they quickly perceive that such behaviors are not in the path toward the goal. This cognitive restructuring, Lewin contends, only describes the behavior of the older children, and occurs more quickly when they are thwarted relatively far from the goal.

Another summary is in order, for the explanation is indeed complex.

Both older and younger children withdraw because the nature of the restraining force alters over time. And, for both groups the tendency is to withdraw faster when far from the goal. Lewin believes that in the case of the older children this withdrawal was due in part to a change in the cognitive structure of the situation. Older children realize sooner that their actions will not lead to the toy when far from the goal. On the other hand, for infants the differential persistence is only a function of the disparate force that is attributable to the perceived differences in psychological distance. Why does Lewin infer that the representation of this situation differs for the younger and older children, when the time spent at the activity was identical? Because only the younger children displayed differential emotionality as a function of distance from the goal. Hence, only for them did conflict, and therefore approach force, vary with decreased distance. Inasmuch as the force over the physical distance was constant for the older children, an additional factor must have been operative to account for their differential persistence. Lewin (1938) concludes:

Fajans' experiment seems to me a good example of a rather important problem in psychological measurements. *To keep a set-up physically constant does not secure psychological constancy.* . . . Measurement of forces in psychology will have to be aware of this basic fact which, as we have seen, is important also in the case of the obstruction box. To my knowledge, only Fajans has attempted to take care of the dynamical questions involved in these "historical changes" by providing additional observations necessary for deciding among the different possibilities [p. 132].

EXPERIMENTS GENERATED BY FIELD THEORY

Few theoretical approaches have been as heuristic as Lewinian field theory. In *Theories of Personality,* Hall and Lindzey (1957) assert that

one widely acknowledged criterion of a "good" theory is the measure of its fruitfulness in stimulating research. In this respect, Lewin's theory is a very "good" theory indeed. Few other theories of personality have been responsible for generating so much experimentation. Lewin himself, although he is known as a brilliant theoretician, was always a working scientist. He took the lead in formulating empirical tests of many of his basic hypotheses, and his great enthusiasm for research has been transmitted to many generations of students in Germany and in the United States. The series of articles in the *Psychologische Forschung* between 1926 and 1930 is one of the most distinguished group of empirical studies in the psychological literature. Moreover, Lewin's ideas and his genius for devising simple and convincing demonstrations of his theoretical conceptions have acted as catalysts for many psychologists who were never personally associated with him. It is impossible to estimate the number of investigations that bear the imprint of Lewin's influence. Their number is surely legion. Whatever may be the fate of Lewin's theory in the years to come, the body of experimental work instigated by it constitutes an enduring contribution to our knowledge of personality [pp. 239–40].

Lewin's research investigated many aspects of behavior. The topics include conflict, memory, perception, group dynamics, social climate, mental retardation, substitution, level of aspiration, ecology, and many others. However, not all of the research is germane to his formal theory. For example, the analysis of social climate has, at best, a remote relationship to his mathematical conception of the determinants of behavior. In the present context only research directly relevant to his formal theory of motivation is discussed. This research falls into four categories: (1) the recall of incompleted tasks; (2) the resumption of incompleted tasks; (3) substitution; and (4) satiation and cosatiation. Criticisms of the research and suggestions for other investigations also are presented.

Task Recall

The investigations of task recall and task resumption were the initial studies relevant to Lewin's conception of personality dynamics. Their importance within the Lewinian system cannot be overemphasized. Lewin (1935) states:

All later experimental investigations are built upon this. It was an attempt to break a first path through a primeval forest of facts and assumptions, using as compass concepts the practical utility of which was still wholly untried [p. 240].

It is said that the idea for the experimental investigation of the recall of incompleted tasks originated from observations in a restaurant. Lewin noticed that a certain waiter did not write down individuals' orders, yet was able to recall what they had ordered when it was time to collect the bill. One day Lewin returned to the restaurant a few moments after he had paid the check and asked the waiter what he (Lewin) had ordered. The waiter no longer retained this information. This observation became the prototypical phenomenon Lewin attempted to account for with his theoretical system.

Lewin (1951) employed these four assumptions, which were hinted at previously, to derive this differential recall of finished and unfinished tasks:

Assumption 1: The intention to reach a certain goal G (to carry out an action leading to G) corresponds to a tension (t) in a certain system (S^G)

within the person so that $t\ (S^G) > 0$. This assumption coordinates a dynamic construct (system in tension) with the observable syndrome popularly called "intention."

Assumption 2: The tension $t\ (S^G)$ is released if the goal G is reached.

$$t\ (S^G) = 0 \text{ if } P^cG \text{ [if } P \text{ completes } G]$$

Assumption 3: To a need for G corresponds a force $f_{P,G}$ acting upon the person and causing a tendency of locomotion toward G;

$$\text{if } t\ (S^G) > 0 \rightarrow f_{P,G} > 0.$$

Assumption 3a: A need leads not only to a tendency of actual locomotion towards the goal region but also to thinking about this type of activity; in other words the force $f_{P,G}$ exists not only on the level of doing (reality) but also on the level of thinking (irreality);

$$\text{if } t\ (S^G) > 0 \rightarrow f_{P,R} > 0$$

where R means recall [pp. 9–10].

These assumptions logically lead to the derivation concerning differential task recall:

Derivation 1: The tendency to recall interrupted activities should be greater than the tendency to recall finished ones. This derivation can be made as follows. We indicate the completed task by C, the unfinished one by U, and the corresponding systems by S^c and S^u respectively. We can then state

   (a) $t\ (S^u) > 0$ according to (A1)
   (b) $t\ (S^c) = 0$ according to (A2)
   (c) $f_{P,U} > f_{P,C}$ hence according to (A3a), on the level of thinking. In other words: there is a greater tendency to recall spontaneously unfinished tasks than finished tasks [p. 10].

Empirical Analysis. To test this derivation, Lewin and his students (Marrow, 1938; Zeigarnik, 1927) experimentally manipulated the degree of task completion. They than compared the recall of incompleted tasks with the recall of the completed tasks. Subjects generally were given 16 or 20 simple puzzles (anagrams, arithmetic problems, and the like) to perform. Half of the tasks were too long to be completed within the allotted time period, while the other half were relatively short and could be finished. The experimenter collected all the puzzles when the time was up. Following an intervening time period of a few minutes or less the subjects unexpectedly were asked to recall the tasks. Zeigarnik (1927) first demonstrated that there was greater recall of the incompleted than completed tasks. The ratio of incompleted/completed tasks (the Zeigarnik quotient) approached 2/1. The tendency to recall a greater percentage of incompleted than completed tasks became known as the Zeigarnik Effect.

Lewin tested a number of additional derivations from his conception of tense systems, employing differential task recall as the dependent variable. The amount of tension remaining within a tense system had been postulated to be a function of the strength of the boundaries around that system and the time the system was in tension. Therefore, the Zeigarnik quotient was expected to decrease over time and in situations in which the strength of the boundaries between the regions had been weakened. In one study Zeigarnik found that when task recall was delayed for 24 hours the Zeigarnik quotient dropped to $1:2/1$. Further, tired subjects and individuals subjected to "strong emotional excitation" prior to recall exhibited a greatly decreased Zeigarnik quotient. The operations of fatigue and induced emotion were expected to decrease the firmness of the inner-personal boundaries. (Why these operations weaken boundaries is not made explicit by Lewin.) In another study Marrow (1938) demonstrated that subjective rather than objective, completion influences task recall. He told subjects that interruption meant they were doing well, while allowing them to finish indicated poor performance. Marrow found greater recall of the subjectively incomplete (objectively complete) tasks than subjectively complete (objectively incomplete) tasks. The findings just discussed and additional derivations and studies are summarized in Table 3:2.

The general pattern of results confirms the predictions derived from Lewin's conception of tension; the experimental findings enhance the validity of the theory. The results are especially supportive of his conception because they do not fit easily into any other theoretical framework. The derivations are unique to the field theoretical approach.

Empirical and Methodological Problems.   A contradiction occurred when studies of task recall were conducted in America. Experimenters such as Rosenzweig (1943) and Glixman (1949) obtained results partially opposed to those of the previous investigations. They found greater recall of completed than incompleted tasks in ego-oriented or stress situations. To explain these data, Rosenzweig postulated that the incompleted tasks are "repressed." Failure was thought to represent a threat to the self or the ego; not remembering incompleted tasks was anxiety-reducing. Therefore, there was relatively greater recall of the successful or completed tasks than the unfinished or failed tasks.

In 1953, Atkinson partially resolved these apparently conflicting results. Atkinson found that subjects classified as high in need for achievement recall more incompleted than completed tasks, given achievement-oriented instructions. Conversely, under those same instructions, subjects low in need for achievement recall more completed than incompleted tasks (see pp. 189–191). Analysis of subjects used by Marrow and Rosenzweig

TABLE 3:2

Summary and Verification of Some of Zeigarnik's Constructs, Assumptions, and Derivations
(adapted from Lewin, 1951, p. 18)

Term	Constructs Operational Definition	Conceptual Properties	Basic Theorems Assumptions	Derived Theorems
Psychological tension (*t*)	Empirical syndrome indicating a "need"	Tendency of spreading to neighboring systems	Relation between intention and need (tension)	Zeigarnik quotient = $\frac{RU}{RC} > 1$
			Relation between tension and force	Decrease of Zeigarnik quotient with time elapsed since creation of need
				Zeigarnik quotient smaller for tired subjects
Psychological force (*f*)	Psychological locomotion	Vector	Relation between tension and force on the level of thinking (tendency to recall)	Zeigarnik quotient smaller for more peripheral systems
				Zeigarnik quotient = 1, if the systems corresponding to finished and unfinished tasks are not separated
Fluidity (*fl*)		Factor determining the velocity of equalization of tension with neighboring systems	Fluidity as a function of tiredness	Decrease of Zeigarnik quotient after emotional shake-up
			Fluidity as a function of degree of irreality	Zeigarnik quotient increases with intensity of need
			Leveling of tensions in different systems by emotional waves	Zeigarnik quotient = 1, if "unfinished" task is psychologically finished
				Zeigarnik quotient = 1, if "finished" task is psychologically unfinished
				Zeigarnik quotient decreased with added tendency created by instruction to recall in definite order

revealed that they were drawn from different subject populations. Marrow used volunteer subjects. Atkinson (1953) cites evidence that volunteer subjects are likely to be high in achievement motivation. Further, it has been found that volunteer subjects exhibit a greater Zeigarnik Effect than nonvolunteer subjects (Green, 1963). On the other hand, Rosenzweig's subjects, who were receiving psychological services at the school clinic, were likely to be high in anxiety and, hence, relatively low in their resultant tendency to achieve success. The contradiction in the results of Marrow and Rosenzweig was attributed by Atkinson to differences in the personality types of the subjects. (For further discussion of this topic see Butterfield, 1964; and Weiner, 1966a.)

While Atkinson did resolve some inconsistencies in the empirical results, he did not attempt to reconcile the data with Lewin's theoretical system. If a large subgroup within the population recalls more completed than incompleted tasks, then the Lewinian notion of tension perhaps has to be modified. Lewin does state that the Zeigarnik quotient is a function of the strength of the force to recall the tasks, and that there are individual differences in the strength of this force. Zeigarnik found that the Zeigarnik quotient is greater for "ambitious" subjects (subjects who would be classified as high in achievement motivation). However, it is difficult for Lewin to conceptualize the greater recall of completed than of incompleted tasks (repression), which Zeigarnik also observed on occasion. Perhaps the underlying difficulty in his and many systems is a relative lack of understanding of avoidance behavior.

One must also question whether the differential recall of incompleted and completed tasks reflects differences in the retention of these tasks. Memory is often conceptualized as a three-stage process. The first stage in the process involves learning, or trace formation. In the second stage, often referred to as the period of trace storage, the trace is available but is not exhibited in behavior. In the third stage, the trace is revived or retrieved by the organism. Only the latter two stages, storage and retrieval, are considered to be memory processes.

To demonstrate that incompleted tasks are retained more than completed tasks, it must be shown that the two types of tasks are learned equally well. That is, inferences about retention functions require equality in the degree of original learning of the materials under consideration (see Underwood, 1964). Lewin and others have assumed that differential retention was being measured in their experiment, although there was no indication that the tasks were learned to an equal degree. Perhaps subjects work longer at the incomplete task, resulting in more learning and better retention. Hence, one cannot discern whether the differences in recall are due to differences in learning or to differences in memory.

Caron and Wallach (1957) tested whether the Zeigarnik quotient reflects differences in learning or in retention. Weiner (1966a) summarizes this research:

Caron and Wallach (1957), reasoned that there is a subgroup of individuals (*F* Group) who will exhibit a Zeigarnik effect under stressful, or ego-involving, conditions. Similarly, there is a subgroup of individuals (*S* Group) who will recall more completed than incompleted tasks in a stressful situation. It is usually theorized that the *F* Group recalls more incompleted tasks because of the persistent tension system directed toward task completion. The *S* Group, however, represses the incompleted or failed tasks and, therefore, recalls more completed than incompleted tasks. Caron and Wallach hypothesize that if these explanations are valid, then the differential recall should be reduced by revealing that the experiment is a hoax and that some of the tasks are insoluble. That is, the *F* Group should subsequently recall fewer incompleted tasks because the tension system associated with an incompleted task is discharged. Correspondingly, the *S* Group should subsequently recall more incompleted tasks. The repressed material would no longer be perceived as threatening, and should reemerge into consciousness.
Caron and Wallach employed the usual Zeigarnik paradigm, with relaxed and stressful conditions. Subjects were classified into *S* and *F* groups on the basis of factor analytic considerations. Results at the immediate-recall period revealed the expected interaction between the experimental conditions and the individual difference classification. The subjects were then informed that the experiment was "fixed," and that some of the puzzles were insoluble. Two additional recalls revealed that there was no shift in the pattern of recall following this feedback. It was therefore concluded that the initial differences in recall were due to selective learning rather than selective retention. Caron and Wallach suggest that differential rehearsal of the material might account for the differences in the degree of learning [pp. 30–31].

The data suggest that differential recall does not reflect differences in persisting tendencies. Thus, the general experimental design and results of the studies investigating task recall neither support the Lewinian conception, nor thus far allow an adequate test of his conception of tense systems. (See Weiner, 1966a, for a further discussion of this point, and Heckhausen, 1968, for experimentation indicating that task recall is a memory phenomenon.)

Task Resumption

The experimental paradigm used in the investigations of task resumption is very similar to the one employed in the study of task recall. The derivations of the hypotheses in the resumption and recall studies are virtually identical; individuals are expected to resume incompleted rather than completed tasks because of the persisting tension in the systems.

The original investigation of task resumption was conducted by Ovsiankina (1928). Children were interrupted before they could finish some tasks and were allowed to complete other tasks. The experimenter then removed herself from the experimental room using some pretense—to answer a telephone, sharpen a pencil, or perform similar errands. During the intervening time period the subjects could "spontaneously" resume some of the tasks. At times the tasks remained in the subject's immediate perceptual field, while in other experiments the tasks were placed out of sight (although available to the subject). Ovsiankina found a significant tendency for individuals to resume the previously unfinished tasks. This occurred whether the tasks were immediately visible or out of sight.

Further experimentation revealed that the tendency to resume unfinished tasks is influenced by many factors. These include:

1. The type of activity. Tasks having no definite end state (such as stringing beads) are resumed significantly less often than tasks which have a definite goal. Clearly, tasks that have no end point cannot be "unfinished."

2. The place in which the activity was interrupted. In general, the closer the subject is to the goal when the interruption occurs, the greater the tendency to resume the task.

3. The duration of the interruption. As the time between the interruption and opportunity to resume increases, the tendency to resume the task decreases. This tends to confirm Lewin's assumption that the amount of tension remaining within a system is, in part, a function of the time that the system is in tension.

4. The attitude and character of the person. According to Lewin, (1951) "Children who had the attitude of being examined and of strict obedience showed little resumption owing to the lack of involvement; they were governed mainly by induced forces" [p. 275]. That is, there was no intrinsic interest among these children to undertake the activities and, therefore, no system that remained in tension. The children performed the task because of an extrinsic source of motivation, or a "force from without."

Since the 1930s there have been extremely few studies of task resumption. It is intuitively reasonable and surely an accepted observation that individuals often tend to finish tasks that have been started and do not tend to "resume" completed activities. The obviousness of an empirical fact does not minimize its theoretical importance. It is evident that most objects fall; it is also an important empirical fact, and a sophisticated theory was required to explain this datum. Lewinian field theory specifies that incompleted tasks will be resumed. And this important empirical fact also will require a sophisticated theory for its explanation. Unlike Lewin's conception, other theoretical approaches have not focused upon the effects of attainment or nonattainment of a goal. The derivation concerning task resumption is unique to Lewinian theory.

More sophisticated questions related to resumption that could further confirm or disconfirm Lewinian theory remain to be raised. For example, does the likelihood of resumption increase as the level of tension within a system increases? Does it also increase as the attractiveness of the goal object increases? If the latter is true, is the theory supported, disconfirmed, or in need of relatively minor modifications?

In addition, data reported by Ovsiankina tend to call into question Lewin's conception. Lewin postulated that following the nonattainment of a goal the tension within the inner-personal region associated with the goal would persist. Tension is defined operationally as the magnitude of a need; theoretically it is relatively independent of psychological distance from the goal. Yet Ovsiankina found that resumption is affected by distance from the goal; greater resumption occurs as a function of nearness to the goal at the time of interruption. This apparently contradicts Lewin's conception of persisting tense systems. The data suggest that a quantity reflecting force, rather than tension, persists. That is, because resumption is affected by psychological distance, which is a determinant of force and not tension, it is more consistent with the data to postulate that a scalar quantity of the aroused force persists following nonattainment of a goal. If the magnitude of aroused tension persisted, then the tendency to resume incompleted tasks should be unrelated to distance from the goal at the time of the prior interruption.

Substitution

As indicated in the discussion of regression, Lewin was strongly influenced by the observations and analyses of Freud. He realized that Freud's insights were not easily put to scientific test, and that experimental evidence in support of Freud's conception was indeed sparse. Lewin (1935) writes,

Experimental studies of the dynamic laws of the behavior and structure of personality have forced us to consider more and more complicated problems. Instead of investigating the single psychological systems which correspond to simple needs and desires, we have to deal with the interrelationships of these systems, with their differentiation and transformations, and with the different kinds of larger wholes built up from them. These interrelationships and larger wholes are very labile and delicate. Yet one must try to get hold of them experimentally because they are most important for understanding the underlying reality of behavior and personality differences. In doing this we often find facts which Freud first brought to our attention, thereby rendering a great service even though he has not given a clear dynamic theory in regard to them [p. 180].

Later, Lewin (1936) added:

In its present state of development psychology must be thought of as a young science. There is only one field in which it is relatively well established and in which it has advanced steadily: this is the psychology of sensation and perception. The scientific character of this field is fully recognized. Its findings are based almost entirely on experimental evidence, and even when its theories are in conflict one feels that as far as method is concerned it stands on relatively firm ground. The situation is different with the psychology of will, of needs, and of personality despite the fact that these fields have always attracted popular interest. As recently as fifteen years ago it was assumed that they, by their very nature, were not amenable to scientific methods. The little experimental work that has been done seemed too artificial and abstract to give an insight into the real processes. It was generally accepted that experimental investigations of these elusive and highly complicated processes were intrinsically impossible, at least in so far as human beings are concerned. Thus in Europe these problems were treated in a half-literary, half-philosophical way, and in America the tendency was to study individual differences by means of tests.

The only approach to deeper problems was the brilliant work of Freud. However, the attempt of the psychoanalysts to base general laws entirely on case studies and therapeutical work seemed methodologically unsound to most scientists [p. 3].

Experimental Studies.   In the experimental investigation of substitution some of Freud's ideas were examined within a Lewinian framework. Freud had postulated that following nonattainment of a goal the tendency to strive for that goal persists. The mechanism responsible for the persisting wish was identified as the "internal stimulus from which there is no flight." According to Freud, this persisting tendency often is inadvertently expressed in dreams, wit, slips of the tongue, daydreams, and the like.

Within the Freudian system the object of the original unsatisfied desire may change; there are "vicissitudes of the instincts." The unfulfilled wish can become directed toward (attached to) objects that have some psychological similarity to the desired goal. Freud also states that ultimately the libidinal tendency may be expressed in cultural activities such as painting, or composing. His analyses of Michelangelo and da Vinci appear to indicate that these great artists had strong unfulfilled sexual urges. Freud calls this deflection of energy into socially acceptable channels "sublimation."

Lewin (1935) also notes that goal objects may change. Behavioral substitution is manifested in many different ways:

There is, for instance, the man who dreams of a palace and brings a few pieces of marble into his kitchen. There is the man who cannot buy a piano, but who collects piano catalogs. Again, we find the delinquent boy who knows that he will not be allowed to leave his reform school but who asks for a traveling bag as a birthday present. And the little boy who threatens and scolds the larger boy whom he cannot beat on the playground. These and a hundred other examples make us realize how important and far reaching the problem of substitution is in regard to psychological needs as well as with reference to bodily needs such as hunger and sex [pp. 180–81].

Ovsiankina and Zeigarnik provided the foundation for the experimental investigation of substitution. It was believed that these investigators had demonstrated that tension persists in a system and is reduced with goal attainment. The question asked in the study of substitution is: Can these tense systems be discharged through some compensatory activity? That is, will there be a decrease in the resumption of previously interrupted tasks following completion of other activities? If so, then this would be a valid experimental demonstration that one goal has substitute value for another goal.

The general experimental paradigm used in the study of substitution follows closely the methodology first employed by Ovsiankina. Subjects are given tasks to complete and are interrupted before task completion. The experimenter then allows the subjects to undertake and finish an interpolated activity. Finally, subjects are tested for the spontaneous resumption of the previously incompleted tasks. Resumption therefore becomes the behavioral criterion for the identification of goal substitutes.

One of the first experimental studies of substitution was conducted by Lissner (1933). In her experiment, children were interrupted while making a figure from clay. Then, after making a different figure, they were tested for resumption. Lissner identified two factors that influence the substitute value of an activity: its similarity to the first activity and its level of difficulty. The more similar and difficult the interpolated task, the greater its substitute value. In another study Lissner told the children that the interpolated activity was "completely different" from the one they had just attempted. In that situation the interpolated activity had little substitute value for the original activity. That is, the percentage of task resumption following the activity did not decrease. Lewin (1935) states, "We find very little substitute value if two activities are psychologically separated through special circumstances of the situation" (p. 185).

Mahler (1933), another student of Lewin's, gave subjects an interpolated activity that could be completed in ways that differed in their proximity to overt behavior (the level of reality). Subjects could think about doing the task, talk through its completion, or actually do it. In general, substitute value varied monotonically with the degree of reality of the action.

The experimental attitude of the subject also has been shown to be an important determinant of substitute value (Adler & Kounin, 1939). If the subject's attitude toward a task is concrete, such as "building a house for Mary," then "building a house for a different person" has little substitute value. However, if the task is conceived more abstractly, such as building a house, then an interpolated task of building another house has substitute value.

Lewin (1935) speculated about the psychological characteristics of feeble-minded individuals from their behavior in substitution experiments. Feeble-minded children exhibit great variance in their behavior following completion of an interpolated task. Either they all tend to resume the original activity after the interpolated completion (no substitution), or virtually none of the children resume the original task (complete substitution). Lewin reasons that feeble-minded children have strong boundaries between their inner-personal regions, but fewer regions (differentiations) than normal children (see Figure 3:13). Therefore, two activities are perceived as identical (complete substitution) or as psychologically separate (no substitution). (See Stevenson & Zigler, 1957; Zigler, 1962, for some objections to this formulation.)

The most extensive experimental work on substitution has been conducted by Mary Henle (1944). Her work concerns the relationship between substitution, valence of the original task, and valence of the interpolated or substitute task. In Henle's studies the subjects first rate the attractiveness of various activities. They then are given a subjectively attractive or unattractive task to complete. Following interruption, an interpolated activity of high or low attractiveness is completed. Again resumption is the behavioral criterion for degree of substitution. Henle found that the greater the valence of the original task, the less the possibility that other tasks can substitute for it. Similarly, the greater the valence of an interpolated activity, the greater is its substitute value.

The studies of Mahler, Lissner, Henle, and others clearly demonstrate that goals can substitute for one another. Further, these studies have identified some of the relevant dimensions and determinants of substitution. The

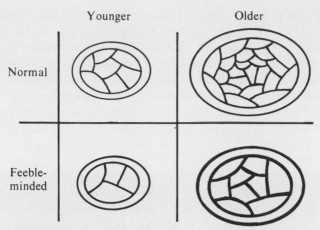

Younger   Older

Normal

Feeble-
minded

FIGURE 3:13. Representation of the development of normal and feeble-minded individuals. Normal children are assumed to have greater differentiation and weaker boundaries between the inner-personal regions than feeble-minded children (from Lewin, 1935, p. 210).

data support Lewin's contention that there are interrelationships, or dynamic communications, between psychological systems. Henle (1944) summarizes her research with a similar conclusion:

In any case, the problem which is raised by the results of the present experiments is that of determining how large a unit is necessary to describe adequately the behavior of the subjects in the experimental situation. It is suggested here that the relevant segment of behavior does not consist simply of activity directed to satisfy a quasi-need to complete a particular task, but must be thought of as activity directed to a more inclusive goal [p. 18].[5]

[5] There are a number of interesting similarities as well as differences between experimental investigations of displacement and the study of substitution. In studies of both displacement and substitution, there is a desire for a goal that is unattainable either because of conflict (the existence of an avoidance tendency) or because of the absence of the goal object. Further, the need instigating the action is then expressed in activities directed toward the attainment of other incentives that derive their attraction because the initial goal was not attained. Theoretically, this shift in goal objects is conceptualized in terms of the stimulus similarity between the goals or via the spreading of tension to neighboring regions. The investigations of displacement primarily examine the direction of the substitute activity—the choice or selection made between the various alternate goal objects. On the other hand, investigations of substitution are concerned with the value of the displaced activity; that is, the degree to which that activity reduced the desire for the original goal. Thus, the study of substitution involves a comparison between the pre- and post-magnitude strength of the need. It is apparent that given substitution, there must have been displaced activity. Given displaced activity, however, there need not have been any substitute gratification.

Evaluation of Substitution Experiments.   Do the demonstrations of substitution provide support for the conception of tense systems presented by Lewin? Yes and no. Yes, in that the Lewinian conception makes one take seriously the notion that needs are not separated psychologically; that is, tension spreads to neighboring regions. Yes, in that the body of empirical work is again uniquely Lewinian and difficult to account for with any other theoretical system. However, clearer conceptualization and additional experimentation is greatly needed in this area. Within a Lewinian framework one might ask:

1. To serve as a substitute, must the valence of the substitute activity be derived from the original task? That is, would attainment of goal *B* reduce the persisting tension for activity *A* if the valence of *B* existed independent of (prior to) the desire toward *A*?

2. Must substitution be conceptualized as a simultaneous reduction in tension in more than one system? Lewin (1936) defines substitution in this way:

An action *b* has a substitute value for the action *a* if the tension of the system corresponding to *a* is released when the tension of the system corresponding to *b* is released [p. 218].

If force at a boundary is function of the difference in tension between two systems, then substitution could be derived by postulating a reduction in only one tense system. If tension flows from system *A* to system *B,* then attainment of *B* reduces tension in that system, increases the difference between the levels of tension in *A* and *B,* and increases the flow of tension out of *A* into *B*. This reduces the amount of tension in *A*. The point of this analysis is that within the Lewinian system there are many ways to capture the notion of substitution, and they should be explored systematically.

An additional problem is connected with the conceptualization of the effects of goal attainment. As Weiner (1965b) states,

Other investigators have suggested that the attainment of goals similar to a desired goal will lead to an increase rather than a decrease in the resultant tendency to strive for the goal. Murray (1954) found a greater frequency of aggressive responses toward significant authority figures as a patient progressed through psychotherapy. He employed Miller's (1944) approach-avoidance conflict model to explain these results. Murray suggested that during therapy sessions hostile responses directed toward individuals similar to a disliked authority figure were not punished. This was represented conceptually as a lowering of the avoidance gradient, which resulted in a subsequent increase in the number of aggressive responses made toward the originally feared authority figure [p. 166].

To demonstrate the instigative properties of goal attainment, Weiner (1965b) also employed the resumption paradigm of Lissner, Mahler, and others. Subjects classified according to strength of their achievement motivation were given a booklet containing ten long (incompleted) and ten short (completed) tasks. Following this activity the subjects were given a longer interpolated puzzle task which one-half of the subjects solved and one-half failed. Time was then allowed for spontaneous resumption of the original tasks. Weiner (1965b) summarized the results of the study:

Results indicate that subjects high (above the median) in *n* Ach [need for achievement] more frequently resumed interrupted tasks following interpolated failure as opposed to interpolated success experiences. . . . Subjects low in *n* Ach more frequently resumed tasks following success rather than failure experiences [1965b, p. 167].

For one subset of the population, goal attainment served as a substitute; that is, it decreased the tendency to strive for the original goal. But for another subpopulation of subjects, the results were opposite; goal attainment acted as an instigator to resume previously interrupted (failed) tasks. These results are difficult for Lewin to interpret and parallel the contradictory pattern of results exhibited by the different subject populations when task recall is used as the dependent variable. The interaction between individual differences in achievement motivation and the effects of goal attainment and nonattainment on subsequent performance provide difficulties for Lewin's system.

Satiation and Cosatiation

Another aspect of Lewin's system that promised to provide evidence for (or against) his theoretical conception concerned the study of satiation and cosatiation. Lewin (1951) writes:

One can distinguish in regard to all or most needs a state of hunger, of satiation and of oversatiation. These states correspond to a positive, a neutral and a negative valence of the activity regions which are related to a particular need [p. 282].

Satiation is related to the general problem of the effects of attainment or nonattainment of a goal and to changes in valence as a result of consumption. Cosatiation refers to a decrement in the valence of tasks related to a satiated task. The question of the interrelations of need systems is involved in the study of cosatiation, just as it was in the study of substitution.

There have been extremely few studies of satiation and cosatiation, with little attempt to relate the results to Lewin's formal system. Karsten

(1927) conducted the most extensive study in this area. She found that central activities satiate faster than peripheral ones. In his customary extension of these findings to observations of human behavior, Lewin (1951) points out, "fashions in women's clothes change faster than in men's clothes" (p. 242) because clothes are more central to women than to men. Similarly, children show faster velocity of satiation than adults. Conceptually, among children there is less differentiation between regions. Hence, acts tend to involve the whole person. From the evidence of Karsten and others, Lewin (1951) concludes:

The phenomena of satiation indicate (1) that there is a close relation between activities and needs, and (2) that an activity can be viewed as a consumption which changes the underlying need and, therefore, the positive valence of the activity into a negative one. As a result of this consumption the valence of "similar activities" also becomes negative [p. 284].

Lewin also believed that fatigue had a large psychological component, rather than being entirely physical. In one investigation he asked subjects to write their names as many times as they could, and to continue at this activity until they were too tired to write their names again. When the subjects finally yielded to fatigue, sometimes after four or five hours of continuous writing, they were told to hand in their papers. Lewin then casually added that the paper should be folded, and asked each subject to write his or her name on the outside for identification purposes. Of course, they were able to write their names again without the slightest sign of fatigue.

The study of satiation is closely related to investigations of resumption and substitution. However, this work is less intimately related to Lewin's system than are studies in the other areas. There is no clear conception to capture Karsten's data concerning satiation in peripheral and central areas. The relationship between satiation, oversatiation and tension is, at best, vaguely specified. The lack of conceptualization and the sparcity of data make it inappropriate to cite this area as supporting or as contradicting Lewinian field theory.

ADDITIONAL AREAS OF INVESTIGATION

Psychological Ecology

Psychological ecology was introduced earlier in this chapter when examining the role of the "foreign hull" in determining behavior. Lewin (1951) states:

The relation between psychological and nonpsychological factors is a basic conceptual and methodological problem in all branches of psychology, from the psychology of perception to the psychology of groups. A proper understanding of this relationship must be achieved before we can answer the many questions raised in efforts to produce an integration of the social sciences. A field-theoretical approach to these problems of "psychological ecology" suggests some of the ways in which these questions may be answered. . . .

Any type of group life occurs in a setting of certain limitations to what is and what is not possible, what might or might not happen. The nonpsychological factors of climate, of communication, of the law of the country or the organization are a frequent part of these "outside limitations." . . . The psychologist studies "nonpsychological" data to find out what these data mean for determining the boundary conditions of the life of the individual or group [p. 170].

Lewin was not personally involved in many studies of ecology. However, one investigation in which he participated attempted to discover the bases of food habits and to find reasons why people eat what they do. One of the main conclusions of this study is that food must pass through many channels or steps before it reaches the table; it must be bought, stored, taken out of storage and cooked, and so on. Entering or not entering each of these steps is primarily determined by a "gatekeeper"—a person who controls entry into each channel. In the case of food, the housewife assumes responsibility for what the family will eat, inasmuch as she controls a great number of the channels. In turn, her decisions are determined by cognitive and motivational factors, such as her perceptions of healthy and edible food, her values concerning health as opposed to taste, and the like. For the other members of the family, particularly the children, eating habits are primarily determined by what is placed on the table by the woman of the household. The members of the family generally "like what they eat, rather than eat what they like" (Lewin, 1951, p. 181).

The most extensive contributions to the study of ecology have been made by Roger Barker and his colleagues. This work has not achieved great fame or widespread acknowledgement among contemporary psychologists, nor is it immediately germane to Lewin's theory per se. However, it is extremely interesting and valuable, and has proven pertinent to the understanding of many behaviors.

T-Data and O-Data. Barker (1965) outlines two methods of data collection that are of interest to psychologists. In one procedure the psychologist acts as an "operator." That is, he is directly part of the action, alters the behavior of the organism, and generates the desired data. For example, questions are asked to determine intelligence, food is placed in a box so the animal will run, barriers are erected between children and toys to observe the effects of frustration, and so forth. Barker refers to the data gathered in this manner as "O-data." O-data are the result of typical experimental methodology. The "experimental method" is advantageous because the investigator has some degree of control over the events, and can focus upon the data of interest to him.

A second type of data, referred to as "T-data," is produced without the intervention of the scientist. He is merely a transducer, transferring and translating the observations. The psychologist merely receives, codes, and classifies the inputs from the environment.

T-data reveal certain facts not ascertainable with O-data. For example, T-data indicate what actually is occurring in the environment. In the study of chemistry, Barker states, it is essential to know such facts as what elements really exist, how abundant they are, and where they can be found. Yet psychologists, he says, tend to ignore the description of the real world. The importance of gathering this type of information is well illustrated by Barker. For example, he finds that surprisingly few incidents of severe frustration occur in the lives of most children. When such frustrations do occur, their effects are often transient. The consequents of frustration observed in the laboratory, such as regression, are rarely observed in the real world. In a second example demonstrating the importance of T-data, Barker comments that in experimental psychology subjects who do not respond generally are not included in the data. Yet not-responding is a characteristic mode of reaction of children. Observing mother-child interactions in a drugstore revealed that children do not respond to close to one-third of the mothers' inputs!

Behavioral Settings.   Behavior in nature, which gives rise to T-data, often occurs in a particular behavioral setting. A behavioral setting has a number of essential properties: it contains physical objects arranged in a special pattern; the behavior exhibited is relatively independent of the particular people located in the setting; the setting may exist unchanged for a great period of time; and the setting generally exists independent of the conscious awareness of the individuals within the setting. For example, the bridge club at the corner is considered a behavioral setting. It has a physical locus and physical properties; the behavior within the club is relatively independent of the particular people; and the club may exist unchanged for a great number of years. Similarly, the baseball field is a behavioral setting. It has physical properties, a certain type of behavior occurs within that setting, and it exists unchanged. In sum, a behavioral setting is visible, involves people, has certain attributes, and greatly influences the behavior that occurs there.

People, of course, are the sine qua non of a behavioral setting. They are part of a setting, and generally essential to its continuation. The local bridge club will not continue if it has no patrons. Yet the individuals within the setting are, to a great degree, equipotential: a fourth for bridge is a fourth for bridge. Further, each setting has an optimal population requirement. The bridge club should have at least four members present, and not more members than table space. Likewise, a game of baseball requires a certain minimal and maximal number of players.

Within these settings a great variety of personal motives are satisfied. The motivations of bridge players can vary from aggression and affiliation to achievement or power. The same is true of the participants in a baseball game. Hence, the unity of the setting is not derived from the unity of the aroused motivations.

The aspect of behavioral settings most thoroughly investigated by Barker and his colleagues is the relation between the number of people available to function within the setting and the psychological implications of that setting. Settings may be undermanned, overmanned, or have an optimal number of members. That is, settings can be classified according to the number of people available to perform its essential functions. This characterization of a setting has far-reaching consequences for the behavior of its members.

Consider, for example, some consequents of participating in a baseball game when your team has only four players instead of the usual nine. The average value of each team member is great, since everyone is needed. There will be less evaluation of individual differences, inasmuch as all the available players are accepted. Further, each person has more obligations; for example, the second baseman must also play first base. This implies that there will be greater variability per person in the displayed behaviors, and that more effort will be required than if the setting were optimally manned. In addition, maximum performance is lessened because of the complexity of the task and the augmented demands on each player. Yet more tension also is aroused, more responsibility assumed, and greater insecurity manifested because of the increased demands and abundant number of decisions that must be made. And, of course, there are more incidents of success and failure.

Wicker (1968) summarizes the effects of undermanned settings as follows:

In undermanned settings, the setting functions are often in jeopardy, and occupants sense the possibility of losing the satisfactions the settings provide. This leads them to invest more time and effort than when occupants are numerous and behavior setting functions are not precarious. Often they take positions of responsibility and engage in a wide range of supportive behaviors. Under pressure to keep activities going, members seek to induce others to participate. Membership requirements are minimized, and attempts are made to bring available personnel to at least the minimal level of performance. Feelings of involvement, success, failure, challenge, responsibility, and insecurity due to dependence upon others are common [p. 255].

Observations of behaviors in small and large cities, and in average towns in America and England, have supported the expectations enumerated in preceding paragraphs. In one series of studies Barker and his co-workers (see Barker, 1960) found that the average town in England has fewer behavioral settings and more people available for those settings than a typical small city in America. Therefore, the average person in the American town holds more responsible positions across the diverse settings. Because the individual is more important to the survival of the settings in America than in England, different patterns of segregation are exhibited by the two nations. In the typical American town far fewer settings are segregated in terms of age, sex, and social class. These are important considerations in understanding the problems of the aged, or in analyzing patterns of juvenile delinquency. Further, because the average English village does not really "need" all its inhabitants, it can afford to send some of its members out of the community. Many children in English towns are educated in boarding schools. This educational practice does not characterize rural America, presumably in part because the younger members of the community are needed to maintain the undermanned settings.

Investigations of the effects of population size and behavioral settings also have been conducted in large and small high schools. Generally, small schools are undermanned while large schools have more individuals than are needed for their settings. Wicker (1968) summarizes the results of this research:

Students of small schools, vis-à-vis students of large schools, (a) enter more different kinds of activities, (b) hold more positions of responsibility in activities entered, . . . (c) use more dimensions or constructs to describe school activities, . . . (d) experience more satisfactions "relating to being challenged, engaging in important actions, to being involved in group activities, and to achieving moral and cultural values (Barker and Gump, 1964, p. 197)," (e) report more internal and external pressures to attend and participate, including feelings of obligation to support the activities [p. 255].

These differences between the behavioral effects of small versus large high schools are not due to size per se, but rather to the fact that in the smaller schools more students are placed in positions of responsibility, and are needed in the various settings. Wicker summarizes:

The processes relating to student experiences in behavior settings [are] represented [in Figure 3:14]. The thick arrows represent the more com-

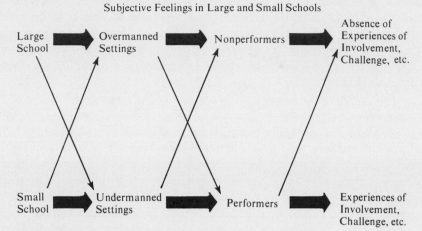

FIGURE 3:14. Flow of events relating school size, degree of under-manning, level of performance, and experiences in behavioral settings (from Wicker, 1968, p. 259).

mon flow of events; the thin arrows, the less common flow of events. While most large-school settings are overmanned, a few are undermanned; the opposite is true of the small school. Regardless of school size, students occupying overmanned settings are more likely to be nonperformers, although some will be performers. Occupants of undermanned settings are more likely to be performers. And since overmanned settings are more characteristic of large schools than small schools, the former will have fewer performances by the average student. Regardless of school size, most of the performers (but not the nonperformers) have the experiences postulated by Barker (1960) [enumerated above]. The average student in the large school, having fewer performances than his small school counterpart, also has fewer of the experiences. Thus school size is an important influence on students' experiences because of its relationship to the degree of undermanning of its settings and the consequent channeling of students into performance or nonperformance roles [pp. 259–60].

In sum, the behavior of students is clarified when the ecological context of the school is made explicit. The investigations of Barker and others on small versus large school settings provide important data and insights.

Total Institutions. A "total institution" also is a behavioral setting. However, it has certain unique characteristics not possessed by the type of settings investigated by Barker. A total institution completely encompasses the individual, providing a barrier to social intercourse occurring outside of the setting. Monasteries, jails, homes for the aged, boarding schools, and military schools are a few examples of total institutions. Analysis of total institutions stems primarily from the work of Goffman and is reported in his book, *Asylums* (1961). Goffman was not a student of Lewin or Barker, nor was he necessarily influenced by their conceptions. However, the problems with which he grapples are similar to those studied by Barker.

Total institutions have certain common characteristics. First, the individuals in such institutions must sleep, play, and work within the same setting. These are generally segmented aspects in the lives of most individuals. But within a total institution life within one sphere of activity influences life within the other spheres. Second, each phase of life takes place in the company of a large group of others. Sleep frequently takes place in a barracks-type room, food is served in a cafeteria, and so on. In such activities all persons are treated alike, and all must perform certain essential acts. Third, activities in the institution are tightly scheduled. There is a time to rise, to eat, to exercise, to sleep, and so forth. That is, a "master plan" embraces the entire time period of the members of the institution. These institutional attributes result in a predominantly bureaucratic society, which requires the hiring of people for surveillance. This leads to a dichotomous split in the people associated with the institution. There is a large, managed group ("inmates") and a small supervisory staff. There tends to be a great social distance between the groups; they perceive one another in stereotyped ways, and communication between the groups is severely restricted.

The world of the "inmate" differs from the normal person's world. When a potential member enters a total institution, previous role relations are greatly disrupted. Roles such as elder brother, son, and the like, temporarily cease. Often the issuance of a uniform, confiscation of belongings, gathering of personal information, and other similar factors result in a depersonalization of the individual. Such subtle devices as doorless toilets, record keeping, and bedchecks also contribute to this depersonalization. Further, residents at some institutions must at times assume humiliating postures, such as standing at attention, lying on the floor, bending over to be spanked, and so forth.

Of course, individual differences are seen in adaptation to this situation. They can be as extreme as psychosis and regression, or as mild as refusal to cooperate. Yet most individuals "adjust" and build up satisfactions within the organization. Among these satisfactions frequently are the development of close friendships and the formation of cliques. Because of this the person faces great problems when he leaves the institution. Often he has not acquired habits he will need in the "outside world." Leaving may be further demoralizing because of a shift from the top of a small society to the bottom of a larger society.

Goffman provides many other fascinating insights concerning total institutions. But the general message of this work is that to comprehend behavior intelligently the environment in which it occurs must be understood.

Level of Aspiration

One of the most influential series of experiments originating from the Lewinian frame of reference concerns "level of aspiration." Level of aspiration refers to goal striving and is a fundamental concept in the analysis of achievement-related behaviors. The grades for which a student strives, his occupational goals, and personal standards concerning how well one should perform in a given situation, all can be considered under the rubric of level of aspiration.

Definition and Basic Terminology.   The most widely accepted definition of level of aspiration is "the level of future performance in a familiar task which an individual, knowing his level of past performance in that task, explicitly undertakes to reach" (Frank, 1935, p. 119). The level of aspiration refers to a statement about goals. Because many goals are possible, one's level of aspiration involves a decision or choice among various alternatives.

Four temporal boundaries are distinguished within a level-of-aspiration situation. (Note that level of aspiration refers here to a methodology. Often the use of the term as a technique as opposed to an attribute of an individual is not clearly distinguished.) The conceptual boundaries for the level-of-aspiration sequence are portrayed in Figure 3:15. For illustrative purposes, assume that an individual is asked to toss rings over a peg from a specified distance. He is first given some familiarization trials, and then ten "test" trials. During the test performance the number of successful tosses are counted. This defines his past performance. In this particular illustration we will assume that he was successful on six of the ten trials. The experimenter then asks this subject to specify his aspiration level for the next trial series. Generally, this question is phrased as: "How many are you going to try to get over the peg in the next series?" Assume that the individual responds, "Eight." This response, in relation to the level of prior performance, is his goal discrepancy score. In this case the person is striving for more $(+2)$ than his previous performance; his discrepancy is described as positive. Of course, he could be striving for less than his prior performance, in which case his discrepancy score would be negative.

associated with success, and a potency linked with failure. A more contemporary view might use the term probability rather than potency. The concept of potency also can be compared to psychological distance; a low potency could be considered as indicating great psychological distance (many steps intervening between the person and his goal), while a high potency could indicate that few instrumental actions are necessary to reach the goal. Lewin, however, did not use the constructs of potency and psychological distance interchangeably. Clearly, one could be many steps from the goal, but each step might have a probability of 1 of being consummated.

Corresponding to each level of difficulty there is a potency of success (Po_s). Similarly, there also is a potency of failure (Po_f) varying with task difficulty. The approach force toward a goal is postulated by Escalona and Festinger to be a function of the valence of success (Va_s) multiplied by the potency of success, while the force away from the goal is postulated to be determined by the negative valence of failure (Va_f) multiplied by the potency of failure. Therefore, the resultant force toward the goal is conceptualized as follows:

$$\text{Resultant force} = (Va_s \times Po_s) - (Va_f \times Po_f)$$

In sum, each alternative can be considered to involve an approach-avoidance conflict between positive and negative forces which are determined by valences and potencies. Choice involves an implicit comparison of all the available alternatives; the choice that has the greatest resultant approach force is expected to be exhibited in action.

A numerical example adapted from Lewin et al. by Atkinson (1964, p. 101) indicates some of the power of this conception. In the example shown in Table 3:3, the valence of success and the valence of failure are given arbitrary values that increase and decrease respectively with the level of task difficulty. Similarly, the potency of success and failure, which range in value from 0 to 100, vary with objective task difficulty. In the illustration it is assumed that on the prior task performance was at level 7. The subsequent choice, that is, the alternative associated with the greatest resultant value, is level 8. Hence, there is a positive goal discrepancy of 1.

It previously was indicated that prior outcomes and motivational dispositions influence the level of aspiration. Two further illustrations are provided to indicate how these factors might be incorporated into the conception. In Table 3:4, we see how choice varies when the potencies of success are systematically increased, as might happen following a success experience. The table shows that the level with the greatest resultant approach force is now alternative "9".

Table 3:5 portrays the situation in which an individual is especially concerned about failure (see Atkinson, 1964, p. 102). The negative

TABLE 3:3

Numerical Illustration of the Determinants of Level of Aspiration (from Atkinson, 1964, p. 101)

Levels of Possible Objective	Tendency to Approach Success Va_{succ}	$\times$ Po_{succ}	$= f_{P,succ}$[1]	Tendency to Avoid Failure Va_{fai}	$\times$ Po_{fai}	$= f_{P,-fai}$[2]	Resultant Tendency $f*_{P,G}$	
15	10	0	0	0	100	0	0	
14	10	0	0	0	100	0	0	
13	10	0	0	0	100	0	0	
12	10	0	0	0	100	0	0	
11	10	5	50	0	95	0	50	Level
10	9	10	90	0	90	0	90	of
9	7	25	175	−1	75	−75	100	aspiration
8	6	40	240	−2	60	−120	120	
7	5	50	250	−3	50	−150	100	Goal discrepancy
6	3	60	180	−5	40	−200	−20	Level of
5	2	75	150	−7	25	−175	−25	past
4	1	90	90	−9	10	−90	0	performance
3	0	95	0	−10	5	−50	−50	
2	0	100	0	−10	0	0	0	
1	0	100	0	−10	0	0	0	

Too difficult (levels 15–12) ↑ · Too easy (levels 3–1) →

[1] Force toward success.

[2] Force away from failure.

[3] Force on the person toward the goal.

TABLE 3:4

Determinants of Level of Aspiration When the Potency of Success Is Relatively High
(adapted from Atkinson, 1964, p. 101)

Levels of Possible Objective	Tendency to Approach Success			Tendency to Avoid Failure			Resultant Tendency $f^*_{P,G}$	
	Va_{succ} ×	Po_{succ} =	$f_{P,succ}$	Va_{fai} ×	Po_{fai} =	$f_{P,-fai}$		
15	10	0	0	0	100	0	0	
14	10	0	0	0	100	0	0	
13	10	0	0	0	100	0	0	
12	10	5	50	0	95	0	50	Level of aspiration
11	10	10	100	0	90	0	100	
10	9	15	135	0	85	0	135	
9	7	40	280	−1	60	−60	220	
8	6	50	300	−2	50	−100	200	Goal discrepancy
7	5	60	300	−3	40	−120	180	
6	3	70	210	−5	30	−150	60	Level of past performance
5	2	80	160	−7	20	−140	−20	
4	1	95	95	−9	5	−45	50	
3	0	100	0	−10	0	−0	−0	
2	0	100	0	−10	0	0	0	
1	0	100	0	−10	0	0	0	

Too difficult ← (levels 15–9)

Too easy → (levels 3–1)

Note: the values of the positive and negative valences of failure are the same as in Table 3:3.

TABLE 3:5
Determinants of Level of Aspiration When the Negative Valence of Failure Is Relatively High
(from Atkinson, 1964, p. 102)

Levels of Possible Objective	Tendency to Approach Success			Tendency to Avoid Failure			Resultant Tendency	
	Va_{succ} ×	Po_{succ} =	$f_{P,succ}$	Va_{fai} ×	Po_{fai} =	$f_{P,-fai}$	$f^{*}_{P,G}$	
15	10	0	0	0	100	0	0	
14	10	0	0	0	100	0	0	
13	10	0	0	0	100	0	0	
12	10	0	0	0	100	0	0	Level of aspiration
11	10	5	50	0	95	0	50	
10	9	10	90	0	90	0	90	
9	7	25	175	−2	75	−150	25	Goal discrepancy
8	6	40	240	−4	60	−240	0	
7	5	50	250	−6	50	−300	−50	
6	3	60	180	−10	40	−400	−220	Level of past performance
5	2	75	150	−14	25	−350	−200	
4	1	90	90	−18	10	−180	−90	
3	0	95	0	−20	5	−100	−100	
2	0	100	0	−20	0	0	0	
1	0	100	0	−20	0	0	0	

Too difficult (levels 15, 14, 13 …)

Too easy (… levels 3, 2, 1)

Note: The values of subjective probability of success and failure are the same as in Table 3:3, but the negative valence of failure is doubled.

valence of failure is doubled in comparison to that shown in the prior illustrations. The table indicates a surprising result. Although fear of failure increases, the level of aspiration actually rises three steps. This captures conceptually the unrealistic goal striving that sometimes is exhibited by individuals with histories of failure and motivational deficiencies in the area of achievement. Level of aspiration will be discussed further in Chapters IV–VI.

In sum, the conceptual scheme of Festinger and Escalona is able to account parsimoniously for much of the reported level of aspiration data.[6] The resultant valence theory proved to be one of the key advances necessary for the analysis of achievement motivation, which is discussed in the following chapter.

SUMMARY

The development of Lewin's theory has been traced, beginning with Gestalt psychology, progressing through the Lewin-Ach controversy, and ending with his formal motivational system. Lewin's conception of motivation contains structural and dynamic constructs for the person and the environment. The concept of tension attempts to integrate the person and environment constructs. Tension results in an environmental object being imbued with a valence. The valence establishes a force field, and the force acts on the person to locomote toward the goal object. Tension is released when the goal is attained, reducing the valence of the environmental object and diminishing the force acting on the person, thus causing a cessation of behavior.

A series of unique experiments was designed to provide empirical support for this conception of behavior. The investigations include the recall and resumption of interrupted tasks (Zeigarnik and Ovsiankina), substitution of goal objects (Mahler and Henle), and investigations of satiation and cosatiation. While these areas of investigation all lend credence to the Lewinian conception, the empirical results are open to criticism. The study of task recall does not provide clear evidence for the postulation of persistent tense states, for the experimental design confounds learning (trace formation) with memory (trace storage and retrieval). In addition, a significant subpopulation of individuals recall more completed than incom-

---

[6] The resultant valence conception is better at postdiction than prediction. It is evident that minor changes in the valence or potency factors in the Tables 3:3, 3:4, and 3:5 would greatly alter the expected choice behavior. Thus, it is easier to "explain" or "understand" aspiration choice than it is to specify subsequent behavior.

pleted tasks (Rosenzweig, Atkinson). Studies of task resumption also provide only questionable support for Lewin's theory, inasmuch as the data suggest that a scalar representing force, rather than tension, persists following nonattainment of a goal. Further, although the investigations of substitution do support Lewin's belief in the interrelationship of need systems, few experimental studies have been conducted. It also appears that goal attainment produces an instigation rather than a decrement in behavior for a subpopulation of persons (Weiner). Finally, the studies of satiation and cosatiation are too few to add any evidence for or against the conception. Thus, it is concluded that the data base for the theory is very weak. In addition, the chapter includes a discussion of research not immediately related to Lewin's formal theory of motivation. These studies pertain to psychological ecology, or the influence of physical factors in the world upon behavior (Barker and Goffman), and an examination of level of aspiration (Festinger and Escalona).

Many similarities and differences between the Hullian and Lewinian schemes have been pointed out. Both conceptions delineate the immediate determinations of action, and include motivational states of the person (drive, tension), the incentive value of the goal (G, K), and a learning component (habit, psychological distance). But the amount of data and the source of evidence supporting the two conceptions greatly differs. Drive theorists primarily have gathered their data from well-controlled experiments with infrahuman subjects. On the other hand, Lewinians have almost exclusively concerned themselves with human behavior. The differences in subject populations, complexity of the observed behaviors, and preciseness of the conceptions are in part responsible for the inequality in the quantity and exactness of the empirical data supporting the conceptions. This disparity is conveyed by the number of tables and figures containing empirical evidence in Chapter II, as compared with this chapter. There is, however, an asymmetry in the extensity of the conceptions which perhaps redresses the empirical imbalance. Lewin incorporated some of the basic results supporting Hullian theory within the framework of field theory, although the more sophisticated predictions from drive theory, such as those derived by Spence in forced versus free-response experiments, are not amenable to explanation within Lewinian theory. However, Hull and Spence would not be able to deal with the Lewinian studies of task resumption and recall, substitution, and so forth. There also is an important difference between the "flavors" of the Hullian and Lewinian scheme. One can sense that Hull and Lewin conceived of a "complete psychology of motivation" in quite disparate ways. Undoubtedly, this is because of the mechanistic versus cognitive orientation of these theorists.

There is no clear alternate conception to explain the data generated by field theorists, such as the role of "pure" associationism in interpretating the data of drive theorists. Further, there cannot be any "definitive" experiments in connection with this conception. Field theory grew little over time, did not have many followers to enhance the formal conception, and gathered a sparse amount of supporting data. Yet the conception is unique. It provided the powerful tool of a new language for motivational psychology, opened up new research areas, and demonstrated that psychodynamics is a legitimate field of experimental study. If drive theorists demonstrated how motivational psychologists "ought" to operate as experimenters, then field theorists pointed out the broader goals of motivational theory—an understanding of complex "everyday" behavior, within a conceptual framework able to explain as well the simple behavior of infrahumans.

IV

Achievement Theory

Achievement theory, like field theory, is a cognitive theory. It assumes that one's beliefs about the likelihood of attaining a goal (success at an achievement task) mediate between the perception of the task stimulus and the final achievement-related response. In the mechanistic tradition of drive theory, however, an attempt is made to predict with great precision a rather limited domain of behavior. Atkinson's model of achievement motivation, which we will discuss in this chapter, is perhaps the only cognitive theory of motivation with this virtue. Yet, as in the Lewinian (field) theory, achievement models pay relatively little attention to cognitive processes, and it is believed that both Lewin's (field) and Atkinson's (achievement) theories are best labeled quasi-cognitive.

HISTORICAL EVOLUTION

The construct of drive came into prominence in the 1920s because the instinct doctrine was no longer accepted by psychologists. Initially drive, like instinct, was related to the common-sense conception of a need; drive and need often were either used interchangeably or were linked somehow. For example, Hull considered drive the psychological manifestation of a need state. Over time, however, drives became identified with states of deprivation, neobehaviorism, and research employing infrahuman organisms, while the concept of need became incorporated by molar personality theorists and began to signify more stable characteristics of individuals.

Henry Murray

Henry Murray is important in the present context because he was a central influence in achievement motivation research and in the development of achievement theory. Murray based his theory of behavior on the concept of "need." The definition of need generally accepted by personality theorists is conveyed in the following quote from Murray (1938):

Though each [need] is unique, observation teaches that there are similarities among them, and on the basis of this, needs may be grouped together into classes; each class being, as it were, a single major need. Thus, we may speak of similar needs as being different exhibitions of one need, just as when we recognize a friend we do not hesitate to call him by name though he is different from the person with whom we conversed yesterday. . . . We may loosely use the term "need" to refer to an organic potentiality or readiness to respond in a certain way under given conditions. In this sense a need is a latent attribute of an organism. More strictly, it is a noun which stands for the fact that a certain trend is apt to recur. We have not found that any confusion arises when we use "need" at one time to refer to a temporary happening and at another to refer to a more or less consistent trait of personality [pp. 60–61].

Murray's Approach to Psychology.   Unlike the systems of Hull and Lewin, Murray's theoretical conception is influenced more by biological than physical models. Murray (1959) writes:

In my persistent efforts to move, step by step, toward an adequate solution to . . . [behavioral] problems, I was greatly assisted by the reported observations and formulations of biologists from Darwin on, and of others, particularly McDougall, who had used the concept of instinct as their tool [p. 20].

At a later point in the same article, Murray cautions against the exclusive use of the model provided by physics to explain psychological phenomena:

Besides many other things, this meant to me (with my memories of chemistry) that a psychologist will bring in less knowledge by viewing a person as a mass-point of indifferent constitution in a field of forces, as Lewin (with his interest in physics and his image of Galileo at the tower) was tempted to do, than he will by viewing him as an entity with a particular conjunction of distinguishable properties. It is, of course, true that in establishing some sorts of lawful relationships between entities it is possible to disregard differences of constitution, but even in physics, how often can one predict the outcome of an experiment without taking into account the internal structure of the molecule or such properties of substances as conductivity or melting point? [pp. 28–29].

Murray did not contend that behavior could be explained given only knowledge of the needs or personality structure of the actor. As in the Lewinian scheme, he considered behavior a function of the characteristics of the environment as well as of the properties of the person. Murray (1938) states:

Since, at every moment, an organism is within an environment which largely determines its behavior, and since the environment changes—sometimes with radical abruptness—the conduct of an individual cannot be formulated without a characterization of each confronting situation, physical and social. It is important to define the environment since two organisms may behave differently only because they are, by chance, encountering different conditions. . . . For these reasons, the organism and its milieu must be considered together, a single creature-environment interaction being a convenient short unit for psychology [pp. 39–40].

According to Murray, the environment can provide the necessary support for the expression of a need, or it can contain barriers that impede goal-directed behavior. The environmental "press" acting in conjunction with a need determines the duration of a "behavioral episode," or the psychological time necessary to attain a goal. Murray, following Lewin, also differentiates the perceived environment (beta press) from the objective environment (alpha press).

Murray's behavioral theory contains many constructs and is more complex than we need discuss here. He draws freely on the insights of Freud and Jung and was influenced by sociologists and anthropologists. Further, he was trained in medicine and biology; he attributes his conception of an active, growing organism to this instruction. His conception is in opposition to the Hullian view of a passive organism responding merely to reduce incoming stimulation.

Although Murray examined many issues within psychology, his main contributions lay in the field of personality assessment. Murray retained an overriding interest in personality description, with his view of the person as "an entity with a particular conjunction of distinguishable properties" (1959, p. 29), and he developed an extensive taxonomy of needs. These needs apparently are derived from physiological deficits, but represent relatively enduring personality characteristics. Included in the list are the needs for achievement, aggression, and autonomy, for example.

The need for achievement, which is the focus of the present chapter, Murray (1938) describes as

the desire or tendency to do things as rapidly and/or as well as possible. [It also includes the desire] to accomplish something difficult. To master, manipulate and organize physical objects, human beings, or ideas. To do this as rapidly, and as independently, as possible. To overcome obstacles and attain a high standard. To excel one's self. To rival and surpass others. To increase self-regard by the successful exercise of talent [p. 164].

To determine the strength of the various needs, Murray advocated a "multiform" method of personality assessment. He believed that full knowledge about a person is ascertained only when that individual is evaluated by many social scientists representing different theoretical viewpoints and utilizing different descriptive techniques. Murray employed this method at the Harvard Clinic, which he directed, and in his well-known assessment program for the Armed Forces Office of Strategic Services (OSS) (OSS Assessment Staff, 1948).

The Thematic Apperception Test (TAT).   Murray is perhaps best known as the originator of the Thematic Apperception Test (TAT). In that method of personality assessment an individual writes or relates stories to ambiguous pictures. The content of the story projections is used to infer the personality and areas of conflict of the story teller. Murray (1938) describes the TAT:

The purpose of this procedure is to stimulate literary creativity and thereby evoke fantasies that reveal covert and unconscious complexes.

The test is based upon the well-recognized fact that when a person interprets an ambiguous social situation he is apt to expose his own personality as much as the phenomenon to which he is attending. Absorbed in his attempt to explain the objective occurrence, he becomes naively unconscious of himself and of the scrutiny of others and, therefore, defensively less vigilant. To one with double hearing, however, he is disclosing certain inner tendencies and cathexes: wishes, fears, and traces of past experiences. Another fact which was relied upon in devising the present method is this: that a great deal of written fiction is the conscious or unconscious expression of the author's experiences or fantasies. [Murray shared with his mentor, Jung, a great interest in literature, and wrote an insightful interpretation of Melville's "Moby Dick."]

The original plan was to present subjects with a series of pictures each of which depicted a dramatic event of some sort with instructions to interpret the action in each picture and make a plausible guess as to the preceding events and final outcome. It was anticipated that in the performance of this task a subject would necessarily be forced to project some of his own fantasies into the material and thus reveal his more prevailing thematic tendencies. As the subjects who took this test were asked to interpret each picture—that is, to apperceive the plot or dramatic structure exhibited by each picture—we named it the "Thematic Apperception Test." Only by experience did we discover that much more of the personality is revealed if the *S* is asked to create a dramatic fiction rather than to guess the probable facts [pp. 530–31].

The TAT ranks among the most widely used instruments of personality assessment in both clinical and research settings. It is employed by David McClelland, John Atkinson, and other workers in the area of achievement motivation to assess the strength of the need for achievement.

McClelland's Theory of Personality and Motivation

David McClelland was greatly influenced by Murray. McClelland's molar approach to personality, his desire to examine all the facts about the person, and his interest in need systems and the measurement of those needs all attest to Murray's formative guidance.

In McClelland's (1951) relatively early work in personality, motives, traits, and schema are distinguished. Motives, he states, determine why people behave as they do; they are the genotypes of behavior. Traits describe "consistencies in behavior or the mode of adjustment which the subject habitually adopts to meet recurrent situations. . . . the trait construct account(s) for the how of behavior" (McClelland, 1956, p. 352). Schema refer to the person's conceptions and attitudes toward the world and himself. Schema involve ideas, values, attitudes, and attributions. In sum, motives are the causes of behavior, traits are the method of motive expression, and schema are cognitions about the self and others.

Inasmuch as motives are conceived by McClelland as "the springs of action" (from James, 1890), they are the central constructs in his analysis of behavior. A motive is construed as "the redintegration by a cue of a change in an affective situation" (McClelland et al., 1953, p. 28). McClelland contends that throughout life certain stimulus situations become associated with affective states. The hot stove elicits fear because it has been associated with pain; tasks are associated with positive affect (pride) or negative affect (shame) because they have led to such feelings in past encounters. The reappearance of meaningful cues, such as the hot stove or an achievement task, arouses affective states that, in turn, elicit instrumental approach or avoidance behavior. That is, anticipatory goal reactions, or emotions, learned from prior cue-affect associations, energize and direct behavior. Hence, "emotions are not motives, but they are the basis for motives" (McClelland, 1951, p. 466). [The reader is referred to Mowrer (1960) for an elaboration of this position.]

McClelland (1951) further believes that motives

involve two points on an affective continuum: a present state (either positive, negative, or neutral) which redintegrates through past learning a second state involving an increase or decrease in pleasure or pain over the present state [p. 467].

Motives, therefore, are aroused in situations in which there are discrepancies between the present affective condition and an expected affective state.

Perhaps McClelland's definition of a motive—"the redintegration by a cue of a change in an affective state" (McClelland et al., 1953, p. 28)—is now somewhat clearer. Stimuli arouse anticipations of affect which may differ from the present affective state. These affective expectations are learned from prior experiences and automatically are reproduced in the presence of stimuli similar to those present during the time of original learning. The discrepancy between the present and future affective states leads to approach or avoidance behavior.

McClelland labels this conception of motivation an *affective arousal model*. In distinction to the drive conception, the model incorporates the hedonic quality of behavior. Behavior is not merely undertaken "in order to" avoid unpleasant states. In further distinction to the drive conception, all motivations, including hunger drives, are learned. Primary and secondary drives, or viscerogenic and psychogenic needs, are not differentiated in his system; complex human needs are not derived from primary need deficits. Finally, motives do not only energize behavior. They also have associative or directional properties, and guide the organism towards particular end states or goals. Thus, motives are conceptually similar to Spence's conception of incentives (r_g-s_g), for incentives also are learned, involve goal anticipations, and direct the organism.

Although McClelland does not conceive of organisms as merely striving to reduce needs, he does employ an equilibrium model. However, equilibrium does not necessitate a reduction in the level of stimulation. McClelland is an "optimal level" theorist. However, unlike Freud and Hull, he believes the optimal level of stimulation is at some point greater than zero. It is postulated that if stimulation is above that level, instrumental action is undertaken to reduce the amount of stimulation, but if stimulation is below the optimal level, action is initiated to increase the amount of incoming sensation (see Hebb, 1949).

The motive most thoroughly examined by McClelland and his colleagues has been the achievement motive, or the need for achievement. This motivational tendency refers to the positive or negative anticipatory goal reactions aroused in situations that involve competition with a standard of excellence, where performance may be evaluated as a success or a failure.

ACHIEVEMENT MOTIVATION

There are a number of different phases in the study of achievement motivation. Initially there was the attempt by McClelland, Atkinson, Clark, and Lowell (1953) to assess individual differences in the strength of the achievement motive, using the fantasy measure (TAT) devised by Murray. Then a vast amount of data was gathered to provide empirical support for the validity of the TAT measure by relating the attained motive scores to various behavioral indices. At the same time, there were attempts to find the childrearing antecedents and the sociological correlates of achievement motivation. Then a theory of achievement motivation was formulated, and a great deal of research was generated to validate that conception. Finally, more recent work has focused upon changes in the initial theory of achievement motivation, the effects of achievement concerns upon economic development, and programs to change an individual's level of achievement needs. This chapter primarily is concerned with the theoretical conception that emerged from the study of achievement motivation, although most of the issues mentioned above are considered. Further, the theory-application gap relatively neglected in the two previous chapters is examined, and the educational implications of achievement theory are probed.

Assessment of the Need for Achievement

Psychologists are more concerned with the study of behavior than with the study of consciousness or thoughts. Further, when interests have turned toward thought processes, the contents of the thoughts generally are neglected in favor of an understanding of the thought process per se. The attempt to measure the need for achievement is a reversal of these research directions, for the method of assessment reveals what a person is thinking about. That is, the *content,* rather than the *process,* of thoughts is being investigated (see McClelland, 1955).

As indicated, McClelland et al. (1953) employ a TAT when measuring the need for achievement. The rationale for this choice is conveyed in the following quotes from McClelland:

To begin with, most clinicians have found that fantastic [unreal] material is the best hunting ground for motivational analyses. Freud got his start in analyzing free associations and dreams; he then went on to apply similar methods of interpretation to other such unrealistic or odd behavior as slips of the tongue, memory losses, parapraxes, etc. Murray, who has been perhaps the most influential exponent of motivational analysis in America, has had his greatest success in analyzing controlled daydreams or imaginative productions produced for his Thematic Apperception Test. The reason for the apparently unique value of imaginative material for dynamic analysis probably lies in the fact that fantasy is by definition less influenced by the autochthonous, culture-pattern variables that produce schemata and less influenced also by the past learned responses (traits) of the subjects [1951, p. 412].

Here again [in the measurement of motives] one may be guided by the experiences of the psychoanalysts. After all, theirs is largely a dynamic or motivational psychology based almost exclusively on a single method of measurement—e.g., content analysis of free associations produced in the therapeutic session. Perhaps it is the method of measurement—informal and intuitive though it often is, to be sure—which led to the best understanding of human motivation as yet available. It was this argument that led to an attempt to use more formally and systematically the psychoanalytic method of measuring motivation [1956. p. 332].

The clinical method employed by therapists to determine the existence of motivations and conflicts was not adopted in toto. The frequent ad hoc interpretations of TAT protocols, at times useful in clinical diagnoses, could not be employed when the instrument was administered to groups of individuals not known to the experimenter. McClelland and his co-workers also realized that many of the principles of measurement specified by psychometrists had to be met for the instrument to be useful in research settings. For example, the measure needed to have inter-rater reliability. That is, judges must agree on the scoring of the fantasy content. Often this is not the case when the TAT is used for diagnostic purposes (see Zubin, Eron, & Schumer, 1965). Finally, a quantitative score or numerical value representing the strength of the need was required so that individuals could be ordered according to the magnitude of their achievement concerns. The numerical value could then be related to other behavioral indicators to discover if a meaningful motivational index had been devised. Such precision generally is not sought in clinical diagnoses. In sum, a number of changes had to be instituted when adopting the TAT as a research instrument. The TAT measurement procedure is first discussed before answering whether McClelland et al. successfully overcame some of the problems associated with the use of this projective technique.

Measuring Procedure.   Atkinson (1964) describes the TAT measure and the method of administration:

The method established . . . has been repeatedly employed, with very minor changes. . . . The procedures developed by Murray for individual testing with the TAT were adapted so that pictures could be projected on a screen in a group situation and stories written instead of told to an examiner. A series of pictures . . . were selected from some of Murray's original set of TAT pictures and from ordinary magazines. Following a general instruction that the task was to construct interesting and imaginative stories, each picture was shown 20 seconds and then withdrawn. The subjects were then given four minutes to write a story about the picture. The general questions that are normally given verbally in clinical use of thematic apperception were printed at equal intervals on otherwise blank story forms to guide subjects through the plot of a story. The guiding questions were:

   1. What is happening? Who are the persons?
   2. What has led up to this situation; that is, what has happened in the past?
   3. What is being thought? What is wanted; by whom?
   4. What will happen? What will be done?

As soon as the four minutes allotted for writing a story was up, another picture was shown. This procedure continued for 16 to 32 minutes, depending upon the number of pictures employed. It produced a substantial "thought sample," or sample of imaginative behavior, induced by certain picture cues under controlled motivating conditions [p. 223].

The TAT protocols are then scored according to a method of content analysis originated by McClelland and his group. The general scoring procedure is similar when measuring any motive (achievement, affiliation, power), although the specific content scored naturally differs for the various motives.

Scoring Procedure.   When scoring the protocols for achievement needs, each story written to a TAT picture receives from minus one to eleven points. An individual's total achievement score is the sum of his scores on each picture. The initial step in the scoring procedure is to decide whether the story written meets the criteria necessary to be considered achievement imagery. If it meets these criteria, then the story receives a score of one, and the scorer proceeds to examine ten achievement subcategories. If the story does not contain achievement imagery, it receives a score of zero or minus one, and none of the subcategories are scored. Thus, the initial imagery decisions greatly determine the inter-rater reliability of the instrument.

A story is considered to have achievement imagery if it contains some reference to competition with a standard of excellence. Atkinson (1958), guided by the scoring procedure outlined in McClelland, Atkinson, Clark, and Lowell (1953), states:

> Competition with a standard of excellence is perhaps most clear when one of the characters is engaged in competitive activity (other than pure aggression) where winning or doing as well or better than someone else is the primary concern. Often, however, competition with a standard of excellence is evident in the concern of one of the characters with how well a particular task is being done, regardless of how well someone else is doing. Any use of adjectives of degree (good, better, best) will qualify so long as they evaluate the excellence of performance [p. 181].

Achievement imagery also is scored if a story includes a unique accomplishment (an invention, an artistic act), a long-term achievement goal (becoming a doctor, being a success in life), or any indication that strong affect and/or instrumental actions are associated with the attainment of achievement-related goals.

The following content analysis illustrates the scoring scheme and criteria. Assume that the story protocol was written in response to the picture depicted here. This particular picture frequently is used for achievement need assessment, although it is possible to use any of a number of specific pictures (see Atkinson, 1958). Many of these pictures were selected from popular magazines, and are not part of the initial set devised by Murray (1943).

> Two inventors are working on a new type of machine. They need this machine in order to complete the work on their new invention, the automobile. This takes place some time ago, and the necessary tools are not available. They are thinking that they will succeed. They want to do a good job, and improve transportation. After years of hard work they are successful, and feel elated (from McClelland et al., 1953, p. 118).

This story is scored for achievement imagery because there is pursuit of a unique accomplishment (invention of the automobile). But it also meets the criteria of achievement imagery because there is positive affect (elation) coupled with an unusual amount of instrumental activity (years of hard work). Thus, the figures in the picture are perceived as competing with a standard of excellence. Although this story was "rigged" for illustrative purposes, it is not unlike actual stories written in response to this particular picture.

After a story is judged as containing achievement imagery, it is scored for a number of achievement subcategories. Each of the subcategories receives a score of one point. Among the ten subcategories represented in the above story are: need (they *want* to do a good job), instrumental activity (years of *hard work*), positive affect (they feel *elated*), positive

Picture often used in the TAT assessment of need for achievement.

goal anticipation (they are *thinking* that they *will succeed*), blocks or impediments in the world (tools are *not available*), and thema (a point given when only achievement motivation is represented in the story). Thus, this particular response would receive a score of seven points, one for achievement imagery plus six for the six subcategories scored.

Four other subcategories scorable in the content analysis of achievement motivation are not present in the above story: negative affect (they *feel unhappy*), negative goal anticipation (they are *thinking* they *will fail*), blocks in the person (they *cannot concentrate* on their work), and nurturant press (someone aids the characters to reach their goal; as, for example, a friend *encourages them* to continue).

The particular content scored is clearly described in McClelland et al. (1953) and Atkinson (1958). Inter-rater reliability, generally considered the degree of rank-order scoring agreement between two judges, can readily attain the rho = .80 to .90 level. Further, each subject receives a numerical score expressing the strength of his achievement needs. Thus, the problems outlined earlier associated with the TAT—that is, the lack of interjudge reliability and the absence of quantitative values—are overcome by this method of content analysis.

The Arousal of Motivation

The initial experiment, which was in part responsible for the development of the scoring scheme for achievement needs, involved the manipulation of hours of food deprivation (Atkinson & McClelland, 1948). Hunger was chosen as the initial source of motivation to manipulate because it is generally agreed that the operational definition of hunger is hours of food deprivation. In the Atkinson and McClelland experiment, subjects wrote TAT stories following either 1, 4, or 16 hours of food deprivation. Recall McClelland specifies that a motive is linked with an affective state aroused by certain stimuli. The cues associated with food deprivation are conceived as persistent internal stimuli. In the history of the subjects it was assumed that these cues have been followed by "the sensory pleasure of eating and the subsequent affective change when food is digested" (Atkinson, 1954, p. 60). Hence, different states of deprivation were expected to arouse different intensities of goal anticipations, or motivation. If the TAT is sensitive to motivational arousal, or need strength, then the differential concerns over food should be exhibited differentially in the content of the TAT protocols.

The results of the study are complex, and do not definitively support the hypothesized need-fantasy relationship. Some of the scoring content categories (such as food imagery) were not systematically related to time of deprivation. But other categories (such as instrumental activity, deprivation thema) increased either monotonically or curvilinearly as a function of deprivation. It might be anticipated that individuals rarely experience 16 hours of deprivation, and thus the greatest affective anticipations would be aroused following 4 hours of deprivation; see the experiment by Birch et al. (1958) discussed in Chapter II. It was therefore concluded that "the general results of this study encouraged the belief that thematic apperceptive content was, indeed, sensitive to motivational influences" (Atkinson, 1964, p. 224).

A series of studies then followed that investigated the relationship between fantasy expression and aroused psychogenic needs. The advance of these studies over prior investigations manipulating hours of food deprivation is noted by Atkinson and McClelland (1948):

It has been shown how these clues [fantasy content] can be combined into a composite numerical score which gives a pretty good indication for most of the Ss of how long they have been without food. Naturally it is hoped that this procedure will have a much wider significance than could be attached to the determination of hunger from the Ss' stories. It would be much simpler to ask the Ss when they last ate! The results become of major importance only if changes occur in the same way in the same categories of response with other experimentally induced needs—particularly psychogenic ones [p. 654].

The general procedure in the subsequent studies arousing psychogenic needs, such as affiliation, power, and learned fear, followed the logic in the original investigation of the effects of food deprivation on fantasy expression. In the study of affilative motivation, for example, affiliation was aroused by having fraternity members rate one another, while all were present, on a sociometric friendship index (Shipley & Veroff, 1952). In addition, each fraternity brother was required to stand and be rated by the other members of the fraternity on a list of trait adjectives. After this rather harrowing experience the TAT was administered, and affiliative need expression was compared with a control condition in which affiliation was not stimulated.

To obtain TAT protocols following the arousal of power needs, students running for a school office wrote stories to TAT pictures immediately prior to the counting of the election ballots. Veroff (1957) believes that this is a valid arousal condition for power motivation because

in the phenomenal sphere of the power motivated individual, he considers himself to be the "gatekeeper" to certain decision-making of others. The means of control can be anything at all that can be used to manipulate another person. Overt dominance strivings can be considered one kind of control execution [p. 1].

It was then determined whether this "real-life" arousal manipulation increased power imagery expression on the TAT relative to a control condition in which power needs were not aroused.

The effects of fear arousal on fantasy expression were investigated by administering TATs to soldiers varying in their physical and temporal proximity from an atomic-bomb explosion (Walker & Atkinson, 1958). It was assumed that lessening the temporal and spatial distance from the blast increases the magnitude of aroused fear (see Chapter II).

The general finding in the affiliation, power, and fear studies was that more need-related imagery is expressed under aroused than neutral conditions. In sum, the TAT reflects psychogenic as well as viscerogenic needs, and apparently is sensitive to a variety of motivational states.

Motive Arousal Cues. The stimuli assumed to arouse affiliation, power, and fear are external to the organism; those associated with hunger, on the other hand, are internal deprivation cues. These internal or external stimuli, in conjunction with the cues on the TAT card, are believed to influence the amount of need imagery in the story protocols. Concerning the multiple sources of cues that affect need expression, Atkinson (1954) comments,

We have pointed to three classes of cues which influence the frequency of imaginative responses from which motive strength is inferred: (1) cues

in the every-day environment or in the relatively autonomous thought processes of the individual; (2) specific experimentally introduced cues; (3)
the controllable cues in a particular picture. Cues of class 1 and 2 were
presumed to arouse a motive by virtue of prior association with affective
changes accompanying certain activities. Picture cues, on the other hand,
were viewed as providing an occasion for the expression of thoughts accompanying the arousal of a motive to the extent that the pictures themselves aroused similar associations [pp. 82–83].

In the arousal studies reviewed above, the experimentally induced
cues are manipulated between conditions, and differences in need imagery
are attributed to the motivational consequences of those stimuli. The controllable picture cues and cues brought into the situation by the individuals
were not varied or investigated. In later studies the individual becomes
the focus of attention, and "cues in the autonomous thought processes"
are of primary concern.

Motive Arousal and Avoidance Tendencies.   An arousal study involving sexual needs (Clark, 1952) yielded additional results having important implications for motivational theory and the assessment of motives.
Clark employed the usual arousal versus nonarousal paradigm to study
the effects of sexual arousal on TAT need imagery. To stimulate sexual
motivation, Clark showed his male subjects pictures of nude females. Then
he administered the TAT and scored the protocols according to the method
of content analysis already described. In contrast to the other arousal
studies, Clark found less need imagery in the arousal than the nonarousal condition. That is, the arousal procedure produced a decrement,
rather than an increment, in the amount of expressed need-related
imagery.

These results led Clark to believe that more guilt feelings (avoidance
motivation) than sexual needs (approach motivation) were aroused by the
experimental procedure. The Miller conflict model discussed in Chapter
II specifies that the gradient of avoidance motivation is steeper than the
gradient of approach. Hence, any movement toward the goal that is beyond
the point of equilibrium increases the avoidance tendency to a greater extent than the increase in the approach tendency. This could result in less
expression of needs, perhaps even on the level of fantasy. Clark contended that the direct sexual confrontation in his experiments suppressed
need expression because the subjects were brought "too close" to the
goal.

To provide evidence for this explanation, Clark conducted the study
again, but slightly modified his experimental procedure. In the second experiment the arousal manipulation occurred in a permissive atmosphere

(a fraternity party) at which alcoholic beverages were served. Because prior research had demonstrated that alcohol consumption reduces the tendency to fear an aversive stimulus (Conger, 1951), it was expected that when students were under the influence of alcohol their sexual anxiety would be minimized and the arousal procedure would result in increased expression of sexual needs on the TAT. Clark's results confirmed this hypothesis.

The Arousal of Achievement Needs

The initial study of achievement needs adhered to the general experimental procedure already outlined. To affect the level of aroused achievement needs two factors were manipulated: the instructions to students before an examination and the feedback from the exam. In the arousal condition, subjects were told that they were about to take tests which would

directly indicate a person's general level of intelligence. . . . in addition to general intelligence, they bring out an individual's capacity to organize material, his ability to evaluate situations quickly and accurately; in short, these tests demonstrate whether or not a person is suited to be a leader [McClelland, Clark, Roby, & Atkinson, 1949, p. 243].

In a second (relaxed) condition the subjects merely were told that some tests were being developed; in a third (neutral) condition there was no experimental attempt to increase or decrease the achievement motivation of the subjects.

There were also three degrees of exam success. This feedback was administered only following the achievement-oriented (arousal) instruction. Subjects in one condition were given false information that they had failed. In a second condition success feedback was given; in a third condition subjects were told they did well on one part of the test but poorly on a second part. Success and failure were varied between conditions because they appeared to provide a direct analogy with the manipulation in the hunger study—failure corresponds to a state of achievement deprivation and success to a state of achievement satiation.

Following the instructions with and without false feedback, the subjects wrote stories to TAT pictures. The general results indicated that achievement scores were higher in the aroused than relaxed condition, with the amount of achievement imagery in the neutral condition falling between these two extremes. Further, achievement imagery was greater following failure than success feedback, although the amount of imagery in the success-failure condition slightly exceeded that in the failure-only condition. Thus, the general pattern of results supported the hypothesis that achievement needs also are reflected in fantasy expression.

Individual Differences in Motive Strength

The studies reviewed above indicate that a variety of motivations (achievement, affiliation, fear, power, sex) are augmented given certain environmental conditions. That is, behavior, or TAT need expression, is a function of the stimulus situation.

The next phase in this research program examined whether the TAT also is sensitive to individual differences in need strength. That is, given the identical environmental cues, are there some individuals more aroused than others? And, if so, would this state of arousal be exhibited in TAT fantasy productions?

The theoretical shift in need research from environmental variation to individual difference inference also characterized the Hull-Spence program of research. Studies generated by the Drive $\times$ Habit conception first demonstrated that response strength is, for example, a function of the intensity of an unconditioned aversive shock stimulus. The strength of the shock operationally defined the level of induced drive. A measure of drive, the MA scale, was then devised to assess an individual's characteristic level of emotional arousal in stressful situations. Given an identical level of shock, it was demonstrated that some individuals react as if that shock were more intense than other individuals.

In sum, both the later research generated by the Drive $\times$ Habit conception, and the study of achievement motivation, adhered to the Lewinian programmatic statement that behavior is a function of the properties of the person and the characteristics of the environment. Both research areas initially manipulated experimental conditions and then moved to the study of individual differences in reaction to environmental stimuli. Although the Drive $\times$ Habit conception preceded the study of achievement motivation, individual difference research in achievement motivation came prior to the development of the MA scale.

THE TAT AS A MEASURE OF ACHIEVEMENT MOTIVATION

Has it been demonstrated that the TAT validly assesses individual differences in the level of achievement motivation? To answer this question we must consider the various types of validity that test constructors have identified and each validity must be examined separately. In the following pages the content, criterion (empirical), and construct validity of the TAT as a measure of achievement needs is examined.

Content Validity

Content validity, according to the American Psychological Association (1954),

is demonstrated by showing how well the content of the test samples the class of situations or subject matter about which conclusions are to be drawn [p. 13].

Although content validity is most appropriate in the evaluation of proficiency measures, it also is an important consideration in achievement motive assessment. Individuals manifest achievement-oriented tendencies in different situations. Athletes strive for success on the athletic field, while scientists work in the laboratory to accomplish their goals. It has been demonstrated that TAT pictures depicting scenes of subjects' major field of concentration in college elicit more imagery than pictures unrelated to their major field (Rosenstein, 1952). Because individuals are differentially sensitive to dissimilar TAT picture cues, an accurate measure of a subject's *general* tendency to strive for success must be free of specific cue effects.

One possible means of obtaining general achievement motive scores free of specific picture content cues is to sample the domain of possible achievement areas and include a picture depicting each or many areas in the assessment procedure. An attempt to sample from a variety of achievement areas apparently has guided the selection of TAT pictures. Atkinson (1958a) writes:

If it were plausible to assume that the expectancies aroused by the distinctive cues of a particular picture were the same for all subjects, it would be reasonable to treat differences in the frequency of a particular kind of motivational content appearing in stories written to that picture as a fair index of the strength of the motive in various individuals. If, in other words, the expectancies aroused by a picture were constant for all subjects, then observed differences in a particular kind of motivational content could be directly attributed to differences in the strength of the motive. We need not make this assumption, however, since the index we use as our estimate of the strength of a motive is the total score obtained from a series of pictures. The total score, as you will recall, is a summation of a particular kind of motivational content which appears in *all* the stories the individual has written. To infer differences in the strength of motive from differences in total motivation score, we need only assume that the *average strength* of a particular expectancy (e.g., the expectancy of achievement, or of power, etc.) aroused by *all* of the pictures in the series is approximately equal for all subjects. When such an assumption is warranted, every subject has had a fair opportunity to reveal his motive in the test as a whole [p. 609].

Later in that chapter Atkinson goes on to state that

If it is actually possible to obtain an independent measure of the particular cognitive expectancies aroused by both the situation and picture cues, the experimenter will be in a position to loosen his control of the physical stimuli and substitute instead his readings taken on the cognitive meanings of these stimuli for particular subjects or particular groups of subjects. *The ideal test of strength of a particular motive may ultimately consist of different pictures for different individuals—pictures more alike in the expectancies they arouse than in their physical properties* [p. 615].

Atkinson's statements reveal that individuals involved in the assessment of achievement motivation are aware of the problem of controlling picture cues, and sampling from the domain of achievement situations. However, the APA's (1954) "Technical Recommendations" specify that

If a test performance is to be interpreted as a sample of performance or a definition of performance in some universe of situations, the manual should indicate clearly what universe is represented and how adequate the sampling is [p. 20].

This level of sophistication is not reached in the assessment of achievement needs. Indeed, it is doubtful that such specificity in the sampling of achievement content is possible. Generally the motive assessment procedure consists of 4 or 6 pictures differing somewhat in their content; for example, a man at a typewriter, men working at a machine, a man in a lab coat looking at a test tube, or a boy on a farm. However, this is the extent of the content "sampling." There is no specification of the "sampling" procedure, nor generally of the rationale behind the choice of the particular pictures selected for any investigation.

The meaning or significance of this deficiency in content validity is not immediately evident. The construct of trait or motive, as well as the entire field of individual difference inference, has recently been called into question (Mischel, 1968). Support for the concept of a motive (need) requires that people behave in a consistent manner across a variety of stimulus situations. The sampling of only a limited domain of achievement situations by the TAT pictures, and prediction within a similarly delimited area, does not provide proof that the need for achievement is a *motive*. (See the discussion of Murray earlier in this chapter.)

The existence of traits, on the other hand, and the value of predicting behavior from the assumption of very general and enduring personality dispositions, as opposed to predictions based upon expected reactions elicited in particular stimulus contexts, is not of primary interest to most researchers in the achievement area. McClelland (1955), for example, contends that

there are those who argue that what we are identifying . . . are not really motives at all, but something else, perhaps habits. I don't want to seem too light hearted about psychological theory, but I should hate to see much energy expended in debating the point. If someone can plan and execute a better research by calling these measures habits, so much the better. If, furthermore, it should turn out that all the interesting findings we have turned up are the result of some theoretical "error" in our thinking, I cannot admit to much regret. The fact of the matter is that we know too little about either motives or habits to get into a very useful discussion as to which is which [p. 43].

In sum, the consequences of inappropriate content sampling, or the relative lack of content validity, remain to be discerned.

Criterion-Related Validity

Criterion-related validity, according to the APA's (1954) "Technical Recommendations," is

demonstrated by comparing the test scores with one or more external variables considered to provide a direct measure of the characteristic behavior in question [p. 13].

McClelland (1958) captures the essence of criterion-related validity in his description of a good motive measure:

The measure of a motive should have relational fertility. It should correlate with many other variables or account for much of the variance in human behavior. . . . Validity, properly speaking, is an *instance* of relational fertility. . . . It is correct to assess the validity of the measure in terms of the *number* and *extent* of its connections to other theoretically-related variables [p. 20].

Early investigations of need for achievement concerned with criterion or empirical validity followed McClelland's dictum and related individual differences in motive strength to a variety of behaviors for which achievement appeared to be a relevant source of motivation. In one of the very earliest investigations, Lowell (1952) required subjects to make words out

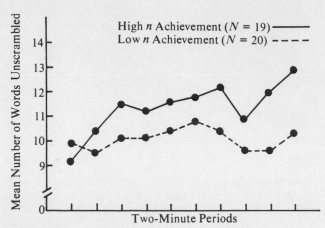

FIGURE 4:1.   Mean output of scrambled words solved for subjects high or low in achievement needs. Increments in learning influence the performance score (from Lowell, 1952, p. 36).

of scrambled letters. The mean output of words per minute for individuals classified as high or low in need for achievement is shown in Figure 4:1. The figure indicates that the rate of output for subjects high in achievement motivation increases over trials, while for individuals classified as low in achievement motivation the intensity of performance remains relatively constant.

A second study conducted by Lowell (1952) investigated the output of addition problems for two groups differing in level of achievement needs. At the overlearned arithmetic task an initial difference in level of performance between achievement groups is exhibited, and this inequality remains relatively stable over trials (see Figure 4:2).

There are many methodological and empirical similarities between two studies conducted by Lowell and the early investigations of the properties of drive. For example, in the experiments reported by Perin and Williams (see Chapter II) animals high in drive, operationally defined in terms of hours of deprivation, exhibit greater resistance to extinction than animals low in drive. Further, differences in extinction trials increase as a function of habit strength, operationally defined as number of prior reinforced trails. In the investigations by Lowell, individuals differing in achievement motive strength, operationally defined as score on TAT, differ in their intensity of performance. The performance disparity increases as a function of number of trials at the activity when learning also is involved.

Yet there also are clear conceptual distinctions between Lowell's studies and those conducted by Perin and Williams. For example, in the

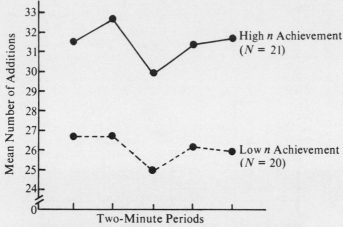

FIGURE 4:2. Mean output of addition problems solved for subjects high or low in achievement needs. Arithmetic tasks are overlearned, and
improved performance is not displayed over trials
(from Lowell, 1952, p. 38).

former, *R-R* relationships are under study (Brown, 1961); that is, responses to one test are related to other responses. However, when drive
is manipulated by withholding food, as in the Perin and Williams experiments, then the independent variable is not a test response, but a manipulated organic characteristic.

Task Recall. Another frequently cited early study providing criterion validity for the TAT measure of achievement needs was conducted
by Atkinson (1953). Atkinson investigated the recall of incompleted and
completed tasks after subjects received relaxed, neutral, or achievement-
related instructions. These three conditions influence the degree of aroused
achievement motivation, and therefore were expected to affect task recall.
The subjects also were classified as high or low in achievement needs. The
results of this study revealed that the percentage recall of completed tasks
did not significantly differ between the three experimental conditions for
the two motive groups. However, the percentage recall of incompleted
tasks was systematically influenced by the arousal instructions. Figure 4:3
shows that for subjects high in achievement motivation recall of incompleted tasks increases from the relaxed to achievement instruction condition. Conversely, subjects low in achievement needs exhibit decreased recall of incompleted tasks as conditions become more closely associated
with achievement concerns. (See also Chapter III.)

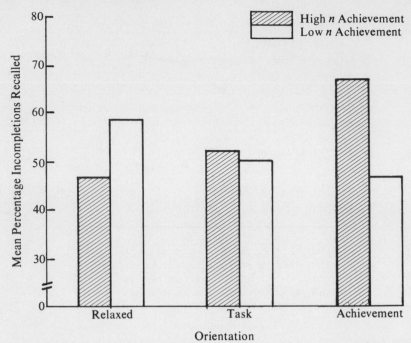

FIGURE 4:3.   Mean percentage recall of interrupted tasks for subjects high or low in achievement needs, given three degrees of achievement arousal (from McClelland, Atkinson, Clark & Lowell, 1953, p. 266.)

Atkinson (1964) interprets the findings for the high achievement-oriented subjects:

There is a significant increase in recall of interrupted tasks (and the Zeigarnik effect) as the instructions and other situational cues increase the likelihood that subjects will perceive completion as evidence of personal success and incompletion as evidence of personal failure. In other words, the strength of the tendency to achieve at these particular tasks was significantly greater among persons having comparably High n Achievement scores when cues in the instructions and other features of the situation led them *to expect* that performance would be evaluated in terms of a standard of excellence than when the situational cues made it patently clear that their performance would not be evaluated [p. 233].

It was suggested earlier that the Zeigarnik effect, or the greater recall of incompleted than completed tasks, may be attributed to differential task learning, rather than to differential memory. The results for individuals high in achievement needs shown in Figure 4:3 are consistent with this point of view. The figure may be interpreted as indicating that subjects high in need for achievement learn incompleted tasks to a greater extent in the aroused than the relaxed condition. The differential learning could be mediated by inequalities in covert rehearsal. In the achievement-oriented condition the subjects high in achievement needs may repeatedly think about the incompleted tasks. In their life history such behavior may have been instrumental to goal attainment. Many psychologists believe that fantasy, daydream activity, and other covert cognitive activities have functional significance and aid in problem solving; see Singer (1966). This continued cognitive activity, or problem-solving behavior, would not be manifested in situations in which the expectancy of achievement attainment is not aroused, as in the relaxed instruction condition.

Further Studies of Criterion Validity. There are many other studies pertaining to the criterion validation of the TAT measure of the need for achievement. The logic of these investigations is similar to that employed by Lowell and Atkinson. Individuals are classified into motive groups on the basis of their TAT achievement score. Then their performance is compared on one or more dependent variables which are sensitive to motivational influence. A few frequently cited findings in this area are reported now to give the reader some familiarity with the extensity and type of relevant investigations.

French (1956) allowed subjects to choose a work partner for a task. One available partner had performed a prior task well, while another was affiliative. French found that individuals high in need for achievement were more likely to choose the "expert" rather than the friendly person as a work partner. On the other hand, subjects high in need for affiliation chose the friendly person rather than the expert as a co-worker. In another investigation, French and Thomas (1958) gave subjects an insolvable achievement-related task to complete. They found that subjects high in achievement needs persist longer in their attempts to solve the task than subjects low in need for achievement.[1]

In still another experimental paradigm, Mischel (1961) related need achievement to delay of gratification. He found that children high in need for achievement are willing to wait and receive a larger reward rather than immediately accept a smaller one. On the other hand, children low in achievement needs prefer the lesser but more immediate gratification. These findings are consistent with the conception of a high achievement-oriented person as one who sets long rather than short-term goals, and

---

[1] French uses the French Test of Insight to assess need for achievement. In this projective test, individuals are given sentence stems (such as Tom always lets the other fellow win) and then write paragraphs that explain this behavior. The stories are scored for achievement motivation with the method of content analysis devised by McClelland et al. The French test appears as valid as the TAT format, although it has not been used as frequently.

has a future time perspective (McClelland et al., 1953; Heckhausen, 1967).

In sum, this small sampling of studies reveals that achievement needs are related to diverse criteria such as intensity of performance (Lowell), task recall (Atkinson), choice of a work partner (French), persistence of behavior (French & Thomas), and delay of gratification (Mischel). Thus, the measure has "relational fertility." (The reader is directed to Atkinson, 1964; Birney, 1968; Byrne, 1966; McClelland et al., 1953; and Weiner, 1970, for far more extensive reviews of research in this area.)

Construct Validity

To examine construct validity requires a combination of logical and empirical attack. Essentially, studies of construct validity check on the theory underlying the test. The procedure involves three steps. First, the investigator inquires: From this theory, what hypotheses may we make regarding the behavior of persons with high and low scores? Second, he gathers data to test these hypotheses. Third, in light of the evidence, he makes an inference as to whether the theory is adequate to explain the data collected [American Psychological Association, 1954, p. 14].

To establish construct validity, a test must be embedded in a clearly stated theory or nomological network (Cronbach & Meehl, 1955). Thus far in this chapter a theory of achievement motivation formally comparable to the Hullian or Lewinian conceptions has not been presented. In 1957 Atkinson formulated a comprehensive theory of achievement behavior. Validation of this theory provides construct validity for the measurement instrument (generally the TAT) employed in the investigations.

ATKINSON'S THEORY OF ACHIEVEMENT MOTIVATION

General Laws and Individual Differences: Introduction to the Theory

In the tradition of Hull, Lewin, Tolman, and other motivational theorists, Atkinson (1957) attempted to isolate the determinants of behavior and to specify the mathematical relationship between the components of the theory. In one respect, however, Atkinson greatly differs from both Hull and Lewin. Atkinson focuses upon the role of individual differences (in achievement needs) for the understanding of motivational processes. The explicit concern with personality structure is characteristic of neither Hull nor Lewin, although both theorists did recognize the need to deal with this issue. Berlyne (1968) accounts somewhat for Hull's neglect of individual differences:

Behavior theory has neglected personality, in the sense of individual differences. . . . Behavior theorists have inherited from their empiricist and associationist forebears of previous centuries a bias towards environmentalism.

Watson was evidently determined not to be outdone by any 17th century *tabula rasa* theory, as witness his famous claim (1924) that any normal child can be turned into "any type of specialist I might select—doctor, lawyer, artist, merchant, thief, and yes, even make a man a thief, regardless of his talents, penchants, tendencies, abilities, vocations and race of his ancestors." No neo-behaviorist has assumed this position, but the fact remains that behavior theorists spend most of their time studying learned behavior and feel that to understand the behavior of the higher mammals means, above all, to understand how learning works. . . .

Preoccupation with learning may lead one to disregard innate differences, which must seem the logical starting point to anyone who wishes to throw light on the dissimilarities among human beings. . . .

It is perfectly obvious that human beings are·different from one another in some respects but alike in other respects. The question is whether we should first look for statements that apply to all of them or whether we should first try to describe and explain their differences. The behavior theorist feels that research for common principles of human and animal behavior must take precedence. This, he would point out, is how scientific inquiry must proceed. . . . Until we can see what individuals of a class or species have in common, we cannot hope to understand how their dissimilarities have come about or even to find the most fruitful way to describe and classify these dissimilarities. . . .

[Hull's] aim was to find some way of handling inter-individual and inter-species differences within the bounds of "a strict quantitative natural-science approach to the theory of behavior." He offered the hypothesis that this could be achieved by "assuming that the *forms* of the equations representing the behavioral laws of both individuals and species are identical, and that the differences between individuals and species will be found in the empirical constants which are essential components of such equations" [pp. 639–41].

It thus appears that Hull's relative neglect of individual differences was a conscious by-product of his philosophy of science. On the other hand, Lewin's basic contention was that behavior is a function of both the person and the environment. Further, in distinction to Hull, Lewin (1951) states,

general laws and individual differences are merely two aspects of one problem; they are mutually dependent on each other and the study of one cannot proceed without the study of the other [p. 243].

But, as Atkinson (1964) points out,

in the theoretical conception and experimental analysis of motivation, Lewinians consider only the momentary and temporary condition of the person, which is represented at $t(S_G)$ [a system in a state of tension]. And in most cases, $t(S_G)$ is assumed to be roughly equivalent for all subjects exposed to the same experimental instructions and arrangements in the course of conducting the experiment [p. 103].

Lewin does have constructs within his theory that can incorporate relatively permanent personality factors. He specified that there are individual differences in the strength of boundaries between regions, in the degree of differentiation of the world, and so forth. However, Lewin habitually studied general laws, and the person was usually considered "a mass point of indifferent constitution" (Murray, 1959, p. 29). Indeed, the following quote from Lewin (1951) indicates that he treated individual differences in a manner quite similar to that of Hull.

To give just one example of the linkage between the study of general laws and of individual differences: The velocity with which an activity is satiated increases, according to Karsten, with the degree to which the activity is psychologically central (as against peripheral). This proposition has the nature of a general law. . . . A law is expressed in an equation which relates certain variables. Individual differences have to be conceived of as various specific values which these variables have in a particular case [pp. 242–43].

Atkinson (1964), instead of using knowledge of individual differences to alter the numerical value of a variable, includes personality structures among the behavioral determinants. His concern with individual differences in the understanding of motivational processes cannot be overemphasized. He states that

A most encouraging development in recent experimental analysis of motivation . . . is the use of tests to assess individual differences in the strength of theoretically-relevant motivational dispositions of humans. Here again, the broad implication of Lewinian ideas is apparent. The guiding hypothesis, $B = f(P,E)$, is now represented in a methodological development that may provide a means of bridging the gap between the study of individual differences in personality and the search for basic explanatory principles which has so far seriously handicapped both enterprises in psychology's relatively short history. . . .
It is to be hoped that contemporary research on n[eed] achievement . . . and contemporary research on individual differences in anxiety, within the context of Drive $\times$ Habit theory, will point the way towards more fruitful systematic use of personality tests in future research on human motivation [pp. 271, 272].

Although Atkinson differs from Hull and Lewin in his focus upon individual differences, his conception is guided by these earlier theorists. In both the Hullian and Lewinian conceptions, behavior is conceptualized as a function of a temporary state of the organism (drive or tension), the properties of the goal object (incentive value or valence), and an experiential or learning factor (habit or psychological distance). Atkinson includes a very similar set of person, environment, and experiential variables among the immediate determinants of action.

Further, Atkinson's theory of achievement motivation is influenced by Miller's conflict model. Achievement-related behavior is conceptualized as a resultant of a conflict situation. It is assumed that the cues associated with competition against a standard of excellence arouse both the hope of success and the fear of failure. The strength of the approach tendency toward the goal (the hope of success) relative to the strength of the avoidance tendency (the fear of failure) determines whether the individual will locomote toward or away from achievement-related tasks.

Hope of Success

The tendency to approach an achievement-related goal, or the hope of success (T_s), is postulated to be a product of three factors: the need for achievement, also known as the motive for success (M_s), the probability that one will be successful at the task (P_s), and the incentive value of success (I_s). It is postulated that these three components are multiplicatively related:

$$T_S = M_S \times P_s \times I_s$$

The Need for Achievement. In this equation of the determinants of approach motivation, M_S represents a relatively stable or enduring disposition to strive for success. The operational and generic definition of the concept, as well as the historical linkage to the work of Murray and McClelland, has already been documented. Atkinson (1964) defines the need for achievement as a "capacity to experience pride in accomplishment" (p. 214). That is, the achievement need is an affective disposition.

The Probability of Success. The probability of success, P_s, refers to a cognitive goal expectancy or an anticipation that an instrumental action will lead to the goal. Atkinson's use of this concept was guided by Tolman's analysis of latent learning.

The studies of latent learning discussed in Chapter II demonstrate that rats exhibit dramatic performance increments following a number of nonrewarded trials if the response suddenly is followed by a reward. This suggested to Tolman and his associates that during nonrewarded trials the animals are learning, even though they are not displaying this "knowledge" in their performance. According to Tolman, during both nonrewarded and rewarded trials animals develop "cognitive maps" of their environment. When an incentive is placed in the maze the animals utilize the information gained on prior trials, and display sudden gains in performance.

In the Hullian scheme learning is represented as the strengthening of a mechanistic bond between an antecedent stimulus and a subsequent response. Further, for this bond to grow a reward must follow the response. Tolman contends that when a reward follows a response, response-reward contingencies, or expectancies, are formed. The animal becomes aware "if I make this response to this stimulus, a reward will follow." Thus, an S_1-R_1-S_2 sequence, where S_2 is the goal stimulus (G_1), is learned. The increment in the R_1-G_1 bond represents the growth of a goal expectancy.

The meaning of P_s as used by Atkinson is very similar to Tolman's notion of expectancy. Atkinson (1964) explains:

What Tolman originally called the *expectancy of the goal* and conceived as a forward-pointing cognition based on prior experience is represented as the subjective probability of attaining the goal. . . . The two terms *expectancy* and *subjective probability* have been used interchangeably in the theory of achievement motivation which . . . calls attention to the fact that the concept of expectancy . . . serves to represent the associative link between performance of an act and the attainment of the goal (*R-G*) [p. 275].

Atkinson is a cognitive theorist primarily because of the incorporation of "expectancy" into his model.

According to Tolman, expectancy increases as a function of the number of rewarded trials. Further, he states that early and late trials exert special influence on the formation of goal anticipations. Atkinson, however, working with human rather than infrahuman subjects, takes much more liberty in the specification of operations that alter expectancy or subjective probability. Any information or contrived stimulus situation that influences a subject's beliefs about winning or performing well apparently can be used to define operationally the magnitude of P_s. The most frequently adopted strategy to manipulate P_s is to supply subjects with some normative information about the difficulty of the task they are attempting. For example, the subject might be told: "Our norms indicate that _____% of the students of your age level and ability are able to solve these puzzles" (see Feather, 1961; Weiner, 1970). Another procedure used to influence P_s is to have subjects compete against varying numbers of others. For example,

Atkinson (1958b) had individuals competing against one another for a monetary prize. Some of the subjects were told that they had to perform better than only one other person to win, while others were informed that they were in competition with twenty others. Still a further operation employed to alter P_s is to vary the actual difficulty of a task. For example, many studies of achievement motivation employ a ring-toss game requiring that rings be thrown over a peg. It is generally assumed that the farther one stands from the peg when playing this game, the lower is his subjective expectancy of success. Finally, altering reinforcement history also is used to produce varying levels of P_s, although this particular strategy has not been used frequently in prior studies. In one experiment (Weiner & Rosenbaum, 1965) different subjects received puzzle booklets varying in the number of soluble puzzles. The perceived percentage of success at these tasks determined the P_s.

The P_s in Atkinson's equation of the determinants of approach behavior represents a subjective probability of success, or a personal belief about the chances of goal attainment. The operations reviewed above to produce a desired P_s level generally are identical for all subjects within an experimental condition. The experimenter assumes that a high correspondence exists between an individual's subjective expectancy and the experimentally induced probability.

The Incentive Value of Success. The third determinant of approach behavior specified by Atkinson is I_s, or the incentive value of success. Guided by the resultant valence theory of Escalona and Festinger it is postulated that I_s is inversely related to P_s: $I_s = 1 - P_s$. Thus, the incentive value of success increases as P_s decreases. Atkinson contends that the incentive value of an achievement goal is an affect labeled "pride in accomplishment." It is argued that greater pride is experienced following success at a difficult task than after success at an easy task. For example, little pride should be experienced by the reader when receiving a grade of "A" in an easy course, but much pride would be felt of this grade were earned in a difficult course. In a similar manner, strong positive affect should be experienced when winning from a superior, rather than a poor, athletic team.

Although the inverse relationship between I_s and P_s may be considered a postulate within Atkinson's system, it has been experimentally investigated and receives strong empirical support. For example, in 1958 Litwin (reported in Atkinson & Feather, 1966) found that the farther one stands from a peg in a ring-toss game, the greater the reward assigned for success (Figure 4:4). In a similar manner, occupations in which the attainment of success is believed to be difficult are accorded greater prestige and salary

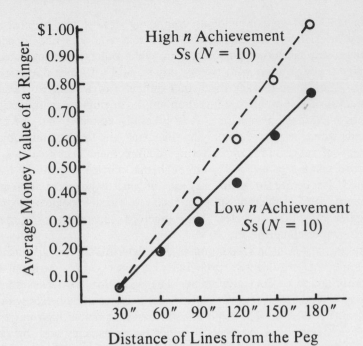

FIGURE 4:4.   Judged mean reward for success at varying distances from the peg (reported in McClelland, 1961, p. 236).

(I_s) than occupations in which success is believed to be relatively easy (Strodtbeck, McDonald, & Rosen, 1957).

In a more direct test of the I_s-P_s relationship, Cook, (1970) allowed fourth and fifth grade male pupils to self-reinforce themselves following success at a puzzle task. Following the task performance the children could reward themselves by taking the amount of poker chips "which you feel your deserve" from a container on their desks. Five different levels of task difficulty were conveyed by varying the complexity of the puzzles and accompanying each puzzle with a false difficulty norm. The relationship between apparent task difficulty and the number of chips taken for a success is shown in Figure 4:5. The figure reveals that task difficulty is linearly related to the amount of self-reward. If one assumes that self-reinforcement is an index of positive affect, then Cook's study also provides support for Atkinson's conception of the relation between pride and success probability.

Because the incentive value of success is conceived as an affect, it complements the concept of the achievement motive, which is an affective disposition or a capacity to experience pride in achievement. Thus, as in the Lewinian scheme, the final valence of a goal is a function of both the properties of the person (motive strength) and the properties of the goal

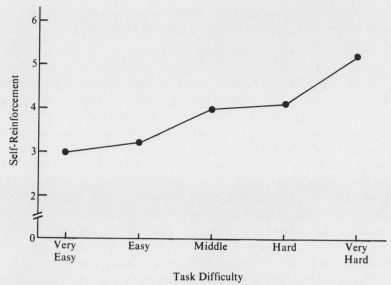

FIGURE 4:5. Mean reward (number of chips taken) for success, given five different levels of task difficulty (adapted from Cook, 1970, p. 45).

(task difficulty). In an investigation already cited that bears upon this point, Litwin (1966) asked individuals to assign a monetary value for success at tasks varying in their difficulty level. Subjects also were classified according to their strength of achievement needs. Figure 4:4 shows that the assigned reward is a function of both M_S and P_s. That is, both personality dispositions and the stimulus situation influence the reward for success. The divergence of the functions for the motive groups shown in Figure 4:4 also indicates that M_S and P_s (or I_s) combine multiplicatively to determine the reward value of success. However, this finding is not well documented (see Karabenick, 1972).

Fear of Failure

Achievement-related activities elicit *positive affective anticipations* because of past successful accomplishments and experienced pride, as well as *negative affective anticipations* learned from prior failures and experienced shame. Thus, a fear of failure as well as a hope of success is aroused in achievement-related situations.

The determinants of fear of failure, or the tendency to avoid achievement tasks, are conceived by Atkinson as analagous with those of the hope of success. It is postulated that the tendency to avoid failure (T_{AF})

is a multiplicative function of the motive to avoid failure (M_{AF}), the probability of failure (P_f), and the incentive value of failure $(-I_f)$:

$$T_{AF} = M_{AF} \times P_f \times (-I_f)$$

The Motive to Avoid Failure. Just as M_S is conceived as a capacity to experience pride in accomplishment, M_{AF} may be considered a capacity to experience shame given nonattainment of a goal (failure). The conception of an avoidance motive, independent of the approach motive, was introduced well after the TAT assessment studies, and a supporting measurement program was not initiated. Generally, Atkinson and other workers in the achievement area employ the Mandler-Sarason Test Anxiety Questionnaire (TAQ) (Mandler & Sarason, 1952) to define operationally the strength of M_{AF}. The TAQ is an objective self-report measure of anxiety. Atkinson therefore employs a projective instrument to assess M_S, and an objective self-report measure to assess M_{AF}. This asymmetry is of interest, inasmuch as self-report measures of M_S generally are ineffective and typically not used by Atkinson and his co-workers (see Atkinson, 1964). There have been some successful attempts to measure the need for achievement with an objective instrument (Mehrabian, 1969), and to assess anxiety about failure with a projective instrument (Heckhausen, 1967, 1968).

The items on the TAQ pertain only to the anxiety aroused in test-taking situations. Anxiety about failure is conceived as a specific associative disposition, in contrast to the Spencian conception of anxiety as a nondirective drive. As we have already indicated, typical items on the TAQ are:

While taking an intelligence test, to what extent do you worry?
Before taking a course examination, to what extent do you perspire?

The questions are answered on Likert-type scales anchored at the extremes (for example, Perspire a lot—Perspire not at all), and a total score attained by summing the scores on the 39 test items. Mandler and Sarason (1952) report a correlation of $r = .59$ between scores on the TAQ and behaviors such as hand and body movements and inappropriate laughter and talking during an exam. These actions interfere with task performance because the responses are incompatible with, or irrelevant to, exam taking behavior. Anxiety as measured by the MA scale and test anxiety assessed by the TAQ correlate from $r = .40$ to $r = .55$.

Mandler and Sarason contend that individuals scoring high on the TAQ have a higher level of drive during test situations, and are prone to make task-irrelevant responses which result in the avoidance of task performance. Thus, test anxiety as conceived by Mandler and Sarason is somewhat similar to the McClelland-Atkinson notion of M_S, which also is conceived as responsive only to task-related cues, and has energizing and directional functions.

Probability and Incentive Value of Failure. Two environmental factors influence the avoidance of achievement activities: the probability of failure (P_f) and the incentive value of failure $(-I_f)$. It is assumed that the incentive value of failure is a negative affect labeled "shame." Greater shame is believed to be experienced following failure at an easy task than after failure at a difficult task. Therefore, I_f is conceived as equal to $-(1 - P_f)$. In contrast to the empirical work concerning the determinants of I_s, there have been few successful attempts reported to support the intuitively reasonable I_f-P_f relationship (see Cook, 1970, for a failure to find the postulated inverse relationship.)

It is further assumed by Atkinson that the probabilities in the model total unity: $P_s + P_f = 1$. Thus, $P_f = 1 - P_s$. It previously was noted that I_s also is equal to $1 - P_s$. Hence, $I_s = P_f$.

Resultant Achievement Motivation

The resultant tendency to approach or avoid an achievement-oriented activity (T_A) is postulated to be a function of the strength of the tendency to approach the task plus the strength of the tendency to avoid the task:

$$T_A = T_S + (-T_{AF})$$

or

$$T_A = (M_S \times P_s \times I_s) + [M_{AF} \times P_f \times (-I_f)]$$

The incentive value of failure has a negative value, and leads to avoidance behavior. The two motivational tendencies therefore are in conflict and may be represented as opposing forces. Thus, the prior equations may be written as follows:

$$T_A = T_S - T_{AF}; \tag{1}$$

or

$$T_A = (M_S \times P_s \times I_s) - (M_{AF} \times P_f \times I_f) \tag{2}$$

It has been indicated that $I_s = 1 - P_s$, $P_f = 1 - P_s$, and that $I_f = P_s$. Simple arithmetic substitution yields:

$$T_A = [M_S \times P_s \times (1 - P_s)] + [M_{AF} \times (1 - P_s) \times (-P_s)]; \tag{3}$$

or

$$T_A = [M_S \times P_s \times (1 - P_s)] - [M_{AF} \times (1 - P_s) \times P_s]; \tag{4}$$

or

$$T_A = (M_S - M_{AF}) [P_s \times (1 - P_s)] \tag{5}$$

Inasmuch as M_S and M_{AF} are uncorrelated within the general population, Equation 5 reveals that there are two degrees of freedom among the personal determinants of behavior. However, there is only one degree of freedom among the four environmental determinants of behavior. Given that P_s is assigned a value, the numerical strengths of I_s, P_f, and I_f are determined. Whether, then, these four variables all can be considered determinants of behavior is a point of theoretical contention.

Further Elaboration of the Model

It is evident from Equation 5 that when $M_S > M_{AF}$, T_A has a positive value. Individuals with this motive constellation, labeled as high in resultant achievement motivation, therefore are attracted to achievement tasks. They should approach achievement-related activities when given the opportunity. On the other hand, when $M_{AF} > M_S$, T_A has a negative value. Individuals with this motive constellation, labeled as low in resultant achievement motivation, should not approach achievement-related activities, and should actively avoid them when able. Atkinson believes that negative motivation merely indicates what an individual will not do. That is, avoidance motivation is conceptualized as an inhibitory tendency. The distinction between an active versus a passive avoidance tendency is not crucial in the discussion that follows, and is neglected here.

It is evident that in our culture the vast majority of individuals engage in some achievement-related actions, such as attending school or working at a job. This apparently contradicts the achievement avoidance behavior expected among individuals in whom $M_{AF} > M_S$. However, achievement-oriented activities are not necessarily initiated to satisfy achievement needs. The sources of motivation may be to avoid punishment, gain power, or satisfy affiliative tendencies. For example, one might study hard at school to impress a girl, to win parental favors, and so on. This is merely belaboring the self-evident truth that behavior is overdetermined, and that many sources of motivation may cause an action.

To capture the overdetermination of achievement behavior, Atkinson specifies that the final tendency to undertake achievement activities is determined by the strength of the resultant achievement oriented tendency, plus the strengths of all other tendencies elicited in the situation that are unrelated (extrinsic) to achievement needs per se:

$$\text{Achievement behavior} = T_A + \text{extrinsic motivation} \qquad (6)$$

It is therefore possible for the model to account for achievement-type behavior exhibited by individuals in whom $M_{AF} > M_S$. Such actions are attributed to the nonachievement sources of motivation operative in the

TABLE 4:1

Resultant Achievement Motivation Classification as a Function of Strength of the Hope of Success (Generally Assessed with the TAT) and Strength of the Fear of Failure (Generally Assessed with the TAQ)

Hope of Success (Need for Achievement)	Fear of Failure (Anxiety)	Resultant Achievement Motivation
High	Low	High
High	High	Intermediate
Low	Low	Intermediate
Low	High	Low

situation. The strengths of the extrinsic motivations presumably are a function of the strengths of other motives, goal expectancies, and incentives.

Combining the Motives

It is reasonable for the reader to ask such questions as: "How can one be classified as high or low in the resultant tendency to strive for success? How can the strengths of M_S and M_{AF} be compared, for they are conceived as independent dimensions and assessed with different instruments?" The procedure generally followed by Atkinson and other researchers in this area is to assign each individual standard scores, or Z-scores, on the basis of his TAT and TAQ score deviations from the means of the population under investigation. By transforming scores on both the TAT and TAQ into Z-scores, it is possible to compare the relative strengths of these motives within any individual. Thus, if an individual scores high on the TAT relative to his comparison group, and low on the TAQ relative to this group, he is classified as high in resultant achievement motivation, or one in whom $M_S > M_{AF}$. One shortcoming of this procedure is that persons scoring high on both measures and those scoring low on both measures are grouped into a common "intermediate" classification (see Table 4:1). However, it is likely that these two intermediate groups have differentiating characteristics.

DERIVATIONS FROM THE THEORY AND SUPPORTING EVIDENCE

Substituting numerical values for the proposed determinants of behavior immediately gives rise to hypotheses that have been tested experimentally (see Table 4:2). In Table 4:2 it is assumed that when $M_S > M_{AF}$, $M_S = 2$ and $M_{AF} = 1$; when $M_S = M_{AF}$ the value assigned to both motives is 1; and when $M_{AF} > M_S$, $M_{AF} = 2$ and $M_S = 1$. The rows in the table indi-

TABLE 4:2

Strength of Resultant Achievement Motivation Related to Task Difficulty (Probability of Success) for High, Intermediate, and Low Achieving Groups

Motive Classification

High ($M_S > M_{AF}$)	Intermediate ($M_S = M_{AF}$)	Low ($M_{AF} > M_S$)
$2 \times .1 \times .9 - (1 \times .9 \times .1) = .09$	$1 \times .1 \times .9 - (1 \times .9 \times .1) = 0$	$1 \times .1 \times .9 - (2 \times .9 \times .1) = -.09$
$2 \times .3 \times .7 - (1 \times .7 \times .3) = .21$	$1 \times .3 \times .7 - (1 \times .7 \times .3) = 0$	$1 \times .3 \times .7 - (2 \times .7 \times .3) = -.21$
$2 \times .5 \times .5 - (1 \times .5 \times .5) = .25$	$1 \times .5 \times .5 - (1 \times .5 \times .5) = 0$	$1 \times .5 \times .5 - (2 \times .5 \times .5) = -.25$
$2 \times .7 \times .3 - (1 \times .3 \times .7) = .21$	$1 \times .7 \times .3 - (1 \times .3 \times .7) = 0$	$1 \times .7 \times .3 - (2 \times .3 \times .7) = -.21$
$2 \times .9 \times .1 - (1 \times .1 \times .9) = .09$	$1 \times .9 \times .1 - (1 \times .1 \times .9) = 0$	$1 \times .9 \times .1 - (2 \times .1 \times .9) = -.09$

cate the value of the resultant tendency to strive for success as a function of the difficulty (P_s) of the task. In this example extrinsic motivations are neglected.

It can be observed in Table 4:2 that when $M_S > M_{AF}$, T_A is positive; when $M_S = M_{AF}$, $T_A = 0$; and when $M_{AF} > M_S$, T_A is negative. Thus, the motive scores may be considered relative weights brought to bear upon the environmental sources of motivation. When $M_S > M_{AF}$, greater weight is given to the combination of $P_s \times I_s$ than to $P_f \times I_f$. On the other hand, when $M_{AF} > M_S$ the negative affect linked with failure is more salient to the individual than is the positive affect associated with success. The model thus implies that affective anticipations, or emotions, are vying against one another for behavioral control. The affective expectation that is strongest dominates the organism and determines the direction (toward or away from) of achievement actions.

Free-Choice Behavior

There is some direct evidence pertinent to the simple prediction conveyed by Table 4:2 that individuals in whom $M_S > M_{AF}$ are more attracted to achievement-related tasks than persons for whom $M_{AF} > M_S$. For example, Atkinson (1953) reports that individuals volunteering to participate in an experiment for which achievement appears to be a source of motivation tend to be high in need for achievement. In an extension of this finding, Green (1963) compared the Zeigarnik effect of volunteer and nonvolunteer subjects. He found that the recall of incompleted relative to completed tasks is greater for volunteer than nonvolunteer subjects. This result is consistent with the finding that individuals high in need for achievement tend to display a greater Zeigarnik effect than do those low in need for achievement (Atkinson, 1953).

One further experiment also provides evidence that the attractiveness of achievement-related tasks is a function of the strength of M_S relative to M_{AF}. Weiner and Rosenbaum (1965) allowed subjects to choose whether they would attempt an achievement-related puzzle task or an "aesthetic judgment" task for which achievement apparently was not a source of motivation. Of the 26 subjects choosing not to perform the achievement task on the initial trial, 19 were in the $M_{AF} > M_S$ motive group.

Forced-Choice Behavior (Risk Preference)

Further analysis of Table 4:2 yields hypotheses more complex than the rather simple predictions concerning free-choice behavior. Inspection of

Table 4:2 reveals that achievement motivation varies systematically as a function of the P_s at the task. Among those in whom $M_S > M_{AF}$, motivation is maximum when $P_s = .50$. Further, the strength of motivation decreases symmetrically as P_s increases or decreases from the level of intermediate difficulty. Neither the incentive value of success nor the expectancy of success are greatest at tasks of intermediate difficulty. But the postulation that $I_s = 1 - P_s$, and the specification that I_s and P_s relate multiplicatively, result in greatest motivation when P_s, and therefore I_s, are equal to .50.

Turning attention to those in whom $M_{AF} > M_S$, it is seen that among these individuals motivation is most inhibited at tasks of intermediate difficulty. All achievement tasks are aversive in that they predominantly elicit fear. But tasks that are very easy or very difficult are mildly aversive in comparison to tasks of intermediate difficulty.

Finally, the resultant achievement tendency for individuals in whom positive and negative affective anticipations are equal is 0. Motivation is unaffected by task difficulty. However, the degree of absolute approach-avoidance conflict decreases as task difficulty departs from the intermediate level. At high or low P_s levels little approach and little avoidance motivation are aroused, while at more intermediate P_s levels both high approach and high avoidance tendencies are elicited.

A number of within- and between-group hypotheses follow from the above analysis. Most frequently tested by Atkinson and his colleagues has been the prediction that, when performance is confined to achievement-related activities, individuals in whom $M_S > M_{AF}$ will select tasks of intermediate difficulty with greater frequency than individuals in whom $M_{AF} > M_S$. Many confirmatory tests of this hypothesis have been reported. For example, Atkinson and Litwin (1960) had subjects attempt to toss rings over a peg. The subjects were allowed to stand at varying distances from the peg, and could change positions following each toss. It was assumed by Atkinson and Litwin that a position close to the target corresponds to a high P_s level, and that P_s decreases as the distance from the peg increases. The subjects also were classified according to strength of resultant achievement motivation on the basis of their TAT and TAQ scores. The data from this study are shown in Figure 4:6. Figure 4:6 reveals that intermediate task preference is greatest for the high motive group, least for subjects in whom $M_{AF} > M_S$, and intermediate for subjects either high or low in both motives. Intermediate difficulty in this study was defined either as intermediate physical distance from the peg or the median of the actual distribution of shots. The two measures yielded comparable results.

Figure 4:6 further reveals that subjects in whom $M_{AF} > M_S$ do not avoid tasks of intermediate difficulty. Rather, they exhibit a less clear

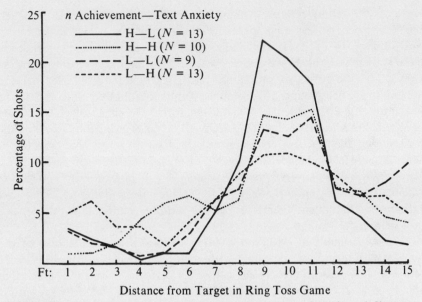

FIGURE 4:6. Percentage of ring-toss attempts as a function of distance from the peg, with subjects classified according to strength of resultant achievement motivation (adapted from Atkinson & Litwin, 1960, p. 55).

preference for tasks at that level. It could be argued that among the college students participating in this experiment few were absolutely high in test anxiety relative to their need for achievement (as Atkinson & Feather, 1966, pp. 22 and 342, suggest about college students). If this were the case, then T_A among all the subjects is positive but differs in magnitude, and the behavior observed in Figure 4:6 would be expected. However, in the vast majority of risk-preference experiments, regardless of the subject population, subjects in whom $M_{AF} > M_S$ do not absolutely prefer easy or difficult tasks. They do, however, select fewer tasks of intermediate difficulty than subjects in whom $M_S > M_{AF}$. These data pose some problems for the theory, yet they do support the broad hypothesis tested.

Level of Aspiration

The analysis of risk preference outlined above is closely related to the conceptualization of level of aspiration proposed by Escalona (1940) and Festinger (1942b), inasmuch as the main theoretical terms in the Escalona-Festinger model are the probabilities and valences of success and failure. Atkinson has obviously incorporated many of these earlier ideas into his theory of motivation (see Atkinson, 1964).

Level of aspiration is defined operationally by Lewin and his colleagues as the setting of a performance goal. It can be contended that such goal setting necessitates a comparison among a number of possible alternatives differing in P_s level, and final selection of one of these alternatives as the subjective goal. For example, when establishing a level of aspiration at an arithmetic series of problems, the individual may believe that the probability of completing 10 problems within the allotted time is .70; 15 problems, .50; 20 problems, .30, and so forth. He then selects the level for which he will strive, knowing that easier tasks are more likely to be attained, but that success at easier tasks is less attractive than success at more difficult tasks. Hence, the setting of an aspired level of performance conceptually is similar to a risk-preference for a task in which selection is made among a number of alternatives differing in difficulty. The level of aspiration paradigm therefore can be readily examined within Atkinson's theoretical framework.

An experiment by Moulton (1965) combines a modification of the usual level of aspiration paradigm with achievement theory. Moulton's subjects were first required to select a task to perform from three tasks that differed in level of difficulty. Task difficulty was manipulated by presenting fraudulent norms indicating that one of the tasks was easy ($P_s = .75$), a second of intermediate difficulty ($P_s = .50$), and a third difficult ($P_s = .25$). Moulton introduced the norms after each subject attempted a preliminary series of tasks supposedly providing the experimenter with information about the subject's ability. Thus, Moulton attempted to establish the norms as subjective, in addition to objective, probabilities. As intimated earlier, this is frequently overlooked by experimenters in this area.

After receiving the normative information, the subjects indicated which task they preferred to do. The particular task involved rearranging letters to form a word. Regardless of their preferences, all were given the task of intermediate difficulty. But if the subject had indicated a preference for the easy task, he was told that he failed at the $P_s = .50$ task; if he had indicated a preference to perform the difficult task, he was told that he successfully completed the $P_s = .50$ task.

After the success or failure experience the subject was asked to select a second task. This time the choice was between the two remaining tasks, which originally had been introduced as easy or difficult. Moulton reasoned that if an individual was successful on the prior trial, the task initially perceived as difficult would now be perceived as closer to the $P_s = .50$ level than the task first introduced as easy. Success should increase P_s, and the probabilities initially symmetrical around the intermediate level (.25 and .75) would now be, for example, .35 and .85. Thus, the difficult task is closer to .50 than the easy task, and is more intermediate in difficulty.

Given this new asymmetry in probability levels, subjects high in resultant achievement motivation were expected to choose the initially difficult task, and subjects low in resultant achievement motivation were expected to select the easy task. Selection of the easy task following success when $P_s = .50$ was considered an atypical response, for the subject is lowering his aspiration level following goal attainment.

In a similar manner, it was assumed that P_s decreases following failure. The subjective probabilities may have shifted from .25 and .75 to, for example, .15 and .65. Thus, the task introduced as easy is now more intermediate in difficulty than the task introduced as difficult. Individuals in whom $M_S > M_{AF}$ therefore were expected to select the easier task, while those in whom $M_{AF} > M_S$ were predicted to make an atypical response by selecting the more difficult task after failure.

The results of this study are shown in Table 4:3. It can be observed that subjects in whom $M_{AF} > M_S$ exhibit more atypical responses than the intermediate or high motive group subjects. Thus, Moulton's hypotheses were confirmed, additional support was provided for Atkinson's conception of motivation, and a further rapprochement was made between level of aspiration and the study of risk-preference.

Moulton examined another derivation from achievement theory in his experiment. Table 4:2 shows that individuals in whom $M_{AF} = M_S$ theoretically have no preferences among tasks that differ in level of difficulty. Hence, when faced with a choice between achievement tasks, they should experience some degree of conflict. On the other hand, individuals high or low in resultant achievement motivation theoretically have task preferences when faced with a choice between tasks of differing difficulty, and should have relatively little conflict.

TABLE 4:3
Type of Shift in Level of Aspiration as Related to Resultant Motivation
(adapted from Moulton, 1965, p. 403)

Motive Classification	Resultant Motivation	Type of Shift		
		Atypical	Typical	N
$M_{AF} < M_S$	Avoidance oriented	11	20	31
$M_{AF} = M_S$	Ambivalent	3	28	31
$M_S < M_{AF}$	Approach oriented	1	30	31
	Total	15	78	93

Avoidance oriented versus approach oriented, $\chi^2 = 8.37$**

Avoidance oriented versus ambivalent, $\chi^2 = 4.52$*

* $p < .05$.
** $p < .01$.

To test the differential conflict hypothesis, Moulton merely asked his subjects whether they had experienced any "difficulty in choice" during their second task selection. Approximately 40 percent of the $M_S = M_{AF}$ group indicated that they encountered such difficulty, while only 20 percent of the subjects in the extreme motivational groups reported choice conflict.

The intermediate motive classification includes subjects in the High-High and Low-Low motive groups. It could be predicted that subjects greatly attracted to and greatly inhibited by tasks experience more conflict than subjects neither attracted to nor inhibited by the available choices. Conflict has been specified to be a function of the absolute intensity of motivation to perform the activities, as well as the difference in motivation to undertake the alternatives (Berlyne, 1961). However, Moulton did not investigate this hypothesis.

Persistence of Behavior in Progress

One additional experiment (Feather, 1961) also is presented here in some detail as supporting Atkinson's risk-preference model. Feather's experiment perhaps best captures the predictive value of the conceptual framework provided by the theory of achievement motivation. Feather created a free-choice situation in which subjects were given an achievement-related puzzle to perform. They were instructed that they could work on the task for as long as they desired and could quit whenever they wished to undertake a different puzzle. The task required subjects to trace over all the lines on a complex figure without lifting the pencil from the paper or retracing a line. Although the subjects did not know it, the task was impossible.

Feather introduced false norms to establish a P_s at the task. In one experimental condition the task was presented as quite difficult ("At your age level approximately 5 percent of the college students are able to get the solution"). In a second condition the task was introduced as relatively easy ("70 percent of the college students are able to get the solution"). Feather then examined the number of trials attempted by the subject, or the persistence of behavior, before quitting the task. Persistence was predicted to be a function of the initial P_s at the task and individual differences in the strength of achievement-related needs.

The derivations of Feather's hypotheses are similar to those outlined in the temporally subsequent level of aspiration study conducted by Moulton. Table 4:4 shows the strength of motivation toward the achievement tasks in the two experimental conditions for subjects in whom $M_S > M_{AF}$ and for those in whom $M_{AF} > M_S$. For ease of presentation, it is

TABLE 4:4

Strength of Motivation to Undertake the Activity in Progress Among Subjects High or Low in Resultant Achievement Motivation, Given the Two Experimental Conditions Employed by Feather (1961)

| | | | Strength of Total Motivation (Achievement plus Extrinsic Motivation) | |
| | | | Subject Classification | |
Experimental Condition	Trial	P_s	$M_S > M_{AF}$	$M_{AF} > M_S$
$P_s = .70$	1	$.70^a$	$2 \times .7 \times .3 - (1 \times .3 \times .7) + .50^c = .71$	$1 \times .7 \times .3 - (2 \times .3 \times .7) + .50 = .29$
	2	$.60$	$2 \times .6 \times .4 - (1 \times .4 \times .6) + .50 = .74$	$1 \times .6 \times .4 - (2 \times .4 \times .6) + .50 = .26$
	3	$.50$	$2 \times .5 \times .5 - (1 \times .5 \times .5) + .50 = .75$	$1 \times .5 \times .5 - (2 \times .5 \times .5) + .50 = .25$
$P_s = .05$	1	$.05^b$	$2 \times .05 \times .95 - (1 \times .95 \times .05) + .50 = .55$	$1 \times .05 \times .95 - (1 \times .95 \times .05) + .50 = .45$
	2	$.04$	$2 \times .04 \times .96 - (1 \times .96 \times .04) + .50 = .54$	$1 \times .04 \times .96 - (1 \times .96 \times .04) + .50 = .46$
	3	$.03$	$2 \times .03 \times .97 - (1 \times .97 \times .03) + .50 = .53$	$1 \times .03 \times .97 - (1 \times .97 \times .03) + .50 = .47$

[a] It is assumed that P_s decreases .10 following failure when the initial $P_s = .70$.
[b] It is assumed that P_s decreases .01 following failure when the initial $P_s = .05$.
[c] Extrinsic motivation is assumed constant and equal to .50.

assumed that when $M_S > M_{AF}$, $M_S = 2$ and $M_{AF} = 1$, and vice versa when $M_{AF} > M_S$. In addition, extrinsic motivation is assumed equal to .50, and the decrement of P_s following failure is .10 in the $P_s = .70$ condition, and .01 in the $P_s = .05$ condition. The table shows that among subjects in whom $M_S > M_{AF}$, motivation on Trial One is greater when $P_s = .70$ and than when $P_s = .05$ (.71 versus .55). Further, following initial failure motivation rises in the .70 condition, for P_s decreases and moves closer to the level of intermediate difficulty. Assuming that the decrement in P_s remains .10, motivation also should increase after the next failure. On the other hand, motivation immediately decreases following failure in the $P_s = .05$ condition, for P_s moves from the level of intermediate difficulty. Further, motivation continues to decrease given repeated failures. Thus, Feather predicted that persistence, or the number of choices of the activity in progress, would be greater in the $P_s = .70$ than $P_s = .05$ condition among subjects in whom $M_S > M_{AF}$.

The right half of Table 4:4 portrays the hypothetical strength of motivation among subjects in whom $M_{AF} > M_S$. The total motivation for these subjects is positive only because the strength of the assumed extrinsic sources of motivation exceeds the achievement inhibition aroused by the task. When $M_{AF} > M_S$, motivation initially is greater in the $P_s = .05$ than in the $P_s = .70$ condition (.45 versus .29), for .05 is farther from the level of intermediate difficulty than is .70. In addition, following failure the motivation in the $P_s = .70$ condition decreases, while it increases in the $P_s = .05$ condition. This is again due to the respective shifting of P_s toward or away from the .50 level. Because repeated failures are experienced, it would be expected that motivation continues to increase in the $P_s = .05$ condition, and approaches asymptote as P_s approaches 0. Hence, Feather predicted that subjects in whom $M_{AF} > M_S$ would persist longer in the $P_s = .05$ than in the $P_s = .70$ condition.

In sum, an interaction was hypothesized between level of resultant achievement needs and task difficulty. Among subjects in whom $M_S > M_{AF}$, greater persistence was predicted in the easy than difficult condition. On the other hand, among subjects in whom $M_{AF} > M_S$, greater persistence was expected at the difficult than easy task. The data from the experiment, shown in Table 4:5, reveal that Feather's hypotheses were confirmed.

Feather also predicted that when $P_s = .70$, subjects in whom $M_S > M_{AF}$ would persist longer than those in whom $M_{AF} > M_S$. The differences in the numerical values of the strength of motivation shown in the upper half of Table 4:4 (.71, .74, .75 versus .29, .26, .25) indicate that the prediction follows directly from the conceptual analysis already presented. Table 4:5 reveals that this hypothesis also received empirical confirmation.

In addition, Feather hypothesized that when the initial P_s at the task

TABLE 4:5

Persistence Following Failure Related to Initial Expectancy of Success and
Motivational Disposition of the Individual: Number of Subjects Who Were
High and Low in Persistence in Relation to Stated Difficulty of the Initial
Task and the Nature of Their Motivation
(adapted from Feather, 1961, p. 558)

n Achievement	Test Anxiety	Stated Difficulty of Task	Persistence Trials	
			High (Above Median)	Low (Below Median)
High —	Low	$P_s = .70$ (easy)	6	2
		$P_s = .05$ (difficult)	2	7
Low —	High	$P_s = .70$ (easy)	3	6
		$P_s = .05$ (difficult)	6	2

is .05, persistence would be greater among those in whom $M_{AF} > M_S$ than
for subjects in whom $M_S > M_{AF}$. This prediction apparently defies common
sense, for the contention is that subjects low in achievement-related needs
will persist longer at achievement-related tasks than subjects high in achievement needs. Yet Table 4:4 indicates that the prediction also apparently
defies the derivations from the model, for the strength of achievement
motivation, even in this low P_s condition, is greater for those high than
low in achievement-related needs (.55, .54, .53 versus .45, .46, .47). Independent of P_s, the achievement model specifies that the strength of achievement motivation will always be higher for the $M_S > M_{AF}$ than the $M_{AF} >
M_S$ motive group, for among the former subjects achievement motivation
is positive, while when $M_{AF} > M_S$ achievement motivation is negative.
Thus, the hypothesis of Feather and the supporting empirical evidence
in Table 4:5 apparently are not consistent with the theoretical analysis.

But there is a reasonable argument to extricate Feather from this
dilemma. Feather specifies that persistence at the activity in progress is
a function of the strength of the tendency to undertake the activity, and
a function of the strengths of the tendencies to undertake any alternative
activities. One interesting derivation from this analysis is that persistence
of behavior and intensity of performance, two dependent variables often
used interchangeably in motivational research, may at times correlate negatively. For example, consider a situation in which one has little motivation
to perform the activity in progress, but no alternative activities are available. There should then be great persistence but poor performance. Con-

versely, one might be highly motivated to perform the activity in progress, but an even more attractive alternative is available. Poor persistence but high performance is then expected. Given these circumstances, there is a negative correlation between two dependent variables that presumably "measure the same thing."

In Feather's experiment the alternative activity also was an achievement-related puzzle task. The instructions had informed the subjects that they could undertake that task whenever they desired. Thus, while subjects in whom $M_S > M_{AF}$ theoretically were more motivated to continue the activity in progress than subjects in whom $M_{AF} > M_S$, they also were more attracted to the alternative achievement task. The P_s at the alternative puzzle task was not stated, but it is not unreasonable to believe that subjects perceive the task as more intermediate in difficulty than the low P_s task at which they experienced repeated failures. Hence, the alternative task may have been relatively attractive to the high motive group and relatively unattractive to subjects in the low motive group. This disparity could have produced the predicted differences in persistence in the $P_s = .05$ condition. In sum, the analysis of this particular between-group hypothesis requires somewhat more conceptual apparatus than was outlined by Feather, but it could be incorporated within his theoretical framework. In a subsequent experiment, Feather (1963) replicated these findings when the P_s at the alternative activity was presented as equal to .50.

One lesson to be learned from the Feather experiments is that in studies of persistence the strength of motivation to undertake all the optional activities must be known. Frequently in studies of persistence the subject merely is told, "quit when you want." But what activity he chooses when he quits, if any, is unstated, thus creating a large source of experimental error.

There is one further issue of conceptual interest in the Feather experiments. Among subjects in whom $M_{AF} > M_S$, motivation theoretically continues to increase once P_s falls below .50. Repeated failures are given and P_s continues to move farther from the level of intermediate difficulty. Thus, if the task is attempted on Trial $n + 1$, and P_s at that trial is below .50, then it should be attempted again on Trial $n + 2$.

Yet the vast majority of the $M_{AF} > M_S$ subjects do not persist until stopped by the experimenter in the $P_s = .05$ condition, and some quit after a number of attempts in the $P_s = .70$ condition (presumably when $P_s < .50$). To account for these findings within the framework adopted by Feather, it would have to be postulated that extrinsic sources of motivation also change over trials. For example, one source of motivation to undertake the puzzles may be curiosity. Curiosity decreases as a function of commerce with the activity in progress (Berlyne, 1961), and may remain constant or increase toward the unknown alternate task. Thus, it is possible to infer that subjects in whom $M_{AF} > M_S$ quit because of non-achievement-related motivations that vary from trial to trial. The experimental design used by Feather and the explanation of the empirical findings necessitates that there be a "changing constellation of forces." Lewin's arguments against such experimental paradigms are outlined in Chapter III.

EDUCATIONAL IMPLICATIONS OF THE THEORY

The theoretical conception formulated by Atkinson has a number of potential applications in educational settings. Vocational aspiration, choice of school courses and major field of concentration, programmed instruction, ability groupings, and the effects of competition on school satisfaction and performance are a few of the areas amenable to conceptual analysis within Atkinson's theoretical framework (see Weiner, 1967). Some of these areas are now considered in detail, for they illustrate how theoretical analysis may give rise to the solution of practical problems.

Vocational Aspiration

Because there are many possible occupations, career choice requires a selection from a number of achievement-related alternatives. Further, each alternative has an associated level of difficulty, as well as a potential payoff. Thus, the conceptual analysis of risk-preference behavior observed in the laboratory is immediately relevant for the examination of vocational aspiration.

Mahone (1960) reasoned that individuals in whom $M_S > M_{AF}$ are realistic in their vocational aspiration. That is, the expectancy of success at their chosen field and their level of ability are relatively congruent. On the other hand, Mahone hypothesized that individuals in whom $M_{AF} > M_S$ are unrealistic in their vocational choice. That is, they either over- or underaspire, as defined by the relationship between their level of ability and the difficulty of their occupational goal.

To test these hypotheses, Mahone asked a group of college students to state their vocational objectives. Trained consulting psychologists then rated the realism of their choices after examining the subjects' grade point averages, college entrance exam scores, and other pertinent information. Table 4:6 shows the relationship between the clinically judged aspiration-ability discrepancy and the level of resultant achievement motivation. As Mahone predicted, greatest realism is displayed by subjects in whom $M_S > M_{AF}$, and the least amount is exhibited by those in whom $M_{AF} > M_S$.

Mahone argued that there are two reasons for the differences between the vocational realism of the motive groups. First, earlier research had demonstrated that groups varying in level of achievement needs also differ in risk-preference behavior. Selection of an occupation congruent with one's level of ability corresponds to a choice of a task of intermediate difficulty, while over- or underaspiration is the selection of high or low P_s risk. Second, individuals high in fear of failure may not expose themselves to information necessary to make an appropriate vocational choice. That is, they may not possess sufficient information about themselves and their own level of ability to make a realistic vocational selection.

To test the risk-preference interpretation of the general findings shown in Table 4:6, Mahone asked the subjects in his experiment to estimate their perceived ability relative to other college students. He also asked the subjects to rate the degree of ability necessary for success at various occupations ("What percent of college students have the ability to attain success at this occupation?"). Perceived personal ability was then compared to the perceived ability necessary for success at the occupation selected as a career choice. This subjective goal discrepancy was greater for the low than the high resultant achievement group (see Table 4:7). Thus, differential risk-preference behavior is exhibited that is independent of the objective skills of the person and the objective difficulty of the task.

To test the differential information interpretation of the vocational choice data, the subjective estimates of own ability were compared with the ability estimates derived from objective percentile scores obtained on college entrance exams. These results revealed that subjects low in resultant achievement motivation are most inaccurate in estimating their own

TABLE 4:6

n Achievement and Debilitating Anxiety Related to Clinical Judgments of Realistic and Unrealistic Vocational Choice ($N = 135$) (from Mahone, 1960, p. 256)

n *Ach*	*Anxiety*	N	Clinical Judgments	
			Realistic	*Unrealistic*
High	High	31	48%	52%
High	Low	36	75*	25*
Low	High	28	39*	61*
Low	Low	40	68	32

* $\chi^2 = 7.96$
$p < .003$

TABLE 4:7
n Achievement and Debilitating Anxiety Related to
Absolute Subjective Goal Discrepancy
(from Mahone, 1960, p. 258)

| n Ach | Anxiety | N | Absolute Goal Discrepancy | |
			Mid-Third	Extremes
High	High	30	30%	70%
High	Low	36	50*	50*
Low	High	28	18*	82*
Low	Low	40	38	62

$* \chi^2 = 7.0$
$p < .005$

abilities, while subjects high in resultant motivation are most accurate. In sum, both the differential risk-preference and differential information interpretations received empirical support, and apparently account for the disparities in occupational realism displayed by the extreme motive groups.

A related investigation utilizing a somewhat different experimental paradigm confirmed Mahone's findings. Morris (1966) reasoned that the subjective probabilities of success at tasks often differ greatly from the objective task difficulties, for individuals have idiosyncratic patterns of actual and perceived ability which produce upward or downward probability biasing. For example, an individual possessing high mathematical but poor mechanical abilities may perceive an objectively difficult math problem as easy, but an objectively simple mechanical task as very difficult. In general, the degree of perceived difficulty of various specific jobs should be a function of the perceived level of competence within the general occupational area in which they are subsumed (see Figure 4:7).

Morris obtained the level of subjective occupational competence among a group of high school boys by having them estimate their probabilities of success at ten general occupations. Included within each of the ten occupations were nine specific jobs. The subjects indicated which job within each of the ten occupational areas they most preferred, and rank ordered the nine jobs within each occupation according to difficulty level. Morris then examined job preference (aspiration level) within the two general occupations at which subjects estimated they had the greatest or least subjective competence. The subjects also were classified according to strength of resultant achievement motivation.

Table 4:8 shows the results of this investigation. For students either high or low in general level of intelligence, unrealistic or "atypical' choices (selection of a difficult job from a low competence occupation, or an easy

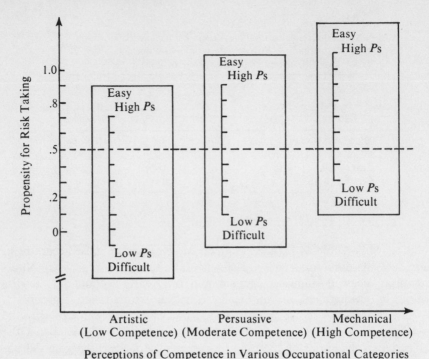

Perceptions of Competence in Various Occupational Categories

FIGURE 4:7.   The effect of expectancy of success in various occupational fields upon expectancy of success in specific jobs within those fields (from Morris, 1966, p. 329).

job from a high competence occupation) are markedly greater among subjects low than high in resultant achievement motivation. These "atypical" preferences are for both overly easy and overly difficult jobs.

Programmed Instruction

In recent years there has been a tremendous growth in the use of programmed instruction as a learning device. Programmed learning has many advantages: each student may proceed at his own pace, feedback and reinforcement are immediate, and the teacher is free for other classroom duties. Most written programs approximate 100 percent reinforcement schedules. The student is guided step by step from easy to difficult problems; students generally are able to answer correctly the question posed.

The reinforcement schedule that is employed has motivational consequences. Translated in terms of the achievement model, when reinforcement is 100 percent, P_s approaches 1 $(P_s \rightarrow 1)$, for the person receives

TABLE 4:8
Frequency of Typical and Atypical Selections for the Group
as a Whole and for Subjects Above and Below the Median IQ
(from Morris, 1966, p. 321)

Group and Job Preference	Resultant Achievement Motivation	
	High	Low
All subjects		
Typical	33	22
Atypical	6	22
High IQ		
Typical	21	10
Atypical	1	9
Low IQ		
Typical	12	12
Atypical	5	13

continual success. Given this reinforcement history, motivation theoretically is maximized for individuals in whom $M_{AF} > M_S$. However, when $P_s \rightarrow 1$ motivation is minimized among those in whom $M_S > M_{AF}$. The achievement model suggests that these high achievement-oriented students might become "bored" given this type of program. To maximize motivation, the model indicates that students in whom $M_S > M_{AF}$ should be given a program in which they initially can answer only half the questions correctly. This hypothesis has not been experimentally tested.

One general implication of the prediction outlined above concerning optimal programs is that in some situations failure can act as a positive reinforcer; that is, it can increase the probability of subsequent achievement-related responses.

Intelligence and Motivation

Many studies have demonstrated that the need for achievement and IQ or other tests of general ability are uncorrelated. On the other hand, anxiety about failure and intelligence are inversely related, $r \sim -.25$ (Sarason, Davidson, Lighthall, Waite, & Ruebush, 1960).

There are many possible interpretations of this particular correlation. It could be contended that individuals generally unsuccessful become anxious about failure. This suggests that intelligence influences the growth of motivational structures. Conversely, it can be argued that anxiety and other motivational factors influence intellectual development. Fear of failure does inhibit the undertaking of achievement-related actions. Thus, individuals high in this motivational disposition may avoid activities that enhance intellectual growth. Sarason, Hill, and Zimbardo (1964) report that the correlation between anxiety and intellectual performance increases with age. This suggests that there is a progressive interference with mental development because of the inhibiting effects of anxiety. Other psychologists (such as Hunt, 1961) also contend that motivational factors such as curiosity influence intellectual development. However, the chicken-egg dilemma—the temporal influence of anxiety on intelligence versus the influence of intelligence on anxiety—remains a moot point.

It also can be argued that the IQ-anxiety correlation is an "artifact" of the testing situation. Scores on IQ or other achievement tests reflect ability factors, but also all the other variables that influence performance. If anxiety impedes performance, as much data indicate, then it also should interfere with achievement performance on an IQ-type test. This interpretation intimates that anxiety may be unrelated to ability per se, but is related to scores on an ability-type exam that arouses concerns about failure. However, this explanation also would lead to the expectation that level of achievement needs and IQ score are correlated. Indeed, the lack of an IQ-need achievement correlation is rather paradoxical.

Still a fourth interpretation of the IQ-anxiety correlation is that individuals with a low IQ are not really smart enough to mask their true feelings about exams. That is, the negative correlation is caused by shortcomings in the use of self-report instruments.

The empirically reliable negative correlation between anxiety and achievement test performance is extremely important in the interpretation of empirical findings in the achievement area. Ability rather than motivational disparities may cause individuals highly anxious about failure to perform differently from those low in anxiety. For example, Mahone (1960) reports that intelligence is significantly related to resultant achievement motivation and to vocational realism. Partial correlation analyses eliminating the possible confounding effects of intelligence in his study did reveal that resultant achievement motivation is predictive of vocational realism. However, the magnitude of this relationship is modulated when the effects of intelligence are eliminated.

Grade Point Average

An experiment by Spielberger and Katzenmeyer (1959) is instructive when considering the joint effects of motivation and ability on performance. These investigators obtained the grade point average (GPA) of students classified as high or low in manifest anxiety. The students were further subclassified into levels of scholastic achievement on the basis of scores on a college entrance exam.

The relationship of GPA to level of anxiety and ability is shown in

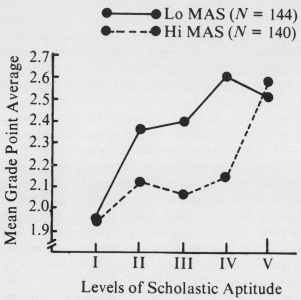

FIGURE 4:8. Mean grade point average for college students at five levels of scholastic ability who are high or low in anxiety (from Spielberger, 1962, p. 423).

Figure 4:8. There is a clear main effect of academic competence, a strong effect due to level of anxiety, and an interaction between these two independent variables. Grade point average does not differ between the groups high or low in anxiety at the extreme ability levels, but is influenced by anxiety at levels of intermediate scholastic ability.

Atkinson (1964) interprets these results within his general theoretical framework. He assumes that for students intermediate in ability there also is an intermediate subjective probability of doing well in school. Thus, motivation should be maximally aroused for students low in anxiety, and maximally inhibitory among highly anxious students. This should result in disparities in GPA. On the other hand, at the extreme ability levels, where P_s is near 1 or 0, hope of success and fear of failure are minimally aroused, and hence do not affect GPA. In sum, Atkinson argues that motivational differences, mediated by the P_s variable in his model, are responsible for the observed GPA differences among students differing in ability and level of anxiety.

Atkinson's interpretation is provocative, but his explanation may be questioned. It is conceivable that very bright students generally perform well in school, regardless of other factors such as motivation. In a similar manner, it is likely that students who are not very bright generally perform poorly, regardless of motivational factors. Hence, performance differences as a function of motivation relatively are confined to groups intermediate in ability. Whether the GPA differences for these groups are then mediated by P_s remains to be demonstrated.

The overall relationship between GPA and anxiety is rather striking in the Spielberger and Katzenmeyer study. On the other hand, the majority of investigations relating need for achievement with GPA find, at best, extremely low positive correlations. Grade point average is an overdetermined motivational index. One may obtain a high grade for any number of reasons, such as to receive a new car from pleased parents or to be deferred from the Army. As intimated previously, as the extrinsic sources of motivation to undertake achievement tasks increase, the relative variance accounted for by achievement needs decrease. It therefore should be expected that need for achievement will be only weakly related to GPA.

Inasmuch as IQ and GPA generally correlate approximately $r = .50$, it should be possible for some combination of motivational factors to significantly predict the remaining GPA variance. However, a definitive study demonstrating a motivation-GPA relationship does not exist. McKeachie (1961) has shown that both need for affiliation and need for power are determinants of GPA. He found that when classrooms are highly cued for affiliation (with, for example, a friendly, warm instructor) individuals high in need for affiliation attain better grades than students low in affiliative needs. In a similar manner, in classrooms structured toward power needs (with a teacher allowing many questions, for example) students high in need for power attain higher grades than those low in this motive disposition. However, McKeachie reports that the relationship between GPA, achievement needs, and classrooms differentially cued for achievement motivation is complex and not entirely interpretable.

Ability Grouping

Atkinson (1964) has pointed out the relevance of his conception of achievement motivation to the current practice of grouping students in classrooms on the basis of equal ability.

The assumption that an individual's knowledge of his own ability (past performance) influences his expectancy of success (P_s) in an academic situation has further interesting implications for understanding motivation in the schools. When the full range of abilities is represented among the students in a classroom, only the students of average ability should be very strongly motivated to achieve and/or to avoid failure, depending upon the relative strengths of their M_s and M_{AF}, the two personality dispositions which they "bring in the door" Neither the very bright nor very dull student should have his achievement-related dispositions aroused, for the competitive achievement situation will seem either "too easy" or "too difficult." What, then, should happen if classes are organized in terms of ability level? The bright student, surrounded by other equally bright students, and the less endowed student, surrounded by peers of comparable ability, should find themselves in an altogether different achievement-oriented situation. If the theory is correct, and the assumption that knowledge of one's own general ability influences the subjective probability of success at any task, there should be an intensification of both interest in achieving and anxiety about failing (depending upon the relative strength of the achievement-related dispositions of personality) when students of nearly equal ability sit in the same classroom [p. 255].

Atkinson and O'Connor (1963; also reported in Atkinson & Feather, 1966) tested hypotheses derived from the above analysis. They predicted that motivation is enhanced in homogeneous as compared to heterogeneous classrooms among students in whom $M_S > M_{AF}$. Conversely, they expected motivation to be inhibited among those in whom $M_{AF} > M_S$ when placed in an equal-ability classroom grouping.

To test these predictions, achievement needs and anxiety about failure were assessed among students either in homogeneous or heterogeneous ability-grouped classes during the sixth grade. Previously, all the students had been in classes not grouped according to ability. Thus, the group defined as "experimental" changed from a heterogeneous to a homogeneous class, while the composition of the control or comparison group remained heterogeneous. The dependent variables in the study included standard achievement test scores obtained during the sixth grade and self-report measures of interest in academic activities and classes.

The interpretation of the findings of this study are complex, for students in the control or heterogeneous group were unexpectedly higher in achievement performance during the fifth grade than the students placed in the homogeneous group. Therefore, Atkinson and O'Connor used growth or change in achievement score between the fifth and sixth grades to infer the effects of ability grouping. However, use of this index is complicated by the fact that students initially scoring high in performance cannot increase as much as those scoring low. These problems merely are mentioned here to indicate some difficulties likely to be encountered in field studies. It is not surprising that the vast majority of psychologists forgo the "field research" so strongly advocated by Lewin.

Atkinson and O'Connor were able to devise a meaningful index of ability growth apparently free of the problems mentioned above. Their findings reveal that individuals in whom $M_S > M_{AF}$ exhibit significantly greater achievement growth in the homogeneous than heterogeneous class.

Contrary to expectation, the direction of the results was the same for students in whom $M_{AF} > M_S$, although for this group the findings do not approach statistical significance.

Self-reports of interest in school activities also provide support for the hypotheses of Atkinson and O'Connor. Students in whom $M_S > M_{AF}$ expressed greater academic interests in the homogeneous class than those in whom $M_{AF} > M_S$. Among the latter group self-reports of motivation were significantly greater in the control than in the experimental class. This is especially interesting, inasmuch as students in whom $M_{AF} > M_S$ actually perform better in the experimental class.

The Atkinson and O'Connor study is in need of replication and extension. The findings are indeed promising, and have significant implications for educational practices. Perhaps the greatest general import of the study is the ease with which the theory of achievement motivation can be brought to bear upon educational practices that intuitively seem reasonable, but may be detrimental to the student.

Major Field of Concentration

When choosing a major field of study students are confronted with a decision between a number of achievement-related alternatives. Once more, the possibility exists that the alternatives differ in perceived level of difficulty, and that choice is a function of difficulty level interacting with a motivational disposition.

To test the hypothesis that achievement motivation and P_s influence one's area of academic concentration, Isaacson (1964) assigned various academic programs in college P_s ratings. This was accomplished by: (1) having students estimate how well they could do in the various programs, and (2) deriving an objective difficulty ratio consisting of the average grades given in a course/the average brightness of the enrolled students. These two indexes were in close accord, and were used to classify major areas of concentration as difficult (low P_s), intermediate (middle P_s) or easy (high P_s). Isaacson also obtained achievement and anxiety scores and chosen field of concentration for approximately 110 male and 110 female students. These students had superior academic records, and nearly 60 percent were enrolled in a highly selective honors program at the University of Michigan.

Figure 4:9 shows the students' choice of field of concentration as a function of the difficulty of the area and resultant achievement motivation. Figure 4:9 portrays the data for male students in the upper and lower 25 percent of the resultant achievement motive distribution. The figure reveals that the observed pattern of choice is in agreement with the general

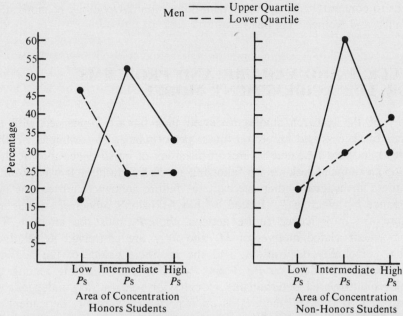

FIGURE 4:9. The percentage of men in the upper and lower quartile of achievement motivation concentrating in low, intermediate, or high probability of success areas. The left-hand portion of the figure describes choices of men in the honors program ($N = 35$); the right-hand portion, choices of men not in the honors program ($N = 20$) (from Isaacson, 1964, p. 450).

predictions derived from the achievement model. Within both the honors and nonhonors prorams, students in whom $M_S > M_{AF}$ are more likely to select a major of intermediate difficulty than those in whom $M_{AF} > M_S$.

None of the predicted relationships between choice and motive classification were confirmed among the female students in Isaacson's investigation. Thus far this chapter has avoided the difficult problem of disparities in the predictive value of the TAT and the theory of achievement motivation for males and females. It is generally true that hypothesis confirmation is much more likely when using male rather than female subjects. Perhaps achievement striving among females is a more complex phenomenon, inasmuch as achievement behavior among women may conflict with the role assigned and ascribed to them by socicty. Some evidence even suggests a fear of success exists among women that may be as potent a determinant of achievement avoidance behavior as the fear of failure. Women tend to perceive negative consequences associated with achievement success, such as loss of friends (Horner, 1966). McClelland (1966) has gone as far as to contend, "Clearly, we need a differential psychology of motivation for men and women" (p. 481).

SUCCESS AND FAILURE AND PROBLEMS FOR THE ACHIEVEMENT MODEL

Many of the research studies reviewed thus far are concerned with the effects of success and failure on future performance. For example, Feather (1961) induced repeated failures in his study of persistence, and Moulton (1965) examined task choice following success or failure. It was assumed by these investigators that success and failure influence subsequent performance by affecting P_s. Indeed, within Atkinson's model, if success and failure are to influence future actions, then P_s must be affected. The achievement-related motives of M_S and M_{AF} are conceived as relatively stable personality dispositions, and the incentive values of the goal are completely dependent on P_s. Thus, P_s is the only variable among the achievement-related determinants of behavior free to vary independently from trial to trial. Further, P_s is an experiential variable, dependent, in part, on the person's past history of success and failure.

A review of the literature pertaining to the motivational effects of success and failure yields results that are very difficult to predict with Atkinson's conception of achievement motivation. Two investigations among the many experiments manipulating success and failure are selected here for discussion because they are methodologically dissimilar, yet their results may be interpreted as being consistent.

Although experiments with somewhat compatible results are selected for examination, the reader should not be lulled into the false conclusion that the data in the success-failure area are either generally reliable or interpretable. Butterfield and Zigler (1965), noting the empirical inconsistencies concerning the motivational effects of achievement outcomes, state that

it is extremely difficult to reconcile the inconsistencies in this body of work, especially since the studies differ in: (a) the method of inducing success and failure experiences, i.e. experimentally manipulating the amount of objective success or failure experienced and/or having the experimenter tell the child that he is doing well or poorly; (b) the degree of success and failure involved in the experimental manipulations; (c) the degree of similarity between the task upon which the subject received success or failure and the criterion measure; and (d) the criterion measures themselves. Despite these methodological differences, it appears extremely unlikely that a single general process, e.g., drive level of the subject, underlies the disparate findings reported above. This very disparity indicates that certain more idiographic variables influence the reactions of children to success and failure experiences [p. 26].

Despite the warning of Butterfield and Zigler, a general empirical deduction is reached here concerning the motivational effects of success and failure. Theoretical extensions of Atkinson's model are then presented that enable the model to explain these data.

The Motivational Effects of Failure

The effects of failure on performance have been examined with a number of experimental paradigms. In one paradigm false information repeatedly is introduced that indicates that the subject is performing poorly. Speed or quality of performance, level of emotionality, and so on, are monitored as the subject receives these reports of failure. In a somewhat different paradigm, the subject is given one or more failure reports during a preliminary series of trials. Then an index of motivation is measured during a subsequent test trial (s).

Lucas (1952), employing the latter experimental procedure, examined the effects of anxiety and failure on immediate memory. Six series of ten consonants were presented to subjects for immediate memorization. The degree of failure was varied between experimental conditions, with failure reported after 6, 4, 2, or 0 trials. Then a test series was administered in which the subjects were asked to remember three lists of ten consonants each. In addition to manipulating the degree of prior failure, the subjects also were classified as high or low in anxiety, determined by their score on the MA scale.

The results of this investigation are portrayed in Figure 4:10. For highly anxious subjects, performance decreases as a function of the degree of prior failure. Conversely, performance increases as a function of the number of past failures for subjects low in anxiety.

Atkinson (1964) discusses this experiment in detail, for he believes that drive theory cannot account for the observed results. Atkinson contends that drive theory perhaps can account for the increments or decrements in performance that individuals highly anxious about failure generally display on easy or complex tasks. Heightened drive theoretically may impede or retard performance for these individuals. However, he argues that drive theory cannot account for the increments in performance which often are displayed by individuals low in anxiety when under stress (failure) (Atkinson, 1960).[2] Atkinson concludes, "to explain this result [the

---

[2] It has been pointed out (Kukla, personal communication) that Atkinson's theory cannot account for the fact that individuals high in anxiety perform better than those low in anxiety on an easy (or successful) task.

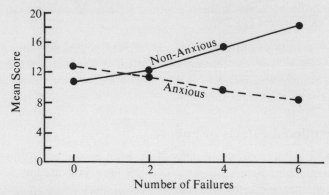

FIGURE 4:10. Mean recall score in four experimental conditions varying in the number of failures, with subjects classified as high or low in anxiety (12 subjects in each group) (from Lucas, 1952, p. 64).

improvement in performance of individuals low in anxiety when under failure stress], we must turn to contemporary research on achievement motivation" (1964, p. 221).

But the data reported by Lucas are also very difficult to explain within the theoretical framework offered by achievement theory. To account for the observed increments and decrements in performance respectively displayed by individuals low and high in anxiety, Atkinson would have to postulate that for both motive groups the memory task initially is perceived as easy, and the P_s remains above .50 for six failure experiences. That is, P_s is slowly moving toward the level of intermediate difficulty. This would result in performance increments for those low in anxiety and decrements for subjects who are highly anxious.

Unfortunately, the initial P_s at the task was not manipulated or controlled by Lucas, and P_s estimates were not obtained following failure. But it is reasonable to argue that the retention of ten consonants is not perceived as an easy task, and that prior to the sixth failure P_s is below .50. If this were the case, then the data contradict the predictions derived from Atkinson's conception. Given the assumption that the task is not perceived as easy, or that P_s falls below .50 prior to trial six, the achievement model leads to the prediction that individuals low in anxiety will display decrements in performance prior to the final trial, and individuals high in anxiety will exhibit performance increments.

Another experimental investigation (Lazarus & Eriksen, 1952) also illustrates the difficulties of the achievement model in accounting for the results in the success-failure area. The subjects in the Lazarus and Eriksen experiment were administered a digit-symbol test and were informed that the test could influence their "status in school." One group was then told that they performed poorly, while a second group was given feedback that they did well. Following these false feedbacks the test was readministered, with the experimenter continually reporting fraudulent information that resulted in further successes or failure experiences.

Individual differences were not assessed in this investigation. However, the subjects were classified as high or low in GPA. The data revealed that in the failure condition the performance of high GPA students was enhanced, while performance of those low in GPA decreased when given repeated failures. If one were willing to accept that high GPA students are relatively low in anxiety and low GPA students relatively high in anxiety, then the data reported by Lazarus and Eriksen are consistent with the Lucas findings. That is, those low in anxiety are motivated by failure, while individuals high in anxiety are inhibited by failure at an achievement-related goal.

Given the achievement model, the displayed pattern of results should only be observed if the digit-symbol task is perceived as easy, and the P_s remains above .50 on the test series. Again, however, there is no evidence to support these suppositions and little justification to maintain that P_s remains relatively high, given the severity of the failure inductions reported by Lazarus and Eriksen. Thus, the data are not readily explainable by Atkinson's achievement model.

Other investigators report similar interactive effects of failure. For example, Mandler and Sarason (1952) conclude that "the optimal condition for a low anxiety group is one in which the subjects are given a failure report" (p. 173). On the other hand, Zeller (1951) found that retention (or speed of relearning) is adversely affected by failure among subjects who would be classified as highly anxious. Further, Weiner (1966) and Weiner and Schneider (1971) report that subjects highly anxious about failure exhibit relative performance decrements when attempting an easy verbal learning task if they are given false failure feedback. Conversely, subjects low in anxiety apparently are motivated by failure and exhibit superior performance when given false failure feedback. The increments or decrements in performance following failure as a function of anxiety level reported by Lazarus and Eriksen, Lucas, Mandler and Sarason, Weiner, Zeller, and others are independent of, or override, the motivational effects of P_s.

The findings reviewed above led this author to the following empirical generalizations:

1. Motivation is enhanced following failure among individuals high in resultant achievement motivation.

2. Motivation is inhibited following failure among individuals low in resultant achievement motivation (see Weiner, 1970).

The Motivational Effects of Success

In success, as in failure, there appears to be an interaction between motivational effects and individual differences in achievement-related needs. The verbal learning experiments discussed at length conducted by this writer (Weiner, 1966; and Weiner & Schneider, 1971) indicate that individuals low in resultant achievement motivation are motivated or encouraged by a success experience (also see Zeller, 1951). On the other hand, subjects high in resultant achievement motivation display relative performance decrements given repeated success. Perhaps the most straightforward test of the hypothesis that success differentially influences behavior as a function of level of achievement concerns is reported by Child and Whiting (1950). These investigators merely asked subjects whether their successful goal attainments are generally followed by relaxation or renewed goal striving. The subjects also were classified according to their expectation of frustration prior to initiating the activity, and their stated history of success and failure at similar tasks. Guided by the definition of achievement motivation, it is assumed here that individuals high in resultant achievement motivation expect to encounter little frustration and have a history of achievement success, while those low in resultant achievement motivation expect to experience failure and perceive that past achievement efforts have not resulted in goal attainment.

The responses to the "striving" versus "relaxation" questions for individuals believed here to be high or low in resultant achievement are shown in Table 4:9. The data reveal that individuals having characteristics associated with high achievement motivation report they often relax after a success, while those with characteristics of individuals low in resultant achievement motivation state they are likely to exhibit renewed goal striving following goal attainment.

The following generalizations summarize the data reviewed above:

3. Motivation is decreased following success among individuals high in resultant achievement motivation.

4. Motivation is enhanced following success among individuals low in resultant achievement motivation (see Weiner, 1970).

Summary of Motivational Effects

An interaction has been observed between the motivational effects of success and failure and personality dispositions in achievement related motives. Success enhances performance of individuals low in achievement concerns

TABLE 4:9
Relation of Renewed Goal Striving to Anticipation of Frustration at the Beginning of the Incident and to Perceived Previous Achievement Experiences When Striving for Similar Goals
(from Child & Whiting, 1950, p. 674)

	Simple Attainment Incidents	
Renewed Goal Striving	Expected Little Frustration[a]	Expected Considerable Frustration[b]
Yes	31	60
No	27	33
	$\chi^2 = 1.5$	
	$p < .50$	
	History of Easy Success	History of Difficulty or Failure
Yes	23	67
No	28	31
	$\chi^2 = 6.6$	
	$p < .02$	

[a] Column describes characteristics of individuals high in resultant achievement motivation.
[b] Column describes characteristics of individuals low in resultant achievement motivation.

while failure further inhibits their achievement strivings. Conversely, success dampens the performance of individuals high in resultant achievement motivation while failure increases their achievement strivings.

A MODIFICATION OF THE ACHIEVEMENT MODEL

The achievement model as formulated by Atkinson in 1957 cannot account for the empirical generalizations outlined above pertaining to the interactive effects of success and failure and achievement related needs. However, an addition to the model of achievement motivation introduced by Atkinson and Cartwright (1964) and elaborated by Atkinson (1964, 1969) helps to overcome this difficulty. This conceptual change apparently was not introduced in response to the contradictory or unexplainable data reviewed above. Rather, the modification was offered because Atkinson and his colleagues noted a theoretical weakness in the prior model.

It is informative to reconsider McClelland's definition of a motive when examining the perceived theoretical shortcoming in the model for achievement motivation. According to McClelland et al. (1953), a motive denotes a "redintegration by a cue of a change in an affective state" (p. 28). Therefore, motives, and the behavior they produce, are aroused by stimuli having emotional significance to the organism. Behavior is stimulus-bound; action is instigated only following the reception of a stimulus. Thus, the criticism of conceiving man as stimulus-bound, which Atkinson (1964) and others had leveled against drive theorists, also is applicable to the conception of man implied by achievement theorists, who view man as being at rest until an achievement-related activity is perceived. This stimulus arouses a latent disposition to succeed and experience pride, and a subjective expectancy of doing well. In addition, the task stimulus arouses fear and a subjective expectancy of failure. Appropriate approach or avoidance activity is then initiated. If the behavior is approach-oriented, then the behavior will persist until some other impinging stimulus arouses a tendency of greater magnitude that changes the direction of behavior.

The conception of a stimulus-bound organism is untenable to Atkinson and Cartwright (1964). They state:

A few decades ago, psychologists frequently got into heated debates over the desirability of attempting to construct a theory of an active organism. The debate has subsided, and as we review the various conceptions of determinants of performance and decision that have been proposed, it is quite clear that psychologists have so far settled for a theory of a reactive organism. Attempts to develop formal statements of how the impetus to act in a particular situation is determined invariably presume that initiation of a tendency to respond resides in a stimulus. The conceptual analysis tends to begin with a stimulus. Just as Aristotle found it impossible to conceive the cause of terrestrial motion without positing the action of external force, psychologists find it difficult to conceive the possibility of an active tendency to perform a response without an immediately present stimulus, somewhere inside or outside of *S*, as the cue or trigger or instigation. Yet neurophysiologists have thrown away the stagnant picture of the brain as a machine designed to turn off excitations from outside. They are beginning to yield a new picture, one in which an active brain selects what shall and what shall not be stimuli for it (Pribram, 1960). Does psychology lag behind in its conceptual and experimental analysis of the determinants of preference and performance? We think so [pp. 575–76].

Theorists prior to Atkinson also conceived of an active organism, not bound by incoming external stimulation (Freud, 1915; Hebb, 1949; Lewin, 1935; Peak, 1958). According to Atkinson, however, the major motivational theorists such as Freud and Lewin did not fully develop this notion. For example, Freud postulates that behavior persists in the absence of an instigating, external stimulus. But action is sustained by the continued presence of internal stimuli (see Rapaport, 1960). Lewin also postulates a persisting tense system that acts as a constant force on the organism. This tense state is not coordinated with or dependent upon any internal or external stimulus. But Atkinson feels that the Lewinian model of motivation does not fully develop the tension conception.

How, then, does Atkinson alter his model so it is no longer stimulus bound? He states (1969):

The seed of the general idea for a psychology of motivation is contained in Freud's assumption that the wish persists until it is expressed or satisfied and in Lewin's attempt to account for the persistence of the *tendency* to complete a task when activity has been interrupted. It is *the idea that the immediate stimulus situation (conceived as an influence that is external to the relatively autonomous process of the brain) does not cause a tendency to act*—that is, does not elicit a certain response tendency from a state of rest—*but operates on already active tendencies to produce a change in their strength.*

Most psychologists would willingly concede that the subject they study is at least as active as a rolling ball. Yet the conceptual schemes which have arisen in objective study of behavior (except for Lewin's) still correspond to an Aristotelian conception of motion, that is, the stimulus (external influence) is viewed as the *cause* of the tendency to act. What would follow if we were to assume, as a *first principle of motivation,* that *a goal-directed tendency, once aroused, persists until it is satisfied?* . . .

Given the assumption that a previously aroused but unsatisfied tendency to attain a goal will persist, we can restate the conception of the immediate determinants of a particular goal-directed tendency at a given time as follows:

$$T_s = (M_s \times P_s \times I_s) + T_{Gi} \text{ [notation mine]}$$

In this assertion, T_{Gi} is introduced to represent the persistent unsatisfied tendency. It might appropriately be called *"the inertial tendency"* to remind us of the physical analogy. By employing the capital G as the subscript on the inertial tendency we mean to imply, for example, that when the tendency to achieve has been aroused in some particular activity and the particular goal is not attained, what persists is the *general* tendency to achieve success. The persistent tendency toward success should enhance the final strength of any particular tendency to achieve that is subsequently aroused. The inertial tendency, T_{Gi}, should, in other words, have a relatively non-specific effect on a whole class of subsequent activities that is comparable, in this respect, to the relatively non-specific effect of a motive, M_s. This means that the persistent tendency to achieve will influence the strength of any subsequent tendency to undertake an activity that is expected to lead to success, but will not influence specific tendencies to undertake activities which are expected to lead to other kinds of consequences (e.g., eating, sexual activity, affiliation, etc.) [1964, pp. 310, 311].

Atkinson (1969) restates this position in a later article:

It should also be apparent that the present scheme implies that Tolman was wrong in stressing that behavior, once initiated, persists until an objectively defined goal is reached. A goal-directed sequence of activities once initiated . . . does not always persist until the goal is attained. Just as often it is interrupted by some other activity.

The present scheme emphasizes the distinction between the argument of Tolman that behavior persists, and the assumption of Freud that the *tendency* (i.e., motivation) persists even when not overtly expressed in behavior. It is the Freudian concept of persistence, persistence of the unfulfilled wish, that is represented in the concept of inertial tendency [pp. 119–20].

Atkinson believes that specifying "inertia" as a first principle of motivation results in a fundamental alteration in the study of motivation. He states: "The focus of interest must turn from the initiation, persistence, and cessation of the single goal-directed episode to the juncture or joint between two episodes that constitutes the cessation of one and the initiation of another" (1969, p. 106). That is, he suggests that change of activity become the central focus for the study of motivational processes. This particular position carries us somewhat farther afield than is necessary here. The reader is directed to the sources of the quotations cited above and to Atkinson and Birch (1970) for a more detailed examination of this issue.

Inertial Motivation

A concrete example, substituting numerical values for the somewhat esoteric concept just introduced, illustrates the significance of "inertial" motivation in predicting achievement-related behavior. Assume that individuals in whom $M_S > M_{AF}$ fail at a task (Task A). For ease of illustration, assume that prior to undertaking Task A the strength of inertial motivation is zero. Further, P_s at Task A = .50, $M_S = 2$, $M_{AF} = 1$, and extrinsic motivation = 0. Hence, the strength of resultant achievement motivation to undertake Task A is

$$[(2 \times .5 \times .5) - (1 \times .5 \times .5)] = .25.$$

These individuals subsequently attempt a different achievement-related activity (Task B). The P_s at Task B is independent of the P_s at Task A, and thus unaffected by the prior success or failure at Task A. Further, the P_s at Task B = .50. The strength of resultant achievement motivation aroused by the immediate task stimulus also is equal to .25. In addition, however, within the context of achievement behavior, failure is the antecedent condition that results in the continuation of previously aroused motivation. The strength of motivation to undertake Task B therefore is augmented by the persisting unsatisfied positive motivation resulting from failure at Task A. T_{Gi} is determined by calculating the positive aroused unsatisfied motivation at the prior trial. The total achievement tendency to undertake Task B is thus equal to .75—(.25 units of motivation aroused by the immediate stimulus plus .50 units of persisting positive motivation, determined by the $M_S \times P_S \times I_S$ value for Task A).

An empirical prediction is now evident: Subjects receiving prior failure at an activity are more motivated to achieve than subjects either not engaging in a prior achievement task, or those who experience success (goal attainment) at a prior task. The preliminary experimental paradigm to assess the motivational effects of unsatisfied achievement striving is shown in Diagram 4:1. The diagram indicates that both control and experimental groups undertake Task B after prior experiences that differentially influence the amount of persisting motivation. Then some motivational index is assessed during Task B performance.

But two problems remain unanswered given this analysis. First, the general prediction that subjects in the experimental (failure) condition will perform with greater vigor than those in the control (success) condition is contradicted by observations of individuals in whom $M_{AF} > M_S$. These individuals perform worse after failure than after success. The prediction that motivation is enhanced more by failure than success is confirmed only among subjects in whom $M_S > M_{AF}$. Second, the assumption that sucess or failure at Task A does not influence the P_s at Task B is generally untrue. Operations that result in the maintenance or decrements of inertial tendencies (failure and sucess) also affect the motivation aroused by the subsequent achievement task by influencing P_s. The dangers of having one operation affect more than one construct in a theoretical system were documented in Chapter II. There it was pointed out that time of deprivation influences both drive level and the internal stimulus state of the organism. This confounding gives rise to difficult theoretical problems when one attempts to interpret the effects of time of deprivation

DIAGRAM 4:1
Preliminary Experimental Paradigm Examining the
Motivational (Inertial) Effects of Failure

	Control Condition 1	Control Condition 2	Experimental (Inertial) Condition
Step 1	No Task	Task A Success	Task A Failure
Step 2	Task B	Task B	Task B

on performance. Thus, an experimental design is required that disentangles the motivational effects produced by P_s from the effects attributable to inertial motivation. The experimental design in Diagram 4:1 is adequate, but the method of separating inertial effects from P_s effects has not been indicated.

Problem One: Explaining Failure Effects When $M_{AF} > M_s$

The inertial motivational tendency is conceived by Atkinson and Cartwright (1964) and Atkinson (1964, 1969) as a continuation of aroused positive motivation, or the persistence of the tendency towards a goal. Weiner (1965a, 1970), on the other hand, suggests that the concept be broadened to include the persistent fear or threat of failure which also is aroused in achievement settings. That is, he suggests that both approach and avoidance tendencies persist following failure.

The distinction between a model specifying that only positive strivings persist, and one postulating the continuation of both approach and avoidance tendencies, is clarified with a numerical example. Table 4:10 shows the strength of achievement motivation among individuals differing in motive classification, given the two different conceptions of inertial motivation.

Consider first the predictions for individuals in whom $M_S > M_{AF}$. It is assumed that for these individuals $M_S = 2$, $M_{AF} = 1$, P_s at both Task A and Task B $= .50$, and the strength in inertial motivation (T_{Gi}) on performance at Task A $= 0$. If only approach tendencies persist following failure at Task A, then the strength of motivation toward Task B is determined by the motivation aroused by that particular task (.25), plus the strength of the persisting positive goal striving, determined by $M_S \times P_s \times I_s$, which is $2 \times .5 \times .5$. Thus, motivation toward Task B is augmented by .50 units of motivation because of the prior failure at Task A, and is equal to .75.

On the other hand, if it is assumed that the threat of failure also persists following failure, then the persisting *resultant* inertial tendency (inertial approach motivation minus inertial avoidance motivation) is composed of .50 units of approach motivation, and .25 units of avoidance motivation. The avoidance motivation is a function of $M_{AF} \times P_f \times I_f$, or $1 \times .5 \times .5$. The persisting *resultant* tendency therefore is positive, and has a value of .25; that is, $.50 - .25$. Given the persistence of both approach and avoidance tendencies the subsequent achievement tendency is augmented by .25 units of motivation, rather than the .50 units of motivation that represent the persistence of only approach motivation.

Although the two conceptions of inertial motivation lead to different

TABLE 4:10

Strength of Achievement Motivation According to Two Conceptions of Inertial Motivation

Motive Classification		Inertial Models	
		Positive Inertial Motivation[a]	Resultant Inertial Motivation[b]
Task A	$M_S > M_{AF}$	$2 \times .5 \times .5 - (1 \times .5 \times .5) + 0^c = .25$	$2 \times .5 \times .5 - (1 \times .5 \times .5) + 0 = .25$
Task B		$2 \times .5 \times .5 - (1 \times .5 \times .5) + .50^d = .75$	$2 \times .5 \times .5 - (1 \times .5 \times .5) + .25^e = .50$
Task A	$M_{AF} > M_S$	$1 \times .5 \times .5 - (2 \times .5 \times .5) + 0 = -.25$	$1 \times .5 \times .5 - (2 \times .5 \times .5) + 0 = -.25$
Task B		$1 \times .5 \times .5 - (2 \times .5 \times .5) + .25 = 0$	$1 \times .5 \times .5 - (2 \times .5 \times .5) + (-.25) = -.50$

[a] Persistence of only approach motivation following failure.
[b] Persistence of approach and avoidance motivation following failure.
[c] Strength of persisting motivation at Task A = 0.
[d] $2 \times .5 \times .5$, or persisting motivation following failure at Task A.
[e] $2 \times .5 \times .5$, or persisting positive motivation, minus $1 \times .5 \times .5$, or persisting avoidance motivation.

expectations concerning the strength of persisting motivation among subjects in whom $M_S > M_{AF}$, both yield the identical directional prediction that performance will be augmented by failure, and will be greater after failure than after success. Hence, the distinction between the persistence of approach versus resultant motivation may not be critical among individuals in whom $M_S > M_{AF}$. However, the distinction between the two conceptions of inertial motivation is decisive when considering the behavior among individuals in whom $M_{AF} > M_S$.

The strength of achievement strivings when $M_{AF} > M_S$ is shown in the lower half of Table 4:10. It is assumed that $M_{AF} = 2$, $M_S = 1$, P_s at Task A and Task B = .50, and that persisting motivation prior to Task A = 0. Again the outcome at Task A is failure. Examination of only the achievement-related sources of motivation reveals that the strength of the tendency to undertake Task A = —.25. Thus, achievement behavior would not be initiated unless extrinsic sources of motivation also were aroused.

Given the assumption that only positive strivings persist following failure, Table 4:10 shows the strength of achievement motivation to undertake Task B after failure at Task A is equal to 0. The increment in motivation, from —.25 at Task A to 0 at Task B, is due to the persisting positive tendency aroused by Task A ($1 \times .5 \times .5$). In this particular example the strength of the persisting positive striving is as great as the inhibition aroused by Task B. On the other hand, if the threat of failure also persists following failure, then the persisting resultant motivation after failure at Task A is inhibitory, $(1 \times .5 \times .5) - (2 \times .5 \times .5) = -.25$. The strength of the tendency to undertake Task B is thus further diminished from —.25 to —.50. The persisting resultant tendency, which is inhibitory and has a value of —.25, adds to the inhibition aroused by the task stimulus (—.25) to yield a value of —.50.

In sum, Table 4:10 reveals that if only positive motivation persists following nonattainment of an achievement goal, then both individuals in whom $M_S > M_{AF}$ and those in whom $M_{AF} > M_S$ are more motivated after a failure. On the other hand, if both approach and avoidance tendencies persist after failure, then only individuals in whom $M_S > M_{AF}$ should exhibit performance increments after failure. Among those in whom $M_{AF} > M_S$, performance decrements are anticipated. Thus, the resultant inertial model predicts an interaction between the motivational effects of failure and individual differences in achievement-related needs. The data previously reviewed reveals that the resultant inertial model is supported by the empirical data.

It is therefore postulated that previously aroused but unsatisfied approach and avoidance motivation continue to exert influence following nonattainment of an achievement-related goal. If the previously aroused approach motivation exceeds that of avoidance motivation, as among individuals in whom $M_S > M_{AF}$, then the persisting tendency augments future performance. That is, prior failure increases achievement strivings. Conversely, if the aroused avoidance motivation exceeds that of the approach tendency, as among individuals in whom $M_{AF} > M_S$, then the persisting tendency dampens future performance. That is, prior failure further inhibits achievement strivings.

Problem Two: Disentangling Stimulus from Inertial Effects

Failure influences P_s as well as being the antecedent condition which theoretically results in the continuation of aroused motivation. Therefore, as already indicated, the motivational effects attributable to a change in P_s must be separated from the effects of failure on inertial tendencies before conclusions can be reached about persisting motivation.

The separation of inertial from P_s effects was first attempted by Weiner (1965a) in a study guided by the experimental procedure developed by Feather (1961). Subjects classified as high or low in resultant achievement motivation were given an achievement task to perform, knowing that they could shift to an activity unrelated to achievement whenever they wished. There were two experimental conditions. In one condition false norms conveyed that the achievement task was relatively difficult ($P_s = .30$); in the second condition the norms indicated that the task was relatively easy ($P_s = .70$). The subjects in the $P_s = .30$ condition received repeated failure; subjects in the $P_s = .70$ condition experienced repeated success. A crucial assumption made by Weiner was that the change in P_s following success is equal in magnitude, but opposite in direction, to the change following failure. For example, if success in this situation increases P_s from .70 to .80, then failure is assumed to decrease P_s from .30 to .20.

Given these experimental conditions, the strength of achievement motivation aroused on the initial trial is identical in the success and failure conditions among subjects with identical motive dispositions. The motivation aroused in the success condition is equal to $(M_S - M_{AF}) \times (.7 \times .3)$, while motivation in the failure condition is equal to $(M_S - M_{AF}) \times (.3 \times .7)$. Further, given the assumption of equal P_s changes following respective success and failure, the motivation aroused by the immediate stimulus remains equal in the two experimental conditions among subjects with the same motivational dispositions. For example, if P_s increases .10 following success and decreases .10 following failrue, resultant achievement motivations on the second trial are

$(M_S - M_{AF}) \times (.8 \times .2)$ and $(M_S - M_{AF}) \times (.2 \times .8)$, respectively. But the failure condition results in a continuation of previously aroused motivation, while in the success condition aroused motivation decreases because there is attainment of the goal. Thus, this procedure equates the motivational effects attributable to the stimulus situation, while varying the strength of inertial motivation between conditions. The experimental design therefore permits an examination of the effects of failure on only persisting inertial tendencies.

The achievement task employed by Weiner (1965a) was a digit-symbol substitution test. This task is frequently used in motivational research (see previously discussed studies by Mandler & Sarason, 1952; Lazarus & Eriksen, 1952), for it is sensitive to motivational influences. There were two dependent variables: speed of performance (number of substitutions per unit of time) and persistence of behavior (number of digit tasks attempted before undertaking the nonachievement-related alternate activity). Failure and success were manipulated by interrupting subjects prior to task completion, or allowing them to finish before an artificial time limit.

It was hypothesized that subjects in whom $M_S > M_{AF}$ would perform with greater intensity and persist longer at the achievement task in the failure than in the success condition. On the other hand, performance and persistence were expected to be greater in the success than failure condition among subjects in whom $M_{AF} > M_S$. These predictions, derived from the resultant inertial model of achievement motivation, contrast with predictions derived from Atkinson's 1957 model. The model first formulated by Atkinson specifies that motivation is equal among subjects with identical motivational dispositions in the success and failure conditions. The motivation aroused by the immediate stimulus situation is assumed to be identical in the success and failure conditions, for P_S is symmetrical around the .50 level. Thus, performance and persistence should not differ between the two experimental conditions.

The general direction of the results confirmed the hypotheses derived from the resultant inertial model. Speed of performance among subjects in whom $M_S > M_{AF}$ was greater following failure than success. Conversely, among subjects in whom $M_{AF} > M_S$, performance intensity was greater after success than after failure (see Table 4:11). (All subjects in the experiment perform more poorly on Trial 2 than on Trial 1 because of fatigue. Thus, only relative comparisons are meaningful.) In addition, the subjects in the high motive group persist longer given repeated failure than given repeated success, while there is a trend among subjects in the low motive group to persist longer in the success than failure condition. In sum, for both dependent variables the Motive $\times$ Condition interaction predicted by the resultant inertial model was exhibited.

TABLE 4:11

Time (in Seconds) to Complete 60 Digit-Symbol Substitutions on
Trials One and Two (adapted from Weiner, 1965a, p. 437)

| | Motive Classification | | | | | | |
| | $M_S > M_{AF}$ | | | | $M_{AF} > M_S$ | | |
Condition	N	Trial One	Trial Two	Dif-fer-ence	N	Trial One	Trial Two	Dif-fer-ence
Success								
($P_s = .70$)	19	60.1	66.6	−6.5	12	60.6	62.8	−2.2
Failure								
($P_s = .30$)	14	60.9	64.3	−3.4	14	60.9	70.4	−9.5

Expectancy Changes Following Success and Failure. A number of
critical assumptions were made by Weiner in the study reviewed above.
Foremost among the assumptions is that the changes in P_s following
success and failure are equal, but opposite in direction. This assumption
is crucial, for if the changes in P_s are greater after success than failure,
then the results also would be in the direction predicted by Atkinson's 1957
model. If P_s is farther from .50 in the success than failure condition,
individuals in whom $M_S > M_{AF}$ should perform better given failure than
success, and the opposite would be true among those in whom $M_{AF} > M_S$.
These are the results reported by Weiner.

Determining the effects of success and failure on P_s is a difficult
problem. In the majority of relevant investigations success and failure
are induced, and the subjects inform the experimenter of their expectancies
of success prior to each trial. Whether this type of verbal-report methodology is adequate remains to be proven. However, when this procedure is
followed, the P_s shifts reported following failure are greater than those
after success (Feather, 1966; Feather & Saville, 1967). In the experiment
most pertinent to the interpretation of the Weiner (1965a) study, Feather
(1966) introduced false norms indicating that the P_s at an anagram
task was either .30 or .70. Some subjects in the $P_s = .70$ condition received a series of initial success trials, while other subjects in the
$P_s = .30$ condition received a series of initial failures. The P_s estimates
on these trials are shown in Table 4:12. The table shows that subjects
in both motive groups greatly bias the "induced" P_s. But more important
for the present discussion, among subjects in both motive groups P_s shifts
following failure are greater than those after success.

Thus, the relative performance decrements exhibited by subjects in
whom $M_{AF} > M_S$ following failure in the Weiner (1965a) experiment
cannot be attributable to the differential shifting of P_s between the success

TABLE 4:12

Mean Estimates of Probability of Success for the First Five Trials at an
Anagram Task (adapted from Feather, 1966, p. 290)

Induced Probability	Motive Classification	Outcome	Probability of Success over Trials					Difference (1-5)
			1	2	3	4	5	
.30	$M_S > M_{AF}$	Failure	.56	.49	.38	.35	.29	−.27
.30	$M_{AF} > M_S$	Failure	.55	.36	.28	.19	.15	−.40
.70	$M_S > M_{AF}$	Success	.67	.66	.69	.74	.75	+.08
.70	$M_{AF} > M_S$	Success	.54	.58	.66	.70	.71	+.17

and failure conditions. Indeed, a consideration of only expectancy changes would result in the prediction that subjects in whom $M_{AF} > M_S$ will perform better following failure than after success. As indicated, this prediction is contradicted by the data. In sum, the results reported by Weiner (1965a) cannot be interpreted using Atkinson's (1957) conception of motivation, and provide evidence that approach and avoidance tendencies persist following nonattainment of a goal.

Further Examination of the Persistence of Behavior

Most research investigations supporting Atkinson's conception of behavior examine choice behavior when the P_s of achievement-related alternatives varies between tasks. Generally, success and failure are not manipulated in risk-preference studies. Therefore, it has not been essential to consider the effects of persisting tendencies when predicting choice behavior. On the other hand, Feather (1961, 1963) examined persistence of behavior when administering repeated failures. Hence, inertial tendencies should have been an important determinant of the observed behavior in his investigations.

To review Feather's hypotheses briefly, Atkinson's 1957 model was employed to predict that individuals in whom $M_S > M_{AF}$, when experiencing continual failure, would persist longer when the initial P_s at a task is .70 than when the initial $P_s = .05$. Conversely, it was hypothesized that those in whom $M_{AF} > M_S$ would persist longer in the $P_s = .05$ than in the $P_s = .70$ condition. These predictions were confirmed.

The model that includes a resultant inertial tendency leads to the same predictions as those made by Feather, but the conceptual representation differs. As Feather states, following failure the P_s in the .70 condition changes toward the level of intermediate difficulty, while the P_s in the .05 condition goes further away from the .50 level. In addition, however.

greater motivation is aroused when $P_s = .70$ than when $P_s = .05$, and in both conditions there is nonattainment of the goal. The persisting unsatisfied motivation, therefore, is greater in the $P_s = .70$ condition than in the $P_s = .05$ condition. Both the environmental and inertial sources of motivation are operating to maximize the differences in persistence between the two P_s conditions. Among subjects low in resultant achievement motivation, the analysis is reversed. For these subjects the inhibition attributable to the immediate stimulus situation is greater following failure at the easy than the difficult task, as Feather indicated. In addition, the persisting resultant inertial tendency is more inhibitory following failure at the relatively easy task than after failure at the task perceived as very difficult. When $P_s = .70$, greater avoidance of achievement tasks is aroused, and persists, than in the condition where $P_s = .05$. Therefore, persistence is expected to be greater following failure at the difficult than at the easy task for subjects low in resultant achievement motivation.

. The analysis employed by Feather and the alternate inertial motivational conception are shown in Table 4:13. For ease of presentation, it is again assumed that $M_S = 2$ and $M_{AF} = 1$ when $M_S > M_{AF}$, and vice versa when $M_{AF} > M_S$. It is also assumed that the change in P_s following failure is $\frac{1}{2}(1 - P_s)$ when the initial $P_s = .70$, and $\frac{1}{2}(P_s)$ when the initial $P_s = .05$. The inertial tendency is assumed to be zero on Trial One. The table presents the strength of resultant achievement motivation for the first and second trials; analysis of the remaining trials would take the identical form.

Table 4:13 shows that in both models the absolute increase in the tendency to persist at the activity in progress is greater for high achieving individuals when the initial P_s is .70 than when the initial P_s is .05. For subjects low in resultant achievement motivation, the $P_s = .70$ condition leads to the greater increase in avoidance of the activity in progress in both models. The implication of the conceptual analysis presented in Table 4:13 is that Feather's results may be due primarily to the failure manipulation per se (T_{Gi}), rather than to the change in P_s that occurs as a consequence of failure.

To examine the role of inertial motivation in Feather's experiment, Weiner (1970) somewhat modified the procedure used by Feather. Subjects classified as high or low in resultant achievement motivation were placed in a free-choice situation in which they could perform either of two activities. One task consisted of the achievement-related booklet employed by Feather. The alternate activity was a nonachievement-related picture-judgment task. Three conditions were created by varying the initial P_s at the achievement task and the subsequent success and failure experiences. In one condition subjects were given continual success at the

TABLE 4:13

Analysis of Feather's Experiment According to Two Models for Achievement-Oriented Behavior (from Weiner, 1970, p. 89)

Model	Trial	Condition	Motive Classification	
			$M_S > M_{AF}$	$M_{AF} > M_B$
1957 (no inertial component)	One	$P_s = .70$	$2 \times .7 \times .3 - (1 \times .3 \times .7) = .21^a$	$1 \times .7 \times .3 - (2 \times .3 \times .7) = -.21$
	Two	$P_s = .70$	$2 \times .55 \times .45 - (1 \times .45 \times .55) = .25^b$	$1 \times .55 \times .45 - (2 \times .45 \times .55) = -.25$
	One	$P_s = .05$	$2 \times .05 \times .95 - (1 \times .95 \times .05) = .05$	$1 \times .05 \times .95 - (2 \times .95 \times .05) = -.05$
	Two	$P_s = .05$	$2 \times .02 \times .98 - (1 \times .98 \times .02) = .02$	$1 \times .02 \times .98 - (2 \times .98 \times .02) = -.02$
Resultant inertial component	One	$P_s = .70$	$2 \times .7 \times .3 - (1 \times .3 \times .7) = .21$	$1 \times .7 \times .3 - (2 \times .3 \times .7) = -.21$
	Two	$P_s = .70$	$2 \times .55 \times .45 - (1 \times .45 \times .55) + .21 = .46$	$1 \times .55 \times .45 - (2 \times .45 \times .55) = .21 = -.46$
	One	$P_s = .05$	$2 \times .05 \times .95 - (1 \times .95 \times .05) = .05$	$1 \times .05 \times .95 - (2 \times .95 \times .05) = -.05$
	Two	$P_s = .05$	$2 \times .02 \times .98 - (1 \times .98 \times .02) + .05 = .07$	$1 \times .02 \times .98 - (2 \times .98 \times .02) - .05 = -.07$

a Strength of resultant achievement motivation.
b All numbers rounded to two decimal points.

achievement task when the initial $P_s = .30$. In a second condition continual success was experienced when the initial $P_s = .95$. The difference between the initial probabilities in these two conditions $(.95 - .30)$ is equal to the difference between the initial probabilities in Feather's experiment $(.70 - .05)$. The predictions derived from Atkinson's 1957 model, as well as the model including the resultant inertial tendency, are similar to those of Feather. Subjects in whom $M_S > M_{AF}$ were expected to choose more achievement-related puzzles when the initial $P_s = .30$, while subjects low in resultant achievement motivation were expected to select more puzzles when the initial $P_s = .95$. These predictions follow from the achievement models because the P_s respectively is shifting toward and away from the level of intermediate difficulty in the two conditions, while T_{Gi} remains zero.

In the third condition subjects received continual failure when the initial $P_s = .05$. Thus, in the second and third conditions the probabilities were symmetrical around .50 (.95 and .05). These conditions essentially repeat those used previously by Weiner (1965a). Subjects in whom $M_S > M_{AF}$ were expected to choose more achievement-related puzzles than subjects in whom $M_{AF} > M_S$ in the repeated failure, but not repeated success, condition.

Comparing Condition One ($P_s = .30$ and success) with Condition Two ($P_s = .95$ and success) in this investigation demonstrated the effect of situational determinants of behavior; the effect of inertial sources of motivation were controlled because continual success is experienced. Comparing Condition Two ($P_s = .95$ and success) with Condition Three ($P_s = .05$ and failure) shows the effect of inertial determinants of behavior; the influence of the environmental sources of motivation was controlled because the P_s is symmetrical around the level of intermediate difficulty.

In sum, this experiment combined Feather's study of the effects of P_s on behavior with Weiner's study of the effects of inertial motivation on subsequent action. Further, the P_s and inertial effects were disentangled from one another.

The results of this experiment are portrayed in Figure 4:11. The figure indicates the percentage choice of the achievement-related activity as a function of the experimental conditions and motive classification of the subjects. The dependent variable was based upon 20 free-choice trials. Examination of choice in the two success conditions reveals that subjects in whom $M_S > M_{AF}$ select more puzzles when the initial $P_s = .30$ than when the $P_s = .95$. Conversely, subjects in whom $M_{AF} > M_S$ choose more puzzles in the $P_s = .95$ than in the $P_s = .30$ condition. Although these findings are in the predicted direction, the differences do not approach

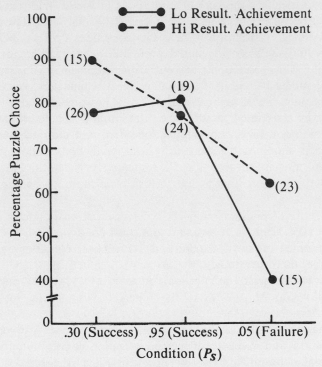

FIGURE 4:11. Percentage choice of the achievement task in three experimental conditions for subjects differing in motive dispositions (from Weiner, 1970, p. 92).

statistical significance. Comparing choice in the .95 success condition and the .05 failure condition between motive groups reveals that only in the failure condition do subjects in whom $M_S > M_{AF}$ select the achievement-related task more frequently than those in whom $M_{AF} > M_S$.

Thus, the general patterns of results in the success conditions replicate Feather's findings and demonstrate the effects of environmental (P_s) determinants of behavior. Comparison of the .95 success condition with the .05 failure condition reveals that the direction of results replicate Weiner's previous findings concerning the influence of inertial motivation. In sum, both situational and inertial sources of motivation need to be included among the determinants of achievement-related behavior.

Comparison of the .95 and .30 success conditions in this experiment indicates that none of the obtained differences within or between motive groups is statistically significant. The analysis in Table 4:13 suggests that Feather's prior results may have been caused primarily by the persisting inertial tendency, rather than the shifting of the P_s level. Therefore, Weiner (1970) suggests that the observed differences in behavior between the .95 and .30 success conditions would be less than the differences obtained by Feather between .70 and .05 failure conditions. However, because of the high percentage of achievement choice exhibited by subjects in the success conditions, it is not justifiable to conclude that Feather's results are predominantly attributable to the inertial motivational component. Another study is needed—one that permits a better test of this hypothesis.

Summary

It has been contended that Atkinson's 1957 model of achievement motivation is inadequate in that it cannot account for data indicating that, independent of P_s effects, failure enhances motivation among individuals high in resultant achievement motivation, while causing performance decrements among persons in whom $M_{AF} > M_S$. The suggestion by Atkinson and Cartwright (1964) that aroused motivation does not decrease given nonattainment of a goal led to the postulation by Weiner (1965a, 1970) of a resultant inertial tendency that persists following failure in an achievement-related context. Addition of this component to the achievement model enables the model to account for the interactive effects of failure on persons differing in achievement predispositions. Further, it is suggested that prior research in the achievement area, particularly the experiments conducted by Feather (1961, 1963) that experimentally induce failure, be reexamined in the light of this new theoretical conception.

The Reduction of Inertial Motivation

It also was indicated that Atkinson's 1957 model is inadequate because it cannot account for data indicating that, independent of P_s effects, success increases motivation for persons low in resultant achievement motivation, while decreasing motivation among individuals in whom $M_S > M_{AF}$. A clear alternative model that can explain the interactive effects of success remains to be formulated. Weiner (1966b) has attempted to account for these data by again employing the conception of inertial tendencies, although this theoretical explanation is in need of further consideration. In the Weiner (1966b) paper it is suggested that following goal attainment there is a decrement in the magnitude of both the persisting tendency to approach success and the persisting tendency to avoid the threat of failure. That is, following success the magnitudes of the persisting approach and avoidance tendencies decrease. The diminution in the strengths of these tendencies is postulated to be proportional to the strength of achievement motivation sustaining the original activity. Among persons in whom $M_S > M_{AF}$, the approach toward achievement is greater than the tendency to avoid achievement activities. Thus, given success, the decrement in the magnitude of the persisting approach motivation is expected to be greater than the reduction in the magnitude of the persisting avoidance motivation. Consequently, these individuals should exhibit decrements in their achievement-striving behaviors following success. Conversely, when $M_{AF} > M_S$, the decrement in the strength of the persisting avoidance tendency is greater than the reduction in the strength of the persisting approach tendency. These individuals therefore should exhibit increments in achievement-oriented behaviors after a success experience. In sum, the notion of differential decrements in persisting tendencies after success can account for the opposing reactions that subjects classified as high or low in resultant achievement motivation exhibit following goal attainment.

In one study supporting this conception, Weiner (1965b) demonstrated that goal attainment has substitute value for persons high in achievement needs (as evidenced by a decrease in their tendency to resume previously interrupted activities), while increasing the likelihood of task resumption among persons low in achievement needs. These findings can be accounted for by postulating differential reductions of the assumed persisting approach and avoidance tendencies. Among individuals high in achievement concerns, the achievement approach tendency exceeds that of avoidance. Hence, success reduces the persisting approach tendency more than the persisting threat of failure, thus decreasing subsequent achievement activity (task resumption). Conversely, among individuals low in achievement concerns, the achievement avoidance tendency exceeds that of approach. Hence, success reduces avoidance more than approach motivation, thus increasing subsequent achievement activity (task resumption).

These ideas may aid in the explanation of some paradoxical empirical findings in other areas of psychological investigation. For example, aggressive fantasy goal attainment sometimes has cathartic value and reduces subsequent aggressive behavior, and at times leads to modeling behavior and a subsequent increase in aggressiveness. These opposing findings may be due to differences in the motivational characteristics of the samples tested. Given overtly aggressive children, as might be found among a lower class sample, it is suggested that fantasy goal attainment will have cathartic value, inasmuch as the magnitude of the aggressive approach tendency exceeds the strength of the fear of aggressive retaliation. On the other hand, given a sample in whom aggressive responses are inhibited, as might be found among middle class children, fantasy goal attainment is expected to result in a subsequent increment in the tendency to act aggressively. In that sample the strength of the avoidance tendency exceeds the tendency toward aggressive expression. In sum, an interaction is anticipated between the effects of goal attainment and the strength of the tendencies initially to approach or avoid the goal object. Data are available that support these expectations (Feshbach & Singer, 1970).

ANOTHER LOOK AT EDUCATIONAL PRACTICES

Programmed Learning

It was submitted that learning programs approximate 100 percent reinforcement schedules, thereby minimizing motivation among students in whom $M_S > M_{AF}$ (see section headed "Educational Implications of the Theory"). The addition of the inertial motivational component in the achievement model extends this argument. Table 4:14 outlines the conditions that theoretically maximize and minimize motivation for individuals in the high and low achievement motive groups. Among individuals in whom $M_S > M_{AF}$, minimum motivation is produced in situations where there is repeated success. That is, where $P_s \to 1$ and inertial motivation $\to 0$. On the other hand, a program of repeated success theoretically maximizes motivation among students in whom $M_{AF} > M_S$. Thus, the current learning program procedure least enhances motivation for those high in achievement needs, and least inhibits motivation for those low in achievement needs. This intimates that performance will tend toward the

TABLE 4:14
The Magnitude of Achievement Motivation Related to Individual Differences
and Sources of Motivation (from Weiner, 1970, p. 80)

Motive Classification	Source of Motivation	Strength of Achievement Motivation	
		Maximal	Minimal
High ($M_S > M_{AF}$)	Environmental	$P_s = .50$	$P_s = 1$ or 0
	Inertial	$T_{G_i} > 0$	$T_{G_i} = 0$
Low ($M_{AF} > M_S$)	Environmental	$P_s = 1$ or 0	$P_s = .50$
	Inertial	$T_{G_i} = 0$	$T_{G_i} < 0$

median for all students. The general intent of this interpretation is to indicate again that individual differences interact with environmental situations, and program formats differing in "reinforcement schedules" (P_s) are needed.

Grades

Teachers frequently adopt strategies concerning grades and apply them indiscriminantly to all pupils. For example, some give low grades on a midterm exam and assume that this increases student motivation. Conversely, others assign high grades and believe with equal conviction that student output will be increased. Goldberg (1965) summarizes these positions:

> The motivational model of the lenient grader may rest on the psychological assumption that pleasure is a more effective motivant than pain, and that optimum learning occurs under conditions of frequent positive reinforcement (coupled with infrequent errors and consequently infrequent non-reinforcement and/or punishment). The lenient grader—that is, the instructor who converts his test score distributions to letter grades such that there is a markedly skewed distribution of high grades—frequently assumes that (a) high grades are positive reinforcements, which in turn (b) affect learning *directly* through an increase in the probability of making a subsequent response similar to that reinforced, and (c) *indirectly* through the effect of generalization of pleasure to *learning as a process.*
>
> The polar opposite of the lenient grader could be viewed as the "strict" grader—who gives, at least on early examinations, mostly Ds and Fs and uses As and Bs sparingly if at all. He typically assumes (a) that most students are working far below the level at which they are capable, and (b) that punishment, in the form of poor grades, is the best motivational inducement to encourage more intensive efforts at learning [p. 18].

It is extremely difficult to verify predictions concerning the interactive effects of grade feedback on later performance in an actual school setting. But one "field-research" attempt to assess the effects of grades on later performance is reported by Goldberg (1965). He employed five different grading policies, including one labeled "strict" and one labeled "lenient" when giving midterm exam feedback. He then examined the effects of the feedback on performance at a second midterm exam. The results showed a very small trend for the strictly graded group to perform better on the second exam than the group leniently graded.

Unfortunately, Goldberg did not include individual difference assessment of achievement-related needs in this study. Thus, the interaction suggested here between individual differences in achievement concerns and grading policy could not be tested. But is has been contended that college students are, on the whole, relatively high in achievement needs (see Atkinson & Feather, 1966, pp. 22, 342). Thus, failure should have been (and was) a more potent motivator than success. Clearly, however, a similar study is called for that includes the needed individual difference measures.

Item-Difficulty Sequence

On most achievement and IQ tests the sequence of items proceeds from very easy to very difficult. The test-taker first encounters a series of success experiences, lulling him into the belief that he can perform well on the test. Then he suddenly encounters a series of failures, and often experiences an accompanying "panic" reaction. Hutt (1947) hypothesized that the ascending-difficulty test format could be detrimental to individuals having low "frustration tolerance." To test this hypothesis he compared IQ performance of individuals classified as high or low in adjustment. He used two IQ formats: the standard ascending-difficulty test, and an "adaptive" format in which the items were mixed. In the "adaptive" format failure never was experienced on six or more consecutive trials. The results indicated that among persons high in adjustment, item-format does not influence test score. However, the group low in adjustment performed significantly better in the adaptive than in the ascending-difficulty test condition.

Kestenbaum and Weiner (1970) repeated Hutt's study, using level of achievement concerns rather than adjustment as the predictor variable. However, they were unable to demonstrate that a random sequence of test items yields different test scores than an ascending-difficulty order. Indeed, on the reading test they employed, the test-retest reliability between the two test formats approximated the reported test-retest reliability of the ascending-format alone.

In sum, the data concerning the effects of item sequence on performance do not yet permit any definitive conclusions. Considering the importance placed upon the results of achievement tests in our culture, the neglect of this issue is both surprising and unfortunate. Clear data in this area could also be used to further the theoretical conceptions already discussed.

Long-Term Goals

A major shortcoming of the achievement model is that the incentive value of success is completely determined by P_s; that is, I_s is operationally dependent on task difficulty. Thus, for example, the amount of aroused achievement motivation and experienced pride given success at a puzzle task in which $P_s = .50$ is equal, theoretically, to the amount of aroused achievement motivation and experienced pride in accomplishment given success at a doctoral exam in which $P_s = .50$. Yet we intuitively feel that greater motivation is aroused and more affect experienced in the latter than the former situation.

It may be that motivation is augmented at the doctoral exam because sources of motivation in addition to achievement are aroused. However, it also is conceivable that the amount of aroused motivation is determined, in part, by the relationship between the immediate activity and long-term achievement goals. Success at the doctoral exam may be essential for career advancement, while success at a puzzle generally is unrelated to long-term achievement goals.

Recently, Raynor (1969, 1970) has elaborated the theory of achievement motivation to include the idea that aroused motivation is influenced by the anticipation of future goals. He suggests that when actions are related to distant goals "the motivation at the task confronting the individual is a function of both future and immediately expected success and failure" (Raynor, 1970, p. 29). He labels such actions as being part of a "contingent path"; motivation at activities in a contingent path is affected by the motivation aroused at other steps in the path.

To test these ideas, Raynor (1970) had students rate the "perceived instrumentality" of performance in the introductory psychology class in which they were enrolled ("How important to you is getting a good grade in introductory psychology for having your career plans work out?"). Subjects were then classified according to strength of achievement needs and the degree of long-term importance of the course. The data indicated that when the perceived instrumentality of the introductory course grade is low, final grades do not differ between the high and low achievement groups. However, when performance at the course is perceived as important for the attainment of career goals, students in whom $M_S > M_{AF}$ receive higher grades than those in whom $M_{AF} > M_S$.

This promising extension of achievement theory has only recently been suggested, and its implications remain to be fully examined. However, Raynor again has demonstrated that the achievement model can be revised to incorporate new data, and has provided further evidence that the theory is readily applicable to academic performance.

CONFLICT

Atkinson and his colleagues have not been as active in this area as the students of Hull and Lewin and their co-workers. Nevertheless, the basic conceptual framework of achievement theory borrows much from Lewin's and Miller's analyses of approach-avoidance conflict. Achievement striving is postulated to be a resultant of an approach and avoidance conflict, with the stronger of the two tendencies being expressed in action.

Perhaps investigations of conflict between motivation generated by the stimulus situation versus motivation produced by prior nonattainment of a goal could aid in determining the relative strengths of these two tendencies, and clarify the inertial model. The model as formulated adds the inertial tendency to the environmental source of motivation to determine the final strength of achievement motivation. In the achievement model the inertial tendency can infinitely grow in magnitude, while environmental motivation varies between 0 and .25 multiplied by the achievement-related motives. This intimates that generally inertial sources of motivation are weighted more heavily than situational determinants of behavior. It is true that with significant deprivation only minimal environmental support is needed for action, as evidenced in "vacuum behavior" or the range of objects having consummatory value when one is under great hunger. But in most situations behavior is *veridical;* that is, greatly influenced by the situational context. The model needs differential weights on the two motivational components to redress the imbalance and give more importance to the stimulus or environmental determinants of behavior. Investigations that oppose these motivations against one another might yield information about the relative strengths or weights of the behavioral determinants.

It also is likely that the motive groups differentially weight the inertial and environmental components. High achieving individuals are considered to be "realistic." That is, they might weight the environmental source more heavily than inertial motivation. On the other hand, pervasive avoidance behavior among highly anxious subjects may indicate that the inertial component exerts a more profound influence on their behavior than does the immediate environment. Thus, investigations of conflict resolution pitting inertial against environmental motivation may aid in the understanding of aberrant patterns of behavior.

FRUSTRATION

The most well-known motivational conception of frustration (Amsel, 1958) was discussed in detail in Chapter II. The main prediction of Amsel's conception is that following nonattainment of a goal there will be an increment in goal striving. That is, frustration has drive or energizing properties that add to the general level of drive and augment response strength. Confirmation of this hypothesis has occurred within an experimental paradigm in which hungry rats are deprived of an expected reward. Assessment of the speed of response following this frustration reveals the

"Frustration Effect," or the subsequent increment in response strength following nonreward.

The inertial conception of motivation yields the same general predictions as Amsel's frustration theory in the experiment reviewed above. If hunger motivation is aroused, and the goal is not attained, then the unsatisfied motivation persists and should be manifested in subsequent food-related actions. That is, the observed increment in speed of response could be due to the persisting hunger motivation, rather than to the frustrative consequences of nonattainment of a goal (see Atkinson & Birch, 1970).

According to achievement theory, nonattainment of an expected reward decreases the expectation that the response will lead to the desired goal. Hence, in both the achievement model and the Drive $\times$ Habit frustration theory two components in the model are influenced by the same operation. Nonattainment of a goal (failure or frustration) decreases approach relative to avoidance associations (expectancy or habit strength), but increases motivational effects (inertia or drive). The observed increment in behavior on trials immediately following nonreward indicates that the increment in motivation (inertia or drive) is greater than the relative decrement in the learned approach response (expectancy or habit strength). Further, the eventual extinction of the response implies that the relative decrements in positive expectancy or habit offset the increments in inertia or drive. Neither achievement theory nor drive theory, however, explicitly states the relative changes in the strengths of the learning versus motivational components. Thus, it is not possible for either conception to specify the trial at which decrements in performance will be exhibited following nonreward.

One difference in the predictions derived from the Amsel conception as opposed to that of Atkinson is that Amsel postulates that the amount of frustration following a nonrewarded trial is monotonically related to the expectation of the reward. In achievement-related situations, however, motivation is most aroused at tasks of intermediate difficulty. Hence, maximum inertial effects are anticipated following failure at a task that has an intermediate expectation of success. There should be a curvilinear relationship between expectancy and the motivational effects of frustration, according to the achievement model.

COMPARISON WITH HULLIAN AND LEWINIAN THEORY

As indicated throughout this chapter, there are both similarities and points of contrast between the approaches to the study of motivation advocated

TABLE 4:15

Comparison of the Determinants of Behavior Included in the
Motivational Models of Atkinson, Hull, and Lewin

Theorist	Construct		
	Person	Environment	Learning
Atkinson	Motive[a] ×	Incentive of success[b] ×	Probability of success
Hull	Drive ×	Incentive ×	Habit
Lewin	Tension,[c]	Valence,[d]	Psychological distance[e]

[a] Represents a stable personality disposition.

[b] Is equal to one minus the probability of success.

[c] Did not specify mathematical relationship between components in theory.

[d] Determined by properties of the goal object, operationally independent of the needs of the person (tension).

[e] The potency of success also is an experiential variable in Lewin's theory.

by Atkinson, Hull, and Lewin. Consider first the determinants of action specified by these three theorists (see Table 4:15). Table 4:15 shows that all three conceptions postulate that behavior is a function of the properties of the person (motive, drive, or tension), the properties of the goal object (incentive or valence), and an experiential or learning variable (probability of success, habit strength, or psychological distance). However, the property of the person is a stable personality attribute in Atkinson's conception, but a temporary state of drive or tension in the Hullian and Lewinian theories. Further, in the Hullian and Lewinian conceptions the incentive value of the goal object has independent operational existence. Within Atkinson's conception of achievement-related behavior, I_s is determined by the value of P_s. (Atkinson, however, does consider achievement to be a special case within a general model in which I_s and P_s are not necessarily related.) Finally, in the Hullian model the learning or associative variable represents a mechanical strengthening of an S-R bond, while for both Atkinson and Lewin the experiential component is conceptualized cognitively and involves foresight concerning the goal event or the consequences of the response. That is, Atkinson and Lewin contend that mental events (expectancies) intervene between stimulus input and the final response.

The disparities in the conceptions of the learning variable primarily are responsible for the classification of Hullian theory as mechanistic and those of Atkinson and Lewin as cognitive. Although Atkinson and Lewin are considered cognitive theorists, both are extremely influenced by physicalistic conceptions, and make use of mechanical concepts such as vector, inertia, and so forth. But despite their use of mechanistic terminology, they conceptualize man as "rational" and able to use mental faculties to aid in reaching desired goals. Thus, Lewin and Atkinson represent a transition between "pure" mechanistic and "pure" cognitive theories.

There are other points of convergence and divergence between the three motivational models. All are hedonistic conceptions. Individuals are believed to act to maximize pleasure and minimize pain, whether this action is caused by rigid stimulus-response connections stemming from the consequences of prior rewards, or by certain positive goal anticipations. In all three conceptions, however, the most positive incentive is not necessarily approached; the probability of goal attainment, or past stimulus-response-reward contingencies, also influence behavior. For this reason, the Lewinian and Atkinsonian conceptions often are classified as Expectancy × Value theories (see Atkinson, 1964). That is, both the expectancy of goal attainment and the reward value of the goal influence behavior, and a decision-making organism chooses the response that maximizes future pleasures (utilities).

Most theories of motivation link hedonism to homeostatic processes. Pleasurable events return the organism to a state of equilibrium. For Hull, as well as for Freud, a state of equilibrium involves no stimulation. All internal stimuli are considered unpleasant, and are to be eliminated. Nirvana is considered a state of zero stimulation, with all needs satisfied and the organism at rest. Lewin also advocated that motivational processes are derived from homeostatic imbalance, although he did recognize that increments in stimulation could be pleasurable. But he did not formally include the pleasure of stimulus increments within his model, inasmuch as all goal attainment reduces tension. McClelland also is a homeostatic theorist. However, in contrast to Hull, Freud, and Lewin, he contends that there is an optimal level of stimulation, and behavior may be directed either to increase or decrease incoming stimulation, depending on the relationship between the present state of the organism and the optimal level of stimulation. Thus, McClelland held to an equilibrium conception, but broadened the behaviors that could be incorporated within the constraints imposed by such a theoretical viewpoint. In contrast to the above theorists, Atkinson apparently has abandoned the concept of homeostasis. It plays no formal role in his theory. Further, by making the motivational property associated with the person a stable trait, rather than a drive or tense state, the behavior initiated cannot dramatically increase or decrease intrapersonal behavioral determinants. With the inclusion of inertia in his model, however, goal attainment is postulated to reduce persisting tendencies. Whether this will bring Atkinson closer to a homeostatic position remains to be seen.

There also are differences between the actual and stated breadths of the theories under consideration. Although the Hullian conception was formulated as a general behavioral theory, the data cited in support of the conception primarily were generated by hungry rats running down a straight alley. It is only with difficulty and great ingenuity that the theory can explain other behavioral data. Lewin, on the other hand, is more of a general theorist. He attempts to explain the data gathered by Hullians, and has conducted his own research in a variety of areas in support of his theory. In contrast to both Hull and Lewin, Atkinson has limited his theory to the area of achievement-related behavior. Virtually all of the data cited in support of his conception involve success or failure at some achievement activity, or a decision in an achievement-related context. Thus, his conception follows a general trend in psychology to predict and understand more accurately circumscribed domains of behavior. It also is true that Atkinson's model may be considered a general theory of action. But when considered as such, the implicit breadth of the theory is greater than its true data base. Whether the model of achievement behavior can also serve as a model for power seeking, affiliative actions, and the like, remains to be demonstrated.

Finally, there are contrasting features concerning the developments of the three conceptions. Hull's theory underwent continual modification as a result of the experimental findings of Miller, Tolman, Spence, and others. Further, Hull's students and colleagues—Miller, Spence, Brown, and others—modified and sharpened the conception before and after Hull's death. In a similar manner, Atkinson's conception has grown over time. The introduction of avoidance as well as approach achievement strivings, followed by the addition of extrinsic motivation, inertial tendencies, and long-term goal anticipations, attest that the conception has not remained static. In contrast to the growth in these theories, Lewin's field theory did not greatly change over time. The majority of Lewin's students and co-workers entered the fields of clinical, social, or applied psychology. Few retained a long-term or overriding interest in furthering his conception of motivation. Perhaps for this reason the conception per se attracts relatively little interest in contemporary psychology.

ACHIEVEMENT MOTIVATION IN SOCIETY

A number of sociological and anthropological investigations that are proceeding outside the laboratory concern achievement motivation. Foremost among these is the monumental attempt by McClelland (1961) to relate achievement motivation to economic growth. This is an ambitious enterprise, to say the least, and one is tempted to accuse McClelland of trying to explain extremely complex and overdetermined phenomena in an oversimplified manner. Yet the data he presents are compelling.

McClelland's argument was guided by findings of Winterbottom (1953) relating need for achievement to child-rearing practices. Winterbottom found that when mothers expected their sons to be self-reliant and independent at an early age, those sons were relatively high in need for achievement. These mothers believed that their sons should know their way around the city, make their own friends, and the like, at an earlier age than did mothers whose sons were low in need for achievement.[3]

McClelland reasons that the relationship between early independence training and the growth of achievement motivation is pertinent to the linkage postulated by Weber (1904) between the Protestant reformation and the growth of capitalism. McClelland (1955) states:

In the first place, he [Weber] stresses, as others have, that the essence of the Protestant revolt against the Catholic church was a shift from a reliance on an institution to a greater reliance on the self, so far as salvation was concerned. The individual Protestant, Lutheran or Calvinist was less dependent on the church as an institution either for its priests or its sacraments or its official dogma. Instead there was to be a "priesthood" of all "believers," in Luther's words. The Protestant could read and interpret his Bible and find his own way to God without having to rely on the authority of the Church or its official assistance. As Weber describes it, we have here what seems to be an example of a revolution in ideas which should increase the need for independence training. Certainly Protestant parents, if they were to prepare their children adequately for increased self-reliance so far as religious matters were concerned, would tend to stress increasingly often and early the necessity for the child's not depending on adult assistance but seeking his own "salvation." In the second place, Weber's description of the kind of personality type which the Protestant Reformation produced is startlingly similar to the picture we would draw of a person with high achievement motivation. He notes that Protestant working girls seemed to work harder and longer, that they saved their money for long-range goals, that Protestant entrepreneurs seemed to come to the top more often in the business world despite the initial advantages of wealth many Catholic families had, and so forth. In particular, he points out that the early Calvinist business man was prevented by his religious views from enjoying the results of his labors. He could not spend money on himself because of scruples about self-indulgence and display, and so, more often than not, he reinvested his profits in his business, which was one reason he prospered. What then drove him to such prodigious feats of business organization and development? Weber feels that such a man "gets nothing out of his wealth for himself, except the irrational sense of having done his job well" (22, p. 71). This is exactly how we define the achievement motive. So again, the parallel seems clear, although there is not space to give the argument in full here. Is it possible that the Protestant Reformation involves a repetition at a social and historical level

---

[3] Although some investigations confirm these general findings; for example, Rosen & D'Andrade, 1959, at present the child-rearing antecedents leading to the development of achievement motivation remain in doubt. The reader is directed to Smith, 1969, for a full discussion of this area.

Hypothetical Series of Events Relating Self-Reliance Values with
Economic and Technological Development

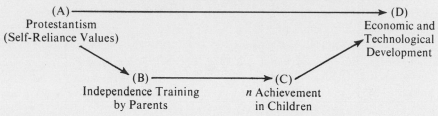

(A) ————————————————————————► (D)
Protestantism   Economic and
(Self-Reliance Values)   Technological
                                                 Development

(B) ————————————► (C)
Independence Training   *n* Achievement
by Parents   in Children

of the linkage that Winterbottom found between independence training and
n Achievement among some mothers and their sons in a small town in
Michigan in 1950?

To make such an assumption involves a breath-taking leap of hy-
pothesizing so far as the average psychologist is concerned, who is much
more at home with a sample of 30 mothers and 30 sons than he is with
major social movements. But the hypothesis seems too fascinating to dis-
miss without some further study. It can be diagrammed rather simply. In
terms of this diagram Weber was chiefly concerned with the linkage between A and D, with the way in which Protestantism led to a change in
the spirit of capitalism in the direction of a speeded-up, high-pressure,
competitive business economy. But the manner in which he describes this
relationship strongly suggests that the linkage by which these two events
are connected involves steps B and C, namely a change in family socialization practices which in turn increased the number of individuals with high
achievement motivation. Thus a full statement of the hypothesis would
be that Protestantism produced an increased stress on independence training which produced higher achievement motivation which produced more
vigorous entrepreneurial activity and rapid economic development [pp.
44–46].

The diagram above indicates four relationships McClelland has examined: (1) Protestantism and early independence training; (2) early independence training and need for achievement; (3) need for achievement
and economic growth; and (4) Protestantism and economic growth. At
this time the relationship between religious training and child-rearing practices (1), and the relationship between child-rearing practices and achievement development (2), remain indeterminate. McClelland cites evidence
available at the time his book was written that Protestant families expect
earlier mastery from their sons than Catholic families, and that early independence training produces concerns about achievement. Since that time
these relationships have been called into question, and an evaluation of
these hypotheses is neglected here.

The great bulk of McClelland's personal investigations concern relationships (3)—need for achievement and economic growth—and (4)—

TABLE 4:16

Average per Capita Consumption of Electric Power, Corrected for Natural Resources, for Protestant and Catholic Countries Outside the Tropics of Cancer and Capricorn (From McClelland, 1961, p. 51)

Countries	Consumption of Electricity kwh/cap (1950)	Usable Water Power hp/cap (1947) (SD = 1.36)	Coal Produced tons/cap (1951) (SD = .99)	Combined Natural Resources in Standard (Z) Scores	Predicted Output kwh/cap	Difference (Predicted— Obtained)	Rank of Difference
Protestant							
Norway	5,310	4.182	.000	+2.73	3,379	1,931	1
Canada	4,120	3.079	1.124	+2.49	3,186	964	4
Sweden	2,580	1.117	.026	−.35	903	1,672	2
United States	2,560	3.88	3.431	+1.42	2,328	232	9
Switzerland	2,230	1.553	.000	+.08	1,253	977	3
New Zealand	1,600	1.405	.675	+.42	1,526	74	11
Australia	1,160	.164	2.505	+.51	1,598	−438	20
United Kingdom	1,115	.023	4.529	+1.86	2,631	−1,566	24
Finland	1,000	.810	.000	−.67	652	348	6
Union S. Africa	890	.203	2.165	+.30	1,430	−540	21
Holland	725	.003	1.238	−.58	724	1	15
Denmark	500	.011	.121	−1.39	74	426	5
Average	1,983	1.078	1.318		1,645	338	10.1

TABLE 4:16 (cont.)

Countries	Consumption of Electricity kwh/cap (1950)	Usable Water Power hp/cap (1947) (SD = 1.36)	Coal Produced tons/cap (1951) (SD = .99)	Combined Natural Resources in Standard (Z) Scores	Predicted Output kwh/cap	Difference (Predicted—Obtained)	Rank of Difference
Catholic							
Belgium	986	.004	3.335	+ .96	1,959	−973	22
Austria	900	.500	.379	− .71	620	280	8
France	790	.289	1.293	− .25	989	−199	16
Czechoslovakia	730	.085	2.837	+ .63	1,734	−1,004	23
Italy	535	.265	.033	− .120	227	308	7
Chile	484	.676	.381	− .53	764	−280	18
Poland	375	.059	3.338	+1.02	2,007	−1,632	25
Hungary	304	.017	1.049	− .70	628	−324	19
Ireland	300	.156	.061	−1.29	154	146	10
Argentina	255	.318	.003	−1.17	251	4	14
Spain	225	.271	.418	− .91	459	−264	17
Uruguay	165	.204	.000	−1.29	154	11	18
Portugal	110	.070	.052	−1.38	82	28	12
Average	474	.224	1.014		771	−208	15.7

Protestantism and economic growth. To investigate the hypothesis that Protestantism is related to economic growth, McClelland (1961) compared the per capita electric power consumption of predominantly Protestant societies with that of Catholic countries. McClelland contends that electric power per capita usage is the best index of economic growth (rather than, for example, the more widely used index of gross national product), because these data are available, the figures are in comparable units between countries, and modern societies are based upon the use of electrical energy. The findings of this investigation are shown in Table 4:16.

Table 4:16 shows the consumption of electricity per capita and the predicted electrical output based on the natural resources of the country. Deviations between the actual and expected consumption are computed and are related to the religious affiliation of the country. Given this index, the table reveals that the level of economic activity of Protestant countries exceeds that of Catholic countries.

The crucial question McClelland then attempts to answer is whether the Protestant-economic activity association is mediated by achievement needs. He hypothesizes that achievement needs precede economic growth and he gathers indicators of these two variables over a wide array of societies and historical periods.

A major problem faced by McClelland and his colleagues was how to assess the level of achievement motivation of a society. Perhaps TAT stories could be collected and scored on a representative sample of the population, or from a sample of business entrepreneurs (who, McClelland believes, are most responsible for economic advancement). But this is not possible when examining the achievement motivation of earlier societies. To assess the level of achievement concerns in past generations, McClelland and his colleagues generally gather samples of the written products of the society. These literary samples are then scored for achievement motivation with the general scoring scheme outlined earlier in the chapter. Frequently the written material is from children's readers, but folk-tales, speeches of the leaders of the countries, poems and songs, and even the shapes of lines on vases have been used as indicators of achievement motivation.

In one investigation, for example, folk tales of more than 50 early cultures were scored for achievement motivation. Achievement scores were then related to various indexes of achievement behavior. The data revealed that 74 percent of the cultures scoring above the median in achievement concerns had at least some-full time entrepreneurs (traders, independent artisans, and so forth), while only 35 percent of the cultures below the median on achievement motivation reported entrepreneurial activity.

In a larger study of more contemporary societies, McClelland compared the difference between the expected and actual gain in electric power consumption per capita between 1929 and 1950 as a function of achievement motivation. Achievement needs were assessed from children's readers published in 1925. The data revealed a dramatically high correlation $(r = .53)$ $(N = 22)$ between achievement score of the society in 1925 and subsequent economic growth. In a similar manner, achievement needs assessed from children's readers published in 1950 predicted economic growth from 1952 to 1958. Table 4:17 shows the countries in the latter

TABLE 4:17

Rate of Growth in Electrical Output (1952–1958) and National *n* Achievement Levels in 1950 (from McClelland, 1961, p. 100)

Deviations from Expected Growth Rate in Standard Score Units					
National n Achievement Levels (1950)		*Above Expectation*	*National n Achievement Levels (1950)*		*Below Expectation*
3.62	Turkey	+1.38			
2.71	India	+1.12			
2.38	Australia	+ .42			
2.33	Israel	+1.18			
2.33	Spain	+ .01			
2.29	Pakistan	+2.75			
2.29	Greece	+1.18	3.38	Argentina	− .56
2.29	Canada	+ .06	2.71	Lebanon	− .67
2.24	Bulgaria	+1.37	2.38	France	− .24
2.24	U.S.A.	+ .47	2.33	U. So. Africa	− .06
2.14	West Germany	+ .53	2.29	Ireland	− .41
2.10	U.S.S.R.	+1.62	2.14	Tunisia	−1.87
2.10	Portugal	+ .76	2.10	Syria	− .25
1.95	Iraq	+ .29	2.05	New Zealand	− .29
1.86	Austria	+ .38	1.86	Uruguay	− .75
1.67	U.K.	+ .17	1.81	Hungary	− .62
1.57	Mexico	+ .12	1.71	Norway	− .77
.86	Poland	+1.26	1.62	Sweden	− .64
			1.52	Finland	− .08
			1.48	Netherlands	− .15
			1.33	Italy	− .57
			1.29	Japan	− .04
			1.20	Switzerland	−1.92
			1.19	Chile	−1.81
Correlation of *n* Achievement level			1.05	Denmark	− .89
(1950) × deviations from expected			.57	Algeria	− .83
growth rate = .43, *p* < .01			.43	Belgium	−1.65

High *n* Achievement

Low *n* Achievement

study, the level of achievement concerns in 1950, and the deviation from the expected rate of growth. The index of achievement motivation in 1950 did not predict growth rate from 1929 to 1950, but did predict development from 1952 to 1958. Thus, McClelland contends that achievement motivation precedes economic development.

Can achievement motivation also predict the economic growth of ancient societies? In one study apparently confirming this contention, McClelland assessed the level of achievement motivation in England during the years 1500–1850. Achievement motivation was determined by a content analysis of popular literature, such as songs, poems, and plays. The relationship between achievement needs and economic activity (operationally defined as gain in coal imports) is portrayed in Figure 4:12. The figure indicates that the productive spurts displayed after 1600 and 1800 are preceded by a growth of achievement needs.

A similar examination was made of the growth and decline of the Greek empire. Level of achievement needs was ascertained by scoring the literary content of leading writers in that era. Three periods of economic growth and decline were differentiated: 900–475 B.C. (growth), 475–362 B.C. (climax), and 362–100 B.C. (decline). The respective achievement scores in the three periods were 4.74, 2.71, and 1.35. Thus, the period

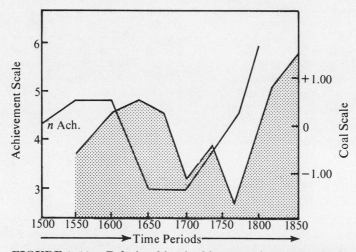

FIGURE 4:12.   Relationship of achievement imagery and subsequent industrial growth (gain in coal imports) for a 350-year period in England (from McClelland, 1962, p. 107). *Note:* Achievement thinking (*n* Ach) = Mean number of achievement images per 100 lines. Rate of industrial growth = Rate of gain in coal imports at London, as deviations from average trend (standard deviation units).

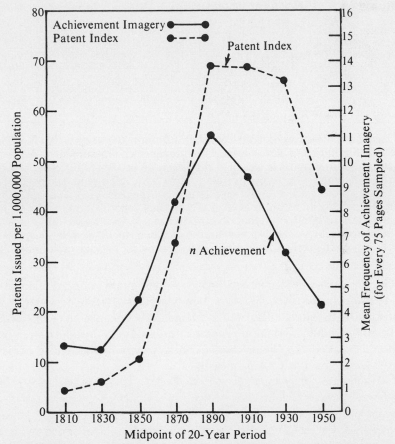

FIGURE 4:13.   Mean frequency of achievement imagery in children's readers and the patent index in the United States, 1800–1950 (adapted from de Charms and Moeller, 1962, p. 139).

of climax was preceded by the highest achievement score, and the decrease in level of economic development followed the decrease in achievement needs.

The reader must be now wondering about the achievement motivation in our culture. Figure 4:13 indicates that achievement needs in America, ascertained from children's readers, increased from 1800 to 1910. Since 1910 achievement concerns have steadily decreased. Does this hint that our economy also is going to decline? Figure 4:13 shows that the patent index, one indicator of unique accomplishments, also is falling. The conclusions from this study of de Charms and Moeller (1962) are evident.

Training in Achievement Motivation

The data reported by McClelland (1961) provide more than suggestive evidence that need achievement is an important factor influencing economic development. Therefore, it would be of utmost importance to determine whether the economic growth of a nation could be accelerated by increasing the achievement motivation of some members of the society. McClelland and Winter (1969) state:

The book [The Achieving Society] ends with the scientist's traditional hope that the knowledge so painstakingly collected will somehow be useful in helping man shape his destiny. At the time it was little more than a pious hope, since it was not all clear how a development specialist or a leader of a new nation could make use of the knowledge accumulated about the achievement motive. If anything, the general import of the findings was discouraging to anyone attempting to accelerate economic growth: the need to Achieve (*n* Achievement) seemed to be a relatively stable personality characteristic rooted in experiences in middle childhood. [pp. 1–2].

McClelland (1965) notes, however, that many nonprofessional as well as professional psychologists are convinced that adult personality and behavior can be altered, and he is attempting to change the achievement motivation of adults. Training programs, primarily for business men, have been initiated and the effectiveness of these programs in altering achievement-related behaviors is being measured.

To increase achievement needs, McClelland and Winter (1969) offer a 3–6-week training course in which the participants learn about the thoughts and actions associated with achievement behavior. They learn to score TATs for achievement motivation, become acquainted with the future time orientation of persons motivated to achieve, and are taught the beneficial consequents of intermediate risk-taking. In addition, the participants undergo a program of self-study in which they describe their life goals, values, self-image, and so forth. The training program assists in the establishment and setting of career goals, as well as suggesting means to assess progress toward these goals. These program "inputs" are in a warm and permissive atmosphere in the company of others, who hopefully will become part of a new reference group. McClelland (1965) describes this as an eclectic method, using all the psychological principles believed to be effective in behavioral change.

The data collected thus far encourage the belief that this program may be an effective behavioral change device. McClelland and Winter present evidence that both American and Indian business men profit from the programs. Course participants display more instances of achievement-related behavior and accomplishments (for example, start a new business, receive an unusual promotion) than control individuals not enrolled in the course.

Using a different subject population, Kolb (1965) had underachieving boys participate in a similar program at a summer camp. The participating students had IQs above 120, but were performing below average in school. The effectiveness of the program, assessed by grade point average, is shown in Figure 4:14. In addition to being classified in the experimental (training) or control group, the students also were subdivided according to their socioeconomic class (SES).

Figure 4:14 indicates that both participating and nonparticipating students unexpectedly exhibit GPA increments. However, only the high SES students participating in the program continue to show academic progress after the first year. Kolb (1965) contends that the values of the subculture of the low SES participants are at variance with the values instilled by the program. These reference group values hinder later development.

The maintenance of the improvement exhibited by the high SES chil-

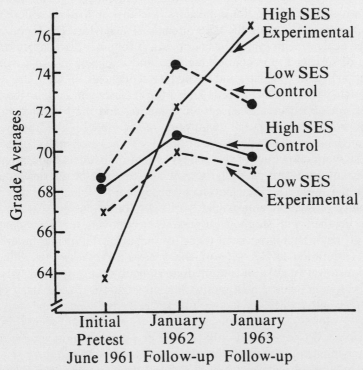

FIGURE 4:14. School grade averages in pretest and follow-up years as a function of socioeconomic class and participation in the achievement training program (from Kolb, 1965, p. 789).

dren provides hope that achievement behavior can be altered, given appropriate intervention techniques. The implications of this possibility are indeed far-reaching. Needless to say, much further evidence is needed before this hypothesis can be fully accepted.

GENERAL SUMMARY

The experimental study of achievement motivation has its origins in Murray's taxonomy of need systems, and his demonstration that fantasy behavior (Theamtic Apperception Test imagery) provides an index of an individual's motivational concerns. The TAT was adopted by McClelland and his colleagues for the measurement of achievement needs, and shown to relate to a variety of achievement behaviors, such as the speed of learning and intensity of performance (Lowell), task recall (Atkinson), and work-partner selection (French).

A theory of achievement motivation, formulated by Atkinson after validation studies of the TAT measure, includes individual differences in achievement needs among the determinants of behavior. The theory specifies that achievement-related behavior is a resultant of a conflict between a hope of success (approach motivation) and a fear of failure (avoidance motivation). The approach and avoidance tendencies, in turn, are a function of achievement-related needs (need for achievement and anxiety about failure), the expectancy of success and failure, and the incentive value of success and failure. A special assumption of the model is that the incentive value of achievement tasks is determined by the probability of success.

The main derivation of this theory is that individuals high in resultant achievement needs are particularly attracted to tasks of intermediate difficulty, while those low in achievement needs are inhibited by tasks whose probability of success approximates .50. Investigations by Atkinson and Litwin, Feather, and Moulton, respectively employing the dependent variables of risk-preference, persistence of behavior following failure, and choice (aspiration level), support the general hypothesis that differential attraction towards tasks of intermediate difficulty are displayed by groups high and low in achievement motivation. In addition, a wide array of education-relevant studies, including investigations of vocational aspiration (Mahone, Morris), field of concentrations (Isaacson), and ability grouping (Atkinson & O'Connor) not only provide empirical support for the theory, but also demonstrate its applicability to educational settings.

A number of deficiencies of the theory were pointed out. The shortcomings include a dependence among the environmental determinants of behavior, a lack of precision in the operational definitions of the expectancy of success, an inability to account for the motivational effects of success and failure, and the conceptualization of the organism as stimulus-bound. Modifications of Atkinson's original model, suggested by Atkinson and Cartwright and Weiner, to include "persisting inertial tendencies" among the determinants of behavior enable the model to overcome some of its insufficiencies.

The chapter concludes with a discussion of McClelland's cross-cultural investigations relating need for achievement to economic growth, and a review of attempts to alter achievement motivation among businessmen (McClelland & Winter) and underachieving students (Kolb).

It was contended previously that drive theorists demonstrated that motivational psychologists could proceed in a scientific and mathematical manner, while Lewin and his colleagues directed attention to the subject matter motivational theorists should investigate. The study of achievement motivation was guided by both these methodological and content concerns. Investigators adopted the procedures and mathematical orientation developed by Hullians, but applied this approach to the study of complex human behaviors observed in "everyday" life.

The theory of achievement motivation, as Lewinian theory, stands at the crossroads between cognitive and mechanistic conceptions of action. Cognitive concepts, such as expectancy of success, are employed side by side with mechanistic concepts, such as inertial motivation. It is contended that individuals consider the probabilities of success at a number of alternative tasks and reach complex decisions that maximize subjective pleasure. Yet one never is informed, for example, how judgments of probability level are formed or how success and failure are perceived. Achievement theory is the most precise of the "cognitive" conceptions of action, yet remains generally unconcerned with mental events.

V

Cognitive Approaches and Attribution Theory

Thus far, the book has advanced from the mechanistic conceptions of Hull and Spence through the quasi-cognitive approaches of Lewin and Atkinson. The main cognitive focus of the latter two theorists is the manner in which past experience (learning) is conceptualized. Lewin and Atkinson initiated few systematic investigations of thought or of the relations between thought and action. Further, concepts such as tension, valence force, and inertial motivation, which form the heart of the Lewin and Atkinson conceptions, have been adopted from the physical sciences. Mechanistic concepts, therefore, seem to have had a greater influence on these theorists than cognitive constructs.

In this chapter we turn to conceptions that have more clearly focused on the relation between thought and action. We begin with a brief introduction to cognitive theory and then present various attempts to relate cognition and motivation. Next we describe the more circumscribed study of the attribution process and introduce the beginnings of an attributional theory of motivation.

In Chapter VI we apply attribution theory to the study of achievement-oriented behaviors, and the theory is briefly extended to the analysis of moral behavior and experimental extinction. We conclude that chapter with an examination of some educational processes from an attributional point of view.

HISTORICAL BACKGROUND OF THE COGNITIVE APPROACH

Cognitive psychology is concerned with how incoming sensory stimulation is "transformed, reduced, elaborated, recovered, and used" (Neisser, 1966, p. 4). Stimuli as conceived by cognitive theorists do not goad the organism or initiate mechanistic chains of thought. Rather, the stimuli are viewed as a source of information. It is frequently contended that the processed information is integrated into a "belief" that gives "meaning" to the external, physical environment.

The study of mental processes, which frequently had been unfruitful, became buried in the psychological avalanche produced by Watson and subsequent behaviorists and neobehaviorists. This was partly fostered by the misconception that only the study of behavior (overt responses) could answer the functionalists' question of how an organism adapts to its environment. Later in this chapter we will argue that cognitive events, such as causal attributions, also have important functional significance. That is, "why" as well as "how" is a functional question.

During the past twenty years the associationistic grip on psychology has greatly weakened. The issue more often raised now by contemporary psychologists is not whether cognitions affect behavior, but how and under what conditions this influence will be manifested. The current acceptance of the study of mediational processes is the result of a multiplicity of factors. Perhaps the main reason for the growth of a cognitive psychology is the general inability of the associationistic and drive positions to explain many behaviors. But Heider (1957) further points out that the vast use of projective testing, the interest in perception by experimental psychologists, and the regard for interperson perception expressed by social psychologists, provided the impetus and climate for the study of higher mental processes. In addition, the advent of information theory and computer models lent scientific respectability to the examination of mental events. These mathematical approaches promised to give more precision and operational anchoring to the often vague terminology associated with the study of the mind. Finally, contemporary cognitive theorists have incorporated the methodological advances and sophistication of behaviorists into their investigations.

The foundations of a cognitive psychology were in part laid by Kant (1781). He argued that there are no absolute sciences, save mathematics, inasmuch as empirical sciences are sciences of phenomena. One can never know the real objects "out there" (*Ding an sich*) for all knowledge, according to Kant, is founded on certain a priori categories of thought which, in turn, condition our experiences.

Phenomenology, the study of subjective experience, is related to the Kantian position. Phenomenologists insist that understanding begins with phenomena. But mediational processes, according to these theorists, are not inferred, nor are they considered hypothetical constructs; they are givens (Van de Geer & Jaspers, 1966). What one asks is how the phenomenological world becomes structured, or how it comes to have meaning (see MacLeod, 1964). Hence, psychological theorists influenced by phenomenology do not accept the Baconian approach to science, which employs the method of abstraction to discover laws existing in nature. Instead, they "construct" a system upon their phenomenological observations in the search for behavioral laws. As already indicated, this is the scientific method advocated by Lewin. Lewin was greatly influenced by Ernst Cassirer, a prominent neo-Kantian.

Gestalt psychologists embraced phenomenology. Boring (1950) notes Kohler's statement: "Never, I believe, shall we be able to solve any problems of ultimate principles until we use the phenomenological method" (p. 601). The phenomenological method is "a description of immediate experience" (p. 18). The methodology of a phenomenological psychology involves demonstrations that convey certain experiences to the viewer, such as the perceptual illusions relied upon so heavily by the Gestaltists, or the causal demonstration of Heider and Simmel (discussed later). The Gestaltists, however, also realized that to advance science one must go beyond a mere description of events.

Both cognitive psychology, with its concern with mediating internal events, and introspectionism, with its concern with immediate experience, are allied to phenomenology. However, there are important differences between these schools. Only the introspectionists endeavor to reduce the experienced event into more basic elements (see MacLeod, 1964, and pp. 4–5 of this book). The reductionistic approach is unacceptable to phenomenologists, because it ignores the meaning of the incoming experience. For this same reason, information theory is rejected by phenomenologists. There are also important differences between cognitive psychology and phenomenology. As Van de Geer and Jaspers (1966) note, cognitive theory ranges from "neobehavioristic mediation to phenomenological interpretation" (p. 148). It is quite possible for one to be interested in cognitive processes while not accepting any of the tenets of phenomenology. Perhaps phenomenology is most directly influential today in certain schools of psychotherapy. Names such as Maslow, May, and Rogers, associated with "existential" or "inner experience" approaches to self-understanding, incorporate the basic phenomenological precepts concerning the significance of inner experience, the irreducibility of those experiences, the salience of meaning, and so forth (see Rogers, 1964).

The general approach of a cognitive theory of behavior is to postulate intervening cognitions between the incoming stimulation and the final response (Baldwin, 1969). The intervening cognition may be an expectancy (Tolman), subjective probability of success (Atkinson), or perceived path to the goal (Lewin). But cognitive theories also are "characterized by a particular flavor in their approach to the problems of psychology at large" (Van de Geer & Jaspers, 1966, p. 146). Thus, although virtually all contemporary associationistic models also postulate that mediating events intervene between the stimulus and final response (such as r_g-s_g sequences, learned drives, or implicit thoughts), they are not considered cognitive theories.

Baldwin (1969) relates the form an idealized cognitive theory of behavior should take:

A cognitive theory of behavior assumes that the first stage in the chain of events initiated by the stimulus situation and resulting in the behavioral act is the construction of a cognitive representation of the distal environment. The later events in the chain are instigated, modified and guided by this cognitive representation. The cognitive representation thus acts as the effective environment which arouses motives and emotions, and guides overt behavior toward its target or goal [p. 326].

The analysis of behavior therefore requires two distinct steps (see Diagram 5:1). First, there is a cognitive representation (schema) of the received stimuli. Second, there is a specification of how the cognition influences the final behavioral response. That is, environmental stimulation is related to mediational interpretations, and behavior is undertaken "because it seemed to me" (Neisser, 1966, p. 4).

Thus, it is apparent that a cognitive theory of action must contain at least the rudiments of a theory of thought in order to fulfill the first of the two steps outlined above. Yet, the "cognitive" theories of motivation that have been presented thus far are little concerned with cognitive processes or mental events. For example, Atkinson never states just how subjective expectancies are formed. Similarly, although Lewin is considered a phenomenologist, his system is "post-perceptual": it does not explain how the world comes to be encoded as it is. The primary cognitive considerations in both Atkinson's and Lewin's models are embodied in

DIAGRAM 5:1
Model of a Cognitive Theory of Behavior

Antecedent Stimuli ⟶ Mediating Cognitive Event ⟶ Behavior

the experiental variables of expectancy, potency, and psychological distance. But, as Festinger (1957b) states,

Certainly, if a person is motivated toward some end, the specific actions in which he engages, will, in part, be determined by his cognition about his environment and about the paths that will lead to the end he desires. But this states only one aspect of the relation between action and cognition [p. 128].

In sum, the major theories of motivation labeled as "cognitive" deserve this title only vis à vis the associationistic (Hullian) position to which they are set in contrast. These so-called cognitive theories generally ignore the relationship between the incoming stimulus and its cognitive representation. They also fail to investigate or even consider the processes of information scanning and selection, information combination and storage, cognitive schema, and perceptions of causality, to name just a few of the other higher processes relevant to action. They take the position that prior experiences are encoded and transformed into a belief system that includes an anticipation of the final goal event—but this position falls short of the requirements of a truly cognitive theory. The concern of theorists such as Atkinson and Lewin with other cognitive functions, such as memory organization and fantasy, are peripheral to their formal systems of behavior, and are not systematically integrated into their conceptions.

It is difficult to speculate why "cognitive" theorists such as Atkinson, Lewin, and Tolman have not been more concerned with cognitive processes and the relationship between thought and action. Atkinson, for one, is heavily influenced by Freud's argument that the major determinants of behavior are unconscious—that individuals cannot even accurately *report* their general level of achievement needs. Thus, many sources of human motivation may not be knowable, given the typical phenomenological or introspective methodology. But it is also true that the major motivational theorists with cognitive orientations were more directly interested in action than thought, and have tended to neglect thought processes in favor of the examination of overt responses.

Many attempts to relate cognition and motivation do not adhere to the motivational model format exemplified in the writings of Atkinson, Lewin, and Tolman. Several theoretical approaches relating cognition and motivation and supporting empirical investigations are now presented: (1) psychoanalytic theory and cognitive controls, (2) cognitive determinants of emotion, (3) cognitive appraisal and coping behavior, and (4) theories of cognitive balance. These areas are selected for review because they are germane to the later discussion of attribution theory, they permit comparisons with the conceptions presented in the prior chapters, and they are influential in the field of psychology. Other important cognitive approaches, such as Blum's (1961) models of the mind and Dulany's (1968) analysis of verbal conditioning, are neglected here.

The general theme under consideration in the following pages is the manner in which cognitions influence affect and action. The reverse temporal sequence: the effect of motivation on cognition, is generally not discussed. Major research areas examining, for example, the effect of drive level on the range of cue utilization, or the many investigations included under the rubric of the "new look" in perception, are not immediately pertinent to the main concerns of this chapter.

PSYCHOANALYTIC THEORY AND COGNITIVE CONTROLS

Psychoanalytic theory often is considered the approach to the understanding of human behavior that is farthest from phenomenology. The emphasis on unconscious motivation by psychoanalytic theorists is incompatible with the descriptive analysis of conscious experience advocated by phenomenologists and introspectionists. Further, the influence of classical mechanics on Freud's thinking, and his associationistic model of thought processes, contribute to the belief that psychoanalytic psychology and phenomenology are antithetical.

On the other hand, Freud formulated a theory of consciousness, and his analysis of dreams and other cognitive processes are well known. The chief determinants of action in his theory of motivation, the instincts, are even conceived as *mental* representations of bodily needs. Klein (1968) also calls attention to the fact that

the germinal insight with which Freud launched psychoanalysis was that it was a forceful *idea*—a cognitive structure—incompatible with other ideas that was the main source of difficulty underlying hysterical neurosis. . . . The conception that the motivational aspect of pathogenesis is essentially a *cognitive* organization tended to be obscured in subsequent theorizing about drives. . . . Even so, it must not be forgotten that to this day the central clinical (that is, psychotherapeutic) *data* about drives are still thought products [p. 7].

Rapaport (1959) also notes that Freud was influenced by Kant and his followers, and distinguishes between "what is perceived and what is conceived, what is real and what is only thought" (p. 61). Thus, it is not unreasonable to consider Freud a cognitive theorist. His theory of motivation specifies clearly that cognitive processes intervene between the onset of the driving stimuli and the final response, and, in part, determine the direction and magnitude of behavior (see Rapaport, 1959).

Psychoanalytic Models of Thought and Action

Within the theoretical framework advocated by Freud, all behavior is instigated by, and derived from, instinctual (id) wishes. These wishes are represented as demands made on the body, and they instigate actions that reduce the instinctual urges. A wish is conceptualized as "cathected" or "bound" energy; this energy or libido is freed when the desired goal is attained. Pleasure is experienced when energy is released, and is thus united with the mechanical principle of entropy, or available energy (see Rapaport, 1959, 1960).

The observational base of the theory is the restlessness displayed by hungry infants, and their subsequent quiescence when the breast is reached:

restlessness — — — — — ➤ sucking at breast — — — — — — ➤ quiescence.

On the theoretical level, this behavioral sequence is conceptualized as:

cathexis — — — — — ➤   action on object — — — — — ➤ discharged cathexis; or

drive — — — — — — ➤   drive action — — — — — — ➤ gratification; or

pain — — — — — — ➤ behavior — — — — — — — ➤ pleasure.

The phenotypic and genotypic sequences depicted above pertain to Freud's primary action model. This model does not account for thought processes, and represents "actions motivated by basic drives without the intervention of psychic structures" (Rapaport, 1959, p. 71). It is therefore a "reflex arc" model, quite similar to Hull's conception of unlearned patterns of behavior.

The primary model of cognition formulated by Freud is conceptually similar to the primary action model. Again, behavior (ideation) is initiated by an instinctual desire, or an unfulfilled wish. However, the drive object is absent, or unavailable, and gratification occurs by means of a hallucination that redintegrates past experiences with the drive object:

cathexis — — — — — ➤ absence of drive object — — — — ➤ hallucinatory idea.

A hallucinatory idea is an example of primary process thinking. Primary process thoughts do not distinguish reality from irreality. Thus, wishing per se, in addition to commerce with the goal object, may serve as a means of gratification. All thoughts governed by primary processes, such as dreams, are therefore wish-fulfillments, and all cognitive processes are derived from basic needs.

Freud's primary models of thought and action coordinate drives or instinctual wishes with immediate expression. There are no intervening processes (ego functions) that aid the organism in its adaptation to the environment. However, Freud notes that at times immediate gratification may result in more pain than pleasure (for example, the threat of castration as punishment for direct sexual expression). Therefore, an "executive," the ego, develops from the energy of the id to further the instinctual aims.[1] The ego intervenes between the driving instinctual stimuli and the prepotent response, imposing delays and altering the direction of behavior. The ego serves the id by attaining the maximum resultant pleasure for the organism. The secondary action model outlined by Freud includes these delay mechanisms:

cathexis ⟶ structuralized delay ⟶ detour activity ⟶ gratification.

The structuralized delays, also called controls or defenses, prevent id discharge and thus fulfill the demands made upon the organism by society. These "secondary processes" are guided by the reality principle, rather than by the pleasure principle that characterizes id functioning. Further, the delay imposed by the ego indicates that there is an organizational hierarchy among Freud's determinants of behavior. The higher center, or ego, can control and inhibit the lower center, or id, even though the ego was created by the id.

The secondary model of thought or cognition outlined by Freud is:

cathexis ⟶ drive object absent ⟶ delay, with thoughts given to plans,
anticipations, and so on,
to reach the goal objective.

The secondary thought model is similar to the primary thought model in that cognitions are initiated by drives, and again there is an absence of the drive object. However, immediate gratification (hallucination) is replaced by thoughtful planning that is instrumental to eventual goal attainment.

In sum, in the secondary models of action and thought, cognitive con-

---

[1] Ego psychologists have called attention to the inconsistency of having an ego created by structures that cannot distinguish reality from irreality (see Hartmann, Kris, & Loewenstein, 1946).

trols (ego structures) intervene between the internal libidinal stimuli and behavior. In the words of Klein (1954), cognitive control,

like a need, . . . directs . . . but its central feature is not a discharge in consummatory actions that bring "gratification." Rather, it functions to resolve an immediately adaptive requirement. . . . When a cognitive control is activated to cope with an adaptive demand and especially when a barrier to need satisfaction is present, such processes of control may also serve a taming function of the need itself; they may engender *delay* of need gratification. Behavior, then, expresses both the pressures of the needs and forces that counteract, qualify, or facilitate their gratification in keeping with the coping strategy that is invoked to meet the requirements and claims of reality [pp. 226–27].

The delay or control mechanisms are conceived as psychic structures. They are slow to change, and represent channels through which gratification may ultimately be attained. Thus, the id-ego (drive-structure) formulation is not dissimilar to the conceptions of behavior already presented. The psychoanalytic model, as in Hullian theory, includes energizing and associative or experiential variables, as well as environmental objects which satisfy needs. Further, in both the Freudian and Hullian models, the energizers of behavior (respectively, libido and drive) are nondirectional, and behavior is undertaken to reduce the internal stimuli associated with drive states. However, the Hull-Freud analogy should not be carried too far (see Rapaport, 1959), particularly because in analytic theory libidinal wishes are conceived as *mental* representations of psychological forces.

It is evident that the differentiating feature between *primary and secondary models* of thought and action in psychoanalytic theory is that in the secondary models the ego intervenes between drive onset and drive expression. Included among the ego or secondary processes are the defense mechanisms, which either raise the threshold necessary before a driving wish is expressed or alter the direction of behavior. Over time, the ego and the mechanisms of defense have taken a more and more important role among the determinants of behavior, while drives per se have become less central in psychoanalytic theory. This is not meant to imply that the instinctual urges are no longer considered important; according to Rapaport (1960) they are the only motivators of behavior in the psychoanalytic conception. However, there is now recognition that behavior is overdetermined, that there is no one-to-one correspondence between the drive stimuli and the goal response, and that the functioning of the id and ego must be considered a constellation. This is often called the Gestalt orientation of Freudian theory (Rapaport, 1959). Because of the intertwining between drive (id) and structure (ego) in the determination of action, Klein (1968) states:

I . . . speak about motivation in terms of properties of a behavioral unit of ideation, affect and action, and not about "drive." To discuss drive as if it were a distinctive entity which "interacts" with thought creates all sorts of mischief. It is only as structured affective-cognitive-motor events that drives are knowable as motivations and definable at all. Inasmuch as motivation involves knowledge, it is cognitive. . . . Conversely, insofar as cognition has direction, it is motivated. . . . Therefore, what is motivating about behavior and what is cognitive about motivation are one and the same thing [p. 5].

The transition point at which the ego and cognitive factors began to play a more central role in Freud's theory came in 1926, with the publication of *The Problem of Anxiety*. There, Freud postulated that his "repression produces anxiety" sequence be reversed to the now famous "anxiety produces repression." Originally Freud argued that anxiety is the result of undischarged libidinal energy. The absence of wished-for objects, or a lack of gratification because of repression, was believed to result in an accumulation of drive energy. The binding of this energy resulted in an affective (anxiety) discharge. Anxiety therefore was considered a product of the id. However, in reversing this sequence to "anxiety → repression," Freud converted anxiety to an ego rather than an id derivative. Freud contended that when drive expression may lead to more pain than pleasure, the ego "inoculates itself" with anxiety. This anxiety serves as a cue or warning that if the organism engages in the expected activity, the ego will experience a greater and perhaps an uncontrollable amount of the anxiety it just felt in mitigated form. Hence, action is initiated (defenses activated) that interfere with and delay drive expression. Freud thus reconceptualized anxiety from an affective id discharge into a cognitive signal. As discussed in Chapter II, this idea was translated into *S-R* terminology, and became one of the most influential formulations in psychology.

Subsequent theoretical analysis suggested that the ego be given its own source of energy, rather than developing out of energy "borrowed" from the id. This permitted psychoanalytic theorists to admit data demonstrating that there are thoughts and actions that are not drive determined and that do not function to reduce stimulation (see White, 1959). The structuralized delays imposed by the ego may thus be learned independent of basic drives, or develop from the *conflict-free* ego sphere (Hartmann, Kris, & Loewenstein, 1946). In addition, it has been postulated that structures developed in the service of basic drives can later become independent of those drives, or attain *functional autonomy*. The conception of permanent cognitive structures, which may or may not develop from or serve driving forces, is the theoretical foundation of research on cognitive styles (controls) conducted by Klein, Holzman, Gardner, and other ego psychologists.

Cognitive Style

Cognitive styles are conceived as individual consistencies in the manner in which persons defend against drive stimuli and adapt to the external world. As already indicated, these stable structures intervene between drive stimuli and the final response. They are hypothesized to influence the manner in which information is registered, encoded, and retained, and serve a variety of other functions (see Gardner, Holzman, Klein, Linton, & Spence, 1959).

Cognitive styles are linked with, but are not identical to, defense mechanisms. A cognitive style denotes a characteristic way of organizing incoming stimulation. This in part determines what defenses individuals are prone to employ. Certain modes of cognitive functioning may be compatible with the use of some defenses, but not with the use of others. Research related to the cognitive style labeled leveling-sharpening illustrates this point.

Leveling-sharpening is conceived as a personality dimension that primarily influences the formation of memory schemata. Levelers are believed to assimilate incoming percepts with prior memory traces. Thus, new percepts do not stand out as "figure," and readily lose their distinct label. Individuals with this mode of cognitive functioning are believed prone to use repression as a psychological defense, for it is relatively easy to "forget" threatening thoughts, and thoughts in general, when their traces are not distinguished. Conversely, sharpeners are believed to organize their memories into distinctive elements. Highly differentiated memories should render it more difficult to employ repression as a defense. Thus, sharpeners may be prone to employ other defenses when protecting themselves from unacceptable drive wishes.

The method of assessment of leveling-sharpening contrasts with both the projective technique exemplified in need achievement assessment, and the objective approach illustrated in the anxiety measures of Taylor (1953) and Mandler and Sarason (1952). To ascertain the disposition to assimilate new percepts with prior memories, subjects are asked to estimate the size of a series of squares. After every fifth trial the smallest of the squares shown drops out. Four of the previously viewed squares, along with one that is slightly larger, are presented in the next series of five trials. Leveling is inferred when the judgment of the square size lags behind the progressive incremental sequence. It is believed that this lag is caused by the assimilation of the new percept with the prior memory traces.

In this assessment procedure the subject is asked to give his most accurate size estimate. Thus, response withholding and response bias, which are inherent in most verbal report measures, are minimized. Further, there is an objective scoring scheme, and the problem of inter-rater reliability, which plagues many projective measures, also is circumvented. Virtually all of the cognitive style assessment devices make use of perceptual tests in which there is a "correct" response. Individual differences in personality structure are then inferred from performance inaccuracies.[2]

Two studies reported by Holzman and Gardner (1959, 1960) suggest that the proposed leveling-sharpening personality dimension is related to the use of repression and to the accuracy of memory. Holzman and Gardner (1959) found that individuals classified as repressors by the Rorschach test (one wishes a performance or behavioral measure was used) also are classified as levelers. However, individuals who are "levelers" are not necessarily high in their usage of repression indicators on the Rorschach (for example, few movement responses, color percepts). Holzman and Gardner argue that factors in addition to leveling determine repression. Thus, a leveler may not be a repressor, but one who represses must function cognitively as a leveler. In addition, Holzman and Gardner (1960) report that levelers are less able to recall the details of a popular children's story with which they were familiar (The Pied Piper) than are sharpeners. Thus, they apparently have less well-articulated memories. These investigators conclude that in investigations of psychological defenses one must also study general cognitive functioning. Clearly, however, more data is desperately needed in this area. Work on cognitive styles has multipled in related areas (see Witkin et al., 1962; and Kagan et al., 1963). But this work is not systematically incorporated into motivational schemes, and is not discussed here.

COGNITIVE DETERMINANTS OF EMOTION

Psychoanalytic theory, including ego psychology, focuses upon the channeling or delay functions of cognitions. Although these "channels" may become permanent structures and attain independence from basic drives, they primarily are important because of their interaction with, and influ-

---

[2] Inferring personality characteristics from IQ batteries and other performance tests also has been attempted, but not with any great degree of success.

ence upon, drive expression. In the following section of this chapter the influence of cognitions on affect and behavior again is discussed, but within frameworks generally divorced from assumptions about drive states.

Cognition, Arousal, and Emotion

Schachter and Singer (1962) contend that emotion is a function of two theoretically separable factors: level of arousal and cognitions about the arousing situation. The general position advocated by Schachter (1964) was summarized by Valins (1966):

> Within his cognitive-physiological theory of emotion, physiological changes are considered to function as stimuli or cues and are represented cognitively as feelings or sensations. These feelings, in turn, arouse further cognitive activity in the form of attempts to identify the situation that precipitated them. Emotional behavior results when the feeling state is attributed to an emotional stimulus or situation [p. 400].

Thus, cognitive factors provide the "steering" function for emotional expression by labeling (ascribing the cause for) the experienced arousal, and guiding the appropriate emotional feeling. Schachter's two-factor theory of emotion has similar properties to the Drive $\times$ Habit conception of behavior. There are distinct energizing and cue components of behavior (emotional expression), and the energizing factor is conceived as also having stimulus properties. Schachter further implies that the two factors are related multiplicatively; if either has a value of zero, then emotions will not be expressed. He cites evidence that pure arousal does not result in emotional expression, and believes that cognitive activity in the absence of arousal also is not emotion-provoking.

In real-life situations the cues that arouse the organism also provide the cognitive structure necessary for labeling the event. For example, the appearance of a birthday cake may raise arousal and is a stimulus for positive affect; the sight of a gun is likely to produce physiological activation and is a cue for fear. However, in laboratory settings Schachter and his colleagues are able to manipulate arousal and cognitive factors independently and apparently have demonstrated their joint effects on emotional expression.

In the first of a systematic series of studies, Schachter and Singer (1962) injected epinephrine into subjects under the guise of studying "how vitamin supplements affect the visual skills" (p. 382). Epinephrine is an activating agent that produces autonomic arousal and symptoms such as heart palpitation and a general "high" feeling. Some subjects were informed about the effects of the drugs, and thus could appropriately label the source of their feelings. Other subjects were either uninformed or misinformed about the drug effects, while control subjects were injected with a placebo. The subjects then waited for their "visual test" in the presence of a stooge subject. The stooge either acted in a very euphoric manner, playing with various objects, or feigned anger at some personal inquiries that were part of a questionnaire administered during the waiting period. During this time interval the behaviors of the subjects were observed and rated for euphoria or anger. The subjects also answered a questionnaire pertaining to their present feeling state.

The main findings of this experiment were that uninformed epinephrine-injected subjects (aroused, but "unlabeled") are angrier in the anger-inducing situation, and more euphoric in the social situation cued for euphoria, than subjects in the other experimental conditions. Thus, emotion is a function of arousal level, and individuals in an aroused state may experience disparate emotions as a function of the social (cognitive) situation in which they find themselves. In sum, Schachter and Singer demonstrated that level of arousal and cognitive processes, when manipulated independently, and contiguously rather than simultaneously, determine the direction and magnitude of experienced emotion.

In a subsequent experiment, Schachter and Wheeler (1962) replicated the effects of arousal level on emotional expression. Subjects were injected with either epinephrine, placebo, or chlorpromazine, a sympathetic blocking agent that dampens arousal. Subjects then viewed a short comedy film. During the film their expressions of amusement were observed. As expected, level of expressed amusement varied monotonically as a function of the induced level of physiological arousal, with greatest expression in the epinephrine condition, and least in the chlorpromazine condition.

The Informational Value of Arousal

Schachter's two-factor theory of emotion has been called into question by a number of experiments conducted by Valins and his colleagues. Valins's studies suggest that cognitions are sufficient to produce emotional behavior, and that internal arousal states are determinants of emotion only because of their cue function. Valins (1966) states:

> Once it is granted that internal events can function as cues or stimuli, then these events can now be considered as a source of cognitive information. They can, for example, result in cognitions such as, "My heart is pounding," or "My face is flushed." As potential cognitive information, however, these events are subject to the same mechanisms that process any stimulus before it is represented cognitively [pp. 400–1].

That is, because the internal arousal state is conceptualized as a stimulus, it can be "denied, distorted, or simply not perceived" (p. 401). For example, sociopaths have high levels of internal arousal, yet generally display little emotional expression (Schachter & Latané, 1964). This apparently contradicts Schachter's conception of the determinants of emotion. However, if the arousal cues are denied, or not utilized, the person could function "as if" his arousal level were indeed low. According to Valins, the nonveridical representation of an arousal state has the same effects as a veridical perception of internal states. It is thus apparent that, given Valin's position, arousal per se does not influence emotional expression.

Valins examines the effects of nonveridical perceptions of internal states by presenting to subjects fraudulent information that conveys they are in a state of arousal. He then investigates the effects of the false evidence on the intensity of emotional expression. Thus, the cue function of internal states is manipulated, while the actual level of arousal remains constant. This reverses the procedure used by Schachter and Wheeler (1962), in which the level of arousal is manipulated while the external stimulus situation remains constant.

In the first of his experiments, Valins (1966) manipulated the extent to which male subjects perceive that their heart reacts to the perception of a slide of a semi-nude female projected on a screen. Subjects were allowed to overhear bogus "monitored heart-rate" information, although they were instructed to "try to ignore the heart sounds" (p. 402). For the experimental subjects half of the slides were associated with a change in heart rate (either acceleration or deceleration). Subjects in a control group also heard the heart-beat sounds, but were told that they were meaningless noise. Following the viewing of the stimuli the attractiveness of the nudes was rated, and subjects selected some photographs of the viewed slides to take home as a reward for their participation.

The results of the study revealed that in the experimental group the nudes associated with a perceived change in heart rate were judged as more attractive and their pictures were more likely to be chosen to take home than were pictures of the nudes not linked with this bogus information. The sound per se did not effect the emotional ratings of subjects in the control group. Valins (1966) therefore concludes,

The results are exactly what one would have expected had heart-rate changes and veridical feelings of palpitation been pharmacologically induced to some slides but not to others. The mechanism operating to produce these effects is presumably the same regardless of the veridicality of the feedback. Internal events are a source of cognitive information and . . . when an emotional explanation is prepotent, they will label their reactions accordingly [pp. 406, 407].

Valins also notes that when subjects are exposed to the fraudulent heart-rate "they seemed to actively persuade themselves that [the nude] was attractive. They report looking at the slide more closely and it is evident that they attempt to justify the feedback" (p. 407). In subsequent investigations of this "hypothesis testing" interpretation of the data, Valins (1972) has found that debriefing about the nature of the experiment does not alter the subjects' posttreatment opinions about the nudes. Thus, subjects apparently are not just passively listening to the heart-rate information that is presented. Further, Barefoot and Straub (1971) found that attractiveness ratings of the stimuli associated with the false arousal information increase when subjects are allowed more time for viewing. It appears that during this time interval they look more closely at the stimuli and find evidence to support their perceived feeling state.

In a replication of his original experiment, Valins (1967) hypothesized that "unemotional" subjects, who presumably ignore their internal arousal cues, would be less susceptible to opinion modification by the heart-rate procedure than "emotional" subjects. Subjects were selected according to their assessed level of emotionality, and placed in the bogus heart-rate experimental setting already described. As predicted, over all subjects pictures associated with heart-rate change were rated more attractive than stimuli not paired with this false information. In addition, the false feedback was a more effective attitude change device for individuals classified as highly emotional.

Valins and Ray (1967) demonstrated that people also infer they are less emotional toward a stimulus when their perceived level of emotional reactivity toward that stimulus is low. Subjects in the Valins and Ray experiment viewed slides of snakes presented in an ascending order of judged fear provocation. Interspersed were slides with the word "shock" printed on them. Whenever the shock slide was viewed, the subject received a mild electric shock which increased in intensity over trials. During the presentation of the shock slide subjects in the experimental group received bogus heart-rate information that their emotional reaction to those slides was increasing over trials. However, the false heart-rate reactions to the snake slides remained constant, although the snakes were objectively more fear-producing over trials. Hence, the subjects were led to infer that they had little fear of snakes. In the control group the heart-rate information was again described as an extraneous sound. Subsequent testing revealed that subjects in the experimental group were less likely to exhibit snake-avoidance behavior (they were more willing to hold a live rattlesnake in their hands) than were subjects in the control group. Valins suggests that the subjects engage in this behavior to prove to themselves that they are not afraid of snakes.

In sum, Valins and his co-workers have shown that arousal per se is not a necessary antecedent of emotional feelings, but that arousal cues are a source of information which individuals use to judge their feeling state (for example, My heart is pounding, I must be angry or euphoric; I feel "high," I must think this movie is funny; and so on). Cognitions appear to be a sufficient condition for an emotional response (assuming, of course, that the cognition of an increased heart rate does not augment one's actual heart rate).

COGNITIVE APPRAISAL AND COPING BEHAVIOR

A third systematic program of research demonstrating the effects of cognition on emotion has been carried out by Lazarus and his associates. Lazarus is primarily concerned with psychological stress and "the external and internal forces or stimulus conditions of stress reactions, and the intervening structures and processes that determine when and in what form the stress reaction will occur" (Lazarus, 1966, p. 13). Like Schachter and Valins, Lazarus believes that the main determinants of emotional reactions (in this particular instance, the threat reaction), are cognitive processes that are instigated following the perception of a threat stimulus. He views his work as "part of a general movement toward psychological models emphasizing cognition and information processing" (1968, p. 199). Lazarus, in contrast to Schachter and Valins, contends that arousal is determined by cognitive appraisal; it is not a prior organismic state to which a cognitive label is applied. Further, Lazarus focuses upon the adaptive or functional significance of cognitive activity. He is interested in how cognitions guide the organism to a "consideration of the nature of one's plight and what might be done to obviate it" (1968, p. 206).

The studies conducted by Lazarus that are most relevant here involve experimental manipulations of cognitive processes, and the effects of these manipulations on emotional reactivity. The general experimental procedure is to present to subjects a film that gives rise to emotional (stress) reactions. Lazarus has used two films that yield similar results: a subincision movie, which shows a stone-age ritual in which adolescent boys have their penises deeply cut, and a safety film, which depicts workshop accidents. While subjects view the movie various measures of autonomic arousal, such as heart rate and galvanic skin response, are continuously recorded.

Lazarus manipulates the cognitive activity during the perception of the film by varying the accompanying sound track. The sound track guides the "cognitive reappraisal" of the perceived stimuli by evoking psychological defenses of *denial* or *intellectualization*. The denial theme indicates that the subincision operation is not harmful, that the participants in the safety film are actors, and so forth. The intellectualization sound track offers a detached view of the situations. The subincision film apparently is narrated by an objective anthropologist merely viewing strange customs, while during the safety film the viewer is asked to take an objective look at the dynamics of the situation. Lazarus then ascertains whether the manipulations of these defensive processes, or modes of thought, influence the manner in which the individual copes with the film. That is, he examines whether the intervening cognitive events reduce the perceived harm or threat inherent in the stimulus itself, and hence lower the emotional reaction to the stimulus. (One assumption of these studies is that the subjects identify with the harmed person; see Lazarus & Opton, 1966.)

Figure 5:1 shows the results of one study that induced the defensive orientation of denial (Lazarus & Alfert, 1964). In this experiment the subincision film was used, and the denial orientation was introduced either prior to or during the film. Both methods reduced the degree of reactivity to the stressor, relative to a control group not receiving the defensive sound track. But it is evident from Figure 5:1 that the "short-circuiting" of the emotional reactivity is most efficient when the defense is introduced in its entirety before the subjects view the film. (Lazarus & Alfert use the analogy of an electrical circuit in their explanation of the processes involved.) Lazarus and Alfert also report that individuals classified as high in a personality disposition toward denial are most benefited by the denial induction. If one's personality structure is compatible with the manipulated defense, then emotional reactions are most reduced. This finding is very similar to results reported by Valins (1967).

In a related experiment conducted by Lazarus, Opton, Nomikos, and Rankin (1965), confirmatory results also were obtained for the basic hypothesis that cognitions affect emotional reactions. In this experiment the safety movie was shown and either denial or intellectualization defenses were aroused prior to the film. Figure 5:2 shows that these defensive interpretations, or cognitive reappraisals, lower the emotional response to the film relative to a control group not exposed to the defensive indoctrination.

In summary, Lazarus and his associates have shown that emotional reactions are a function of the cognitions concerning the perceived stimulus event (see again Diagram 5:1). Lazarus (1968) therefore suggests that emotions be treated as responses rather than as motivators. He believes

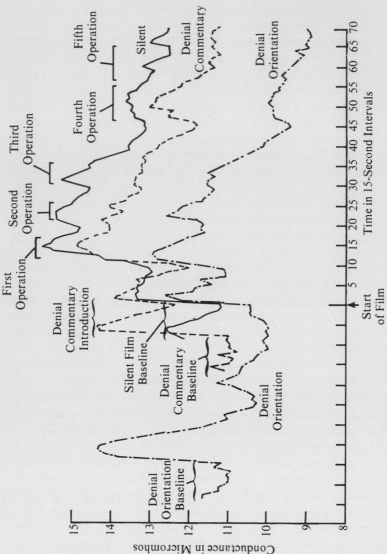

FIGURE 5:1. Skin conductance curves during orientation and film periods under three experimental conditions. Denial orientation indicates that the sound track was presented in its entirety prior to the film onset. Denial commentary indicates that the denial sound track accompanied, rather than preceded, the film. The control condition is designated as "silent," that is, there is no accompanying sound track (from Lazarus & Alfert, 1964, p. 199).

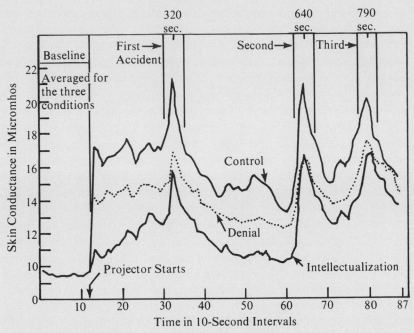

FIGURE 5:2. Effects of experimental conditions on skin conductance, given the defensive orientations of denial or intellectualization (from Lazarus, Opton, Nomikos, & Rankin, 1965, p. 628).

that his position contrasts with the viewpoint of many motivational theorists. For example, within the Drive $\times$ Habit conception of behavior anxiety is conceived as an internal emotional reaction that is important because it energizes behavior. Anxiety is studied only because it is a motivator of other responses. In a similar manner, McClelland and Atkinson conceive of motives as based upon emotions or emotional anticipations. The affects are only important in their role as determinants of achievement-related responses. The Lazarus studies, however, suggest that the postulated emotion-motivation sequence be altered, and motivation and emotion both be viewed as responses following the cognitive appraisal of the stimulus situation. Emotions then become important for their own sake, and motivation becomes more closely allied with cognition than with affect.

THEORIES OF COGNITIVE CONSISTENCY

It is generally acknowledged that "the problem of cognitive dynamics is *the* social psychological problem of the decade" (Zajonc, 1968, p. 338).

Cognitive dynamics refers to the tendency toward change brought about when cognitions are in conflict; that is, when they are inconsistent or "do not fit." In the last twenty years a number of theories of cognitive consistency have been formulated. These theories, although labeled differently (they are variously called balance, congruity, or dissonance), "all have in common the notion that the person tends to behave in ways that minimize the internal inconsistency among his interpersonal relations, among his intrapersonal cognitions, and among his beliefs, feelings, and action" (McGuire, 1966, p. 1). The validities of the various theories, however, have been tested with different reference experiments, and they attempt to account for disparate data that range from attitude change and communication acts to resistance to extinction and the amount of water consumed when thirsty.

There are evident distinctions between the cognitive consistency theories of motivation formulated by social psychologists and the cognitive approaches to motivation followed by personality (clinical) psychologists such as Klein, Lazarus, and Rapaport. Among the latter group, cognitions are allied (but not exclusively) with psychological defenses. The cognitions are adaptive mechanisms; they bind drive expression, control stress reactions, reduce anxiety, and so on. These structures interact with real or potential behavioral activators to determine the final behavioral response. Further, the structures may be permanent, and in some theories are considered basic personality dimensions. On the other hand, consistency theories focus upon the motivational properties of cognitions per se. The cognitions do not interact with motivators, nor are they activated as a response to threat. Rather, motivation is directly derived from the relations between the structures. The "goal" of this motivational state is to change the structures themselves so that they are more consistent with one another.

It is not possible to review in detail the vast amount of data in this area of growing specialization (see Abelson, Aronson, McGuire, Newcomb, Rosenberg, & Tannenbaum, 1968; Feldman, 1966; Zajonc, 1968). Two consistency theories are selected for discussion: cognitive balance and cognitive dissonance. Cognitive balance was the first of the consistency theories, and many of the subsequent approaches borrowed or modified its precepts. Further, the originator of this conception, Fritz Heider, also is the prime influence in attribution theory. Cognitive dissonance, on the other hand, was formulated later than many of the consistency theories. However, it has generated the most data. Some of the investigations concerning dissonance employ predictions derived from Hullian theory, a number of studies demonstrate the inadequacy of Hull's conception, and many of the experiments are pertinent to the attributional model of motivation presented later in the chapter.

Cognitive Balance

The basic assumption of the theory of cognitive balance is that the laws of perception for physical objects specified by Gestalt psychologists can be applied to the perception of social stimuli. Heider (1946) states that a cognitive configuration including social objects can be classified as a steady (balanced) or an unsteady (imbalanced) state. Balanced states, or "good figures," are believed to be preferred to imbalanced states. Hence, "balanced states will be realized either in such a mental reorganization as wishful thinking, or in an actual change through action" (Heider, 1960, p. 167). That is, where balance does not exist, the situation will tend to change in the direction of balance. Further, Heider argues that if an incomplete structure exists, new relations will be formed according to the principle of balance. Heider, following Lewin, thus accepts the notion of disequilibrium as the basic principle of motivation.

What constitutes a state of balance or imbalance? According to Heider, (1946, 1958) cognitive configurations consist of a number of entities having certain relations with one another. One such relation is sentiment (liking or disliking); another is that of a "unit." A unit formation exists if two factors are perceived as belonging together (for example, a person and his deeds, possessions, or attitudes). (The formation of units is one of the central Gestaltist concerns, and in object perception is determined by factors such as similarity and proximity.) In balanced states the "relations among the entities fit together harmoniously" (Heider, 1958, p. 201). Harmony characterizes a dyadic system if, for example, the two entities have the same sentiments toward one another. Thus, if a likes b (aLb) and b likes a (bLa), or if a dislikes b (a-Lb) and b dislikes a (b-La), then it is postulated that a state of balance exists. Imbalance occurs if aLb and b-La, or vice versa.

Of greater interest and more complexity are configurations containing three entities. The most discussed triadic configuration consists of two persons (p and o) and an object (x). A balanced state is said to exist when there are either zero or two negative relations between the elements in the system; that is, when the product of all the relations is positive. For example, if pLo, and both p and o have a positive attitude toward x, then the system is in balance. All the relations between the entities are positive. (The attitude toward x held by p and o is described as a positive unit, pUx and oUx). On the other hand, if pLo and pUx, but o-Ux (o and x do not form a unit, or o takes the opposite attitude toward x), then the situation is not in balance. For example, if George likes Mary, and George likes movies but Mary does not, then the situation is not in balance. If o holds an opposing attitude, then p's affect toward the whole configuration is negative. Either his sentiment toward *o* should change and become negative, (George begins to dislike Mary) or the parts of the *o-x* unit should become segregated from one another so they are no longer perceived as belonging together (Mary has no opinions about movies). Heider does not specify which of these alternatives toward the resolution of imbalance will be taken, or under what conditions one change might be preferred over the other. In general, however, it is believed that a change toward positive sentiments is more likely than a change in a negative direction.

Other examples of balanced and imbalanced configurations are illustrated in Figure 5:3. In Figure 5:3, the direction of the arrows indicates the direction of the relationship: *p* and *o* correspond to persons, *x* to an entity; the solid lines represent positive bonds and the broken lines negative relations or bonds. Structures a, c, d, and f in Figure 5:3 are balanced (the products of the relations are positive), while b and e are imbalanced (the products are negative). Subsequent mathematical formalization has enabled theorists to apply the balance notion to figures with more than three elements, and to determine the degree of balance and imbalance, rather than merely specifying an all-or-none relationship.

Virtually all the research generated by the balance model have been "attempts to demonstrate the validity of the basic principle" (Zajonc, 1968, p. 353). Zajonc suggests that this research constriction may have been caused by a premature formalization of the theory. In one early study, Jordan (1953) presented subjects with a number of triads characterized by different unit and sentiment relations. Subjects imagined that they were

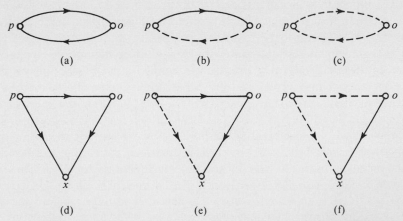

FIGURE 5:3.   Examples of dyads and triads representing balanced and unbalanced configurations. The direction of the arrow indicates the direction of the relationship; solid lines represent positive relationships; broken lines, negative relationships (from Zajonc, 1968, p. 343).

p in the situation, and rated each of the triads for pleasantness and unpleasantness. In accordance with the hypothesis, balanced triads were rated as more pleasant than imbalanced ones. However, Zajonc (1968) points out that the direction of the sentiments per se, and agreement versus disagreement, also influence positive feelings. Positive social relationships are more pleasant than negative ones, and agreement among friends is more pleasant than disagreement among enemies, although these systems are equally balanced (Zajonc, 1968, p. 351). Thus, attitudinal "forces" are extremely important in determining the affect expressed towards a situation, and are perhaps as (or more) important than the forces toward balance.

In summary, cognitive balance is postulated as a principle of motivation because imbalance corresponds to a state of disequilibrium, is unpleasant, and produces behaviors instrumental to the attainment of a balanced state. There is good evidence that balance does influence feelings towards a situation. There is a paucity of research, however, directly assessing the motivational, rather than affective, consequences of disharmonious cognitions. There are few studies, for example, that examine the direction, magnitude, or persistence of behaviors generated by imbalanced stimulus configurations. Perhaps this is in part attributable to Heider's belief that balance "is not meant to be a general theory of motivation, but has developed mainly with respect to interpersonal relations" (Heider, 1960, p. 166). It certainly is not clear at this time whether inconsistency between cognitions should be conceptualized as a drive, motive, need, tense state, or something else (see McGuire, 1966). That is, the conceptual analysis of the motivational properties of imbalance has been neglected in favor of the pursuit of defining what constitutes a balanced or imbalanced state, and then relating this state to a measure of affect or preference. McGuire (1966) fully perceives this imbalance, and states, "We feel that a classification of the concept [of inconsistency] and heuristic suggestions for future research will come more from motivational analyses of need for consistency than from any other single endeavor" (p. 34).

Cognitive Dissonance

The best known of the consistency approaches is the theory of cognitive dissonance. Zajonc (1968) indicates the importance of this conception in the field of social psychology:

No theory in social psychology has stimulated more research than the theory of cognitive dissonance. . . . If there is any one theoretical formulation that has captured the imagination of social psychologists during this decade, it is beyond any doubt Festinger's theory of cognitive dissonance [p. 359].

Dissonance theory, as cognitive balance theory, is concerned with the motivational effects of the relationships between cognitive elements. The elements in dissonance theory refer to "beliefs" or "knowledge." These elements may be unrelated to one another, or be related in a consonant or dissonant manner. According to Festinger (1957a), two cognitions are postulated to be in a state of dissonance if "the obverse of one element would follow from the other" (p. 13). For example, the knowledge that one smokes and that smoking causes cancer are dissonant cognitions. Similarly, if one buys a car and then reads that the car is overpriced, the cognitions do not fit. If one believes smoking causes cancer or perceives a car is over-priced, then it follows that one does not smoke or buy that car. Festinger postulates that dissonance is a motivating state, producing behaviors that reduce the dissonance by altering the discrepant parts.

Zajonc (1968, pp. 360–61) outlines dissonance theory in nine concise propositions:

1. Cognitive dissonance is a noxious state.
2. In the case of cognitive dissonance the individual attempts to reduce or eliminate it and he acts so as to avoid events that will increase it.
3. In the case of consonance the individual acts so as to avoid dissonance-producing events.
4. The severity or the intensity of cognitive dissonance varies with (a) the importance of the cognitions involved and (b) the relative number of cognitions standing in dissonant relation to one another.
5. The strength of the tendencies enumerated in (2) and (3) is a direct function of the severity of dissonance.
6. Cognitive dissonance can be reduced or eliminated only by (a) adding new cognitions or (b) changing existing ones.
7. Adding new cognitions reduces dissonance if (a) the new cognitions add weight to one side and thus decrease the proportion of cognitive elements which are dissonant or (b) the new cognitions change the importance of the cognitive elements that are in dissonant relation with one another.
8. Changing existing cognitions reduces dissonance if (a) their new content makes them less contradictory with others, or (b) their importance is reduced.
9. If new cognitions cannot be added or the existing ones changed by means of a passive process, behaviors which have cognitive consequences favoring consonance will be recruited. Seeking new information is an example of such behavior.

RESEARCH IN COGNITIVE DISSONANCE

The relatively straightforward propositions listed above had led to a number of interesting observations of "real-life" behavior. For example,

Festinger (1957a) notes that one way of reducing the dissonance created by the smoking–smoking causes cancer linkage is to persuade oneself that the latter cognition is false. (Of course, another way to reduce this dissonance is to discontinue smoking, but that often cannot be accomplished.) In one government survey study, individuals classified according to the strength of their smoking habit were asked whether they thought that the alleged link between smoking and cancer had not been sufficiently proven. The respondents were categorized into four groups on the basis of their smoking habits: nonsmokers and light, medium, and heavy smokers. The percentage of respondents reporting that they do not think the evidence conclusive was 55 percent, 68 percent, 75 percent, and 86 percent, respectively. Apparently, when cognitions are not in harmony processes are instigated that help bring cognitive structures into consonance.

Attaining social support for one's beliefs is another method employed to reduce the dissonance between cognitions. In the book *When Prophecy Fails,* Festinger, Riecken, and Schachter (1956) report on the behavior of a group of cultists who predicted the world was about to come to an end. When their expectation was not confirmed, they dramatically increased their proselytizing behavior. In so doing they apparently could bolster their own belief system and reduce the dissonance created between their beliefs and the cognitions of the events in the real world. There is not a great deal of data supporting the idea of proselytizing after a belief has been invalidated. But McGuire (1966) notes, "This notion would explain some historical occurrences of more than a little importance that have puzzled many. It is an appealing proposition that deserves to be true" (p. 18).

Although some evidence gathered in field studies supports predictions from dissonance theory, by far the vast majority of the investigations conducted have been in laboratory settings, under controlled experimental conditions. A number of specific reference experiments have emerged, and the research clusters within a few experimental paradigms. As must be expected, in addition to a vast amount of new and reliable knowledge, research breeds controversy, and issues arise that are never quite resolved. Some of the laboratory reference experiments in dissonance research will now be outlined, but the controversies surrounding each area are generally neglected (see Abelson et al., 1968; Feldman, 1966; Zajonc, 1968).

Forced Compliance and Insufficient Justification

This research area pertains to public actions that are discrepant with the private opinion of the actor. Further, the actions are performed for relatively small rewards. It is hypothesized that in such situations forces are aroused that act upon the individual to justify the prior action.

This hypothesis was first tested in a classic (and controversial) study by Festinger and Carlsmith (1959). In their investigation, subjects participated in an extremely boring "psychological experiment." The subjects were then requested to tell future participants that the experiment was interesting and fun. For this task, half the subjects were offered $20, and the other half were offered $1. Afterwards, the experimenters asked the subjects to rate how interesting the experiment actually had been. The results indicate that the subjects in the one dollar condition rate the objectively boring experiment more interesting than subjects in the $20 condition. That is, the smaller reward produced greater liking of the experiment than the larger one. Festinger and Carlsmith (1959) argue that behavior contrary to one's beliefs is not dissonant when there is a strong external inducement (a large reward) to commit the action. However, if the reward is small, the discrepant behavior is seen as not sufficiently justified and dissonance is created. In the Festinger and Carlsmith experiment this dissonance apparently initiated processes that modified the cognitions (attitudes) concerning the intrinsic value of the experiment.

The insufficient justification paradigm was later extended to the study of punished actions. Aronson and Carlsmith (1963) reason that

if a person is induced to cease the performance of a desired act by the threat of punishment, his cognition that the act is desirable is dissonant with his cognition that he is not performing it. A threat of severe punishment, in and of itself, provides ample cognitions consonant with ceasing the action. If a person ceases to perform a desired action in the face of a mild threat, however, he lacks these consonant cognitions and, therefore, must seek additional justification for not performing the desired act. One method of justification is to convince himself that the desired act is no longer desirable. Thus, if a person is induced to cease performing a desired action by a threat of punishment, the milder the threat the greater will be his tendency to derogate the action [pp. 584–85].

To test this hypothesis, Aronson and Carlsmith (1963) prevented children from playing with attractive toys, using either a mild or severe threat. Both before the threat and after a period of not playing with the toys, attractiveness ratings were obtained. Table 5:1 indicates that the relative attractiveness of the toys is greater in the severe than the mild threat condition, supporting the Aronson and Carlsmith prediction.

The general advice offered by Festinger (1957a) for both rewarding and punishing situations is: "If one wanted to obtain private changes in addition to public compliance, the best way to do this would be to offer just enough reward or punishment to elicit overt compliance" (p. 95). The proposition contradicts the reinforcement approach to attitude change, which states that opinions vary monotonically as a function of their per-

TABLE 5:1
Change in Attractiveness of Forbidden Toy
(from Aronson & Carlsmith, 1963, p. 586)

Strength of Threat	Rating		
	Increase	Same	Decrease
Mild	4	10	8
Severe	14	8	0

ceived reward value, and inversely as a function of their perceived aversive consequences. Thus, a lively controversy has ensued between dissonance and reinforcement theorists. In addition, other interpretations of the data reviewed above have been put forth and the experiments have been criticised for methodological reasons. Some have asked, for example, if subjects in the Festinger and Carlsmith experiment really believe that they will be paid twenty dollars and, if so, does this produce other psychological consequences that account for their behavior? (See the references already cited for a detailed discussion of these issues).

Post-Decisional Dissonance

A potentially dissonant situation is created whenever an individual is in conflict and must make a choice between the available alternatives. The dissonance is produced following conflict resolution because some features of the selected alternative are negative, while some aspects of the unselected alternative are positive. It therefore follows that when the alternatives are equal in relative attractiveness, the dissonance created by the choice is maximal. More formally stated, Festinger (1964) postulates that the degree of aroused dissonance is in part a function of the degree of conflict in a choice situation.

Although dissonance is related to conflict, Festinger (1964) contends that conflict resolution (pre-decisional processes) and dissonance resolution (post-decisional processes) differ dramatically from one another.

When a person is faced with a decision between two alternatives, his behavior is largely oriented toward making an objective and impartial evaluation of the merits of the alternatives. This behavior probably takes the form of collecting information about the alternatives, evaluating this information in relation to himself, and establishing a preference order between the alternatives. . . .

When the required level of confidence is reached, the person makes a decision. Undoubtedly, the closer together in attractiveness the alternatives are, the more important the decision, and the more variable the information about the alternatives, the higher is the confidence that the person

will want before he makes his decision. It is probably this process of seeking and evaluating information that consumes time when a person must
make a decision. . . . Once the decision is made and the person is com-
mited to a given course of action, the psychological situation changes de-
cisively. There is less emphasis on objectivity and there is more partiality
and bias in the way in which the person views and evaluates the alternatives. . . . Certainly, objectivity remains, but something more is added—
namely, dissonance and the pressure to reduce the dissonance [pp.
152–55].

One method of reducing the choice-created dissonance is to reevaluate
the attractiveness of the alternatives after a decision is made. If the chosen
alternative is perceived as more attractive or the unselected alternative perceived as less attractive, then dissonance is reduced. In the first study examining post-decisional attitude change, Brehm (1956) had subjects rate
the attractiveness of various manufactured products. After the ratings the
subjects were told they would receive one of the products as a reward
for participation. They could select from either two equally attractive products (high dissonance condition), or one attractive and one unattractive
product (low dissonance). After the choice had been made, a second attractiveness rating was obtained. As predicted, the chosen alternative, relative to the unselected option, increased in attractiveness following the
choice. That is, the relative attractiveness of the products offered for
reward differed more following the choice than prior to it. Further, the
shift in attitudes was greater in the high than the low dissonance condition.
Subsequent research, however, has not been able to determine clearly
whether the post-decisional change is due to an increment in the attractiveness of the selected object, and/or a decrement in the perceived attractiveness of the unselected alternative.

Post-Decisional Dissonance and Achievement Theory.   Heckhausen
(1970) employed a variant of this procedure to test contrasting predictions
derived from dissonance and achievement theory. Individuals classified according to level of achievement needs failed at a task near intermediate
difficulty. Both prior to and following the failure the attractiveness of the
task, and an unattempted alternate task, were measured. According to
achievement theory, failure is expected to increase the attractiveness of
the performed task for subjects high in resultant achievement motivation
(labeled by Heckhausen "hope of success" subjects) but decrease the task
attractiveness for subjects labeled as high in fear of failure. In addition,
the task performed was either assigned to the subjects or selected by them.
It was anticipated that failure following a volitional choice is dissonance
producing, while failure in the no-choice condition does not arouse dissonance. (Brehm and Cohen, 1962, in a generally accepted modification

of dissonance theory, specify that volitional choice is a necessary condition for the arousal of dissonance.) According to dissonance theory, the relative attractiveness of the selected task should increase following failure in the free-choice but not the forced-choice condition.

Comparisons between the predictions of the two theories in the four experimental conditions (2 levels of achievement needs $\times$ 2 levels of dissonance) are shown in Figure 5:4. In three of the four conditions the models lead to different predictions. Further, among the fear-of-failure subjects in the free-choice condition, opposite predictions are derived from the two models. According to achievement theory, the task should be less attractive for these subjects after failure. Conversely, Heckhausen contends that dissonance theory predicts the task will be more attractive after failure given a volitional choice.

The results of this study did not definitely support either theory, but

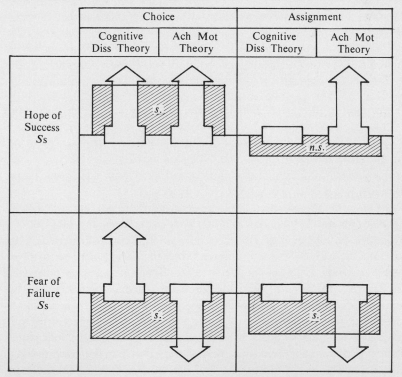

FIGURE 5:4.   Change in attractiveness of tasks after failure, shown for choice versus assignment conditions for subjects high and low on resultant achievement motivation. Arrows compare outcome predictions of cognitive dissonance and achievement motivation theories. Shading shows the obtained results (from Heckhausen, 1970, p. 195).

did favor achievement over dissonance. Dissonance theory best predicted the behavior of subjects high in resultant achievement motivation (see Fig. 5:4, top row). But in the condition where opposite predictions were made (fear-of-failure subjects given a free choice), achievement theory was upheld.

Selective Exposure.   One plausible method to facilitate the spreading of the attractiveness of the alternatives following a decision is to selectively expose oneself to positive or negative information about the alternatives. Reevaluation processes conceivably are aided by environmental information supporting the behavior taken. While there is some data that individuals do engage in such selective exposure (for example, new car owners read more ads about their purchased car), the evidence in this area is conflicting, and does not clearly confirm the expectations of dissonance theorists. Further, it is not clear that selective exposure facilitates dissonance reduction. For example, Brehm (1956) exposed some of his subjects to information consonant with their selection between the first and second attractiveness ratings. The exposed group displayed *less* dissonance reduction, as inferred from the spread in attractiveness ratings, than a control group not exposed to this information.

Pre- versus Post-Decisional Reevaluation.   One of the most controversial arguments related to the post-decisional dissonance investigations is whether the obtained results are due to processes operative before rather than after the decision is reached. When a conflict exists, the individual may attempt to differentiate the choices before a final selection. Thus, reevaluation may occur prior to the actual decision.

In one experiment attempting to separate the pre- versus post-evaluation issue, Jecker (1964) independently manipulated the amount of pre-decisional conflict and the amount of post-decisional dissonance. Subjects first rated the attractiveness of musical records. They were then informed that for participating they would receive either one or two records. The number of records was to be determined by drawing lots, although in one group the probability of receiving two records was very high (.95), while in a second group the probability was presented as very low (.05). Prior to this drawing, the subjects were shown two records they had rated as equally attractive, and were asked to select the one they wanted in the event that they "lost" in the drawing. It was assumed that during this choice the subjects in the .95 group experience little conflict, since both records are anticipated, while those in the .05 group are in high conflict, for only one of the records is expected. Dissonance was manipulated by giving some subjects both records (low dissonance) and others only one

TABLE 5:2
Mean Change in Attractiveness Ratings Favoring the
Chosen Alternative (Increase for Chosen plus
Decrease for Rejected Alternative)
(from Festinger, 1964, p. 26)

	High Conflict	*Low Conflict*
Dissonance	+1.0	+0.6
No Dissonance	+0.2	+0.3

record (high dissonance). Then new ratings of the attractiveness of the records were obtained from the subjects.

The results of this study are shown in Table 5:2. A positive rating indicates that there is a spread in the attractiveness of the alternatives between the pre- and post-decision ratings. The data indicate that this spread is displayed in all four experimental conditions. However, the divergence is greater in the dissonance than the no-dissonance condition. Further, the attitude shift is exhibited in both the conflict and the low conflict dissonance conditions. Conflict without dissonance does not produce significant reevaluation, but dissonance with low conflict does. Jecker thus concludes that dissonance reduction is a post-decision phenomenon. [Although Festinger (1964) believes that "we may thus regard this theoretical question as settled" (p. 30), there is still much controversy about this issue; see reviews already cited.]

Motivational Research

The theory of cognitive dissonance has given rise to a great deal of research concerned with traditional motivational questions. Dissonance is treated as a drive, with the same conceptual status as hunger, thirst, and other physiological states of deprivation. Like other drives, it is postulated to energize and direct behavior, and its offset is reinforcing. Festinger (1957) states: "successful reduction of dissonance is rewarding in the same sense that eating is rewarding" (p. 70). Further, like other deprivation states, dissonance is aversive, and the theoretical optimal state is one of zero dissonance.

Hunger-Thirst.   Investigations demonstrating the motivational consequences of dissonance employ some variation of the public compliance-insufficient justification paradigm first introduced by Festinger and Carlsmith (1959). Brehm (1962), perhaps most responsible for the work in this area, reports a series of studies in which feelings of hunger and

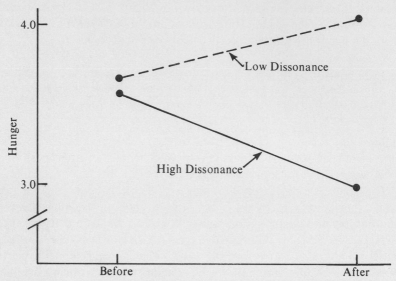

FIGURE 5:5.   Mean self-ratings of hunger for selected subjects, before
and after the dissonance manipulation (from Brehm, 1962, p. 62).

thirst, as well as actual water consumption, are assessed following an insufficient justification procedure. In the first of these investigations, Brehm,
under the guise of examining the effects of deprivation on intellectual and
motor functioning, asked subjects to refrain from eating breakfast and
lunch. Prior to the task performance subjects rated their degree of hunger.
After completion of the required tasks the subjects were asked to undergo
continued deprivation and return later for additional testing. In the low
dissonance condition five dollars was offered as a reward for further participation, while in the high dissonance condition no additional incentive
was offered. Thus, conditions of sufficient and insufficient justification were
established. After a volitional commitment to continue deprivation, hunger
ratings again were obtained. Figure 5:5 shows the results for subjects equal
in their initial hunger ratings. The figure indicates that low dissonance subjects perceive themselves as hungrier after the commitment, while high
dissonance subjects report feeling less hungry. Presumably in the high dissonance condition continued deprivation is justified by altering the cognition related to the perceived discomfort of hunger.

In a subsequent replication and extension of this study, subjects were
deprived of water rather than food (too many of the prior subjects were
happy to have the opportunity to diet for a day.) In addition, after the
second thirst rating the subjects were allowed to drink some water before
leaving the experimental room to undergo continued water deprivation.

The amount of water consumed is shown in Figure 5:6. As predicted, less water is drunk in the insufficient justification (high dissonance) condition.

In the light of these findings, Brehm (1962) concludes:

It is only what the organism "knows" about its motivational state that affects learning, performance, perception, and so on. Noncognitive components of motivation, such as the physiological state of the organism, could then affect behaviors like learning only to the extent that they affected the cognitive components. That is, a state of deprivation, short of killing the organism, would have to have cognitive representation in order to have any kind of psychological effect at all.

Another way of proposing the same view is to say that a theory of cognition about motivation may prove to be adequate for our understanding of the role of motivation in psychological phenomena. A cognitive approach may be able to handle determinants such as deprivation as well as the additional, cognitive, determinants that we have been discussing [p. 75].

This position is very similar to one expressed later by Valins (1966). That is, veridical or nonveridical perceptions about internal states are equally

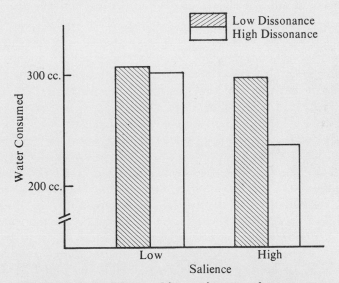

FIGURE 5:6. Mean cubic centimeters of water consumed as a function of dissonance and salience of the thirst manipulation. In the high salience condition water was in the stimulus field during the experimental manipulation, while in the low salience condition, environmental cues pertinent to the deprivation state were not visible (from Brehm, 1962, p. 73).

effective in controlling behavior. Only beliefs count; actual deprivation or physiological conditions control behavior only through their effects on higher mental processes.

Fear.   Experimental paradigms similar to those reported by Brehm also have demonstrated the cognitive control of pain. In one illustrative study (Grinker, 1967; reported in Zimbardo, 1969) subjects were given 20 trials of classical aversive eyelid conditioning. Recall that in this procedure a conditional stimulus, such as a tone, is paired with an aversive puff of air to the eye, and subsequent responses to the stimulus are measured. Following the 20 trials the subjects were told that on future trials the air puff would be more intense. Earlier studies had demonstrated that this stress warning increases classical aversive conditioning.

To create high and low dissonance conditions, different degrees of verbal justification were given for participating in the experiment, although all subjects voluntarily participated. A control group was given neither choice nor justification.

Figure 5:7 shows that in this investigation the change in response strength from the pre- to the post-dissonance trials is a direct function of the degree of aroused dissonance. It appears that dissonance suppresses

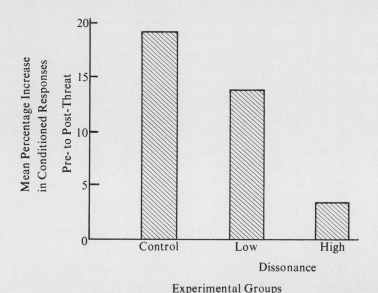

FIGURE 5:7.   Mean percentage increase of conditioned responses from trials 11–20 to trials 21–30 (pre- and post- threat) for control and dissonance groups (from Grinker, 1967; reported in Zimbardo, 1969, p. 130).

the fear response and conditioning by inducing subjects to *think* that the puff is not very intense.

Dissonance and Nondirective Drive.   One further study (Cottrell and Wack, 1967) reveals that some experimental manipulations employed by dissonance theorists are very similar to paradigms used by drive theorists espousing the Hull-Spence motivational position. In this study, subjects were exposed to unfamiliar foreign words for 1, 2, 5, 10, or 25 trials. The differential exposure established different degrees of verbal habits. During the subsequent test trials subjects were required to identify which of these words was presented tachistiscopically. On the critical trials none of the prior stimuli were flashed; verbal responses on these "pseudo-recognition" trials were the critical dependent variable.

High dissonance was created again by using an insufficient justification procedure. Some subjects were given the false information that they could not receive credit for participation, while others were not. As in prior experiments, subjects were not required to participate, although pressures to do so were brought to bear by the experimenter.

The verbal responses on the pseudoconditioning trials for the high and low dissonance groups are shown in Figure 5:8. The figure indicates that in the high dissonance condition the emission of the prepotent habit—the habit highest in the response hierarchy—is enhanced. That is, there is a significant interaction between habit strength and "drive" level. Cottrell and Wack (1967) contend that "the results of the present study support the view that cognitive dissonance has nonspecific energizing effects" (p. 137). The energized responses were not instrumental to dissonance reduction, as were the responses in the Brehm and Grinker studies. Thus, dissonance is given the conceptual status of the Hullian D.

Interpretation of Motivational Research.   Why do subjects feel less hungry in the high dissonance condition in the experiments by Brehm, or act as if they are less fearful in the insufficient justification condition employed by Grinker? Conceptually, dissonance is a drive, with energizing and directional properties. Further, the study of Cottrell and Wack suggests that dissonance is a nondirective drive that activates all habit tendencies. Thus, cognitive dissonance is closely linked with the Hull-Spence conceptual analysis of behavior.

This association with Hullian theory is paradoxical, for the experimental results cited above demonstrate the cognitive control of motivation, and are antithetical to the Hullian mechanistic conception of behavior. The data of experimenters such as Brehm even cast doubt upon the operations for producing drive states; hours of deprivation or the intensity of an aver-

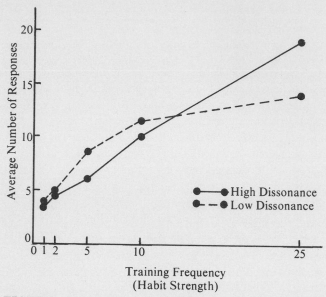

FIGURE 5:8.   Number of responses of different training frequency classes (habit strength) emitted on the pseudo-recognition trials for subjects differing in aroused dissonance (drive level) (from Cottrell and Wack, 1967, p. 135).

sive air puff may or may not be motivating, depending on the associated cognitions.

Further, if dissonance is a nondirective drive, as Cottrell and Wack suggest, then why do subjects in the dissonance conditions in the Brehm and Grinker experiments exhibit *decreases* in their consumption of water and in their probability of responding with a conditioned eye-blink? If dissonance were a nondirective drive, then increases in the magnitudes of these prepotent responses should be exhibited.

Of course, it is possible to conceive of dissonance as a specific drive. But this raises additional questions (How many specific drives can be postulated? How are such specific drives inferred? to name but a few). Perhaps it can be argued that a modification of the Hullian model could be maintained despite the difficulties indicated above, for if dissonance is a drive state, then it also has cue properties that direct behavior. Inasmuch as dissonance is established by cognitions, it seems particularly reasonable to assume that the cues associated with dissonant states direct the organism.

If one focuses upon the steering or cue functions of dissonant cognitions, rather than their supposed energizing properties, a number of explanations for the Brehm and Grinker experiments are plausible. It could be contended that dissonant states can control motivation and bind drive expression, either through reappraisal, raising thresholds, rechanneling drives, or other methods. Clearly this explanation is similar to conceptions by Lazarus and Rapaport reviewed previously. A binding or reappraisal conception would indicate that there is a hierarchical control order reminiscent of the id-ego relation in the Freudian system, and that the stimuli arising from visceral states interact with higher central processes in controlling behavior.

An alternate, albeit similar, explanation is that the organism utilizes many sources of information to infer its level of deprivation. Usually the most salient and accurate stimuli are those arising from the viscera. However, these can be contradicted by other information (cognitions) emanating from higher centers. The "higher" information is weighted more heavily in such conflict situations. This suggestion is similar to the positions held by Brehm and Valins. The drive suppression versus information explanations suggested here have common features. However, the information approach perhaps has greater generality because it can be applied to situations in which drive stimuli are not a source of information.

It appears to this writer that a cognitive approach to motivation adopted a Hullian type framework, and this framework does not fit. The unfortunate drive position of dissonance theorists implies that dissonance theory is subject to all the questions and criticisms invoked about drive theory (Are all states of disequilibria unpleasant? Are drives nondirective? Is drive reduction necessary for learning? Under what conditions do drives enhance response strength?). Most contemporary spokesman in this area do not want to conceptualize dissonance as a general drive (see Abelson et al., pp. 301–46). Thus, dissonance theory will have to develop its own motivational scheme, perhaps independent of notions of drive, and certainly separate from a Drive $\times$ Habit theory, to resolve the difficulties mentioned above. It is fitting that a theory of cognitive elements be embraced within a cognitive conception of behavior.

Resistance to Extinction

One further area of dissonance research deserving mention concerns resistance to extinction. This work has important implications within general experimental psychology, and is pertinent to the attributional model presented later in this chapter.

The insufficient justification paradigm used by Festinger and Carlsmith and others is created by having the extrinsic rewards for "forced" behavior not congruent with the significance of the action. This analysis has been extended to situations in which the subject performs instrumental responses that are somewhat aversive, and the intrinsic value of the reward is not sufficient given the "output" of the subjects. It is postulated that in such situations dissonance is aroused and can be reduced if the reward or incentive value of the goal is perceived as greater than it really "is." In the first demonstration of this principle, Aronson and Mills (1959) had females volunteer to join a group discussion concerning sex. Half of the volunteers first participated in a lengthy and embarrassing "initiation" that included the repeating of "dirty" words (high dissonance). A second group was given an easy initiation procedure (low dissonance). The girls then listened to a rather boring group discussion about sex. Aronson and Mills (1959) found that the subjects in the high dissonance condition rated the discussion more interesting, liked the participating girls more, and so forth, than did subjects in the low dissonance condition. In sum, the cognition "I have experienced pain to attain an unattractive object" is dissonant; dissonance is reduced by perceiving the attained object as attractive.

Lawrence and Festinger (1962) applied this analysis to experimental procedures employed primarily in infrahuman research that apparently arouse dissonance. Included among these dissonance-creating procedures are partial reinforcement, delay of reward, and requiring effortful responses to obtain a reward. These are situations that animals (and humans) would avoid, if possible. Thus, responses under these conditions are dissonance arousing relative to conditions in which there is 100 percent reward, no delay of reinforcement, and so on. Again, the dissonance may be reduced by perceiving "extra" rewards in the goal situation and experiencing a resulting increase in the attractiveness of the goal object.

A number of interesting empirical findings have been generated by this analysis. Lawrence and Festinger (1962) contend that dissonance is experienced on every trial in which an organism is not rewarded after an instrumental response. Thus, they predict that resistance to extinction will be a function of the number of unrewarded trials. The generally accepted position in psychology is that extinction is related to the percentage of reinforcement; number of unrewarded trials versus percentage had not been clearly differentiated in prior research. Experiments by Lawrence and Festinger (1962) in which the number and percentage of reinforced trials are independently manipulated support the dissonance position (see Figure 5:9). Figure 5:9 indicates that resistance to extinction in rats in a straight runway is directly related to the number of unrewarded trials, but independent of the percentage of reinforcement.

Resistance to extinction also has been demonstrated by Lawrence and Festinger (as well as other investigators) to be related directly to the effortfulness of an instrumental response. In one confirming experiment,

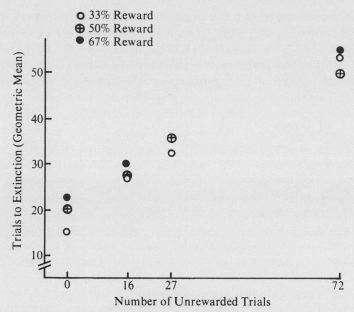

FIGURE 5:9. Resistance to extinction as a function of the number of unrewarded trials, within conditions differing in the percentage of reinforced trials (from Lawrence & Festinger, 1962, p. 91).

rats were required to traverse up inclines differing in steepness to receive a food reward. The group expending the greater effort took longer to extinguish, and ran faster during the extinction period, than the group expending less effort during the learning period (see Table 5:3). Subsequent experiments conducted by Lawrence and Festinger demonstrate that effort results in greater resistance to extinction regardless of the reward schedule, and that with minimal effort the absence of reward still increases resistance

TABLE 5:3
Average Running Time on Extinction (in Seconds) for
Different Effort Conditions (from Lawrence &
Festinger, 1962, p. 143)

	Effort Condition	
	25° Incline (N = 31)	50° Incline (N = 31)
Last day of acquisition	1.8	2.0
First day of extinction	7.1	3.8
Second day of extinction	26.1	16.4
Third day of extinction	37.2	31.0

to extinction. Lawrence and Festinger also manipulated effort and the number of nonreinforced trials independently within the same experiment, and found that they summate to produce increased responding when the reward is withheld. In sum, the "extra" rewards produced by dissonance-creating conditions increase the resistance to extinction.

General Summary

The diversity of the dissonance research and the ingenuity of the experimental techniques indicate the great heuristic value of dissonance theory. Dissonance is a determinant of motivational states rather than a formal theory of motivation. It has not illuminated the functioning of cognitive processes nor has it provided a clear or new theoretical framework for motivation. But it has led to experimental results that are an impressive contribution to the cognition-motivation area.

ATTRIBUTION THEORY

Attribution theory, another cognitive approach to the understanding of behavior, was not formulated as a theory of individual motivation. It is, in part, a theory of how people perceive motivation—"how a typical observer infers a person's motivations from his action" (Kelley, 1967, p. 193). Attribution theory concepts therefore are most relevant to the relationship between person perception and interpersonal behavior, and usage is generally (although not exclusively) confined within social psychology. However, attributional concepts can be employed in the study of self-perception and in the formulation of a theory of individual motivation (see Heider, 1958, p. 79). The role of causal ascription in intrapersonal motivational processes is the main concern of this chapter.

What, then, is attribution theory? "Attribution theory concerns the processes by which an individual interprets events as being caused by a particular part of a relatively stable environment" (Kelley, 1967, p. 193). Thus, attribution theorists deal with "why" questions, or the relationship between phenomena (effects) and the reasons (responsible agents) for those events. The perception of causality is an ascription imposed by the perceiver; causes per se are not directly observable. You can only infer, for example, that an individual stepped on your toe because "he is aggressive" or because "it was an accident." Hume (1739) argues that causality is not an inherent property of sensory events. To use Hume's example, one can see that upon impact of Ball A, Ball B moves. One might then conclude that A caused B to change location; that is, one can attribute the moving of B to the impact of A. But one does not "observe" causes.

Hume (and later Kant, 1781) contends that they are constructed by the perceiver and they render the environment more meaningful.

The prevalence of causal constructions is dramatically illustrated in experiments reported by Heider and Simmel (1944) and Michotte (1946). In the Michotte experiments, a red and a black disc (*A* and *B*) are presented as moving on a screen. Object *A* approaches and "bumps" *B*. If *B* immediately moves, individuals have the "causal impression" that the withdrawal is due to *A*. Michotte labels this the "Launching Effect." Perception of the Launching Effect is extremely influenced by the interval between the arrival of *A* and the departure of *B*. Figure 5:10 shows that if the interval between *A*'s arrival and *B*'s departure is longer than 125 milliseconds, then an "immediate launch" interpretation is not given by the subjects. "Delayed launching" is the most probable interpretation if the delay interval approximates 100 milliseconds. If the delay time is longer than 200 milliseconds, then subjects in this setting do not perceive that *A* caused *B* to move. Michotte also notes that if *B* moves in the direction of *A* after impact, then it is believed to be "carried along" or "joined" with *A*. He labels this the "Entraining Effect."

The Heider and Simmel (1944) experimental paradigm is similar to that used by Michotte, although they employ three moving figures rather than two. The figures are a large triangle, a small triangle, and a circle.

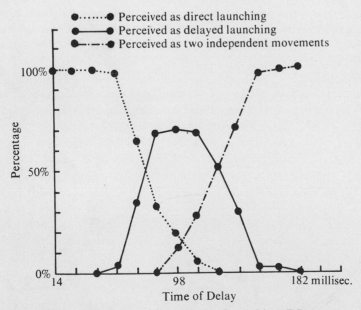

FIGURE 5:10. Perception of the Launching Effect as a function of the interval between the bumping by *A* and *B*'s departure (from Michotte, 1946, p. 94).

Thus, the stimulus configuration is more complex than that employed by Michotte, and interpersonal dramas apparently unfold from the movements. For example, impacts are often interpreted as fights; joint movements generate themes of "belonging," and so forth. Heider and Simmel note the "great importance which causal interpretation plays in the organization of events" (p. 251). This organization is largely determined by motives that are attributed to the figures. Self-induced actions lead to different interpretations than behaviors perceived as induced by others.

The experiments of Heider and Simmel (1944) and Michotte (1946) blur the distinction between physical and person perception. Objects are perceived as "people" with motives, emotions, and so forth. Well before these experiments, Hume had reasoned that all perceptions of causation are constructs; he did not differentiate between a causal analysis of physical and psychological events.

General Theoretical Orientation of Attribution Theory

The basic assumption of attribution theorists is that man is motivated "to attain a cognitive mastery of the causal structure of his environment" (Kelley, 1967, p. 193). He wants to know why an event has occurred—to what source, motive, or state it may be ascribed. Heider (1958) explains:

The causal structure of the environment, both as the scientist describes it and as the naive person apprehends it, is such that we are usually in contact only with what may be called the offshoots or manifestations of underlying core-processes or core-structures. For example, if I find sand on my desk, I shall want to find out the underlying reason for this circumstance. I make this inquiry not because of idle curiosity, but because only if I refer this relatively insignificant offshoot event to an underlying core event will I attain a stable environment and have the possibility of controlling it. Should I find that the sand comes from a crack in the ceiling and that this crack appeared because of the weakness in one of the walls, then I have reached the layer of underlying conditions which is of vital importance for me. The sand on my desk is merely a symptom, a manifestation that remains ambiguous until it becomes anchored to dispositional properties—cracks and stresses in this case. . . . The search for relatively enduring aspects of our world, the dispositional properties in nature, may carry us quite far from the immediate facts or they may end hardly a step from them. That is, there exists a hierarchy of cognitive awarenesses which begin with the more stimulus-bound recognition of "facts," and gradually go deeper into the underlying causes of these facts. . . . Man is usually not content simply to register the observables that surround him; he needs to refer them as far as possible to the invariances of his environment. . . . The underlying causes of events, especially the motives of other persons, are the invariances of the environment that are relevant to him; they give meaning to what he experiences and it is these meanings that are recorded in his life space, and are precipitated as the reality of the environment to which he then reacts [pp. 80–81].

The assumption of man as an information seeking or "knowing" organism is not unique to Heider. Festinger's (1954) theory of social comparison, for example, includes the fundamental proposition that

there exists, in the human organism, a drive to evaluate his opinions and his abilities. . . . A person's cognition (his opinions and beliefs) about the situation in which he exists and his appraisals of what he is capable of doing (his evaluation of his abilities) will together have bearing on his behavior. The holding of incorrect opinions and/or inaccurate appraisals of one's abilities can be punishing and even fatal in many situations [p. 117].

It is evident from the Heider and Festinger quotations that we are now considering the "rational man." This does not imply that attributional errors are not made, nor that ego-enhancing and ego-defensive processes are not operative which render judgments fallible. Despite the existence of some "motivated" errors in judgment and decision, it is postulated that man wants veridically to comprehend his environment (see Kelley, 1971). Attribution theory thus completes the rationalism-mechanism-rationalism cycle in psychological explanation. Pre-Darwinian thought often appealed to the rationalism of man. Then the Darwinian revolution and the advent of behaviorism gave rise to influential mechanistic conceptions of human behavior. Mechanism now is giving way to rationalism—but to an experimental study of the relationship between mental events and overt action. Darwin noted that in the evolution of man an inhibitory mechanism must have been operative preventing his return to the water. Perhaps psychologists were inflicted with a similar mechanism that prevented a return to the study of consciousness, the mind and its processes. But now this stage also has passed.

Fritz Heider

Fritz Heider is generally acknowledged to be the founder of attribution theory. He considers his work an "investigation of common-sense psychology" (1958, p. 79) inasmuch as he is concerned with how the "common man" thinks about causality. The language he employs and many of the basic concepts in attribution theory are taken from common vernacular. Words such as give, take, receive, keep, ought, and may are the foundation of Heider's conceptual analysis. Heider states his goal is "to clarify some of the basic concepts that are most frequently encountered in an analysis of naive descriptions of behavior" (p. 14).

The general theoretical framework employed by Heider is strongly influenced by Gestalt psychology and Kurt Lewin. Heider (1958) contends that

we could go about this [building a conceptual framework suitable to some of the problems in the field of interpersonal relations] in the Baconian way, that is, by seeking further empirical and experimental facts. We side, however, with those who think that we shall not attain a conceptual framework by collecting more experimental results. Rather, conceptual clarification is a prerequisite for efficient experimentation. . . . Systematization is an important feature of any science and reveals relationships among highly diverse events. Lewin's field-theoretical approach known as topology (Lewin, 1936, 1938) has been in the background of much of the thinking in the present theory of interpersonal relations. Though not many of the specific concepts of topology have been taken over, they have helped in the construction of new ones with which we have tried to represent some of the basic facts of human relations [p. 4].

The Conceptual Analysis of Action. The most fundamental distinction made by Heider (1958, p. 82) is stated as follows:

In common-sense psychology (as in scientific psychology) the result of an action is felt to depend on two sets of conditions, namely factors within the person and factors within the environment. . . . One may speak of the effective force (*ff*) of the person or of the environment when one means the totality of forces emanating from one or the other source.

The action outcome, *x*, may then be said to be dependent upon a combination of effective personal force and effective environmental force, thus: $x = f$ (*ff* person, *ff* environment).

The Heiderian equation of the perceived determinants of action is manifestly similar to the Lewinian statement that behavior is a function of the person and the environment: $B = f(P, E)$. However, Heider is referring to the perceived causes of behavior, and not to the determinants of force actually acting upon the person or influencing an outcome (although he frequently slips into the "motivation" rather than "perceived motivation" usage). The science of motivation and the ethnoscience of motivation may yield quite diverse laws. That is, the "true" laws of behavior, and what are perceived as the causes of action, may not be isomorphic, although they should be interrelated.

A simple example taken from Heider clarifies the person versus environment differentiation. Assume that one is rowing across the lake on a windy day. The final outcome (reaching the other side) is perceived as due to factors within the person (ability, effort, fatigue) and factors in the environment (wind, waves). Whether the opposite shore is reached depends on a combination of these two sources of causation. In a similar manner, success at a test could be perceived as due to personal factors (ability, amount of time spent studying) or factors in the environment (an easy test, grading policy). Heider believes that the internal and external forces combine additively to determine behavior. In the rowing example, either the wind or personal factors such as ability may be sufficient to produce the desired consequence. If the effective environmental forces are zero, then the outcome is dependent only upon personal causal factors. Conversely, "without personal intervention . . . the wind (could) carry the boat to the shore" (Heider, 1958, p. 82).[3]

The distinction between personal versus environmental causes of behavior is implicit in all the theories discussed in this book, although again in the prior theoretical conceptions the actual, not the perceived, determinants of behavior are under consideration. Hull, for example, postulates that behavior is in part determined by independent drive (person) and incentive (environment) factors. Thus, instrumental action to attain food might be undertaken because the organism is very hungry (push), or because the goal object is especially attractive (pull). Lewin also specifies that the valence of the goal is a function of needs of the person and properties of the goal object. The physical properties of the goal conceptually are represented as part of the foreign hull; that is, they are physical factors in the real world that have behavioral effects. And according to Atkinson's theory of achievement motivation, individuals differing in resultant achievement motivation (personal factor) differentially work to achieve success at easy versus intermediately difficult tasks (environmental factor). In sum, both the person and the environmental contributions influence action. But Heider, as opposed to Hull, Lewin, and Atkinson, stresses *the consequences of differential ascriptions* to internal versus external factors.

Consequences of Internal versus External Attributions. One quality that differentiates external from internal determinants of behavior is that only sources of action attributed to the person (internal) can be labeled "intentional." This has important implications in the field of interpersonal relations. More important in the present context, differential allocation of causality between the two factors also results in disparate affective experiences, future expectations, and behaviors. For example, if the rower in the example perceived that reaching the other side was due to the aid of the wind, he might only row on windy days, or not attempt to cross the lake again. In a similar manner, if success at a test is perceived as due to personal factors, such as ability, then the person might, for example, expect to do well in other classes, feel more pride, enroll in more difficult courses, raise his occupational aspiration, or study less hard.

[3] Note the slippage in this example between actual and perceived causation.

The behavioral consequences of person versus environment attribution is discussed at length by Heider (1958):

Our judgment of a situation and its possible future development may depend greatly on whether we attribute the psychological phenomenon to the subject or to the object. If a person enjoys an object it may be because the object is very enjoyable or it may be because of very personal reasons located in him.

If the former, any person who has commerce with the object will find it satisfying. This is a judgment about the value of an object and refers to a more invariant disposition of the object. Once this judgment is made, a host of expectations that guide our actions are possible. If I want to make a person happy, I will present him with the object, for instance. If I want to annoy him, I may prevent him from obtaining it. Believing that the object is desirable, I may attempt to make someone envious by flaunting it. I may welcome identification as its creator in order to be admired or liked. I myself will attempt to interact with the object again, the interaction taking various forms depending on further conditions. I may try to have physical contact with the object or I may talk about it or think about it. It will be recorded in my belief-value matrix as something I like. These are some of the implications of the attribution of enjoyment to the object, implications that encompass an ever-widening field as one investigates the network of conditions and effects. In all of them, the enjoyability of the object remains constant, and the varied possible effects of this object-disposition form the expectations of many kinds of behavior.

If p believes that the source of enjoyment is located in o [another person] and not in the object, however, very different expectations arise. They depend upon the presumed facts about o implied by the enjoyment. . . .

Attribution to the person could . . . mean that o is easily satisfied, that he is a peculiar person, that he has sophisticated taste, that he is like me, etc. These "facts" implied by the enjoyment of o are personality traits, the dispositional properties upon which expectations are based. Thus, if I attribute o's enjoyment to his sophistication, then I may expect him to enjoy a different but equally artistic object, to dislike something that is trite, to enjoy the company of a connoisseur, etc. In each of these expectations, it is the object or situation that varies, but the dispositional property of the person remains the same. . . .

If we correctly analyze the raw data . . . we know much more about the event itself and about future occurrences. A highly general statement that can be made is: If we know that our present enjoyment is . . . attributed to our own personality, then at most we can expect only persons who have a similar personality to enjoy it. . . .

Without such attribution, enjoyment remains an ambiguous local experience. The enjoyment of a satiated person eating something very appetizing and the enjoyment of a hungry person eating something less appetizing may represent the same degree of biological elation or tension [an identical phenotype], but the equivalence of the two experiences ends as soon as identification with one or the other of the two poles is made [different genotypes]. Thus, an event that remains undefined as to its dispositional character tells us very little. One whose dispositional character is further defined by attribution to causal factors tells us much.

. . . if a person has adequately analyzed past enjoyment into the subjective and objective poles, the fact that he has profited from this learning is demonstrated in his use of the experience for producing future enjoyment. Let us assume that once, in a very hungry state, he enjoyed a particular food very much, but erroneously attributed the enjoyment to the food. Later, wanting to pamper himself again, he eats the same food, but is disappointed in the gustatory results, not realizing that the experience had originally depended largely on his own appetite. In order to profit from experience, one has to analyze the event correctly into the underlying invariables, otherwise no adaptation to the environment is possible—unless, as Brunswik [1956] puts it, the mediation is channelized. Then a number of conditions are constant and the true source is correlated on a one-to-one basis with the experience.

It is our opinion . . . from the point of view of the psychological meaning of action (motion) it may make all the difference whether *A* moves and *B* is still or vice versa, whether Mohammed goes to the mountain or the mountain moves to him [pp. 147–51].

Summary.   Heider has formulated a cognitive model of behavior in which the stimulus is the perceived outcome of an event, the intervening cognitions a particular causal schema, and the consequences a wide array of expectancies, affects, and behaviors that are influenced by the causal cognitions. The model clearly is subsumed within the general framework outlined in Diagram 5:1. In contrast to the cognitive models discussed thus far, the intervening cognitions do not bind or regulate drive expression. They are a form of appraisal—an appraisal of causality, rather than of "threat." As in the prior cognitive models, these cognitions are functional, and aid the organism in adapting to his environment.

INTERNAL AND EXTERNAL ATTRIBUTIONS

Inasmuch as attributions to subject versus object poles are of such importance, it is essential to determine the conditions under which ascriptions are made to one or the other of these two factors. Heider (1958), guided by Mill's method of inquiry, contends that attributions are reached according to the rule "that condition will be held responsible for an effect which is present when the effect is present and which is absent when the effect is absent" (p. 152). Thus,

if I always experience enjoyment when I interact with an object, and something other than enjoyment when the object is removed (longing, annoyance, or a more neutral reaction, for instance) then I will consider the object the cause of the enjoyment. The effect, enjoyment, is seen to vary in a highly coordinated way with the presence and absence of the object. . . .

If I sometimes enjoy the object and sometimes do not, then the effect varies, not with the object, but with something within me. I may or may not be able to define that something, but I know that the effect has to do with some fluctuating personal state. It may be my mood, my state of hunger, etc., which though temporary in character, are often detectable as the conditions highly related to the effect. Notice that in this type of attribution, a temporary state and therefore a more or less nondispositional property of the person is singled out as the source of the pleasure. . . .

When enjoyment is attributed to a dispositional property of the person, additional data pertaining to the reactions of other people are necessary. Concretely, if I observe that not all people enjoy the object, then I may attribute the effect to individual differences. . . . That is to say, the effect, enjoyment in this case, depends upon who the person is. With o enjoyment is present, with q it is absent. We sometimes, then, speak about differences in taste. The important point is that the presence and absence of the enjoyment is not correlated with the presence and absence of the object, but rather with the presence and absence of different people. Therefore o is felt to enjoy x and q to be dissatisfied with x because of the kind of person each is [pp. 152–53].

Heider also warns against the tendency to attribute action to one or the other of the dichotomous causal factors.

Kurt Lewin has proposed the general formulation that behavior is a function of the person and the environment. This may appear to be a truism, yet it must be held to the fore as a constant reminder lest the tendency to unipolar attribution lead to the neglect of one or the other factors. How often do we feel that we have only to describe the person or the object to explain the enjoyment or other behavior in question [p. 154].

Kelley (1967) has systematized the factors that result in causal attribution to person versus environmental factors. Assume, he writes, that an individual enjoys a movie. The question then raised is whether the enjoyment, or "raw data," is attributed to the person (for example, he is easily pleased), or to the perceived properties of the entity (it is a good movie). Kelley (1967) reasons that the responsible factor may be determined by examining the covariation of the effect and causal factors over "(a) entities (movies), (b) persons (other viewers of the movie), (c) time (the same person on repeated exposures), and (d) modalities of interaction with the entity (different ways of viewing the movie)" (p. 194). Attribution of the enjoyment to the entity (movie) rather than to the person or self is most likely if the individual responds differentially to movies, if the response to this movie is consistent over time and modalities, and if the response agrees with the social consensus of others. Thus, the probability of attribution to the movie is maximized when the individual enjoys only that movie, when he enjoys it on repeated occasions and over different modalities (on TV, at the theater), when all others also like the movie. "In sum, we might say that the subjective criteria for the possession of valid knowledge about the external world are distinctiveness of the response coupled with consistency and consensus" (Kelley, 1967, p. 196).[4] On the other hand, if the individual likes all movies, that is, his response to the entity is not distinctive, if his enjoyment of this movie varies, and if no one else likes this particular picture, then we will ascribe the enjoyment to temporary or stable attributes of the viewer.

Kelley likens the ascription of causality to the analysis of variance procedure employed by scientists. When attempting to attain a valid picture of the world, the distinctiveness of the response represents the numerator in a typical F-ratio, and consistency over time, modality, and persons represent the denominator or error term. A person is surest of his understanding of the world when the response is distinctive (high numerator, or between-entity variance), and when there is greatest consistency (agreement) over the other three variables (low denominator, or little within-entity error variance). Kelley (1967) suggests that the factors of differentiation and stability can be used to index a persons' "state of information regarding the world" (p. 198). If the distinctiveness/stability ratio is low, Kelley reasons that the person will have "informational dependence" and will seek information from others, especially if he believes these others can raise his information level. Kelley employs this line of reasoning to illuminate social psychological processes of communication, persuasion, the Asch conformity effect, and so forth.

Attribution and Emotional Expression

The experimental investigation of emotional reactions conducted by Schachter and Singer (1962) generated a number of studies bearing upon the relation of attribution to emotional expression. Recall that in the Schachter and Singer investigation experimental subjects are injected with epinephrine, an activating agent. Some of these subjects are correctly informed about the symptoms produced by this drug, while others are either uninformed or misinformed. In subsequent testing, aroused subjects in the latter two groups act more euphoric or angry in appropriate stimulus situa-

---

[4] It seems reasonable to attribute enjoyment to the movie even if the person likes it less on subsequent viewing. Heider (1958) indicates that "Static structures are not the only ones that can serve as reference points for understanding. Processes may also provide a basis for understanding as long as they show relatively constant coordination to changes in underlying structure or to other processes" (p. 80). Thus, if satiation accompanies repeated exposure, the original enjoyment is still likely to be ascribed to the movie, and subsequent nonenjoyment to the satiation process.

tions than subjects who can attribute their arousal symptoms to the epinephrine. That is, misattribution of the arousal symptoms to the external stimulus situations produces behavior disparate from that observed when the arousal is drug attributed. Subsequent studies by Valins demonstrated that arousal per se does not affect emotional responses; rather, it is the cognition of arousal that influences affective expression. It further appears that cognitions of arousal convey not only information about the organism's internal state, but also information concerning the source of the arousal. As Schachter and Singer demonstrated, when causal information is lacking the individual finds an appropriate "reason" for the arousal. Often this is referred to as the "plasticity" of the interpretation of bodily states.

Recent studies have investigated directly the effects of causal attributions on emotional responses. The studies are similar in that they generally arouse fear by informing subjects they are about to receive a series of electric shocks. Then an external agent, such as a pill or a loud noise, is introduced. Reactions to these agents are described as similar to the symptoms experienced when frightened. Thus, the subjects can attribute their fear reactions to the nonshock external sources. The misattribution of the fear symptoms results in a reduction of the fear itself.

An experiment by Nisbett and Schachter (1966) closely conforms to the experimental paradigm outlined above. Subjects in that experiment were given a placebo after being told that they were about to receive a series of electric shocks. All of the subjects were informed that the placebo had side effects. In one condition the side effects were described as tremors, shaky hands, pounding heart, a feeling of "butterflies" in the stomach, and so on. That is, the side effects were identical with fear arousal symptoms. In a second condition the side effects were described as itching, headache, and other reactions unrelated to fear symptoms.

Subjects were then given a series of shocks progressively increasing in intensity. The dependent variables included the point at which pain was first experienced and the intensity at which the shock was reported unendurable. The data revealed that, within the range of shock at which the subjects reasonably could attribute their arousal symptoms to the two possible causal sources, the individuals in the pill-attribution condition report first experiencing pain at a higher level of intensity, and have a higher tolerance level, than subjects who apparently attribute their arousal reactions to the fear of shock. Nisbett and Schachter (1966) conclude:

Earlier studies [for instance, Schachter & Singer, 1962] have demonstrated the cognitive manipulability of bodily states produced by the injection of epinephrine. The present study demonstrates that, within the limits of plausibility, the labeling of naturally occurring bodily states is similarly manipulable [p. 236].

A subsequent study by Ross, Rodin, and Zimbardo (1969), guided by the theoretical analysis of Nisbett and Schachter, reported:

Our basic assumption follows directly from Schachter's theory: Any physiological state that is causally attributed by a subject to an emotionally relevant cognitive source will be perceived emotionally and "labeled" in a manner consistent with the cognitive source. Any physiological state that is causally attributed to an emotionally irrelevant cognitive source will be perceived nonemotionally [p. 281].

Ross and his associates tested these ideas using a modification of the procedure introduced by Nisbett and Schachter. Subjects again were led to expect electric shocks. A loud noise was then presented during the experiment. For half of the subjects the noise was described as producing the fear-related symptoms listed earlier, while for the remaining subjects the reactions to the noise were described as unrelated to the fear response. Ross et al. employed a behavioral dependent variable to infer the effects of causal misattribution, rather than relying on self-reports of pain, as had Nisbett and Schachter. Subjects were allowed to work on either of two tasks; success at one of the tasks was instrumental to shock-avoidance, while success at the other task was expected to result in a monetary reward. It was assumed that "a subject's perseverance on the 'shock-puzzle,' while ignoring the reward puzzle, provides behavioral data to test the main hypothesis" (Ross et al., 1969, p. 281)—that attribution of arousal symptoms to the noise lessens fear.

The data reported by Ross et al. support the general hypothesis. The most dramatic of the findings is illustrated in Figure 5:11, which shows the percentage of subjects who worked on the shock-avoidance puzzle over time. It is evident that subjects who attribute their naturally occurring arousal to fear maintain a high rate of behavior instrumental to shock-avoidance. On the other hand, subjects who are led to misattribute their fear symptoms to the loud noise display decreasing shock-avoidance behavior.

In both the Nisbett and Schachter and Ross et al. studies the subjects are exposed to a threatening stimulus while under different attributional "sets." The subjects are believed to experience differential levels of fear because of the cognitive control of motivation provided by the causal attribution. These procedures are quite similar to the threat paradigm employed by Lazarus and his colleagues. Indeed, the only clear difference between these studies and those of Lazarus is that causal attributions, rather than "defenses," are manipulated prior to the onset of the threatening stimulus. The investigations appear even more similar if it is believed that defenses include causal attributions.

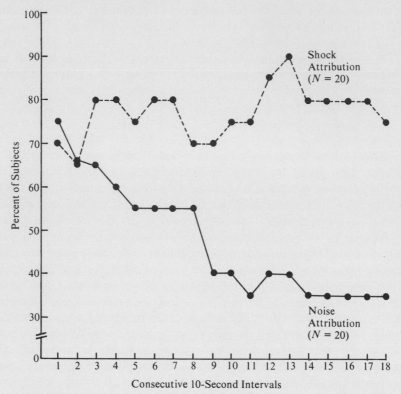

FIGURE 5:11. The percentage of subjects in the shock attribution and noise misattribution conditions working to solve the shock-avoidance puzzle over time (from Ross, Rodin, & Zimbardo, 1969, p. 286).

Davison and Valins (1969) altered this procedure so the subjects received shock under identical attributional belief systems. In their experiment, the subjects' pain thresholds were determined first. Then a placebo, described as a "fast-acting drug," was administered, and a new pain threshold was ascertained. During the new determination the shocks were reduced in intensity so it appeared the subjects were able to endure more pain. Half of the subjects then were told that the administered drug was in fact a placebo. The "undrugged" subjects therefore could not attribute their "improved" shock-tolerance to the drug. The performance during the second threshold thus could be self-attributed. In the final stage of the experiment a third threshold was determined. The data revealed that subjects in the "undrugged" condition now tolerate more pain than the "drugged" subjects. Davison and Valins suggest that debriefed subjects reevaluate their prior behavior on the basis of their actions. That is, the subjects could conclude: "If I tolerated more shock, then I must not be afraid of shock, or perhaps shocks are not as painful as I thought."

One interesting aspect of the theoretical analyses and supporting data in the studies by Ross et al. and by Davison and Valins is the immediate relevance of this work to psychotherapy. For example, Davison and Valins discuss the possibility that the use of drugs during psychotherapeutic treatment might hinder improvement. The patient could attribute any alleviation of his symptoms to the drug rather than to himself, and then experience a relapse when the drug is withheld. Indeed, there is an abundance of evidence concerning the transient effects of drug treatment. Valins and Nisbett (1971) also point out that if aberrent behavior is maintained while the person is under prescribed drugs, it is likely the individual will infer that he is getting worse. The general intent of these suppositions is to point out that some attributions are more adaptive than others, and that existent treatments should pay attention to the causal ascriptions of the patient. Perhaps an attribution therapy could be devised that focuses upon changes in causal attribution (see Strong, 1970). For example, Valins and Nisbett (1971) note that the attribution of bodily pain to somatic sources, rather than to "foreign agents invading the body" could be a key step in the recovery from a paranoid psychosis. Note how this rational approach to motivation and behavior contrasts with Freudian assumptions.

In one direct application of attributional principles to behavioral change, Storms and Nisbett (1970) attempted to alter the sleep behavior of insomniacs. Individuals reporting that they had problems going to sleep were given a placebo that supposedly would produce alertness, mind racing, and other symptoms reported by insomniacs during periods of wakefulness. Self-reports of sleep indicated that subjects in this pill-attribution condition go to sleep *sooner* than subjects unable to attribute their wakefulness to the pill. Conversely, subjects given a placebo "relaxation" pill take longer to fall asleep.

Storms and Nisbett reason that during periods of nonsleep the insomniac introspects about his neuroticism, inferred from his inability to sleep. These thoughts of self-inadequacy further interfere with sleep. Attribution of the wakefulness to the pill breaks the postulated wakefulness-introspection-wakefulness cycle, enabling the insomniac to sleep. This analysis evidently is not the exclusive province of professional psychologists, as indicated in the accompanying cartoon by Jules Feiffer (Figure 5:12).

Attribution and Cognitive Dissonance

Attributional language also has been employed to explain cognitive dissonance phenomena. Consider, for example, the Festinger and Carlsmith

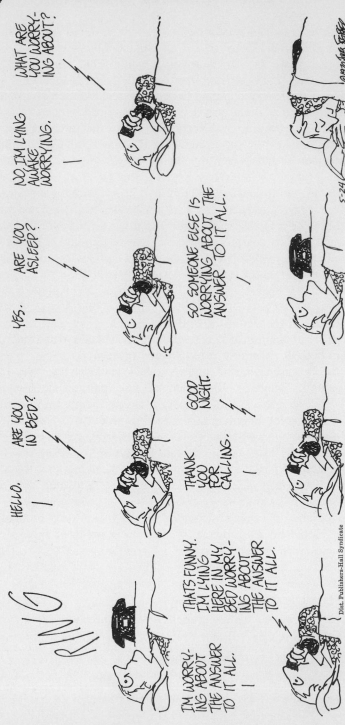

FIGURE 5:12. Attribution and insomnia. Sleep follows the realization that others also cannot sleep, and the inference that "I must be normal" (courtesy of Jules Feiffer, 1970).

(1959) insufficient justification paradigm reviewed in detail earlier. Some subjects in that experiment were offered a large monetary reward to comply with a request to praise an experiment publicly. This positive evaluation of the experiment was contradictory to their private opinion. These subjects maintain their private unfavorable opinion of the experiment following the compliance. On the other hand, subjects given only a small reward for compliance alter their private opinion so it is more consistent with their public behavior. It is assumed that the attitude change resulting from the insufficient justification brings the cognitive elements into greater consonance.

Attribution language leads to the interpretation that in the Festinger and Carlsmith experiment the subjects in the large reward condition attribute their behavior to external factors (the reward). Conversely, subjects in the small reward condition cannot ascribe their actions to the external situation. Therefore, they attribute their compliance to internal determinants, such as an altered belief system.

The attributional approach to dissonance-reducing behavior rests heavily on the data on Valins (1966) and Davison and Valins (1969) and the theoretical analysis of Bem (1967), that individuals infer their attitudes from their behavior. For example, when individuals perceive that their heart is pounding, they infer that they are attracted to a nude picture (Valins, 1966). In a similar manner, when they perceive that they have tolerated a great deal of shock, they conclude that they are not bothered by shock (Davison & Valins, 1969). The parallel argument used to explain the findings in dissonance research is that the individual perceives that he acted given insufficient justification. He then infers from his behavior that the act must have been justified, or had intrinsic merit. The subject is thus making an attributional error in explaining his past behavior.

Thus, a key problem in dissonance experiments is first to elicit the behavior despite insufficient justification. As Kelley (1967) points out, the subjects have only the "illusion of freedom" in the insufficient justification paradigm, for virtually all comply with the experimenter's request, although the situation is presented as one of free choice. Kelley (1967) reasons:

The successful experiment is one in which strong situational demands, entirely sufficient to produce total or near-total compliance, are successfully camouflaged by a network of cues as to self-determination. From an attribution point of view, the situation surrounding the behavior is misleading . . . when the subject in the low-incentive condition reviews his recent behavior it does not occur to him to attribute it to the situation and it is possible for him plausibly to make an entity attribution. Apparently having been free to speak his mind at that point, and having addressed himself to the entity, the subject views his response as having been entity-caused. In the high-incentive condition, the salient fact of the large payment suggests to him a situation-attribution for his behavior [p. 229].

The general explanation of dissonance phenomena by attributional theorists is that the less the extrinsic forces are consistent with behavior, and the less able the subject is to identify the reasons for his action, the more likely the action will be attributed to internal factors, such as the intrinsic self-value of the action. Nisbett and Valins (1971) have extended this analysis to situations in which the extrinsic reward is consonant with the performed act. They reason that the greater the extrinsic reward for behavior consonant with one's true beliefs, the less the likelihood that the behavior will be then ascribed to internal factors (the belief). Thus, being paid to state a belief consistent with one's true feelings might result in a *weakening* of that belief. Nisbett and Valins review a number of published and unpublished studies supporting this general supposition. For example, it has been found that subjects paid a relatively large sum of money to read a speech consistent with their private opinion (overly sufficient justification) are later more likely to be dissuaded from that opinion than subjects paid only a small amount of money to read a speech conveying their beliefs (Kiesler & Sakumura, 1966).

Nisbett and Valins (1971) conclude that the attributional (informational) approach to explain dissonance-type phenomena has more generality than the Festinger-guided motivational explanation. When the behavior in question is insufficiently justified, the dissonance theorist can argue that this knowledge is painful and that attitude change is a motivated process rather than a passive, inferential process. But Nisbett and Valins contend that if the behavior is justified, the situation is not dissonant, and dissonance theory cannot make predictions. An information-processing approach, however, can explain the data.

Attribution in Animal Experimentation

Some experiments that have been conducted with infrahuman subjects can be interpreted from an attributional framework. Of course, the question immediately raised is whether infrahumans can make ascriptions to the self as opposed to external factors. In discussing the cognitive capacities of infrahuman organisms (rats), Festinger (1961) states,

All that is meant by cognition is knowledge or information. It seems to me that one can assume that an organism has cognitions or information if one can observe some behavioral difference under different stimulus conditions. If the organism changes his behavior when the environment changes, then obviously he uses information about the environment and, equally obviously, can be said to have cognitions.

Now for the question of whether or not rats reduce dissonance as humans do. . . . I suspect that the rat is a rather stupid organism and does not reduce dissonance nearly as effectively as the human being does. I suspect that the mechanisms available to the rat for dissonance reduction are very limited and that the amount of dissonance which gets effectively reduced is relatively small. Still, I suspect that they *do* reduce dissonance. At any rate, if we find that the theory of dissonance can make valid predictions for rat behavior, this will be evidence that they do, indeed, reduce dissonance [p. 4].

Psychological processes in humans often are inferred from infrahuman behavior. It seems just as reasonable to reverse this procedure, and speculate about infrahuman processes from the study of human action. Of course, there are dangers in this neglect of Morgan's Canon (see p. 3), and restraint must be exercised.

A simple taxonomy of the arousal studies reviewed in the prior pages aids in the selection of animal investigations pertinent to attribution theory. The proposed taxonomy of arousal studies concerned with self versus environmental ascription includes two dimensions: the subjective (perceived) and the objective (veridical) origins of causality. Within the two dimensions are the self versus environmental attribution poles. A combination of these two dimensions yields four experimental classifications, as shown in Diagram 5:2.

Consider first Quadrant I in Diagram 5:2. This quadrant includes situations in which both objective (veridical) and subjective (perceived) causality are ascribed to the person. Generally, the control groups in the arousal studies fall within this quadrant. For example, individuals are about to experience something threatening (shock), have arousal symptoms, and ascribe those symptoms to their fear. Veridical perception also is subsumed within Quadrant IV. In that quadrant the ascription, and the objective source of arousal, are external to the organism. This is illustrated by the condition in the Schachter and Singer investigation in which subjects were injected with epinephrine and correctly informed of the symptoms it produces. Consequently, when aroused by the injection, the subjects correctly ascribed their fast heart rates, shaking hands, and the like, to the drug.

The remaining cells in Diagram 5:2 portray attributional errors. Arousal that is self-generated is ascribed to external factors, or vice versa. For example, Nisbett and Schachter (1966), Ross et al. (1969), and Storms and Nisbett (1970) told subjects that their arousal symptoms are to be attributed to a pill or to a loud noise. In reality, the symptoms are naturally occurring reactions to impending shock or to their "anxious"

DIAGRAM 5:2

Taxonomy of Arousal-Emotion Studies

Subjective (Perceived) Causality

		Self	Environment (External Agent)
		(I)	(II)
Objective (Veridical) Causality	Self	Control Groups	Experimental Subjects Nisbett and Schachter (1966) Ross et al. (1969) Storms and Nisbett (1971)
		(III)	(IV)
	Environment (External Agent)	Experimental Subjects Schachter and Singer (1962) Schachter and Wheeler (1962)	Experimental Subjects Schachter and Singer (1962) (epinephrine informed)

state. Thus, perceived causality is external, while the veridical reason is "internal" (Quadrant II).

The reverse of this attributional error, that is, attribution of externally (drug) produced symptoms to the self, is exemplified among the uninformed or misinformed subjects in the Schachter and Singer (1962) and Schachter and Wheeler (1962) experiments. Subjects in those conditions aroused because of an external agent (a drug) ascribed their arousal to their immediate cognitive state. Studies by Valins (1966) and Davison and Valins (1969) also can be loosely classified in Quadrant III. Subjects in those experiments attributed false "arousal," or lack of arousal, to themselves, when in fact this cognitive information was fraudulent and experimentally induced.

A similar taxonomic scheme can be used to classify pertinent studies employing infrahuman organisms (see Diagram 5:3). Following Mill, and the Heider and Kelley adaptation of his principles, assume that causation is inferred from a systematic covariation of antecedents and consequents. If an effect occurs given one set of antecedents, and does not occur when those antecedents are absent, then it is assumed that the effect is perceived as caused by those particular antecedents. For example, if food always follows a lever press, and does not appear when the lever is not pressed, it is postulated that the responding organism will ascribe the presence of food to the instrumental lever press. Thus, a simple instrumental learning paradigm is classified within Quadrant I: the outcome objectively is controlled by the organism, and causation is perceived as due to personal factors.

Now consider Quadrant IV in Diagram 5:3. Inasmuch as outcomes are externally controlled, any response the animal makes should not covary with an effect. The effect sometimes occurs in the presence of a particular response, sometimes in the absence of that response, and at other times in the presence of different responses. This apparently corresponds to the classical conditioning paradigm. In a classical conditioning procedure the reward or punishment, or the presentation of unconditioned stimulus, is independent of the organism's response.

Maier, Seligman, and Solomon (1969) describe a classical aversive conditioning procedure, and its effects on the organism:

In a situation where shock is neither escapable nor avoidable . . . shock termination is not dependent on either the occurrence or the non-occurrence of a response. Sometimes the dog does something and shock

DIAGRAM 5:3
Taxonomy of Experimental Paradigms (Infrahuman Subjects)
Pertinent to Attribution Theory

Subjective (Perceived) Causality

Objective (Veridical) Causality		Self	Environment (External Agent)
		(I)	(II)
	Self	Simple instrumental learning	Instrumental escape learning following classical aversive conditioning
		(III)	(IV)
	Environment (External Agent)	Reward following experimenter-established time interval (superstitious behavior)	Simple classical conditioning

happens to terminate. Sometimes the dog does something and shock does not terminate. Sometimes shock terminates when the dog has not done something. The shock programmer is not influenced by the subject. . . .

It follows that, when shock is inescapable, the conditional probability of shock termination, given the presence of any response, is equal to the conditional probability of shock termination, given the absence of that response. Thus, the statement that shock termination is not dependent on responding means that these two conditional probabilities are equal.

We propose that a dog can learn that reinforcement is independent of the presence or absence of responding: "Nothing I do matters." In the case of inescapable shock, the dog learns that shock termination is independent of his behavior. More specifically, we think that the animal is sensitive to the fact that the conditional probability of shock termination, given the presence of any response, does not differ from the conditional probability of shock termination in the absence of that response. Furthermore, we are suggesting that dogs are sensitive to the conjoint variation of these two probabilities. Independence is simply the special case in which these two conditional probabilities are equal [pp. 325–26].

If the arguments put forth by Maier et al. are accepted, then classical conditioning procedures would be included within Quadrant IV. The outcome is caused by factors external to the organism, and the organism is aware of this.

Superstitious Behavior.   The remaining two quadrants in Diagram 5:3 again represent situations in which attributional errors are made. Quadrant III includes experimental paradigms that induce the outcome to be perceived as caused by the self, when, in fact, the outcomes are under environmental control. Beliefs labeled *"superstitious"* can be described as attributional errors, and are included in Quadrant III. The experimental paradigm resulting in such misattribution generally involves the presentation of food to a hungry animal following some experimentally determined time interval. Prior to the reception of the food the animal happens to be engaging in some response, and errs in ascribing the appearance of the reward to his behavior. Subsequently, he tends to repeat this "superstitious" response, believing that it caused the desired effect.

In sum, because a response has inadvertently preceded a reinforcement, the animal makes the false (but not unreasonable) inference that the reward was caused by the response. This attributional error receives repeated confirmation, for repetition of the behavior is at times accompanied by reception of the reward. But rather than labeling this as superstitious behavior, it may be better understood as an honest error in information processing and inference making. The animal apparently weights the response-reward covariation more heavily than the information gained during response-nonreward sequences. What is needed to correct this false causal inference is information that the reward also will appear in the absence of the "superstitious" response. The animal may then discover that the reward is not contingent upon any self-generated behavior.

An animal placed on a partial reinforcement schedule, or a schedule in which one of every given number of responses is rewarded, is acting rationally when making goal responses. Yet an animal engaging in virtually the same behavior, given a different experimental procedure, is labeled as superstitious. In both instances the animals are responding in the absence of a one-to-one correspondence between each single response and a reward; the information available to the organisms regarding response-reward contingencies is virtually identical in the two situations. But in the superstitious-behavior paradigm further evidence is available which would reveal to the organism that his inference is incorrect. To attain this evidence the perceived instrumental response must cease. But hungry animals

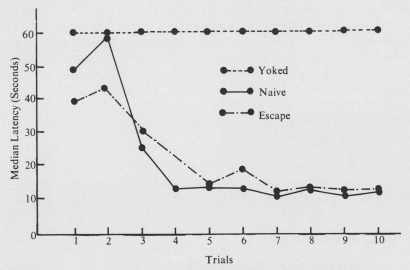

FIGURE 5:13. Effects of matched escapable and inescapable shocks on later escape learning. This figure shows the median escape response latencies in the shuttle-box for three groups of dogs: (a) those given escape training in the shuttle-box as naive subjects; (b) those given prior escape training in harness, panel-press apparatus; and (c) those given prior inescapable shocks in the harness (yoked), but matched in duration and temporal distribution to the shocks for the panel-press, escape training group. The arbitrary criterion of failure to jump was a 60-second latency (50 seconds of shock) (from Maier, Seligman, & Solomon, 1969, p. 328).

are not likely to stop trying to get food. In the superstition paradigm reward would continue if the perceived "instrumental" response was withheld, while in the truly instrumental paradigm the reward would cease.

Learned Helplessness. The reverse attributional error—attribution of an outcome to external agents when the outcome is or may be self-determined (Quadrant II)—has apparently been experimentally demonstrated. Maier, Seligman, Solomon (1969) maintain that in classical aversive conditioning paradigms the animal learns that "Nothing I do matters" (p. 326). When dogs given this training (the "yoked" group in Figure 5:13) subsequently are placed in an instrumental avoidance paradigm in which they may terminate shock, they do not engage in appropriate shock-termination instrumental behavior. The performance of these dogs, as compared with naive dogs or dogs given prior instrumental training in a different stimulus situation, is shown in Figure 5:13. Figure 5:13 reveals that dogs first trained with a classical aversive conditioning procedure do not display performance gains over trials in the subsequent instrumental avoidance learning situation. Indeed, the majority of the previously conditioned animals never learn the escape response. Apparently the dogs are making attributional errors, and have "learned helplessness." They are generalizing their prior conclusions about the inescapability of shock, and making the incorrect inference that in this new situation shock termination is independent of their personal behavior. (This interpretation is the subject of much recent debate. Others have argued the escape response is not learned because of the prior stress situation.)

INDIVIDUAL DIFFERENCES IN CASUAL BELIEFS

Social Learning Theory

The first systematic examination of individual differences in causal attribution was undertaken by Julian Rotter and his colleagues. Rotter's concern with causality followed the development of a "social learning theory" that has much in common with the models of motivation proposed by Lewin and Atkinson.

Rotter (1954) chose the label "social learning" because the theory "stresses the fact that the major or basic modes of behavior are learned in social situations and are inextricably fused with needs requiring for their satisfaction the mediation of other persons" (p. 84). Three basic constructs are included in social learning theory: *behavior potential, expectancy,* and *reinforcement value.* These constructs are very similar to other terms already introduced in this book. *Behavior potential* is comparable with Hull's construct of effective reaction potential (*sEr*), Lewin's concept of force, and Atkinson's notion of a behavioral tendency (*T_A*). Rotter defines behavior potential as "the potentiality of any behaviors occurring in a given situation or situations as calculated in relation to any single reinforcement or set of reinforcements" (p. 105). *Expectancy* is used by Rotter in the manner of Tolman and Atkinson: it is "the probability held by the individual that a particular reinforcement will occur as a function of a specific behavior on his part in a specific situation" (p. 107). Finally, *reinforcement value* is identical with the general construct of incentive, and may be considered the worth of an external reinforcement.

Rotter's formal theory of motivation states that behavior potential (*BP*) is a function of the expectancy (*E*) of a goal and the reinforcement value (*RV*) of the goal:

$$BP = f(E \ \& \ RV)$$

In contrast to Atkinson's view, expectancy and the reward value of a goal are assumed to be independent.

The expectancy variable in Rotter's theory is a function of two independent determinants: A specific expectancy (*E'*) based upon the reinforcement history of the particular response under consideration in a specific stimulus situation, and a "generalization of expectancies (*GE*) from other related behavior-reinforcement sequences" (p. 166). Thus,

$$E = f(E' \ \& \ GE)$$

Rotter persistently has investigated the effects of luck versus skill task situations on the formation of general and specific expectancies. In a chance or luck situation the reward is externally determined. Thus, the probability of a reward is unaffected by the response of the organism. On the other hand, in skill situations the reinforcement is dependent upon the organism's behavior; reward is, in part, internally determined. Hence, the attainment of a reinforcement in situations perceived as determined by chance may result in changes of expectancy that differ from the changes given goal attainment in a skill-defined setting. Rotter, Seeman, and Liverant (1962) relate:

It is a matter of common sense that most individuals who would find a $5 bill on a given street would not return and walk up and down the street many times to find more $5 bills because they consider the event that occurred to be a matter of chance. On the other hand, should someone take up ping pong and be told that he plays an excellent game for someone just learning, he is quite likely to increase the number of times he plays ping pong. In the first case, the reinforcement appears to be a matter of chance, controlled in some way by people or forces outside the individual, and in the second instance, the reinforcement appears to be dependent on some characteristic or quality of the person which he can label as a skill. In the latter case, the reinforcement, in a sense, is understood as occurring because of his own behavior [p. 474].

In sum, the cues associated with luck and skill situations are linked with different patterns of reinforcement, and hence also produce disparate goal anticipations and approach behavior.

Skill versus Chance, Reinforcement Schedules, and Resistance to Extinction

In a series of systematic investigations, Rotter and his colleagues independently manipulated skill versus chance task perceptions and examined how these variables interact to influence expectancy of success and resistance to extinction. In the first of these studies, Phares (1957) contended, like Rotter, Seeman, and Liverant (1962), that in skill situations similar outcomes are expected on past and future occasions. On the other hand, in chance-determined situations covariation of prior and future reinforcement is not anticipated. Hence, Phares hypothesized that the frequency and magnitude of increments and decrements in expectancy would be greater in skill than chance situations following respective success and failure. However, a greater number of "unusual" shifts (increments in expectancy after failure, or decrements after success) were anticipated in chance than in skill situations.

To test these hypotheses, subjects were given a discrimination task that was ambiguous with respect to the objective determinants of success and failure. In one condition the outcome was described as determined by skill, while in a second condition performance was said to be entirely a matter of luck. Prior to each discrimination trial the subjects indicated how many of ten chips they would be willing to bet on their next performance. Expectancy of success was inferred from the magnitude of the reported bet. Subjects in both the skill and chance conditions received the same relatively random reinforcement schedule on the thirteen test trials.

Phares found that his hypotheses were generally confirmed. In the skill condition there were more typical expectancy shifts, and the shifts were of greater magnitude, than in the chance condition. For example, following success, subjects in the skill condition were more likely to increase their bet on the next trial, and by a greater amount, than subjects in the chance condition. On the other hand, there were a greater number of atypical shifts in the chance than skill condition. The atypical shifts are often known as the "gambler's fallacy." The gambler's fallacy indicates that there is a perceived dependence imposed on independent outcomes, and that a loss is expected to be followed by a win, and vice versa.

James and Rotter (1958) extended the Phares study to include different reinforcement schedules, as well as differences in chance versus skill instructions. Subjects participating in an "ESP" experiment were asked to identify whether an "X" or an "O" was flashed during a tachistiscopic exposure. In fact, nothing was shown, and the experimenters manipulated the feedback to the subjects during the pseudo-identification trials. Subjects in a 100 percent reinforcement condition were first given continuous reinforcement, followed by an extinction series. In a 50 percent reinforcement condition, subjects were "correct" on a random series of half the trials and then underwent experimental extinction. Luck and skill task perceptions were manipulated by informing half the subjects, "There is evidence that some people are considerably skilled at this," while others were told, "Scientists have shown so far that this is entirely a matter of luck" (James & Rotter, 1958, p. 359). Prior to each trial the subjects estimated their probability of success on a ten-point scale. The dependent variable, resistance to extinction, was inferred from the probability of success. It was assumed that extinction would occur when the probability of success was .10 or less on three consecutive trials.

The trials to extinction for the four experimental groups (2 levels of reinforcement $\times$ 2 levels of instruction) are shown in Table 5:4. The table indicates that extinction is faster in the 100 percent than the 50 percent condition, given chance instructions. This finding replicates the general pattern of results in extinction studies that employ infrahumans as subjects. On the other hand, given skill instructions, extinction is faster in the 50 percent than the 100 percent condition.

TABLE 5:4
Trials to Extinction
(from James & Rotter, 1958, p. 401)

Group	Trials	Standard Deviation
(100% chance)	15.55	9.86
(50% chance)	29.05	9.41
(100% skill)	22.90	4.84
(50% skill)	19.75	7.27

The explanation of the Instruction $\times$ Reinforcement schedule interaction suggested by James and Rotter (1958) is not clear. The experimenters employ some combination of the cognitive and cue conditioning interpretations of partial reinforcement that are found in the animal literature. Later, Rotter (1966) summarized:

Under chance conditions the extinction series was interpreted as a change in the situation, a disappearance of previous lucky hits in the 100% reinforcement condition but not in the 50% reinforcement conditions. For the subjects with skill instructions the greater the previous reinforcement the longer it took the subject to accept the fact that he was not able to do the task successfully [p. 6].

Subsequently, Rotter, Liverant, and Crowne (1961) combined the study of expectancy shifts and resistance to extinction in one investigation. Again instructions to the subjects indicated that the task (raising a platform with a ball on it) was influenced either by luck or by skill. Subjects were trained with a 100 percent, 75 percent, 50 percent or 25 percent reinforcement schedule, and then underwent experimental extinction. Expectancies were reported prior to each trial, and extinction again inferred when the verbal expectancies were less than .10.

The number of trials to extinction in the eight conditions (4 levels of reinforcement $\times$ 2 levels of instruction) are shown in Figure 5:14. It is evident that given skill instructions, resistance to extinction is monotonically related to the percentage of reinforcement during training. Conversely, in the chance condition extinction trials are greatest given 50 percent reinforcement. In addition, the pattern of results concerning expectancy shifts replicated the prior findings of Phares. Expectancy shifts were more numerous and of greater magnitude in the skill than in the chance condition. However, the instructions did not influence the number of unusual shifts.

In sum, the findings reported by Rotter and his colleagues (1961) relating chance versus skill environments to expectancy shifts and extinction are generally consistent. However, the explanation of the data remains rather ambiguous. It has been contended, for example, that "if [a] subject regards a task as being controlled by luck or chance, he is likely to 'learn' less about future behavior-reinforcement sequences from the occurrence of a reinforcement" (p. 162). Similarly, Phares (1957) contends that chance situations do not provide a basis for generalization about future performance. But these explanations ignore the information and decision-making processes that occur in situations perceived as determined by luck. The lack of recognition of the information processing capacities and causal judgments of subjects in the chance conditions are evident in the general

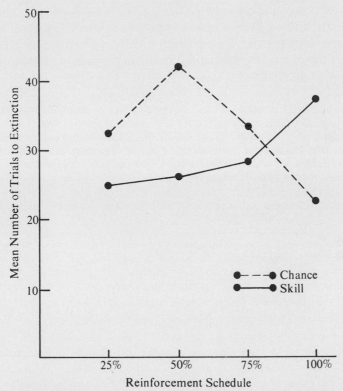

FIGURE 5:14.   Mean number of trials to extinction for skill
and chance groups under four reinforcement schedules (from
Rotter, Liverant, & Crowne, 1961, p. 172).

experimental procedure. For example, some subjects in the luck conditions
are given 100 percent reinforcement during training. But this reinforcement
schedule contradicts the instruction that the outcome is only a matter of
chance. This point is discussed in detail in the next chapter.

Individual Differences in Locus of Control

The data of Rotter and his colleagues indicate that chance versus skill environments differentially affect behavior. The question then raised by this
research group was whether, given identical environments, some individuals
would act as if the task were influenced by luck or chance more than
others. That is, are there individual differences in the perception of outcomes (reinforcements) as determined by skill as opposed to chance? If

so, these individual differences would be a determinant of generalized expectancies, and thus influence the subjective probability of goal attainment and subsequent behavior.

Concerning the individual difference dimension in social learning theory, Rotter (1966) states that

an event regarded by some persons as a reward or reinforcement may be differently perceived and reacted to by others. One of the determinants of this reaction is the degree to which the individual perceives that the reward follows from, or is contingent upon, his own behavior or attributes versus the degree to which he feels the reward is controlled by forces outside of himself and may occur independently of his own actions. The effect of a reinforcement following some behavior on the part of a human subject, in other words, is not a simple stamping-in process but depends upon whether or not the person perceives a causal relationship between his own behavior and the reward. A perception of causal relationship need not be all or none but can vary in degree. When a reinforcement is perceived by the subject as following some action of his own but not being entirely contingent upon his action, then, in our culture, it is typically perceived as the result of luck, chance, fate, as under the control of powerful others, or as unpredictable because of the great complexity of the forces surrounding him. When the event is interpreted in this way by an individual, we have labeled this a belief in external control. If the person perceives that the event is contingent upon his own behavior or his own relatively permanent characteristics, we have termed this a belief in internal control [p. 1].

In sum, the internal-external control construct "relates to whether or not the individual [perceives that he] possesses power or lacks power over what happens to him" (Lefcourt, 1966, p. 207).

Assessment Procedure. Individual differences in the tendency to perceive events as being internally or externally controlled are assessed with a 29-item self-report inventory. The 23 keyed items on this test measure an individual's beliefs about the nature of the world. The test, called the internal-external control scale (I-E scale), has a forced-choice format in which an internal belief is pitted against an external belief. This test format was used because

behavior in complex social situations is usually not a matter of making absolute judgments (I agree or disagree), but a relative matter of deciding that I prefer this alternative to that one. Consequently, forcing a discrimination on the part of the subject may be more representative of "real" life situations than the responses required by single-stimulus items. This may have the salutory effect of producing higher validity coefficients [Rotter et al., 1962, p. 505].

The test construction is thus based upon Rotter's contention that a test itself is a complex stimulus, and that test responses are sensitive to the entire testing situations, including the context within which items are presented.

Some exemplary items, and their keyed responses (keying is in the direction of externality) are:

1. a. Many of the unhappy things in people's lives are partly due to bad luck.
   b. People's misfortunes result from the mistakes they make.
2. a. The idea that teachers are unfair to students is nonsense.
   b. Most students don't realize the extent to which grades are influenced by accidental happenings.

The items on the scale are classifiable into six general subcategories, primarily on the basis of the types of needs they portray and the characteristics of the described goals: academic recognition, social recognition, love and affection, dominance, social-political, and life philosophy (Rotter et al., 1961). The breadth of the items indicate that they often tap far more than the "functionally-related behaviors" which Rotter specifies as comprised within the concept of general expectancy.

Validity.   It is reasonable to anticipate that the validation of the scale would be in the areas of resistance to extinction and expectancy shift. But this is not the case. The few published studies that relate I-E scores to resistance to extinction fail to find significant results (for example, Battle & Rotter, 1963). In addition, the expected greater frequency and magnitude of typical shifts, which has been clearly shown to differentiate chance from skill situations, has not been displayed differentially by subjects high or low on the I-E scale.

As a general rule, the closer the test-taking situation to the situation in which behavioral data are gathered, the more likely that the test will be "validated." Responses to a measure that includes, for example, questions about happiness in life bear little immediate relevance to expectancy shift paradigms. Thus, it is not surprising that the I-E scale has not successfully predicted expectancy shifts. This is not to say that internality-externality is or is not a trait, or a personality dimension having trans-situational predictive power. Rather, conceptually there is too great a gap between the I-E test items (predictor variable), the notion of general expectancy, the concept of specific probability, and expectancy changes in laboratory tasks (criterion variable).

It also seems reasonable to suppose that I-E scores are related to achievement strivings. Individuals who perceive that outcomes are under personal control might be expected to engage in more achievement-related behavior than individuals who believe that outcomes are externally controlled. Again, however, the empirical relationships in this area are weak. There is some evidence that the scale correlates with measures of need for achievement, but frequently the reported correlations are not significant, and the highest correlation is less than —.30 (that is, individuals high in need for achievement are low in externality). There is evidence that individuals high in internality prefer tasks of intermediate difficulty (Liverant & Scodel, 1960), but in the Liverant and Scodel study internals also preferred easy tasks and less risk in general. Thus, there is no clear parallel between the risk-preference behavior of persons high in need for achievement and the probability preferences of individuals who are internal in locus of control.

One finding that does appear reliable is that individuals scoring high in externality on the I-E scale also score high on anxiety. The magnitude of this correlation has been reported as high as $r = .80$ (see the review and a study reported by Watson, 1967). However, it does not seem reasonable to expect that these two constructs have a true relationship of that magnitude. Constructs such as a "fear from a sense of helplessness" have been suggested (Mowrer & Viek, 1948), and it has been contended that individuals who believe they are powerless anticipate that their activities will not be completed, and this leads to anxiety (see Watson, 1967). But at present the meaning of the externality-anxiety correlation remains unclear, and is probably accounted for by test-taking response biases.

The I-E scale has had more success predicting behaviors that generally involve attempts to better one's life through action on the environment. In such activities there is less environmental constraint or dependence on specific probabilities as determinants of action. General expectancies should be more predictive of these broad social actions than of behavior in controlled laboratory settings.

In one series of studies, Seeman and Evans (1962) and Seeman (1963) respectively report on the information seeking and retention of personally relevant information among individuals confined within "total institutions." Seeman and Evans find that, among hospitalized tuberculosis patients, individuals classified as internals know more about their illness and ask doctors more questions than patients who are external in locus of control. Seeman also reports that prisoners who are internals retain more information pertinent to parole than do externals. In sum, among both patients and prisoners the behavior displayed by those who are high in internal control may be instrumental to improving their life situations.

Scores on the I-E scale also have been related to ethnic classification and social action. A number of investigators report that lower class

Negroes are especially external in locus of control, and that internality among Negroes is related to social action (see literature reviews by Lefcourt, 1966; Rotter, 1966). The conception of an external-control Negro as one who does not take part in activities instrumental to social betterment has led to some controversy. Gurin, Gurin, Lao, and Beattie (1969) note that when there are objective barriers in the environment it may be instrumental to blame the lack of positive reinforcements on the system rather than the self. These authors distinguish between internal versus external personal control and system versus individual blame (race ideology); they report these are independent factors. (A system-blame Negro responds positively to assertions such as: "Many Negroes who do not do well in life have good training, but the opportunities just always go to whites"). Gurin et al. (1969) and Lao (1970) find that personal control predicts school grades, educational aspiration, and confidence in school. However, system-blamers participate more in civil rights activities and prefer collective social action. Lao (1970) contends that personal control and race ideology are additive rather than interactive factors.

> Internality in a personal sense relates to competent behavior in the academic domain; externality in an ideological sense relates to innovative behavior in the social arena [p. 270].

The I-E scale has been found to predict a number of other behaviors that are not clearly related to the concept of expectancy, such as conformity, reward value of a goal, political attitudes, and the like (see reviews already cited). Thus, the scale has had great heuristic value. Frequently, however, the findings are unrelated to social learning theory (or to any systematic approach), and stray far from the concept of causality, which is the concern of this chapter.

OTHER WORK IN CAUSAL ATTRIBUTION BASED ON INDIVIDUAL DIFFERENCES

Origin-Pawn as a Causal Determinant

A distinction by de Charms (1968) between "origin" and "pawn" is similar to Rotter's differentiation of internal and external control. De Charms (1968) states:

> We shall use the terms "Origin" and "Pawn" as shorthand terms to connote the distinction between forced and free. An Origin is a person who perceives his behavior as determined by his own choosing; a Pawn is a person who perceives his behavior as determined by external forces

beyond his control. . . . Feeling like an Origin has strong effects on behavior as compared to feeling like a Pawn. The distinction is continuous,
not discrete—a person feels *more* like an Origin under some circumstances
and *more* like a Pawn under others.

The personal aspect is more important motivationally than objective
facts. If the person feels he is an Origin, that is more important in predicting his behavior than any objective indications of coercion. Conversely,
if he considers himself a Pawn, his behavior will be strongly influenced,
despite any objective evidence that he is free. An Origin has a strong feeling of personal causation, a feeling that the locus for causation of effects
in his environment lies within himself. The feedback that reinforces this
feeling comes from changes in his environment that are attributed to personal behavior. This is the crux of the concept of personal causation and
it is a powerful motivational force directing future behavior. A Pawn has
a feeling that causal forces beyond his control, or personal forces residing
in others, or in the physical environment, determine his behavior. This
constitutes a strong feeling of powerlessness or ineffectiveness [pp.
273–74].

De Charms associates the concept of origin with intrinsically
motivated behavior (own forces), freedom of movement, and the perception of situations as challenging. Conversely, the concept of pawn is linked
with extrinsically motivated behavior (induced forces), restriction of
movement, and the perception of situations as threatening. Thus, the
origin-pawn dimension goes far beyond the already broad confines of locus
of control.

Experiments have been conducted manipulating situational factors
which influence the feeling of being an origin or a pawn. The general approach in these experiments is to induce "freedom" in one experimental
condition and constraint in a comparison condition. In one experiment,
for example, children were given a task of building models (Kuperman,
1967; reported in de Charms, 1968). In the pawn condition the subjects
were told exactly what to do; in the origin condition they proceeded in
any manner they desired. Subsequent questionnaire data revealed that
origins enjoyed the task more and were more interested in continuing the
activity than were the pawns. However, significant differences were not
observed in the behaviors of children in the two conditions. A similar experiment conducted by de Charms (1968), yielded comparable results,
and some additional between-condition differences, such as the name of
the model being remembered more by origins than pawns. However, not
all of the reported data are readily interpretable.

It is too early to evaluate the scientific contribution of the origin-pawn
conception. Like other hypothetical constructs, the antecedent conditions
that produce this phenomenological state, and its behavioral consequences,

will have to be clearly stated. In addition, the concept should be embedded in some theoretical framework. Further, it is not clear how the experimental manipulation discussed briefly above differs from those employed in the investigation of democracy versus autocracy or other similar psychological dimensions. That is, the boundary conditions in which the origin-pawn belief is expected to influence behavior must be considered. However, the intuitive appeal of this variable, and the evident fact that the situations described by de Charms produce different feelings and attitudes, indicate the importance of distinguishing origin from pawn perceptions in the understanding of human behavior. Further, recent investigations by de Charms suggest this dimension is an important determinant of school achievement.

Intellectual Achievement Responsibility

Another area of study related to Rotter's investigations of locus of control has been the attempt to assess the perception of responsibility for achievement-related outcomes (Crandall, Katkovsky, & Crandall, 1965; Crandall, Katkovsky, & Preston, 1962). The program of research undertaken by the Crandalls and their associates has been directed primarily toward the identification of the child-rearing antecedents that produce intellectual achievement responsibility. Although Rotter influenced the inception of this work, there has been little systematic attempt to assimilate the findings within social learning theory or to investigate resistance to extinction or other variables of special interest to social learning theorists.

Among the contributions of this research program are the distinctions drawn within the general concept of locus of control. The differentiations are evident in the measure devised to assess intellectual achievement responsibility, although they have not been explicitly examined by the Crandalls. Guided by the I-E scale, a self-report inventory to assess intellectual achievement responsibility (the IAR scale) has been constructed in which an internal belief is paired with an external interpretation of an event. All of the items on the IAR scale pertain to achievement activities. Half of the items on the scale describe positive achievement outcomes ("When you do well on a test . . ."), while the other half present negative outcomes ("If you cannot solve a puzzle . . ."). Crandall et al. (1965), Weiner and Kukla (1970), and Weiner and Potepan (1970) report that correlations between items with positive and negative achievement outcomes are generally low and often are nonsignificant (see Tables 5:5 and 5:6). Thus, an individual who attributes achievement success to internal factor may or may not also attribute failure to himself. The relative con-

TABLE 5:5

Correlations of the Internal Success and Failure Subscale Scores on the Intellectual Achievement Responsibility Scale (Crandall, Katkovsky, & Crandall, 1965, p. 101), and on a Modified Version of that Scale (Weiner & Kukla, 1970, p. 10)

Crandall et al., 1965			Weiner & Kukla, 1970			
Grade	N	I+ versus I−	Grade	Sex	N	I+ versus I−
3	102	.14	3 & 4	Male	87	.15
				Female	99	−.08
4	103	.11				
5	99	.11	5	Male	33	.17
				Female	21	.15
6	166	.38**	6	Male	26	.03
				Female	28	−.13
8	161	.40**				
10	183	.43**	10	Male	112	.24*
12	109	.17				

Note: $I+$ = internality for success, $I-$ = internality for failure.
* $p < .05$.
** $p < .001$.

sistency of the success versus failure data reported in the above three studies strongly suggests that locus of control is not a unidimensional construct.

The internal stems on the IAR scale allocate the positive and negative outcomes to ability or effort. Two items on the scale which illustrate the success-failure, ability-effort distinctions are:

1. When you do well on a test at school, is it more likely to be
    (a) because you studied for it, or
    (b) because the test was especially easy.
2. If you can't work a puzzle, is it more likely to happen
    (a) because you are not especially good at working puzzles, or
    (b) because the instructions weren't clear enough.

Item 1 of the two examples presents a success situation, pairing an internal effort ascription against an external task ease attribution. Item 2 describes a failure situation, pairing an internal ability attribution against an external causal interpretation.

Weiner and Potepan (1970), using a modified version of the IAR scale, found that the correlations between ability and effort ascriptions are low and at times significant in a negative direction (see Table 5:6). Table 5:6 indicates the internal ascriptions of success to ability $(A+)$ and motivation $(M+)$ are not significantly related $(r = -.10)$, while attributions of failure to lack of ability $(A-)$ and lack of motivation $(M-)$ are significantly correlated in a negative direction $(r = -.40)$. Table 5:6 also shows

TABLE 5:6

Correlations of Resultant Achievement Motivation and Ascriptions for Success and Failure, $N = 107$ (from Weiner & Potepan, 1970, p. 148)

Variable Number	Variable	Variable Number					
		1	2	3	4	5	6
1	Resultant achievement motivation						
2	Success ascribed to ability $(A+)$	.35					
3	Success ascribed to motivation $(M+)$	.12	−.10				
4	Internality for success $[(A+) + (M+)]$	.36	.72	.62			
5	Failure ascribed to ability $(A-)$	−.33	−.37	−.14	−.37		
6	Failure ascribed to motivation $(M-)$	.08	.16	.30	.16	−.40	
7	Internality for failure $[(A-) + (M-)]$	−.26	−.24	.11	−.24	.67	.42

that internal ascription of success to high ability correlates negatively with internal attribution of failure to low ability ($r = -.37$). That is, if one attributes success to high ability, one does not ascribe failure to low ability. This certainly is consistent with the notion of ability as a relatively stable self-percept. It also again demonstrates that internality cannot be discussed without differentiating positive from negative outcomes. On the other hand, there is some evidence that if one ascribes success to heightened effort, he is prone to attribute failure to a lack of effort ($r = .16$). In sum, the overall concept of locus of control does not do justice to the complexities found *within* internal or external attributions.

Investigations conducted by the Crandalls and their colleagues have shown that internality for achievement outcomes is positively related to time spent in free-play activities, the intensity of those activities, intelligence-test performance, and grade-point average. The findings are often complex because of interactions with the sex of the respondents. However, the relations reported are encouraging. It is to be expected that the IAR scale has better success in predicting achievement behavior than the I-E scale, inasmuch as all the test items on the IAR scale pertain to beliefs about achievement activities. These relationships perhaps would be enhanced if success and failure ascriptions as well as those of ability and effort were separated in the data analyses.

Ability versus Effort as Perceived Causes of Behavior. The distinction between causal ascription to ability versus effort captured in the IAR

DIAGRAM 5:4
Perceived Determinants of Action, with Power
Grouped Either with Personal
Forces or with "Can"

Personal Forces
$\wedge$
Outcome = f(trying, power, effective environment)
$\vee$
Can

scale was first clearly articulated by Heider (1958). Recall Heider's postulation that the outcome of an action is a function of the effective personal force, and the effective environmental force:

outcome = f(effective personal force, effective environmental force)

The effective personal force, in turn, is allocated to two factors: power and motivation. Power often refers to ability, although other relatively stable personal attributes (strength, or any trait) also determine power. Motivation refers to the direction of a person's behavior (intention) and to how hard he is trying (exertion). Thus:

outcome = f(trying, power, effective environment)

Heider believes that trying and power are related multiplicatively. Neither ability without exertion, nor exertion without ability, are able to overcome environmental obstacles. If either of the two factors has a strength of zero, the effective personal force also is zero.

Heider (1958, p. 84) regroups the three perceived determinants of action so that power and motivation are separated (see Diagram 5:4). Diagram 5:4 indicates that the relation of power to environmental factors determines whether a goal "can" be attained. For example, one's intelligence, in relation to the difficulty of a test, determines if one "can" pass the test. In a similar manner, physical strength, in relation to the width of the lake, wind resistance, and so forth, connotes if one "can" or "cannot" row to the opposite shore. But whether "can" is exhibited in action depends on motivation, or "try." Heider (1958) summarizes:

Relating the roles of "can" and "try" in the action outcome to the effective forces of the person and of the environment, we can state the following: When we say, "He can do it, but fails only because he does not try sufficiently" then we mean that the effective personal force is smaller than the restraining environmental force only because the exertion is not great enough; with greater exertion he would succeed. The concept "can" means that if a person tries to do x, no environmental force away from x is likely to arise that would be greater in its resultant effects than the effective personal force of p toward x [p. 86].

Inasmuch as the effective personal force is determined by both power (ability) and exertion, the greater one's ability, the less the effort needed to overcome environmental obstacles (considered here the difficulty of a task):

$$\text{exertion} = f(\text{difficulty}/\text{power})$$

This means that where different people have the same power, the minimum exertion needed to succeed in a task will vary with the difficulty. It also follows that if the task is held constant, the person who has less power or ability will have to exert himself more to succeed. The greatest exertion will be needed when the person has little power and the task is difficult [Heider, 1958, p. 111].

Simple mathematical transposition also yields:

$$\text{power} = f(\text{difficulty}/\text{exertion})$$

Heider (1958) continues:

Thus, if two people exert themselves to the same degree, the one who solves the more difficult task has greater power. The one who has to exert himself more to solve a task of given difficulty has the lesser power. And the greatest power or ability will be shown by the person who solves a difficult task with little exertion. This, by the way, is the theoretical basis for including timed problems in tests of intelligence. The person who can solve a problem quickly does so with less exertion than the one who takes considerably longer and therefore should be given added credit toward his total intelligence score [p. 111].

Attribution of "Can" to the Person or the Environment. The foregoing discussion reveals that "can" refers to a relation between the person and the environment. *Can* or *cannot* therefore may be relatively ascribed either to the person or to the environment. For example, holding exertion constant, one may ascribe success at a task to high ability or to the ease of the task. In a similar manner, failure can be attributed to a lack of ability or to the difficulty of the task.

In one investigation bearing upon this point, Weiner and Kukla (1970, Exp. VI) gave subjects information concerning the outcome of an achievement task (success or failure). They also included social norm information revealing the percentage of others successfully completing the task (99, 95, 90, 70, 50, 30, 10, 05, 01). The subjects then rated whether the outcome in the 18 conditions (2 levels of outcome $\times$ 9 levels of information) is or is not attributable to the hypothetical person who attempted the task. Ascriptions were indicated on a Likert-type scale anchored at the extremes (outcome due/not due to the person).

The results of this investigation are shown in Figure 5:15. It is evi-

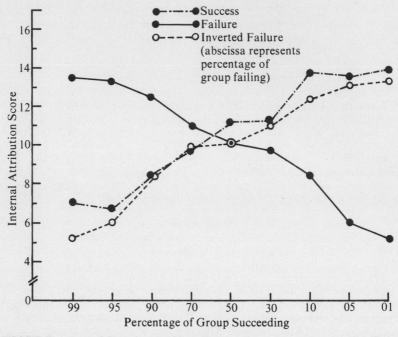

FIGURE 5:15.   Mean internal attribution score for success and failure outcomes as a function of task difficulty (from Weiner & Kukla, 1970, p. 18).

dent that the greater the consistency between outcome and the performance of others, the less the attribution to the person (or the greater the inferred attribution to task difficulty). That is, if one succeeds and so do most others, or fails when most others fail, then the outcomes are ascribed to an easy or hard task, respectively. But if one succeeds when others fail, or fails when others succeed, then the outcomes are attributed to the person. Social norms are therefore one source of information that allows an individual or an observer to determine whether can or cannot is attributable to the person or to the environment.

With characteristic insight, Heider (1958) predicted the findings shown in Figure 5:15. He discussed these relationships in terms of freedom of movement and unit formation.

The unit forming character of attribution is clearly seen in judgments concerning task difficulty. If p is the only person who can do a certain act, or if there are only a few other people who can do it, then the task is difficult and the action belongs in a peculiar way to p. A strong unit between the possibility of success in this action and p is formed. If, however, the task is felt to be so easy that anyone could do it, then the possibility of the action lies in the environment. Speaking topologically, some regions of the individual's space of free movement are common to the spaces of free movement of many people; others have a closer connection to the person [p. 90].

The attribution of can to the person or to the environment is of utmost functional significance. As discussed earlier, if success at a task such as passing a course is ascribed to task ease, then the individual might enroll in other courses given by that teacher, not study for the next exam, and so forth. On the other hand, if success is ascribed to high ability, then he might expect to do well in other courses, raise his level of aspiration, and the like.

The possibility of attributions of can to the person or to the environment may give rise to attributional errors. Errors in ascription were previously discussed in the taxonomy of animal experiments, and in the attributional interpretation of cognitive dissonance phenomena. One "nonmotivated" cause of such errors is the unavailability or misuse of relevant information. For example, one may be unaware that all others who attempt a test fail. Thus, personal failure may be attributed to the self (lack of ability or low effort) rather than to the difficulty of the task. Still other attributional errors may occur when the information is available but is ignored or is misleading (see Kelley, 1967). For example, Kelley notes that during periods of inflation business gains may be ascribed by a businessman to his acumen rather than to the favorable economic circumstances. This error is fostered by the tendency for rewarded responses to be repeated. The repetition of the response-reward sequence provides evidence of their covariation, and results in a self-responsibility causal inference. On the other hand, during a depression it is likely that unfavorable economic conditions are blamed for decreasing profits. Regardless of the individual's actions, business declines. Thus, there is no covariation of response with outcome, and the consequences are apt to be externally ascribed (see discussion of Maier et al., 1969, in this chapter).

Other attributional errors to the self versus the environment may be "motivated," and labeled as ego-defensive or ego-enhancing. These errors, by definition, are displayed when the outcome under question has affective consequences. The vast majority of pertinent research concerning motivated errors are in the area of interperson perception, and will not be discussed in detail here (see Jones & Davis, 1965). For example, Pepitone (1950) led subjects to believe that their ideas about athletics could be instrumental to the attainment of desirable athletic tickets. Three judges (stooges) questioned the subject, and varied in their expressions of approval and apparent power to make the ticket-granting decision. The data revealed that the subjects rated the judges expressing approval of their ideas as more powerful in making the final decision than relatively disapproving judges.

Heider (1958) relates the following example of causal ascription errors in self-perception:

If one person A antagonizes several persons one after the other and there arise difficulties between him and them, then an onlooker observing only the difficulties, will attribute them to A as the constant factor in the situation. However, A himself may be reluctant to put the reason for his negative reception into his own person; that would undermine his self-esteem. So, in order to explain the common attitude, he may come to the conviction that there is a conspiracy among the others, or that one person has contaminated all of them by spreading untrue stories about him. If they all independently came to dislike him, that would leave only himself as the source. In this way the affective significance of the event is seen to markedly influence its causal determination [p. 171].

Figure 5:15 reveals what might also be labeled a "motivated" attributional error. The figure shows that success is more likely to be ascribed to the person than is failure. This occurs even though the judgments made in the Weiner and Kukla study (1970, Experiment VI) did not refer to the respondent. What might be called ego-enhancing patterns of attribution may generalize to the perceptions of others. Differential attributions of success and failure to the self rather than to the environment, and to ability rather than to effort, are the basis of the attributional theory of achievement behavior that follows in Chapter VI.

AN ATTRIBUTIONAL MODEL OF ACTION

Two distinct approaches manipulating intervening cognitions of causal ascription have yielded systematic results. One research paradigm links causal ascription to affective expression (Nisbett & Schachter, 1966; Schachter & Singer, 1962; Valins, 1966). The second paradigm relates causal attribution to expectancy of success (Phares, 1957; Rotter et al., 1961). A general attributional model of action therefore must incorporate the influence of causal ascription on both affect and expectancy. It is postulated that the model assume the following form:

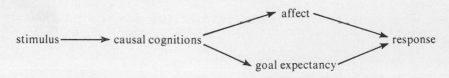

The model indicates that a stimulus arouses cognitions about the causes of a behavioral outcome. The cognitions determine affective responses and goal expectancies (see again Diagram 5:1) as well as subsequent behaviors.

The mediating ascriptions in the above cognitive model of motivation are both predictive and postdictive (see Diagram 5:5). Within achievement-related contexts, for example, a task stimulus gives rise to anticipations concerning the causal determinants of success and failure. If a task is perceived as completely decided by chance, then luck is inferred as the only causal determinant. On the other hand, in situations believed to be skill-determined, power, motivation, and task difficulty may be included among the determinants of outcome. The calculation of "can," in conjunction with expectations about effort and luck, determines the expectancy of success at the task, as well as influencing affective anticipations. The affective anticipations need not positively covary with beliefs about success. Indeed, Atkinson has argued that within achievement-related context these variables are inversely related.

After the instrumental action is completed, the outcome of the behavior is evaluated as a success or a failure (in the "purest" achievement case). The processing of the outcome information results in a reconsideration (postdiction) of the causal determinants. Postdiction must occur, for it has been shown that outcome information significantly affects the perceived causes of success and failure (Crandall et al., 1965; Weiner & Kukla, 1970). Thus, the Task Evaluation Stage relates to perceived

DIAGRAM 5:5
Cognitive and Behavioral Sequence Depicted in an
Attributional Model of Motivation

Stage 1. Task Evaluation

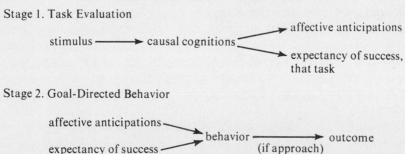

Stage 2. Goal-Directed Behavior

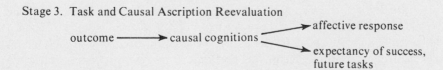

Stage 3. Task and Causal Ascription Reevaluation

control ("Am I in power?"), while the Task Reevaluation Stage relates to perceived causality ("Why did it happen?") (see Fontaine, 1972).

Diagram 5:5 shows that the Task Evaluation Stage influences the behavior toward the particular task initiating the causal cognitions. Note that this is quite similar to the earlier conceptualizations of achievement-related behavior. That is, behavior is a function of P_s and the incentive value (affective anticipation) associated with the goal object. Thus, Diagram 5:5 portrays an Expectancy $\times$ Value model. The Task and Causal Ascription Reevaluation Stage influences behavior toward future tasks. Both the affective response (pride or shame, for instance) and the goal expectancy determine subsequent behavior. It is later argued that incentive (affective) effects and reinforcement (expectancy) effects are conceptually and operationally distinct, and need not positively covary (see Chapter II for a discussion of the reinforcement-incentive confounding in drive theory).

SUMMARY

This chapter was preceded by a review of the Drive $\times$ Habit mechanistic (associationistic) conception of behavior, and by reviews of Lewin's field theory and Atkinson's achievement motivation theory. In the latter two conceptions of behavior cognitive processes are represented in the experiential or learning variables in the models. In this chapter other cognitive approaches to motivation are presented in which cognitive processes have functions other than the acquisition of knowledge.

Psychoanalytic theory, particularly ego psychology, is included among these cognitive approaches because cognitive controls (ego processes) are posited to influence the processing and retention of information (Rapaport, Klein). These mental functions intervene, or mediate, between incoming stimuli and the final behavioral response and they determine, in part, the defense mechanisms used to cope with affective stimulation. Defense mechanisms or coping processes, have been manipulated in experimental situations (Lazarus), and influence affective reactions to stressful stimuli through a postulated process of reappraisal. Finally, theories of balance also represent cognitive approaches to motivation. Dissonance theory (Festinger) has been especially heuristic, and has generated research demonstrating the cognitive control of biological need states (Brehm) and fear and pain. In contrast to Hullian theory, these studies indicate that motivation is a function of an individual's beliefs about his need states.

Attribution theory, also presented in this chapter, is yet another cognitive approach to motivation. Attribution theorists have particularly considered why an event occurs, or the allocation of responsibility for an action. Heider, the founder of this theoretical framework, distinguishes between internal and external determinants of causations. Among the internal causes of behavior, power (ability) and motivation are contrasted. Causal ascriptions to internal or to external factors differentially influence affective reactions (Schachter & Singer, Nisbett & Schachter, Valins), and attributions to ability (internal) versus luck (external) sources differentially influence the subsequent expectancy of goal attainment (Rotter). A general motivational model was proposed in which causal cognitions influence affective anticipations and goal expectancies. Further, following the behavioral action a reappraisal process occurs that determines affective reactions and subsequent goal expectancies.

VI

Achievement Motivation and Attribution Theory

The general attributional model of action presented at the end of Chapter V, Diagram 5:5 is now incorporated within the context of achievement-related actions. First, the perceived causes of success and failure are delineated and a classification scheme of these causal determinants is outlined. Then the antecedent stimulus conditions (information) that give rise to various causal interpretations are outlined. Finally, the effects of causal beliefs on affective responses, future expectations, and subsequent achievement-related behavior are discussed. This leads to a reanalysis of Atkinson's theory of achievement motivation, and a reinterpretation of data cited in support of that conception.

THE PERCEIVED CAUSES OF SUCCESS AND FAILURE

Following Heider, it is postulated that there are four perceived causes of success and failure at achievement tasks: ability (power), effort, task difficulty, and luck. This is not an exhaustive list. Surely individuals often assign causality to sources not readily classifiable within these four categories. For example, failure might be attributed to fatigue (which is distinguished from effort expenditure), bias (which is distinguished from task difficulty), misread instructions (which is distinguished from bad luck), and so forth. It is contended, however, that the four causal elements listed above generalize to all achievement tasks, and account for the major sources of variance when considering the perceived causes of success and failure (see Weiner, Frieze, Kukla, Reed, Rest, & Rosenbaum, 1971).

The more specific attributional model for achievement behavior is shown in Diagram 6:1. In the Task Evaluation Stage, the perception of an achievement-related task evokes attributions concerning the potential causes of success and failure. This causal analysis, in turn, determines the future expectancy (P_s) of success or failure, as well as affective anticipations (hope of success and fear of failure). The affective anticipations or anticipatory emotions and the goal expectancies result in approach or avoidance behavior, and success or failure (Stage 2). Then, in Stage 3, the causal attributions are reevaluated as a function of the achievement out-

DIAGRAM 6:1
Cognitive and Behavioral Sequence in an Attributional
Model of Achievement Behavior

Stage 1. Task Evaluation

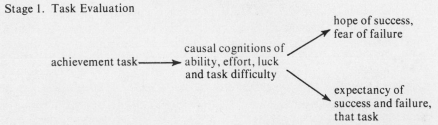

Stage 2. Goal-Directed Behavior

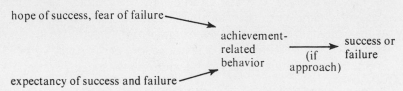

Stage 3. Task and Ascription Reevaluation

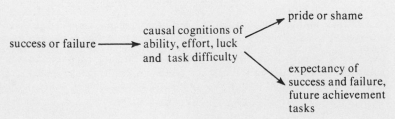

TABLE 6:1
Classification Scheme for the Perceived
Determinants of Achievement Behavior

Stability	Locus of Control	
	Internal	*External*
Stable	Ability	Task difficulty
Unstable	Effort	Luck

come and new information gained as a result of commerce with the task. The attributions in part determine the achievement-related affects (pride or shame) produced by attainment or nonattainment of the goal, as well as future expectancies of success at this and similar tasks.

A Classification Scheme of the Causal Determinants

The four perceived causes of success and failure (ability, effort, task difficulty, and luck) can be comprised within two causal dimensions: locus of control (internal or external) and stability (fixed or variable). Table 6:1 shows that, within the control dimension, ability and effort are classified as internal determinants of action, or, as Heider states, personal forces. Task difficulty and luck are classified as external determinants of success and failure.

Considering the dimension of stability, it is postulated that one's perception of his general ability, as well as his beliefs about specific ability after sufficient commerce with an activity, are relatively invariant (stable) over time. Similarly, task difficulty is conceptualized as an unchanging (stable) factor. Effort and luck, on the other hand, are assumed to be variable (unstable) factors. Exertion may increase or decrease from moment to moment or from one task to another, just as luck may be good at one time and poor at another. Summarizing Table 6:1, it is postulated that ability is an internal, fixed factor; effort an internal, variable factor; task difficulty an external, fixed factor; and luck. an external, variable factor.[1]

The locus of control and stability dimensions of causality have been confounded in prior experimental studies. For example, Rotter and his

[1] Some shortcomings of the classification scheme are immediately evident. For example, individuals may perceive themselves as either diligent or lucky. Thus, the unstable factors of effort and luck may be included among stable determinants. Also, the model does not sufficiently distinguish general from specific ability. And systematic change processes, such as gaining of skill with commerce at a task (learning), are not incorporated. These are among the problems that must be considered in future theoretical developments.

colleagues have demonstrated that expectancy shifts are more frequent, and of greater magnitude, in skill than in chance situations. They equate skill with ability and internal control, and chance with external control. But comparisons of the behavioral effects of ability (Quadrant I, Table 6:1) with luck (Quadrant IV) confound the locus of control and stability dimensions. Ability is both internal and stable, and luck is both external and variable. It is reasonable to predict, for example, that attribution of an achievement outcome to task difficulty, an external causal element, produces expectancy shifts of equal frequency and magnitude as attribution to ability, an internal element. On the other hand, attribution of an achievement outcome to ability might well result in differential expectancy shifts than attribution to effort, although both are conceived as internal factors. Whether expectancy changes are to be linked with the stability or the control dimension is impossible to determine, given the theoretical analyses and experimental comparisons of Rotter and his associates.

In a similar manner, affective expression may be a function of the control or stability dimension. Further, in situations in which expectancy shifts are identical, affective responses might be quite disparate. For example, failure at a task perceived as difficult should result in less negative affect (shame) than failure perceived as due to low ability, although both attributions may be followed by similar decrements in the expectancy of future success. Inasmuch as both expectancy and affect determine immediate and future behaviors, the causal dimensions of stability and locus of control must be considered a constellation. Each of the four causal elements are located along two axes; often it is not meaningful to consider one of the dimensions and not the other.

Antecedent Conditions

The perception of an achievement task is assumed to redintegrate past experience with the task, and an array of other pertinent information. This knowledge allows the calculation of inferences about the causal determinants of the outcome, as well as the expectancies of success and failure.

Ability Inferences.   It is postulated that general ability is inferred from the number, percentage, and pattern of success experiences at prior achievement activities, considered in conjunction with the perceived difficulty of the attempted tasks. Thus, if a task is perceived as reflecting a general level of ability, then immediate success or failure at the task is not likely to significantly alter one's perception of ability. This outcome is merely one more bit of evidence in the entire life history of the organism—all of which is used to infer ability level.

On the other hand, the number, percentage, and pattern of immediate performance at the particular task confronting the individual, and tasks similar to it, should be heavily weighted in reaching inferences about specific task ability. This is particularly true if the task is rather unusual and the individual has had little commerce with such tasks. For example, Weiner and Kukla (1970) had subjects determine whether a 0 or a 1 was the next number in a digit series. Unknown to the subjects, the numbers were arranged randomly and the outcome was entirely a matter of good or bad luck. Following fifty trials at the task with continuous performance feedback, the subjects rated the extent to which their outcome was a function of task ability. Weiner and Kukla (1970) and later Kukla (1970) report that correlations between perceived ability and either objective or subjective performance approximate $r = .45$. These results are included in Tables 6:5 and 6:6 (see also Jones et al., 1968).

Investigations of person perception have demonstrated that the pattern as well as the level of immediate performance is an important cue for ability inferences. In a study by Beckman (1970), student teachers conveyed new math to two grade-school pupils. The children allegedly were sitting behind a one-way mirror, watching the teacher as she presented the material. The teacher, however, was unable to view the children. At the end of each of four teaching periods the children supposedly completed a short exam, which was graded by the teacher. There were, in fact, no pupil participants, and Beckman manipulated the exam information to the teachers. The effects of level and pattern of performance feedback on teacher attributions for success and failure were then examined.

Four experimental conditions varied in the level or pattern of pupil performance. Exam feedback concerning one of the two pupils was high over the four exam periods (H–H condition). The performance of the second pupil either ascended from low to high (L–H), descended from high to low (H–L), or remained constantly low (L–L). Following the completion of the last exam the teachers were questioned concerning the causes of the pupils' behaviors. In addition to the participating teachers, a group of "observers," not directly participating in the teaching interaction, were given the same pattern of feedback information received by the teachers and were asked similar causal questions.

The attributional data revealed that both teacher and observer ability inferences vary directly with total performance score. H–H students are judged as having the highest ability, L–L pupils are perceived as least competent, and the inferred ability of the pupils in the H–L and L–H conditions falls between these extremes. These results are really not very surprising; outcomes indicate what an individual "can" do. (See Jones et al., 1968, Experiment I, for a similar finding.)

The data concerning ability judgments in the ascending and descending conditions in Beckman's study also are of interest. The overall performance of pupils in these conditions are identical. Yet the H–L pupils are rated as higher in ability than the L–H pupils by the "uninvolved" observers (although the judgment did not characterize the participating teachers).

Heider's analysis of action provides a reasonable explanation for the differential ability judgments in the H–L and L–H conditions. If the performance outcome is successful, then the individual, by definition, "can" perform the task. Thus, subsequent performance decrements are likely to be perceived due to unstable factors, such as the amount of effort expended. Phenomenologically, H–L pupils perhaps "can" perform as well as the H–H pupils. This is not true, however, for the students in the L–H condition. The later appearance of "can" indicates that they have less ability than pupils in the H–L condition.

A series of experiments by Jones et al. (1968) yields clearer conclusions regarding the effects of pattern of performance on ability inferences than the study by Beckman. In the studies reported by Jones et al. (Exps. I–V) a subject competes against, or merely observes, the performance of a second (stooge) subject. Experimental conditions are created by varying the pattern of performance of the stooge. In one condition there is an ascending pattern of success, in a second condition a descending pattern, and in a third condition the successes are randomly dispersed. The overall performance levels in the three experimental conditions are identical, with correct solutions attained on 15 of the 30 experimental trials. When competing against the stooge rather than merely observing him, the subject receives success feedback on 10 trials. Figure 6:1 shows the patterns of

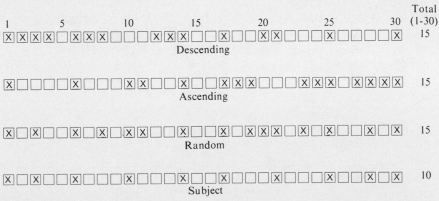

FIGURE 6:1. Feedback patterns employed. Each box indicates a trial and each "X" a success (from Jones, Rock, Shaver, Goethals, & Ward, 1968, p. 321).

success for the stooge in the three experimental conditions and for the subject.

The subjects then are asked to predict the trial-by-trial performance of the stooge over the next series of 30 trials. On the second series feedback is not given. The subjects also rate the intelligence of the stooge, and are asked to recall how many problems the stooge correctly solved on the initial 30-trial series. Jones et al. (1968) consistently find that in this situation the performers in the H–L condition are expected to solve more problems, are rated as more intelligent, and are believed to have solved more problems on the prior series, than the stooges in the ascending or random conditions. Table 6:2 includes the data for the expectancy, intelligence, and recall variables in five experiments conducted by Jones et al. (1968).

Jones et al. therefore conclude that judgments of ability are strongly affected by order of information. Early information influences impression formation more than later information does. This "primacy effect" in im-

TABLE 6:2
Summary of Major Ability Attribution Data: Experiments I–V
(from Jones et al., 1968, p. 335)

Experiment	Prediction Summary[a]	Intelligence	Recall[b]
I			
D	20.2]**]***	7.0	17.8]*
A	17.2]	7.4	15.2]
R	16.4]	7.2	16.9
II			
D	18.7]**]***	7.5]**]*	16.8]**]*
A	15.8]	6.4]	14.7]
R	16.0]	6.8]	14.8]
III			
D	17.3	8.6]**	16.7]***]***
A	16.7	7.6]	14.0]
R	16.9	8.4]**	13.7]
IV			
D	18.1	7.7]**	20.6]***]***
A	17.4	5.6]	12.5]
R	18.4	6.7	14.6
V			
D	17.6]*	7.3]***	16.8]***
A	16.6]	6.5]	13.0]

Note: Abbreviations: D = descending, A = ascending, R = random.
[a] No. of expected right answers.
[b] No. of correct solutions recollected on first 30 trials.
  * $p < .05$.
 ** $p < .01$.
*** $p < .001$.

pression formation also has been extensively reported in judgments of personality traits (see Jones & Goethals, 1971). One conceivable explanation of the primacy effect in the competitive situation is that the high initial performance of the stooge in the H–L condition results in the cessation of social comparison by the subject. Hence, later performance information may not be processed, and this may result in overestimation of expectancy, errors in recall, and the like.

However, the parallel findings in the competitive and noncompetitive conditions led Jones et al. to suggest a "nonmotivated" explanation of the data. The authors reason that early success produces a greater mean expectancy of success over all trials than late success. Consider, for example, a task with three problems. Individual A solves Task 1 but not Task 2, while Individual B solves Task 2 but not Task 1. Further, assume that the expectancy of success on any trial is a function of the number of success trials/total trials. Thus, the probability of success on Task 2 for Individual A is $1/1$, or 1, while the probability of success for Individual A on Task 3 is $1/2$, or .50. Excluding the unknown probability on Trial 1, the mean expectancy of success over the tasks for Individual A is .75, or $(1 + .50)/2$. For Individual B the probability of success is 0 on Task 2, $(0/1)$ and .50 on Task 3, $(1/2)$. Thus, his mean expectancy of success is .25. In sum, although both performers have the identical mean performance level, Individual A, with the earlier success, is associated with a higher mean expectancy of success on Task 3 than Individual B. Jones et al. suggest that this method of information processing and calculation of expectancies may be responsible for the observed primacy effect in ability judgments.

An unpublished study by Rosenbaum demonstrates still another performance cue for ability inferences. Rosenbaum compared the judged ability of two hypothetical individuals varying in their maximal performance scores. The performance information (percentage of correct responses at an unspecified problem) over a series of three trials was specified as 60 percent, 80 percent, 60 percent for one of the to-be-judged individuals, and 70 percent, 60 percent, 70 percent for the other. Thus, the mean performance scores in the two conditions were identical. However, subjects judged ability greater in the former condition, where the maximal performance score is higher. This finding is in accord with common sense and intuitive judgments. For example, if we observe a mental patient performing a complex task on only one occasion, we assume this performance indicates his true level of ability. Nonperformance on subsequent occasions is attributed to other factors, such as his emotional state.

Summarizing the studies presented above, it has been demonstrated that the number (percentage) and pattern of success, and maximal performance are cues for ability inferences. High ability is inferred from repeated success, early success, and a performance peak.

Task Difficulty.   Subjective task difficulty is postulated to be a function of the perceived performance of others at the task. If many others succeed, then the task is "easy"; if few succeed, then it is "difficult." Attribution of *can* to the person rather than to the environment is determined primarily by ability cues considered in conjunction with social consensus (task difficulty) information. If an individual consistently succeeds at a task while others fail, then his successes are self-attributed. On the other hand, repeated success when others also succeed is attributed to the task, rather than to the individual (see Figure 5:15).

It is likely that objective characteristics of the task, such as length, complexity, and novelty, also influence initial judgments of task difficulty. But this information receives relatively little weight in relation to outcome data. If everyone correctly performs a task, then it is of little importance that it "appears" to be difficult. Perhaps task characteristics are most important in judgments of outcomes at clearly difficult activities, for the assumption is made that "ordinary" individuals could not perform the task. For example, failure in climbing a high mountain is likely to be attributed by observers to task difficulty, even though most individuals actually attempting the task succeed. It is quite possible, however, that a climber who fails will attribute the outcome to himself, judging difficulty not on the basis of task characteristics, or norms over the whole population, but rather on the basis of performance of others in his reference group. In general, the difficult problem of the dependence of task difficulty inferences on reference groups is not tackled in this chapter.

Luck.   In psychological experiments luck ascriptions are usually induced by specific instructions; subjects merely are informed that the outcome at a task is entirely due to chance (for example, Phares, 1957). But generally, the most salient cue for luck attributions is the structure of a task. Flipping a coin, drawing a playing card from a shuffled deck, or guessing where the ball will drop in a roulette wheel logically result in luck ascriptions for success and failure. The more valid information for luck ascriptions, however, are the patterns of outcomes. Independence and randomness of outcomes indicate that luck is the causal determinant. If a coin repeatedly turns up heads, or a card player consistently draws an ace, then luck will no longer be perceived as the sole causal outcome determinant despite the task structure.

Individuals overestimate the expected fluctuations in random patterns, and interesting attributional errors may result from the evident fact that the pattern of outcome at times supercedes task structure in determining luck attributions. Observers may incorrectly infer that a task is not solely determined by chance on the basis of the perceived repetitions in the data. In addition, the belief is prevalent that pure chance tasks have a personal causal component (witness roulette or slot-machine players).

Unique events also give rise to luck attributions. For example, finding money on the street or experiencing failure after a series of successes often results in attributions to luck. If the event repeatedly recurs, however, that ascription is likely to be altered.

Effort. It might be anticipated that one "knows" how hard he has tried, and that proprioceptive feedback or introspective knowledge provides sufficient information to reach conclusions about effort expenditure. But this is not the case. For example, there is clear experimental evidence that individuals use performance (outcome) information to infer how hard they tried. The Weiner and Kukla (1970, Exp. V) and Kukla (1970) experiments discussed under "Ability inferences" are pertinent here. Subjects in those experiments anticipated whether 0 or 1 was going to be the next digit in a number series that was actually random. The subjects then rated their effort expenditure. It was found that successful individuals perceive that they tried harder than unsuccessful individuals, even though outcome is entirely a matter of chance. There is little reason to believe that lucky guessers in fact expend more energy than the unlucky guessers. A similar finding is reported by Jenkins and Ward (1965). It is likely that in one's life history effort and outcome covary. Therefore, given a positive outcome one infers the presence of effort, while given a negative outcome one infers the absence of effort. It is believed that in the Weiner and Kukla and Kukla experiments a logically derived attributional inference results in an incorrect causal ascription.

Pattern of performance also is a cue for effort attributions. In an experiment reported by Jones et al. (1968, Exp. VI), subjects receive ascending, descending, or random patterns of success. Although these outcome patterns do not influence *self-perception of ability,* they do systematically influence self-perception of effort expenditure. Subjects in the ascending condition believe that they tried significantly harder than subjects in the other conditions. Again it is to be remembered that the outcome is entirely under the experimental control, and is independent of actual effort.

It is reasonable to contend that in the experiments of Jones et al., Kukla, Jenkins and Ward, and Weiner and Kukla, success induces subjects to try harder (although this is not consistent with the literature concerning the behavior of high-achieving individuals). If so, then effort actually is covarying with outcome, and the conclusion that effort causes success is

TABLE 6:3

Cues Utilized for Inferences Concerning the Causes of Success and Failure

Causal Elements	Cues
Ability	Number of successes, percentage of successes, pattern of success, maximal performance, task difficulty.
Task difficulty	Objective task characteristics, social norms.
Luck	Objective task characteristics, independence of outcomes, randomness of outcomes (pattern of performance), uniqueness of event.
Effort	Outcome, pattern of performance, perceived muscular tension, sweating, persistance at the task, covariation of performance with incentive value of the goal, task difficulty.

logical; that is, there is an apparent covariation between antecedents and consequences. Indeed, this supposition is as reasonable as the causal inferences of "superstitious" rats, who believe that their responses "cause" the outcome (see Chapter V). In studies of other-perception, however, there is some evidence that performance decrements over trials are ascribed to a lack of effort (Beckman, 1970). It seems that the order of information per se, and the logic concerning the relationships between can, try, and outcome, determine effort inferences, rather than the effects of outcome on actual effort expenditure.

It also is probable that external manifestations of effort, such as muscular tension, sweating, persistence of behavior, and the like, result in effort attributions. In addition, perhaps covariation of performance with the incentive value of the goal will result in causal ascriptions to effort. In general, it is contended that if a task is perceived as skill determined, and the environment is constant, then variation in performance is likely to be ascribed to motivation.

Summary. A number of cues are employed to reach inferences concerning the causes of success and failure. The list in Table 6:3 is by no means definitive. But these cues are expected to have salience in achievement contexts, and to generalize across most achievement tasks.

Empirical Investigations of Cue Utilization in Achievement Contexts

Frieze and Weiner (1971) examined some of the rules of information utilization and combination in forming judgments about the causes of success and failure. In one reported experiment, subjects were given cues relevant to inferences about another's ability (percentage of success on prior trials at this task: 100 percent, 50 percent, or 0 percent; and percentage of success on prior trials at similar tasks: 100 percent, 50 percent, or 0 percent). They also were provided with a cue used to infer task difficulty (percentage of others successful at the task: 100 percent, 50 percent, or 0 percent). In addition, the subjects were informed that the individual who was to be judged attempted the task again and either succeeded or failed. The subjects then ascribed the immediate success or failure to ability, effort, task difficulty, or luck. The four causal elements were assigned a value of 0–3 points on each of the 54 judgments (3 levels of past performance, same task × 3 levels of past performance, similar task × 3 levels of social norms × 2 levels of outcome). For example, the subjects were informed that an individual who succeeded on 100 percent of past trials at the same task, and 50 percent of past trials at similar tasks, attempted the task again and succeeded. Further, they were informed that 0 percent of other individuals were able to succeed at the task. The subjects then ascribed the causes of the immediate success to the four specified factors. The cues of past performance and social consensus were selected for manipulation because they are specified by Kelley (1967) as important information in allocating causation to the self or the environment.

The data reveal that all of the information was used to reach causal judgments. Considering first the cue of prior performance at the task, it was found that consistency of the present outcome with prior performance results in attributions to ability or task difficulty, while discrepancies between past and present performance result in ascriptions to luck and effort (see Figure 6:2). For example, if the individual always failed in the past, and failed again, the cause was the difficulty of the task or the lack of ability of the person, or both. But if repeated failure is followed by a success, then the success is ascribed to good luck or extra effort. These findings are in accord with the postulation of ability and task difficulty as fixed or stable factors, and effort and luck as variable or unstable factors. Thus, when immediate and past performance are consistent, attributions are to the two fixed factors; when immediate and past performance are inconsistent, attributions are to the two unstable factors. Parallel findings are reported by Frieze and Weiner (1971) when the information pertains to performance on similar tasks, although the statistical significance of the results is reduced.

The data also reveal systematic usage of the task difficulty cue. Inconsistency between the immediate outcome and the performance of others results in ascriptions to ability and effort, while consistency between immediate outcome and the performance of others gives rise to task difficulty attributions (see Figure 6:3). That is, if one succeeds and so do all others, or fails while all others fail, then ascriptions of the cause of the outcome

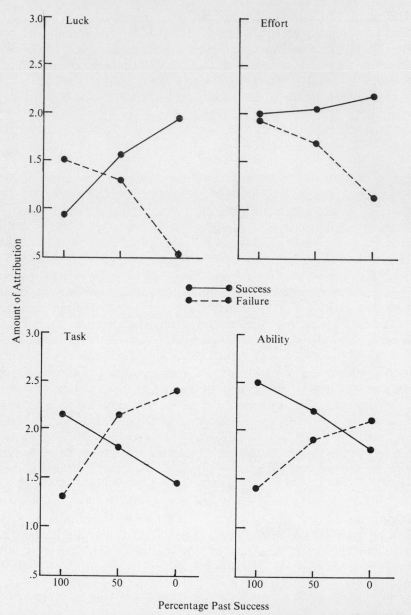

FIGURE 6:2. Attributions to ability, effort, task difficulty, and luck as a function of the consistency of the immediate outcome with past performance at the task (adapted from Frieze & Weiner, 1971).

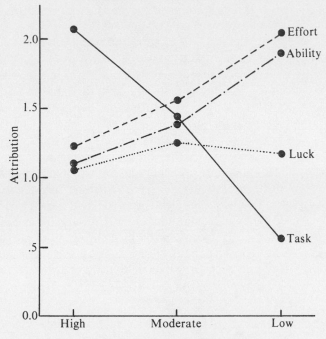

FIGURE 6:3. Attributions to ability, effort, task difficulty, and luck as a function of the consistency of immediate outcome at the task with the performance of others (social consensus) (from Frieze & Weiner, 1971, p. 594).

are respectively to an easy or hard task (external). But if one fails while others succeed, or vice versa, the implication is that the individual is responsible. Either he has (lacks) ability, or has (has not) tried hard enough (see also Figure 5:15).

Considering next outcome information, the data reveal that success tends to be attributed to internal factors (effort and ability) while failure is ascribed to the difficulty of the task (see Figure 6:4). These findings correspond to data reported by Weiner and Kukla (1970, Experiment VI, Figure 5:15), and indicate either the generality of "ego-enhancing" and "ego-defensive" attributional tendencies or a systematic information-processing error in usage of outcome information.

There also are complex interactions among the cue variables, and great usage of configural patterns. The reader is directed to Frieze and Weiner (1971) for detailed discussion of these data.

A second experiment reported by Frieze and Weiner (1971) yields similar conclusions when less extreme percentage values of the cues (80 percent and 20 percent, rather than 100 percent, 50 percent, or 0 percent) are used. Further, in this second experiment two new cues were introduced: time spent at the task and task characteristics of luck or skill. In addition, responses of each subject were separately examined with analysis of variance techniques. The individual data analysis shows great individual differences in both the amount of information used and the manner in which information from the disparate cues is combined. Table 6:4 illustrates the contrasting usage of information and judgment strategy by two of the subjects. The table shows that Subject A uses all of the available information, and that the cues are differentially employed to make inferences about the different causal categories. Outcome information is used to determine luck attributions, percentage of past success provides information about task difficulty, social consensus is used to infer ability level, and so forth. In addition, Subject *A* exhibits great usage of cue configurations. Subject *B*, on the other hand, bases ability, effort, and luck ascriptions on the type of task (luck versus skill). Type of task also is a factor

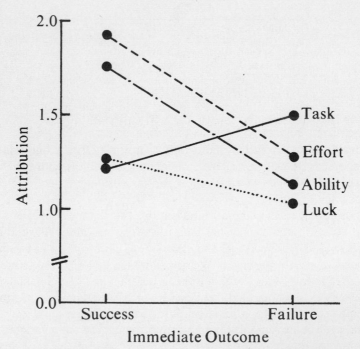

FIGURE 6:4. Attributions to ability, effort, task difficulty, and luck as a function of success or failure at the task (from Frieze & Weiner, 1971, p. 596).

TABLE 6:4

Cues Used by Two Individual Subjects (from Frieze & Weiner, 1971, p. 602)

Cue	Ability	Effort	Luck	Task
Outcome (O)			A	
Percentage Past Successes (P)	A			A
Percentage Successful Others (Sc)	A			B
Amount of time Spent (T)		A	B	
Type of Task (J)	B	B	AB	
OP			A	
OSc		A		
OT			A	
PT				A
ScT				B
TJ			B	
OTJ	A			
OPJ			A	
PTJ		A		
PSJ		B		
PScTJ	A	B		

Note: A = Term significant for Subject A, B = Term significant for Subject B.

in three of his four configural patterns. Subject B, for the most part, ignores information provided by outcome and the percentage of prior success at the task.

In sum, individuals are able to use a variety of cues in a systematic manner to infer the causes of success and failure. In addition, given the identical information, there are wide individual differences in informational usage and causal judgments. It is contended in the following sections of this chapter that individual differences in achievement needs are associated with differential probabilities of ascription to the four causal elements. Divergent achievement-related actions are, in part, a consequence of disparate attributional dispositions.

ACHIEVEMENT NEEDS AND CAUSAL ASCRIPTION

It was previously indicated that attempts to relate need for achievement to locus of control, as assessed by the Rotter I-E scale, have been generally unsuccessful. However, the I-E scale is made up of predominantly non-achievement-related items, and does not distinguish between success and failure outcomes or ability and effort ascriptions. In addition, the possibility that achievement needs are related to the stability of the attribution, rather than, or in addition to, locus of control, has not been considered in past investigations. A number of investigations that take into account the success-failure, ability-effort, and stability-locus of control distinctions reveal that individuals differing in achievement needs have contrasting attributional dispositions.

Weiner and Kukla (1970, Exp. IV) report significant relationships between locus of control and achievement needs when success and failure outcomes are distinguished. The IAR scale devised by the Crandalls and their colleagues, as well as measures of resultant achievement motivation, were administered to grammar and high school students. The data for the male subjects only, classified according to level and achievement needs and grade in school, are shown in Figure 6:5. The data indicate that overall grade levels male pupils high in resultant achievement needs are more likely to ascribe success to themselves than males low in resultant achievement needs. These attributional differences reach statistical significance in all three age groups beyond the fourth-grade level.

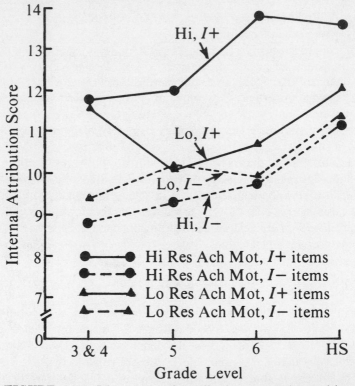

FIGURE 6:5. Mean internal attribution scores for positive ($I+$) and negative ($I-$) outcome items on the Internal Achievement Responsibility scale, with subjects classified according to resultant achievement motivation and grade level (from Weiner & Kukla, 1970, p. 14).

Unfortunately, ability and effort ascriptions are not differentiated in this study. Thus, it can only be concluded that males high in achievement concerns are more likely to attribute success to high ability and/or high effort (internal factors) than individuals low in achievement needs. Figure 6:5 also shows that males low in achievement needs exhibit greater attributions to internal factors in situations of failure than males high in achievement needs. However, these differences approach significance only among the fifth-grade sample. Finally, Figure 6:5 reveals that males high in achievement needs employ differential causal ascriptions for success and failure, while outcome is not as salient a causal cue for subjects in the low motive group. None of the differences between males high and low in achievement motivation approach significance among the female sample.

A subsequent correlational study by Weiner and Potepan (1970) separated the relationship between achievement needs and attributions to ability as opposed to effort in situations of success and failure. A modified version of the IAR scale appropriate to a college population and a measure of resultant achievement motivation were administered to 107 male and female college students. The correlations between resultant achievement motivation and the attributional elements are shown in Table 5:6. The table indicates that achievement concerns are positively related to ascription of success to ability $(A+)$ $(r = .35)$, and positively related to ascription of success to effort $(M+)$ $(r = .12)$. On the other hand, achievement-related motives are negatively related to attribution of failure to low ability $(A-)$ $(r = -.33)$, but positively related to attribution of failure to a lack of effort $(M-)$ $(r = .08)$.

Summarizing the data in Table 5:6, individuals high in resultant achievement needs attribute success to the presence of effort and failure to the absence of effort. On the other hand, individuals low in achievement needs, relative to subjects in the high motive group, do not perceive effort as an important determinant of outcome. Concerning ability, individuals high in resultant achievement motivation ascribe success to high ability, while those low in achievement concerns ascribe failure to lack of ability. In general, individuals high in achievement motivation persistently attribute relatively high ability to themselves, while those low in achievement needs perceive themselves as relatively low in ability. Weiner and Potepan (1970) find these relationships among both male and female subjects.

An experiment reported by Weiner and Kukla (1970, Experiment V) further elucidates and generally substantiates the relationships discussed above, although some contradictory data also were found. Recall that in this study subjects were asked to judge whether 0 or 1 is the next digit in a number series. After each trial the subjects were told the correct solution and graded their answer right or wrong. The numbers were arranged randomly, but subjects believe that there are patterns in the data and that they can learn to anticipate the digits correctly.

Following 50 trials the subjects added up their scores, then estimated (1) how many points of that total were due to "skill rather than lucky guessing" and (2) how hard they tried to succeed. Perceived effort expenditure was indicated on a Likert-type scale anchored at the extremes ("I did not try at all"—"I tried as hard as I possibly could"). For scoring purposes the scale was subdivided into ten equal intervals.

The male subjects were divided at the median into level of resultant achievement motivation, and classified into success, intermediate, or failure "conditions" on the basis of their total number of correct responses. The number of self-assigned skill points and perceived effort are given in Table 6:5. The table shows that given success, individuals high in resultant achievement motivation attribute more of their total points to skill and believe they tried harder than subjects in the low motive group. That is, they attribute success to internal determinants. Given failure, on the other hand, the individuals high in achievement concerns believe that they tried less hard, and assign themselves fewer skill points, than subjects in the low motive group.

Thus, three of the four relationships reported in prior studies are replicated, while one finding is a reversal of prior data. The replicated findings include the attribution of success to high ability and high effort, and the attribution of failure to low effort, displayed by subjects in the high motive group. But, in contradiction to the prior data, the present results indicate that individuals high in achievement needs relatively ascribe failure to a lack of ability.

This study was conducted again because of the inconsistency of the findings related to ability attributions. In the second experiment (Kukla, 1970), ratings for all four causal determinants of success and failure were obtained following performance evaluation. In addition, the task outcome was defined by subjective success or failure, also inferred from responses on a Likert-type scale, rather than from the objective performance.

TABLE 6:5
Mean Skill Points Assigned and Effort Rating as a Function of Motive
Classification and Performance Outcome
(adapted from Weiner & Kukla, 1970, p. 14)

Performance	Skill Points		Perceived Effort	
	Hi Ach Mot	Lo Ach Mot	Hi Ach Mot	Lo Ach Mot
Success	17.5	11.8	8.2	7.7
Intermediate	10.5	9.5	7.4	6.7
Failure	4.7	8.0	5.3	7.1

TABLE 6:6

Mean Attribution Ratings in the Success and Failure Conditions for Ss Classified
as High (Above the Median) or Low (Below the Median) in Resultant
Achievement Motivation (from Kukla, 1970)

Condi-tion	N	Ability			Effort		Task Difficulty		Luck	
		High	N	Low	High	Low	High	Low	High	Low
Success	37	7.0*	35	6.6	7.1	6.3	5.4	4.8	5.2	5.2
Failure	33	5.9	33	4.9	5.8	6.4	5.0	5.8	4.4	4.4

* High numbers indicate high ability, high effort, a difficult task, and good luck.

The results of this study are given in Table 6:6. Examining only the
ability and effort ascriptions, it can be observed that the subjects high in
resultant achievement motivation, relative to subjects in the low motive
group, attribute success to high ability and effort expenditure. When these
subjects fail, those in the high motive group perceive that they are deficient
in effort, while those in the low motive group ascribe their failure to a
lack of ability.

Kukla (1970) reports that among subjects either high or low in resultant achievement motivation, the correlation between perceived skill and
subjective performance approximates $r = .45$. The motive groups equally
evaluate the effects of ability upon outcome, although they perceive that
they have unequal amounts of ability. Conversely, only individuals in the
high motive group perceive that effort is a determinant of outcome
($r = .45$ between perceived effort and performance outcome). Among
subjects low in resultant achievement motivation, the correlation between
perceived outcome and perceived effort expenditure is $r = .08$.

In sum, the data reported by Kukla (1970) are consistent with the
prior findings. The data of each of the individual experiments reported
above (Kukla, 1970; Weiner & Kukla, 1970, Experiments IV and V;
Weiner & Potepan, 1970) are not definitive. However, the pattern of results over all four studies leads to rather unambiguous conclusions concerning the differential causal ascriptions to ability and effort that are displayed
by the contrasting achievement motive subgroups. Individuals high in
achievement needs, relative to those low in achievement needs, attribute
success to ability and effort, and failure to a lack of effort. Individuals
low in achievement needs, relative to those with high achievement motivation, ascribe failure to a lack of ability, and in general perceive themselves
as low in ability. They also do not differentially employ effort or a perceived
causal factor for success or failure. Still further evidence concerning the
attributional dispositions of individuals differing in achievement motivation
is presented when examining the effects of causal ascriptions and attributional dispositions on achievement-related behaviors.

The antecedent conditions that are attributional cues, including individual differences in achievement-related needs, and an attributional schema, have been outlined. The effects of attributions on affect, expectancy, and behavior are now examined. That is, attention is turned from antecedent conditions and mediating cognitions to behavioral consequences (see Diagram 5:1).

CAUSAL ATTRIBUTION AND AFFECTIVE EXPRESSION

The investigations of Nisbett and Schachter (1966), Ross, Rodin, and Zimbardo (1969), Schachter and Singer (1962), Valins (1966), and others convincingly demonstrate that internal versus external attributions of arousal symptoms markedly influence affective experiences such as euphoria, fear, pain, and the like. It is therefore postulated that, *within achievement-related contexts,* affect is determined primarily by attributions to internal versus external factors. The hypothesized relationships between the achievement-related affects of pride and shame and causal attributions for success and failure are depicted in Figure 6:6. The figure shows that

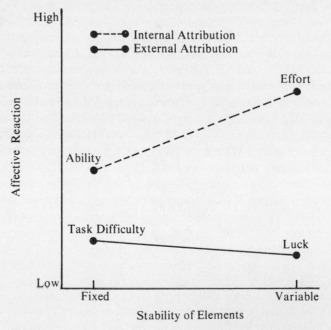

FIGURE 6:6. Hypothesized magnitude of affective reaction to success and failure as a function of causal ascriptions.

affect is maximized when success and failure are attributed to the internal elements of ability and effort. It also is contended that it is of little affective consequence which of the two external elements are perceived as causative agents. Both failure that is perceived as due to a difficult task or bad luck and success that is ascribed to an easy task or good luck produce equally little positive or negative achievement-related affect. It is expected, however, that among the internal elements, causal ascriptions to effort produce greater affective reactions than attribution of success or failure to ability. (Of course, much positive affect is experienced given success at tasks that are completely determined by luck. You would feel very good about winning a lottery. But this emotion differs from the pride experienced for excellence at achievement tasks.)

Inferred Empirical Evidence

Atkinson has contended, and empirical evidence has been gathered to support the position, that the incentive value of success is inversely related to the probability of success (task difficulty): $I_s = 1 - P_s$ (see Figure 4:4). Atkinson further postulates that the incentive value of failure is inversely related to the probability of failure: $I_f = 1 - P_f$. In addition, self-attribution for success and failure are related to task difficulty: self-attribution for success $= 1 - P_s$, and self-attribution for failure $= 1 - P_f$ (see Figure 5:15). That is, success is self-attributed given a difficult task, and failure at an easy task is self-ascribed. It is therefore reasoned that the incentive value of success and failure and self-attribution are positively related: I_s and $I_f = f$(self-ascription). It is contended that greater pride is experienced given success at a difficult task, and greater shame experienced given failure at an easy task, because of the mediating attribution of the outcome to the self. On the other hand, it is suggested that one experiences little pride for success at an easy task, and little shame for failure at a difficult task, because the outcomes are externally attributed (see Figure 5:15).

Direct Empirical Evidence

A number of investigations have examined directly the association between affect and the causal attributions depicted in Figure 6:6. In an experiment devised by Lanzetta and Hannah (1969), subjects acted as "trainers" with the power to reward or punish others during performance at a discrimina-

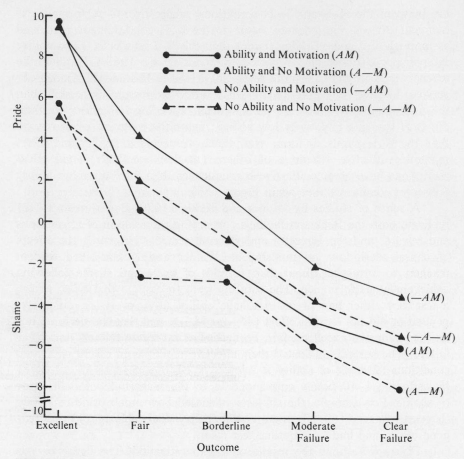

FIGURE 6:7.   Introspective reports of pride and shame as a function of ability, effort, and exam outcome (from Weiner & Kukla, 1970, p. 6).

and shame are a function of how much one feels personally responsible for success or failure. These findings have been replicated in other investigations in which subjects dispense reward and punishment to others (hypothetical pupils), rather than introspecting about their own personal feelings (Weiner & Kukla, Experiments I and II; Heckhausen, unpublished study).

In sum, the experiments of Beckman, Lanzetta and Hannah, and Weiner and Kukla provide evidence that causal ascriptions mediate between task outcome and rewards and punishments from others, as well as between task outcome and feelings of pride and shame. The clearest empirical result in these data is that perceived effort is the most important determinant of affective reactions to success and failure.

Achievement Needs, Causal Inferences, and Affect

Inasmuch as achievement needs are, in part, attributional dispositions, it is logical to hypothesize that individual differences in achievement concerns will be related to affective expressions for achievement outcomes. That is, achievement concerns are linked with particular causal attributions which, in turn, determine affective responses.

Two studies have examined the relationships between achievement needs, causal ascription, and the affective consequences of success and failure. Meyer (1970) gave 72 high school students a series of 15-digit progressions to solve. Following their performance the subjects estimated how many of the problems they answered correctly. Success and failure were manipulated by providing false feedback that two fewer or two more of the problems were solved than anticipated. The subjects then indicated "how much luck or accident played a role" in the outcome, as well as "how much ability played a role." Responses were on a 10-point scale anchored at the extremes. In addition, subjects in the success condition reported their experienced pride, while those in the failure condition indicated how much shame they felt. Affective responses were recorded on a 20-point scale. The subjects also were classified according to strength of resultant achievement motivation.

Table 6:7 shows the relations between causal attributions for success and failure and individual differences in achievement needs. Positive numbers indicate greater attributions to ability than luck, while negative numbers indicate greater attribution to luck than to ability. The table shows that individuals high in resultant achievement motivation ascribe success to high ability and failure to bad luck, while individuals low in resultant achievement needs attribute success to good luck and failure to a lack of ability. These findings generally support the previously reviewed research of Kukla (1970), Weiner and Kukla (1970; Exp. IV), and Weiner and Potepan (1970) concerning the relationship between achieve-

TABLE 6:7
Mean Differences Between Ability Minus Luck
Attributions for Success and Failure, with
Individuals Classified According to Strength
of Resultant Achievement Motivation
(from Meyer, 1970)

| | Motive Classification | |
Experimental Condition	High*	Low*
Success	1.91	−0.27
Failure	−3.40	0.38

* $p < .02$, differences within motive groups, between conditions.

TABLE 6:8
Correlations Between Affective Reactions and Causal Ascription for
Success and Failure (from Meyer, 1970)

	Causal Attribution		
Affect	Luck	Ability	Ability − Luck
Pride in success ($N = 41$)	− .43*	.39*	.54**
Shame in failure ($N = 31$)	− .25	.01	.19

* $p < .005$
** $p < .001$

ment motivation and internal versus external ascriptions for success and failure.

Table 6:8 gives the correlations between positive affect for success, negative affect for failure, and causal attributions to luck and ability. As hypothesized, affects generally are more intense when causal ascriptions are internal (ability) rather than external (luck), thus supporting the hypothetical relationships in Figure 6:6. That is, the more one ascribes outcomes to luck, the less the experienced affect, and vice versa given ability ascriptions. In addition, achievement needs are related to affective intensity, although these findings fall short of statistical significance.

Cook (1970), employing an experimental paradigm quite different from Meyer's, also examined the relationships between causal ascriptions, achievement needs, and affective reactions to success and failure (reported in Weiner, Heckhausen, Meyer, & Cook, 1972). In Cook's study, male children in the fourth and fifth grades ($N = 63$) were placed in a free operant setting in which they determined their own reinforcement for achievement performance. The subjects were given a set of achievement-related puzzles to solve, with half of the puzzles actually unsolvable. On the desk in front of the subjects was a bowl containing poker chips. The subjects were told to reward themselves by taking as many chips as they felt they deserved following each success. In a similar manner, after every failure they were to punish themselves by returning as many chips as they felt they should. A number of precautions ensured that the subjects did not run out of chips, failed and succeeded on an equal number of trials, perceived the puzzles in the success and failure conditions as equally difficult, and so forth. Two months before the experimental manipulation the IAR scale had been administered to the subjects.

Among the findings were data to indicate that resultant self-reward (reward for success minus punishment for failure) varies as a function of causal ascriptions to effort. Greatest resultant reward is exhibited by subjects who are predisposed to attribute success to effort, but do not ascribe failure to a lack of effort. Conversely, the least self-rewarding be-

TABLE 6:9
Individual Differences in the Disposition to Ascribe
Success to Effort, Minus the Disposition to Ascribe
Failure to a Lack of Effort, Related to Self-,
Reinforcement for Achievement Performance
(from Weiner, Heckhausen, Meyer, & Cook, 1972)

| Resultant Reward | Causal Ascription | | |
	High*	Medium	Low
Above median	16	11	6
Below median	8	10	12

* Indicates subjects attribute success to effort, but not
failure to a lack of effort.

havior is found among subjects who have a tendency to attribute failure
to low effort, but not success to heightened exertion (see Table 6:8). Of
the 24 children in the high resultant effort attribution group (high attribution of success to effort, low attribution of failure to lack of effort), only
2 (8 percent) self-punish more than self-reward. In the low attributional
group (low attribution of success to effort, high attribution of failure to a
lack of effort), on the other hand, 7 of the 18 subjects (39 percent) return
more chips following failure than they take out following success.

In addition, Cook reports that achievement needs and total resultant
internality for positive outcomes (internal attribution for success minus
internal attribution for failure) also are systematically related to self-reinforcement behavior. Individuals who are predisposed to attribute success
to self and failure to external factors, as well as those high in achievement
concerns, are most self-rewarding.

General Summary

Considering the relevant studies reviewed, it can be stated with some confidence that causal ascriptions for success and failure influence achievement-related affects. Internal attributions result in greater affect (pride or
shame) than external attributions, and effort is a more potent determinant
of affect than is ability. In addition, achievement needs are related to
causal inferences, and thus to affective expression.

CAUSAL ATTRIBUTION AND
EXPECTANCY CHANGE

Affective responses are determined primarily by ascriptions to internal
versus external locus of control. On the other hand, it is postulated that
expectancy change is determined primarily by ascriptions to stable versus

unstable factors. Figure 6:8 indicates that following success or failure attributions to ability or task difficulty respectively increase or decrease expectancy of success to a greater extent than attributions to effort or luck. More specifically, for example, if an individual perceives that success is caused by his high ability, or the ease of the task, then the increments in expectancy of success on the subsequent trials at that task will be greater than if the prior success is perceived as due to unusual effort or good luck.[2]

It also is contended that expectancy shifts given the identical task are equal when attributions for the achievement outcome are made to ability or task difficulty. That is, among the stable elements, attribution to internal versus external control does not influence expectancy shifts. However, expectancy of future success at tasks that differ from the one performed might be affected more by ascriptions to ability than by ascriptions to task difficulty, for ability may be perceived as having greater generalizability than task characteristics.

It further is postulated that, within the unstable elements, attributions to effort produce greater expectancy shifts than luck ascriptions. Individuals are likely to believe that their effort expenditure is more constant than is their luck, because effort may have a trait-like connotation (for instance, "I am lazy," "I am industrious," and so forth).

Empirical Evidence

The studies most relevant to hypotheses derivable from Figure 6:8 compare expectancy shifts in skill versus chance situations. For example, in a study already summarized, Phares (1957) gave subjects a matching task and described the outcomes as determined by either luck or skill. In both groups subjects received success feedback on about one-half of the trials. Prior to each trial the subjects wagered on their next performance; changes in the subjective probability of success were inferred from the shifts in the amount of money bet. As hypothesized, Phares found that there were more frequent expectancy shifts, and they were of greater magnitude, in the skill than in the chance situation.

The results of other investigations corroborate these findings (Rotter et al., 1961, for instance). In addition, the existence of the gambler's fallacy, or the atypical increments in probabilities after failure or decrements after success in luck situations, are well documented. Thus, the

---

[2] The expectation that effort attributions relatively decrease or modulate subsequent expectancies of success given a positive outcome is in some doubt, for one may intend to continue to exert great effort. The inferences are clearer if one considers the case of failure. In situations of failure, expectancy decrements should be relatively modulated given ascriptions to a lack of effort, *and an intent to succeed*. Effort attributions in situations of success would be most likely to retard subsequent expectancies if the outcome was attributed to "superhuman" effort, which could not be matched in the immediate future.

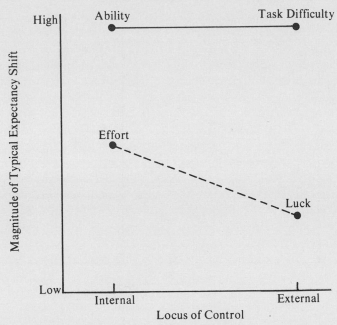

FIGURE 6:8. Hypothesized magnitude of expectancy change (increase after success and decrease after failure) as a function of causal ascriptions for outcome.

differential shifts of expectancy in chance versus skill situations are rather clear cut, although there have not been a great number of investigations in this area.

While the research studies cited above support hypotheses derivable from Figure 6:8, the investigations confuse the locus of control and stability dimensions, for expectancy shifts given skill ascriptions (an internal, stable element) are compared with shifts given luck attributions (an external, unstable element). Meyer (1970) was the first to compare expectancy shifts between stable and unstable attributions. In Meyer's experiment, male high school students, classified according to their level of achievement needs, were given five repeated failures at a digit-symbol substitution task. Following each trial the subjects attributed their failure to low ability, bad luck, low effort, or task difficulty. In addition, they estimated their probability of successfully completing the next trial. The attributions were in percentage figures and were required to total 100 percent. Therefore, the causal ascriptions were not independent of one another.

Figure 6:9 shows the relationship between achievement needs and attributions for failure over the five experimental trials. The figure shows that individuals high in resultant achievement needs ascribe failure to low

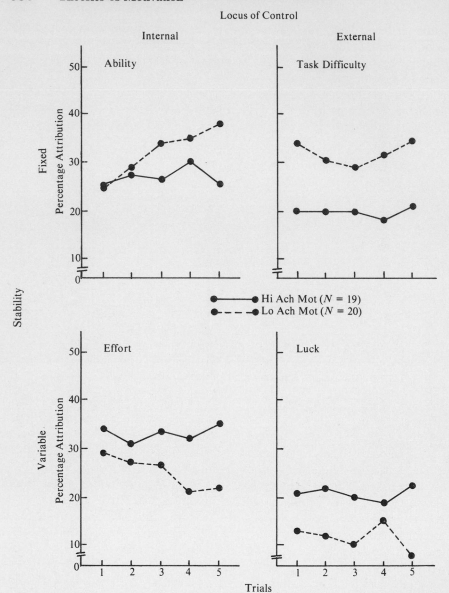

FIGURE 6:9.   Causal attributions given repeated failure for groups high or low in resultant achievement motivation. High percentage attribution indicates ascription to lack of ability, lack of effort, a hard task, and bad luck (adapted from Meyer, 1970).

effort and bad luck, while those low in resultant achievement motivation ascribe their failures to low ability and high task difficulty. The general findings again confirm the motive $\times$ attributional disposition linkage documented previously.

The relationship between causal ascription and expectancy of success is shown in Figures 6:10 and 6:11. Figure 6:10 compares the expectancy

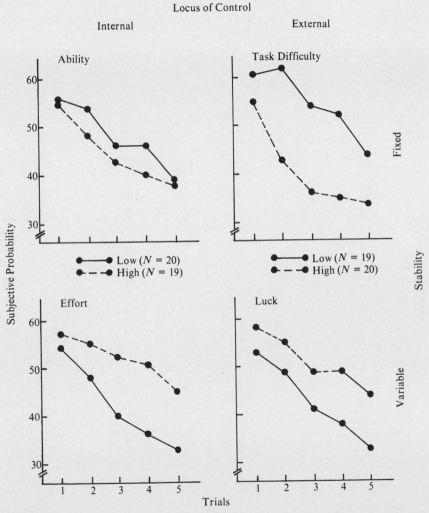

FIGURE 6:10. Expectancy of success as a function of above versus below median ascription to the four causal elements. High ascription indicates lack of ability, a difficult task, lack of effort, and bad luck (adapted from Meyer, 1970).

changes given high versus low attribution to the individual elements, while Figure 6:11 portrays expectancy changes given high versus low attribution to the combined stable elements. (Because of the dependence of the attributional ratings, high attribution to stable elements is isomorphic with low attribution to the variable elements, and vice versa.) The figures reveal that expectancy decrements following failure are most evident when ascriptions to low ability and task difficulty are high and when attributions to lack of effort and bad luck are low. That is, expectancy decreases most when one believes that low ability and/or a hard task, not lack of effort and/or bad luck, are the causes of failure. Combining the data over the locus of control dimension, rather than the stability dimension, would eliminate the expectancy difference between causal groups. A replication of these results using a different experimental procedure is reported by McMahon (1971).

The relationship between subjective probability of success and achievement needs closely corresponds to the findings shown in Figure 6:10. High achievement needs may be considered as represented by the curves depicting low attributions to the stable elements, and low achieve-

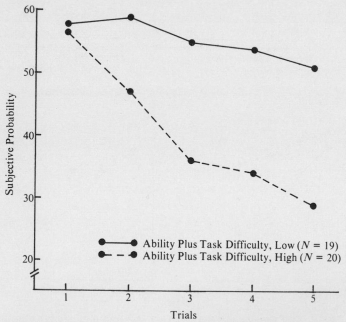

FIGURE 6:11. Subjective probabilities given repeated failure for groups high or low in ascription to stable factors (lack of ability plus task difficulty) (adapted from Meyer, 1970).

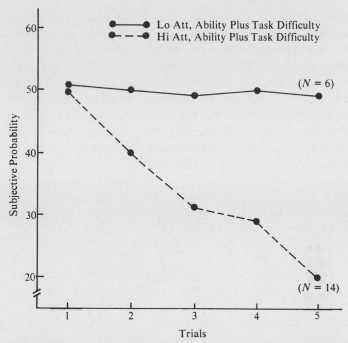

FIGURE 6:12. Subjective probabilities given repeated failures among subjects low in resultant achievement motivation, also classified as high or low in ascription to the stable factors (adapted from Meyer, 1970).

ment needs are closely represented by the curves depicting high attribution to the stable factors.

In addition, Meyer subdivided the subjects *within* motive groups on the basis of their attributions for failure. Figure 6:12 shows that, among subjects low in resultant achievement motivation, probability of success is a function of causal ascription to the stable elements. Probability decrements for individuals low in achievement needs who do not ascribe failure to low ability and task difficulty are minimal, and closely correspond to the expectancy decreases exhibited by subjects high in resultant achievement needs. Thus, the differential probability shifts exhibited by the two motive groups are mediated by the causal ascriptions for failure.

General Summary

It has been argued that affective reactions in achievement contexts are strongly influenced by attributions of success and failure to internal versus external factors. Conversely, it is contended that expectancy shifts following success and failure primarily are a function of ascriptions to stable versus unstable factors. Thus, after a successful achievement outcome, one might experience positive affect and increase future expectancy of success (attribution to high ability), experience little affect and increase expectancy (attribution to task ease), experience very positive affect and moderately increase expectancy (attribution to effort), or experience little affect and not increase expectancy (attribution to good luck). Reinforcement (expectancy) and incentive (affective) consequences of goal attainment are thus separable, and their independent influence on subsequent performance theoretically is determinable.

ATKINSON'S THEORY OF ACHIEVEMENT MOTIVATION

The experimental evidence cited in support of Atkinson's theory of achievement motivation may be categorized into four groupings: (1) free choice (behavior not confined within achievement-related alternatives), (2) persistence of behavior in progress, (3) intensity of performance, and (4) forced choice (risk-preference among achievement tasks). These data are explainable using the attributional model introduced in the previous pages in conjunction with the effects of causal attribution on affect and expectancy.

Free Choice

Experiments have demonstrated that individuals high in resultant achievement motivation are more likely to initiate achievement activities than individuals low in resultant achievement motivation (see Chapter IV). In addition, it has been well documented that individuals high in achievement concerns ascribe success to ability and effort to a greater extent than individuals low in achievement concerns. Individuals in the high motive group therefore should experience more pride in success, for internal attributions heighten affective responses. The augmented positive affect is believed to increase the subsequent likelihood of undertaking achievement behaviors:

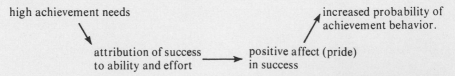

It is not clear whether the differential patterns of ability and effort attributions displayed by the two motive groups also produce disparate expectancies of success at future tasks. The greater attributions of success to ability by the high motive group should especially increase subsequent probabilities of success. However, this increment may be opposed by attributions to the unstable element of effort, although, as noted in footnote 2 of this chapter, ascriptions of success to effort accompanied by a continued intent to succeed need not modulate the increase in the expectancy of success following a goal attainment.

In addition, individuals high in achievement needs ascribe failure to lack of effort, while those low in achievement needs attribute failure to lack of ability. Although both are internal ascriptions, the individuals in the high motive group should experience somewhat greater shame for failure. (This supposition is opposite to a derivation from Atkinson's achievement theory). However, ascription of failure to low ability produces a greater increment in the expectancy of failure on future tasks than ascription to a lack of effort. Thus, even though the low motive group *may* experience less negative affect for failure, they should be less likely to approach subsequent achievement tasks:

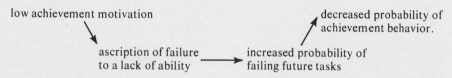

In sum, it is suggested that individuals high in resultant achievement motivation are more likely to undertake achievement-related activities than individuals low in resultant achievement motivation because they have experienced greater positive affect for success, and their expectancy of success remains high following failure.[3]

Persistence of Behavior

The finding that persistence in the face of failure is greater among individuals high in achievement needs than among those who are low can be dismissed with little additional discussion. Individuals high in resultant achievement needs ascribe failure to a lack of effort. Thus, their expectancy of success following failure remains relatively high, and they continue striving for the goal. On the other hand, the attribution of failure to low ability maintained by individuals low in resultant achievement needs decreases the expectancy of success and results in a cessation of goal-directed activity.

[3] This analysis further shows the need for determining the separate as well as joint (weighted) influence of affect and expectancy on behavior.

Intensity of Performance

Experimental studies demonstrate that individuals high in resultant achievement needs work harder, that is, display greater intensity of performance, than individuals low in resultant achievement needs. In addition, there is evidence that intensity of performance is maximal at tasks of intermediate difficulty (Atkinson, 1958a).

The attributional analysis advocated here again provides an alternate explanation of these data to that offered by Atkinson's achievement model. Only among individuals high in resultant achievement motivation is there a perceived relationship between effort and outcome. Inasmuch as individuals in the high motive group believe that effort is instrumental to goal attainment, they simply work harder in achievement-related contexts.

Meyer (1970) has demonstrated that causal attributions are related to intensity of performance. In an experiment previously discussed, subjects attempting a digit-symbol task receive five consecutive failures. After each outcome the failure is attributed to the four causal elements, and

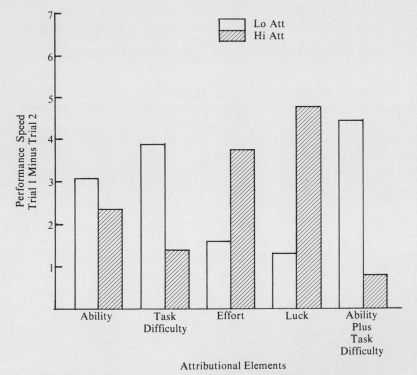

FIGURE 6:13. Intensity of performance in seconds (Trial 1 minus Trial 2) as a function of attribution to the four causal elements, and to the combined stable factors (adapted from Meyer, 1970).

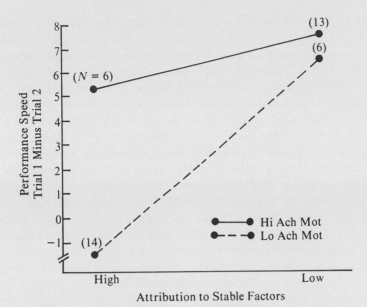

FIGURE 6:14. Intensity of performance (Trial 1 minus Trial 2) as a function of resultant achievement motivation and attribution for failure to the combined stable elements. High numbers indicate increments in speed as Trial 2 (data from Meyer, 1970).

expectancy of success indicated for the next trial. Meyer induced failure by interrupting subjects when they had completed approximately 75 percent of a digit-symbol task. The time taken to reach that degree of task completion (intensity of performance) also was measured.

Figure 6:13 shows the relationship between the difference in performance on Trial 1 minus Trial 2 and the causal attributions for failure following the initial trial. Attributions to bad luck and lack of effort, the unstable elements, relate positively with relative performance increments. If the subject believes that he failed because he did not try hard enough, he then works with greater intensity on the next occasion (completes the measured portion of the task sooner). On the other hand, attributions to the stable elements of low ability and task difficulty are negatively associated with performance change. If the subject thinks that he cannot perform the task (low ability and/or high task difficulty), he relatively disengages from behavior (effort expenditure) instrumental to goal attainment. The correlation between increments in performance and attribution to the combined stable elements is $r = -.43$. That is, the greater the increment between Trial 2 and Trial 1, the less the attribution of failure to stable elements.

Figure 6:14 shows the relationships found by Meyer between the change in performance speed (Trial 1 minus Trial 2) and the joint classification of subjects according to level of resultant achievement needs and causal attributions for failure. The figure illustrates the relationships between causal attribution and performance pointed out in Figure 6:13: High attribution of failure to stable elements (low ability and high task difficulty) results in lesser increments in speed on Trial 2 then does low attribution to the stable factors. In addition, Figure 6:14 shows that individuals highly motivated to succeed perform with greater intensity following failure than those low in resultant achievement motivation, thus replicating earlier findings in the achievement area. Of immediate interest, however, is the interaction between the two predictor variables. Individuals low in resultant achievement motivation not attributing failure to stable elements, and those high in resultant achievement ascribing failure to stable elements, exhibit relatively equal increments in speed on Trial 2. Greatest increments in speed of performance are exhibited by individuals high in achievement needs ascribing failure to unstable elements, while only subjects low in achievement needs attributing failure to low ability and/or high task difficulty display actual performance decrements from Trial 1 to Trial 2.

Motivation as a Function of Probability of Success. An attributional analysis of the relationship between task difficulty and intensity of performance also is based upon perceptions of effort as an outcome determinant. It is suggested that task difficulty is a cue that gives rise to differential attributions to effort as a determinant of achievement outcome. At an easy task effort may be perceived as unnecessary for success, while at a very difficult task effort could be perceived as a "waste of energy." Thus, effort may be considered most important at tasks of intermediate difficulty.

To examine the perceived relationship between effort and task difficulty, Weiner, Heckhausen, Meyer, and Cook (1972) asked subjects to evaluate the "importance of effort as a determinant of outcome" (not differentiating success from failure outcomes) in five tasks that varied according to the percentage of others succeeding at the task (10 percent, 30 percent, 50 percent, 70 percent, and 90 percent). Thus, the cue function of task difficulty in the Task-Evaluation or predictive stage was investigated. Later in this experiment the subjects also were asked at what task it would be most functional to expend effort. On both questions the subjects rank-ordered the five alternatives differing in task difficulty (P_s).

The results of this investigation are shown in Figure 6:15. Effort is judged the most important determinant of outcome at tasks of intermediate difficulty, and it is believed that the best performance strategy is to try hard at intermediate difficulty tasks. The remaining P_s conditions are relatively symmetrical around the $P_s = .50$ level.

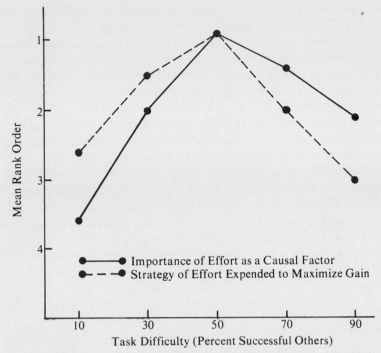

FIGURE 6:15.   Perceived importance of effort as a causal determinant of achievement outcome, and beliefs concerning the functional value of effort, as a function of task difficulty (from Weiner, Heckhausen, Meyer, & Cook, 1972).

Because individuals low in achievement needs do not perceive that effort determines outcome, they too often may have encountered very easy or very difficult tasks in which effort indeed does not covary with outcome. On the other hand, individuals high in achievement motivation may be more exposed to tasks of intermediate difficulty in which effort is an important determinant of success and failure. Thus, the relationship between intensity of performance and achievement needs, mediated by the differentially perceived (and perhaps veridical) effort $\times$ outcome correlations that characterize the high and low achievement motive groups, may be a result of contrasting risk-preference behavior or of contrasting demands made by socializing agents.

Risk Preference (Forced Choice)

Individuals highly motivated to achieve choose tasks of intermediate difficulty more often than individuals low in achievement motivation. In attributional language, selection of tasks of intermediate difficulty has a number of consequences that do not characterize choice of easy or hard tasks. When hard tasks are chosen, respective success or failure (the most frequent outcomes) result in task attributions (see Figure 5:15). Conversely, the selection of intermediate difficulty tasks, over all occasions, most likely results in internal attributions. Choice of tasks of intermediate difficulty therefore indicates a preference for internal rather than external ascription situations.[4]

When attributions are internal, there are increments in the amount of information gained about oneself. Preference for internality may be expressing a desire for feedback about one's capabilities and effort expenditure. Conceptualizing an individual highly motivated to succeed as one desiring feedback about himself is consistent with current thinking in the achievement area. For example, McClelland (1961) writes:

From the psychological point of view, it does not automatically follow that all kinds of people like to have concrete knowledge of results of their choices of action. Such knowledge is a source of anxiety because it cuts both ways: it provides not only proof of success, but also inescapable evidence of failure. . . . There is every theoretical reason to suppose that . . . subjects with high Achievement . . . should be drawn to activities in which they have a chance to show objectively how they can do [pp. 231, 233].

In addition, because tasks of intermediate difficulty most frequently result in self-attributions, the intensity of affective experiences, as well as the variance in affect, are maximized. The strategy of attempting tasks where $P_s = .50$ also may produce the greatest resultant pleasure for individuals high in achievement motivation, as Atkinson (1964) suggests. But whether hedonic value per se guides response selection is a moot point. In any case, the pleasure-pain principle is likely to be only one among a number of principles responsible for the differential risk-preference behavior exhibited by the high and low achievement motive groups. As conceptualized here, the achievement motive is a cognitive, not an affective, disposition.

Summary of Behavioral Consequences of Causal Ascriptions and the Attributional Analysis of Achievement Needs

It has been argued that individual differences in achievement motivation are one antecedent that systematically influences causal judgments. The

[4] This particular analysis differs from those previously discussed, in that the behavior is derived *to obtain* a particular attributional account of the situation, rather than *deduced from* a particular attributional schema.

causal inferences, in turn, determine the direction, magnitude, and persistence of behavior:

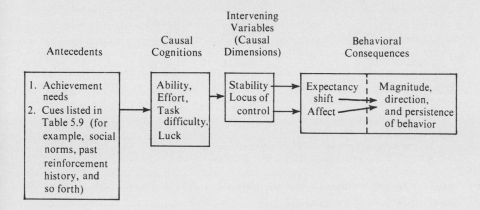

It is also presumed that individuals high in resultant achievement motivation prefer to be in environments that are likely to result in self-attributions for the consequences of their behavior. This results in the selection of tasks of intermediate difficulty, effort $\times$ outcome covariation, and the learning that effort is an important determinant of outcome. This causal predisposition in part produces the tendencies to work hard in achievement settings, to persist in the face of failure, and so on.

The salience of effort attributions as a determinant of choice and performance also may lead to the development of a special sensitivity to effort cues, including such cues as the perceived difficulty of the task. Two studies have examined the behavioral effects when effort cues are present or absent (Kukla, 1970). Kukla told subjects is one experimental condition that "this task is . . . a measure of ability . . . relatively unaffected by effort." In a second experimental condition subjects were informed that "This task . . . is heavily influenced by the amount of effort a person puts into the task." The effects of these instructions on intensity of performance and risk preference were then examined.

The data of the two experiments conducted by Kukla are reported in Table 6:10. The table indicates that only individuals high in resultant achievement motivation are differentially affected by the instructional sets. They perform with greater intensity, and exhibit greater preference for intermediate risk, in the effort than the non-effort conditions. Indeed, given the noneffort instruction, the behaviors exhibited by subjects in the two motive groups are virtually identical. It therefore is again contended that behavioral differences generally displayed by the disparate achievement

TABLE 6:10

Intensity of Performance and Risk-Preference Among Individuals High or Low in Resultant Achievement Motivation, as a Function of Attributional Instructions Regarding the Efficacy of Effort (from Kukla, 1970)

Experi-mental Condition	Dependent Variables			
	Intensity		Risk-Preference	
	High Ach Mot	Low Ach Mot	High Ach Mot	Low Ach Mot
Effort[a]	13.9[b] (N = 17)	9.9 (N = 29)	14.1[c] (N = 10)	7.1 (N = 14)
No effort	10.7 (N = 28)	10.7 (N = 17)	6.6 (N = 12)	6.7 (N = 10)

[a] Instructions indicate that task outcome is a function of effort, or not influenced by effort expenditure.

[b] Number of anagrams solved in a five-minute time period.

[c] Number of intermediate risks taken over twenty trials.

motive groups primarily are mediated by differential causal attributions to effort.

In sum, it is suggested that individuals high in resultant achievement motivation:

1. Prefer situations in which the consequences of their actions can be ascribed to the person (hypothesized),
2. Have learned to attribute outcome to effort (demonstrated), and
3. Are sensitive and reactive to cues indicating the importance of effort expenditure (demonstrated).

Interaction of Achievement Needs and Task Difficulty. The general supposition of Atkinson's (1957) model of achievement-related behavior is that individual differences in achievement-related needs interact with task difficulty to determine behavior. Inasmuch as task difficulty is a cue for effort ascriptions (Weiner, et al., 1972), it may also be stated that achievement-related motives interact with environments differing in their likelihood of eliciting effort attributions. Individuals high in achievement needs are especially motivated to achieve in an environment (P_s = .50) which indicates that effort is the main determinant of outcome. Perhaps, then as already suggested, individuals low in achievement needs are not as sensitive or reactive to such cues, or prefer situations in which effort is not the salient determinant of success and failure.

LOCUS OF CONTROL REEVALUATED

Experiments by Rotter and his colleagues (see Chapter V) have demonstrated that expectancy shifts are a function of skill versus luck task perceptions, and that these task variables interact with the percentage of reinforcement to influence resistance to extinction. Rotter contends that the perceived nature of a task (skill versus chance) affects locus of control or the perceived responsibility for reinforcement. The responsibility for reinforcement, in turn, influences generalized expectancies of success and resistance to extinction.

It already has been intimated that Rotter errs in linking expectancy shifts with locus of control, rather than with the causal dimension of stability. In the experiments conducted by the Rotter research group, ability and luck instructions are varied between experimental conditions. Thus, the effects of internal, stable attributions are compared with the consequences of external, unstable attributions. The two dimensions of causality are confounded.

The attributional model outlined here also leads to a different interpretation of the interaction between schedules of reinforcement and extinction in chance versus skill tasks than that reported by Rotter and his colleagues. Data presented in Table 5:4 and Figure 5:14 reveal that, given the perception of a task as skilled determined, resistance to extinction is greater given 100 percent than 50 percent reinforcement during training. In tasks perceived as chance determined, on the other hand, resistance to extinction is greater given 50 percent than 100 percent reward prior to the extinction period.

In the skill situations of the Rotter experiments, success and failure at the task are described as determined by ability. Presumably luck is not a salient determinant of success or failure (although it may influence outcome given a multiple-choice response, which Rotter at times uses). Further, the attributional significance of effort in determining outcome also is reduced in the tasks used (for example, perceptual sensitivity). Subjects in the 100 percent reinforcement condition thus receive information that they are considerably skilled at the task, while subjects in the 50 percent reinforcement condition are led to believe that they have a relatively small amount of ability. Extinction procedures (0 percent reinforcement) are then initiated. It is assumed that when subjects perceive that they are unable to perform the task, extinction will occur. The change in self-perception from high to low ability requires more information (takes more failure trials) than the shift in self-perception from moderate to low ability. That is, beliefs consistent with later ascriptions of failure to low ability are more likely to be produced in the 50 percent than in the 100 percent reinforcement condition. As expected from this analysis, extinction is monotonically related to the percentage of reinforcement during training (see Figure 5:14).

The extinction data reported by Rotter and his colleagues given chance tasks are less readily amenable to attributional explanations.

Among subjects in the 50 percent reinforcement condition, two sources of information, the instructions and the actual program of rewards, indicate that outcome indeed is a matter of good or bad luck. But in the 100 percent reward condition the schedule of reward is incompatible with the task instructions. Just as a coin's repeatedly turning up heads is not compatible with the belief that the outcome is determined by luck, repeated success at the task indicates that something in addition to luck is causing the outcome. Further, the shift from partial or continuous reward to nonreward during extinction also indicates that task outcome is not just a function of luck. Thus, the initial chance instruction, and the repeated reward in the 100 percent reinforcement condition followed by extinction procedures, are antithetical.

Given this informational analysis of the Rotter procedure, greater variability during extinction is anticipated in the chance than in the skill conditions, for subjects in the chance conditions are more confused about the true causes of success and failure. This expectation is borne out; in both the James and Rotter (1958) and Holden and Rotter (1962) experiments the variance in the chance conditions, particularly given the 100 percent reward schedule, far exceeds the variance in the skill conditions. However, predictions concerning trials to extinction between the experimental conditions are not possible with this attributional interpretation. It is suggested that extinction occurs sooner in the 100 percent reward condition given chance instructions merely because the subjects in that condition believe they are being deceived, and find the entire experimental situation aversive (or confusing).

EXPERIMENTAL EXTINCTION

The studies conducted by Rotter and his colleagues were the first to call attention to a possible relationship between causal ascriptions and experimental extinction. The demonstration of such an association would greatly broaden the empirical foundations of attribution theory. In addition, it would extend this cognitive approach beyond the present confines of personality, clinical, and social psychology.

It has been stated frequently in this chapter that the stability or instability of the perceived causal factors influence the expectancy that the behavioral outcome of an action will change or remain relatively unchanged on subsequent occasions. Attribution by an actor to ability or task difficulty implies that outcomes on prior trials will again be manifested, while attributions to luck and effort implies that on later occasions the outcomes might be different. It is therefore suggested that resistance to extinction is a function of attributions to the causal dimension of stability during the period of nonreinforcement. More specifically, ascription of nonreinforcement during the extinction period to bad luck or a lack of effort are hypothesized to retard expectancy decrements and result in slower extinction than attribution of nonattainment of a goal to high task difficulty or lack of ability.

There are data in the experimental literature that may be interpreted as supporting this hypothesis. For example, Lawrence and Festinger (1962), marshalling evidence to support their cognitive dissonance explanation of extinction, report that resistance to extinction is positively related to the effortfulness of a response. Response-reward contingencies linked with heightened exertion take longer to extinguish than responses requiring little effort (see Chapter V). It is suggested here that nonattainment of a reward during the extinction period is ascribed to a lack of effort by subjects in the high exertion condition. Thus, the expectancy of reward following nonattainment of the goal is relatively unchanged and extinction is prolonged. With repeated nonreward, however, the ascription shifts from effort to ability and/or task difficulty, and expectancy decreases and extinction occurs.

Another theory of extinction (Amsel, 1958) postulates that nonreward following a series of rewarded trials elicits frustration. Extinction occurs because the anticipation of frustration eventually results in the withholding of the approach response. In a study by Amsel and Roussel (1952), which frequently is cited in support of Amsel's frustration theory, a 100 percent reward schedule is instituted during initial learning. Following the first few nonrewarded trials performance intensity increases, presumably demonstrating the energizing properties of frustration.

The attributional analysis advocated here also may be applied to these data. It has been demonstrated that nonreward following repeated reinforcement is ascribed to bad luck and/or lack of effort (see Figure 6:2). Hence, the observation of enhanced response strength following nonreward may be considered evidence that the animal has made an attribution to these unstable elements and this inference results in increments in subsequent performance (see Figure 6:13). Continued nonreward, however, will shift the attribution to stable elements and result in experimental extinction. It also has been demonstrated that the increments in response strength during the initial phase of extinction are positively related to the number of rewarded trials and to the length of the runway. These manipulations intuitively increase the likelihood of the attribution of nonattainment of the goal to a lack of sufficient effort.

Similarly, it is suggested that greater resistance to extinction is displayed given 50 percent than 100 percent reward because in the former condition the outcome is, in part, ascribed to good or bad luck. A random pattern of outcomes is one cue used to infer luck as a causal factor. Ascription of nonattainment of a goal during extinction to bad luck most retards expectancy decrements (see Figures 6:8 and 6:10). In general, it is suggested that the relationship between reward schedule and resistance to extinction is mediated by perceptions of causality, which, in turn, influence the expectancy of success:

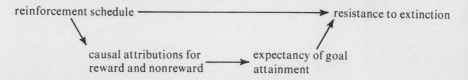

reinforcement schedule   resistance to extinction

           causal attributions for   expectancy of goal
           reward and nonreward   attainment

Experimental Studies

Experiments by this author and his associates (Weiner, Frieze, Kukla, Reed, Rest, & Rosenbaum, 1971) have yielded promising results concerning extinction, although the work is still at a primitive stage. The experimental studies were guided by the investigations of Rotter and his colleagues. Luck and skill instructions were not given, however, and the task employed was ambiguous regarding its chance versus skill structure. Thus, the shortcomings of the Rotter experiments concerning the believability and compatibility of the pairing of instructions and reinforcement schedules is overcome.

In one of these experiments, subjects received a booklet of line-tracing puzzles (see Feather, 1961, and Chapter IV of this book). Although this task is used in studies of achievement motivation, completion at times appears to be a matter of luck. Three experimental conditions were created by varying the percentage of solvable puzzles the subjects received prior to the initiation of extinction. For one group of subjects, all the puzzles were solvable (S condition); for a second group, half were solvable and half unsolvable (R or Random condition); a third group received all unsolvable puzzles (F condition). After eight learning trials, extinction procedures were initiated, with all puzzles unsolvable. There were seven extinction trials.

Prior to every trial the subjects estimated their P_s on a scale ranging from 0 to 10. Then, following success or failure at the task, attributions for the outcome were made on seven-point scales for all four causal elements.

Figure 6:16 shows the P_s estimates of the subjects in the three reinforcement conditions. It can be seen that the experimental manipulation systematically affected the P_s ratings. Subjective expectancy of success

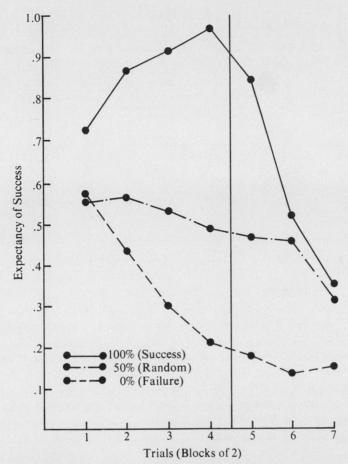

FIGURE 6:16.   Mean expectancy of success over trials given three schedules of reinforcement. Solid vertical line indicates the onset of extinction (from Weiner, Frieze, Kukla, Reed, Rest, & Rosenbaum 1971, p. 22).

increases in the S condition, remains relatively constant and near .50 in the R condition, and steadily declines in the F condition. During extinction the P_s declines in all conditions.

Table 6:11 gives the mean attribution ratings during extinction for the four causal elements. There are significant effects for task difficulty and luck, while the ability and effort main effects approach statistical significance. Inspection of the total pattern of results reveals that in the F condition the subjects infer that stable factors (low ability and high task difficulty)

TABLE 6:11

Mean Attributional Ratings During Extinction as a Function
of Reinforcement Schedule

	Reinforcement Schedule		
Attribution Dimension	(N = 9) 100% (S)	(N = 15) 50% (R)	(N = 11) 0% (F)
Ability	2.3*	3.0	3.4
Task difficulty	5.6	6.2	6.8
Luck	2.1	2.9	1.3
Effort	1.7	2.8	2.1

* High numbers indicate attributions of failure to low ability, difficult task, bad luck, and lack of effort.

are the causes of failure. In addition, they are least likely to believe that the outcome is attributable to a composite of the unstable factors of low effort and bad luck. This overall attributional pattern suggests that subjects in the F condition would be the first to stop responding, for they should not expect the outcome to improve on subsequent occasions. Figure 6:16 does indicate that during extinction the lowest P_s ratings are displayed in the failure condition.

The attributional pattern of subjects in the S condition reveals that they are likely to infer that failure is not due to the stable attributional elements. That is, relative to others they maintain a high ability-easy task inferential pattern. Conversely, the subjects in the R condition most believe that bad luck and lack of effort, the unstable elements, are responsible for their failures. Thus, differential resistance to extinction for subjects in the success and random conditions is indeterminate, inasmuch as subjects in each condition endorse two elements that theoretically retard extinction. That is, subjects in one condition do not attribute failure to low ability or task difficulty; the subjects in the second condition do attribute failure to lack of effort and bad luck. The P_s estimates support this post-hoc null hypothesis (no difference in trials to extinction between the S and R conditions). Subjective expectancy of success in the S and R condition are virtually identical following Trial 10.

Although there are no phenotypic differences in the P_s estimates between the S and R conditions during the final extinction trials, the attributional data indicate that there are genotypic disparities between the two conditions. That is, the subjects may be persisting for different reasons. These genotypic differences should become visible given different instructions. On the one hand, skill directions are expected to result in greater weighting of the ability-task factors and to produce slower extinction for the 100 percent reward condition. Conversely, chance instructions should result in greater salience of the luck dimension, and cause slower extinction in the 50 percent reward condition. These, of course, are the findings reported by Rotter and his colleagues in their skill versus chance instructional conditions.

Achievement Dispositions and Reinforcement Schedules: A Comparison

We have contended that achievement motives and reinforcement schedules can both be considered antecedents that affect mediating cognitions concerning the causes of behavioral outcomes. These mediational processes influence, in part, expectancy of success and overt action. Specifically, individuals high in achievement motivation persist longer given failure than individuals low in achievement motivation. In addition, resistance to extinction is greater given 50 percent than 100 percent reinforcement in infrahuman experimentation. These antecedent-consequent relationships are believed to be mediated by attributions of nonattainment of the goal to unstable elements (lack of effort and bad luck), which then retard expectancy decrements and give rise to persistent behavior:

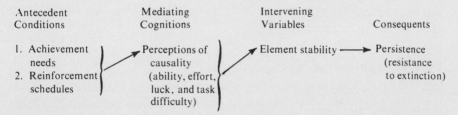

Antecedent Conditions	Mediating Cognitions	Intervening Variables	Consequents
1. Achievement needs 2. Reinforcement schedules	Perceptions of causality (ability, effort, luck, and task difficulty)	Element stability	Persistence (resistance to extinction)

MORALITY

The attributional analysis of achievement behavior intimates that the growth of achievement is contingent upon the learning of cognitive structures that represent the causal importance of effort. It is possible that the expression of other sources of motivation also require the building of mediating effort structures. For example, power-related behavior may necessitate the belief that one must work hard to attain power-related goals. Indices that assess the relative ascriptions of goal attainment to exertion would then yield an ipsitive scale of an individual's motivational tendencies. For example, a person stating that gaining power is matter of "pull," that gaining friendships is primarily luck and a little effort, and that achievement satisfactions are entirely a function of hard work, is respectively low, medium, and high in power, affiliative, and achievement dispositions.

Attributional analyses of other sources of motivation, such as power and affiliation, remain to be formulated. There is evidence, however, that causal ascriptions mediating moral concerns are similar to those associated with achievement behavior. In one experiment illustrating this point, Schmitt (1964) created hypothetical situations in which an act was not committed either because of the actor's lack of willingness (try) or because of the absence of ability (can). For example, a situation was described in which a person did not repay a debt either because he did not want to or because he did not have the money. Subjects indicated the degree to which the borrower was morally obligated to return the money. The data from this investigation are shown in Table 6:12. The table indicates that subjects invoke moral sanctions primarily when the person is able but unwilling to repay. These moral obligations are invoked when the person is unwilling, even when the person is unable to repay. Thus, moral judgments are linked with attributions to intention, rather than with ability. In a similar manner, reward and punishment for achievement behavior are more linked with effort than ability ascriptions (Weiner & Kukla, 1970, Experiments I–III). It is more functional to reward and punish effort (intent) rather than ability, for effort is an unstable variable under personal control. Effort is modifiable, whereas ability generally is not. Note that in Schmitt's study the able person is "punished" more than the unable one, as in the achievement data.

Piaget's Analysis of Moral Judgment

The developmental growth sequence preceding the intentionality-moral judgment linkage has been subject to much discussion. Although the exact

TABLE 6:12

Comparative Frequency Distribution of the Number of Times Subjects Selected the Invocation of Moral Obligation for Incidents
(from Schmitt, 1964, p. 306)

Number of Times an Individual Invoked Moral Obligation	Experimental Variation			
	Willing-Unable	Willing-Able	Unwilling-Able	Unwilling-Unable
4	0	0	15	1
3	1	1	9	0
2	1	3	2	6
1	4	11	0	11
0	20	11	0	7
N	26	26	26	25

progression of this sequence is uncertain, there is some agreement that Piaget's (1932) intuitions and observations are broadly correct (also see Kohlberg, 1963). According to Piaget, there is an invariant sequence of cognitive change through which a child progresses in his moral development. These stages are hierarchical, with the higher stages more integrated and differentiated than the lower ones.

The initial stage of moral development is labeled "heteronomous." In this stage the rules of conduct set forth by adults are accepted as fixed and unchangeable. "These rules not only [are] obligatory . . . but also [are] inviolable" (Piaget, 1932, p. 104). Piaget characterizes morality during this period as one of constraint. Punishment in the heteronomous stage is "expiatory"; the goal is retaliation and the severity of the punishment is a function of the consequences (outcome) of the moral transgression. On the other hand, in the final (autonomous) moral stage, adults are rejected as restraining forces. Social interaction with peers produces a new kind of morality; a morality of cooperation. Further, punishment is restitutive, rather than retaliatory. The punishment restores the status quo and indicates to the wrongdoer the effects of his actions. The intensity of the punishment is a function of the subjective intentions of the wrongdoer rather than of the subjective consequences of his behavior.

Morality and Achievement Motivation

Inasmuch as both achievement and moral evaluation among adults are linked with "try" attributions, they may also follow similar developmental courses. It is therefore suggested that among younger children, achievement-related actions are initially rewarded or punished according to outcome, or the units of of behavior that are labeled as right (good) or wrong (bad). Only in the later developmental stages will effort emerge as the salient evaluative dimension. Perhaps the neglect of the stage hypothesis is one reason for the present unclarity concerning the developmental antecedents of achievement motivation.

In one test of this hypothesis, Weiner and Peter extended an experiment previously reported by Weiner and Kukla (1970). They asked subjects aged four to twelve to pretend that they were teachers, and to reward and punish children in an achievement-related situation. The children to be judged were described as attempting to complete a puzzle. They had (A) or did not have ($A-$) ability, tried hard (E) or did not try ($E-$), and succeeded (S) or failed (F). Thus, the subjects rewarded or punished a pupil presumed to have ability, but who did not try, and failed. The subjects evaluated all eight possible experimental conditions (2 levels of ability $\times$ 2 levels of effort $\times$ 2 levels of outcome) by assigning one to five gold stars (reward) or one to five red stars (punishment). The same subjects also evaluated children within the context of a moral situation. The story context involved a small boy or girl asking an older child for directions. The older child being judged by the subjects did or did not know the correct directions (ability), did or did not want to help (intent), and the smaller child either did or did not arrive home (outcome). Again, all eight possible experimental outcomes were considered by each subject.

The results of this investigation are shown in Figure 6:17. The figure shows the evaluative significance of the three attributional dimensions (ability, effort, and outcome) for both achievement and moral situations as a function of the age of the subjects. Only the main effects are represented, that is, the outcome effect refers to the reward for success (arrival home) minus the punishment for failure (did not arrive home).

Figure 6:17 shows that in the moral situation, outcome is the primary evaluative determinant of the younger children. However, among older age groups evaluation is based upon intentionality; outcome becomes only a minor determinant of moral judgments. Among older subjects, even if the child does not find the way home, the person *wanting* to help is rewarded. A similar developmental sequence describes the achievement evaluation data. In the earlier developmental stages, success or failure determines whether achievement activities are rewarded or punished. But as development proceeds, and new cognitive structures emerge, achievement evaluations are based upon effort more than upon outcome. In contrast to the moral situation, however, outcome does remain a significant evaluative factor.

Ability was not used as an evaluative dimension in either the achievement or moral context. However, it is suggested that at some time following the onset of logical or formal operations, which is thought to be around the age of eleven, lack of ability will emerge in the achievement context as positively evaluated. Weiner and Kukla (1970) and Lanzetta and Hannah (1969) demonstrated this fact with adult samples.

Additional similarities and differences exist between achievement and moral systems (see Kelly, 1971). For example, behaviors labeled as moral or immoral—that produce social rewards and punishment—are *person* attributions. Reward and punishment for achievement actions also are contingent upon person (internal) attributions. In addition, both moral judgments and inferences about the causes of success and failure necessitate social consensus information. But generally what is moral is what other people do (Heider, 1958, notes that "is" tends to be confused with "ought"), while achievement accomplishments often are defined as what others cannot do (Kelley, 1971). Further, moral systems primarily utilize punishment to control behavior (if one does not do what others do, punishment is given). Conversely, achievement systems primarily are based upon

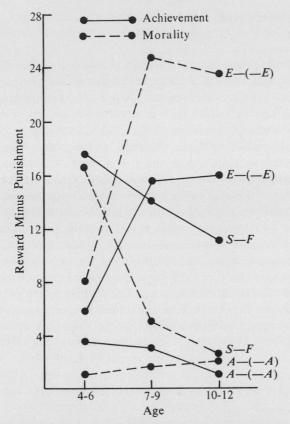

FIGURE 6:17. Evaluative significance of outcome, effort, and ability in achievement-related
and moral contexts, as a function of the age of the
subjects.

rewards (if one does what others cannot or have not done, then reward
is given). There are, however, also moral ideals few individuals attain,
and approximations of such ideals are highly praised (witness idols such
as Schweitzer or Gandhi), just as achievement may be punished if the individual "can" accomplish more than he actually does.

Because social comparison information is necessary for valid attributions, the unavailability or misinterpretation of this information is likely
to give rise to attributional errors. For example, masturbation may induce
guilt because the actor perceives that he alone engages in such actions
(Strong, 1970); this error is due to "pluralistic ignorance," or the tendency
to perceive one's actions as unique (Heider, 1958). Similarly, failure at
any given task may cause an individual to experience shame if he is unaware that other individuals also are not able to complete the same task.

Societal Development: An Attributional
Comparison of Piaget and Karl Marx

There is an interesting parallel between the development of morality as discussed by Piaget, and the historical change in social structure envisioned by Marx. Marx (1875) states that the change in allocation of the resources of society will proceed "from each in accordance with his ability, to each in accordance with his needs" (p. 119). That is, in the early (but not first) stages of social development, the distribution of wealth is based upon individual differences in ability, endurance, and other "can" factors that correlate with productivity. Because of the debasing characteristics of many tasks, individuals in these societies differ in their intentions and effort expenditure toward work. However, in a truly socialistic society, which is a higher level of social progress, rewards will be subjectively equal. They will no longer be a function of outcome. Further, in such a society each person will expend maximal effort, and fulfill himself through his labors. This can be interpreted to mean that subjective (need-fulfilling) rewards are based upon effort or intention, which is equally positive between persons.

The Marxian hypothesis thus has much in common with the stages and growth of moral judgments discussed by Piaget. A moral society, as a moral individual, evaluates not objective outcome, but subjective intent. On the other hand, in the early moral stages of development of individuals and societies, objective outcome determines social reward. Although Marx's work preceded Piaget's, it appears that Marx postulates a *recapitulation* theory of social change: The presumed moral change in society recapitulates the actual moral change within the person. In contrast to the familiar "ontogeny recapitulates phylogeny," which Piaget advocates, Marx offers a theory in which social evolution recapitulates individual growth.

In addition, Marx, like Piaget, hypothesized that change follows a fixed sequence. Each stage of society is built upon the foundations of the earlier levels of advancement. The stages are qualitatively different; modes of thought are displaced and new social characteristics emerge. Whether the speed of progress toward the attainment of a socialistic state can be increased, and stages skipped by means of military revolution, for example, is a central and unsettled issue in the Marx-Lenin thoughts about social change. In a similar manner, whether the speed of moral growth and development can be enhanced by introducing new experiences, or rewards and punishments, also is a moot point. Of course, these analogous questions arise because of the "stage" hypothesis held by both theorists.

To illustrate the similarity in the thinking of Piaget and Marx, selected quotes from Piaget (1932) are presented. With slight changes in wording (for example, government for adults, society for morality, workers for children). Marx easily could be perceived as the author of the quotes.

1. The ethics of authority, which is that of duty and obedience, leads in the domain of justice to the confusion of what is just with the content of established law and to the acceptance of expiatory punishment (p. 203).

2. A sort of communion (that is, community) of submission to seniors and dictates of adults [exists] (p. 310).

3. The child finds in his brothers or sisters or in his playmates a form of society that develops his desire for cooperation. Then a new type of morality will be created in him, a morality of reciprocity and not of obedience. This is the true morality of intention (pp. 133–34).

4. Rule . . . no longer is external law sacred in so far as it has been laid down by adults; but is the outcome of a free decision worthy of respect in the measure that this enlisted mutual consent (p. 57).

5. As the solidarity between children grows we shall find this notion of justice gradually emerging in almost complete autonomy (p. 196).

6. Solidarity between equals appears once more as the source of a whole set of complementary and coherent moral ideas (p. 203).

7. A sense of justice . . . requires nothing more for its development than the mutual respect and solidarity which holds among children themselves (p. 196).[5]

Achievement needs also may be related to the Marx-Piaget analysis, although the exact nature of the relationship is ambiguous. It has been argued that achievement needs develop as causal structures representing effort emerge. Further, it is contended that achievement motivation is responsible for the rise and maintenance of capitalism (McClelland, 1961, Chapter IV of this book). Thus, cognitive structures that Marx considers a prerequisite for a socialistic society—that is, those that make salient intent ascriptions—perhaps may produce a capitalistic rather than a socialistic system. One question that then arises is whether Marx is referring only to an achievement system, or whether he is a "moral" theorist. Further, one wonders if achievement needs are incompatable with, or actually are part of, a socialistic social structure.

EDUCATIONAL IMPLICATIONS

Ascriptions to Ability or to Effort

It has been demonstrated that attributions of success and failure to ability versus effort influence the rewards and punishments given for achievement outcomes. For example, failure perceived as due to low effort among persons believed to be high in ability results in maximal punishment (Lanzetta

[5] It is of interest to note that both Marx and Piaget were greatly influenced by biological models and Darwin. Marx actually dedicated *Das Kapital* to Darwin.

students associated with fraudulent norms are likely to be told that their failures are due to insufficient effort. However, individuals low in achievement motivation are disposed to attribute failure to a lack of ability. Thus, according to this analysis, pupils low in achievement motivation who happen to be placed in the fraudulent norm condition should experience a conflict following failure between their general attributional disposition and the information they receive from the teacher.

Other instances of conflicts between individual predispositions in causal inferences and environmental information can be readily illustrated. For example, individuals high in achievement needs are disposed to ascribe success to effort and ability. But information that all members of a reference group succeed at a task generally results in ascription of success to the ease of the task (Frieze & Weiner, 1971). Therefore, when an individual high in achievement motivation is successful at a task that all others also complete, an atributional conflict is generated. One possible method of resolving this conflict is to perceive the task as more difficult than it really "is." That is, in opposition to current thoughts about achievement motivation, it is suggested that persons high in achievement needs may, given proper circumstances, bias P_s downwards. This increases the environmental support for the attribution of success to the self, thus creating a "balanced" attributional system.

Student-Teacher (*Self-Other*) *Conflict.*   Jones and Nisbett (1971) contend that individuals tend to perceive their own behavior as determined by stimulus factors, or valences in the environment, while the behavior of others is perceived as due to personal traits. Thus, consistency in the behavior of others across stimulus situations, but variability in self-behavior, may be anticipated.

What might account for the hypothesized opposing attributional inferences? First, one has more information about his own intentions and behavior than about the intentions and actions of others. He may be aware of the many occasions in which he expressed different behaviors in the same or in different stimulus situations. On the other hand, he may have observed the other person in only one particular type of social setting. Thus, it is likely that consistent behavior in others is observed, and person or trait attributions are made. In addition, Jones and Nisbett (1971) point out that when an individual acts, the environment is the "figure" in his perceptions, while the behavior itself is "ground." Conversely, when observing the actions of others, the behavior is "figure" and the environment in which the behavior is expressed is "ground." Thus, contrasting salient perceptual aspects of the behavior-environment unit may also be responsible for the proposed differential attributional inferences in self-other comparisons.

Jones and Nisbett suggest that the great amount of work in psychology devoted to the isolation and measurement of traits may merely be another manifestation of the tendency to look for traits in others. This may be an attributional error. As Mischel (1968) notes, consistency in behavior is not often found across different stimulus situations, and "traits" or personality factors frequently account for little of the observed variance in behavior. Needless to say, at present this is a most controversial position to hold.

The above discussion suggests that effort, which has been conceptualized as an unstable personal causal element, may be perceived as a stable attribute when making judgments about others. That is, we may see others as "industrious" or "lazy." Self-predictions of achievement performance therefore may differ from the expectations of others in situations where effort is believed to be an important causal determinant of outcome. The reader surely can recall a conversation with another student who professed he would study harder in the future and succeed (self-perception of effort as an unstable attribute), while the reader anticipated that the student would perform in his usual apathetic manner (other-perception of effort as a stable characteristic). Or perhaps the reader has found himself in a similar attributional conflict with an instructor. While he implored that he would work hard in the future and do better, the instructor expressed lack of confidence in his future actions.

Participant-Observer Conflict.   This type of conflict has been documented in the prior discussion of attributional errors (see experiments by Johnson et al., 1964; Beckman, 1970). Apparently ego-defensive and ego-enhancing attributional errors are likely to be made when individuals are directly involved with the success and failure of others. Imagine a teacher-mother conference in which opposing defensive attributions are made for the poor performance of the student. The mother thinks that her child is able but the teaching is deficient, while the teacher believes that the child is lazy or not able and that her teaching is good.

Observer-Observer Conflict.   Not all attributional conflicts are ascribable to flagrant misuse of information or to motivational factors. Frieze and Weiner (1971) have demonstrated that there are great individual differences in the information used to infer the causes of success and failure, as well as in the manner in which information is combined to reach causal inferences. Individuals use identical information in very disparate manners. For example, some persons use information about how long an individual has spent at a task to infer ability level, others use time spent as a cue for effort attributions, and others may not use this information at all. That is, an individual may believe that another person is bright (or not bright) because he spends much time at a task, while others may just infer that this person tries hard, and still others think that this information reveals nothing about the observed person.

Teaching Programs

In Chapter IV it was suggested that teaching programs do not motivate individuals high in achievement motivation, for the programs approximate 100 percent reinforcement schedules. High probability of success seems to "bore" individuals high in achievement concerns. Furthermore, one wonders whether attributions for success when working with teaching machines are ascribed by the person to himself or to the adequacy of the apparatus and the program. If the latter, then positive affect for success is minimized, for ascriptions are to an external source of causality. Thus, it is possible for individuals to experience success while their probability of undertaking future achievement activities remains relatively unchanged. In some institutions progress through the teaching program is posted for all students to see. Interperson comparisons are then possible and relative success (and failure) may be self-attributed.

Surveillance, Trust, and Grades

Inferences about the dispositions of others are most certain when the observed behavior is not constrained by the social context in which the behavior occurs. For example, one is likely to attribute an aggressive disposition to a job applicant acting in a hostile manner, while he may be unsure if the applicant is "submissive" if he acts in an overly polite manner during the interview (see Jones, Davis, & Gergen, 1961).

Similarly, individuals might work hard to achieve at school, yet a teacher or parent will believe that this behavior is due to the fear of parental or teacher punishment. The effects of surveillance and potential punishment on attributions have been examined in an experimental setting (Strickland, 1958). A subject was assigned to be a supervisor over two other (fictitious) students supposedly performing a dull task. The supervisor had the power to observe and punish one of the workers more than the other. The supervisor was given feedback that the two workers exhibited identical satisfactory performance, and punishment was not administered. The causal determinants of the subordinates' performances were then indicated by the supervisor. In addition, a subsequent task was performed in which the supervisor was free to monitor the performance of either worker. Trust was inferred from the relative amount of time spent observing the two subordinates, as well as from self-reports obtained in questionnaire items. In discussing this study, Strickland (1958) reasoned that:

1. If an individual has high power vis à vis a subordinate, and
2. he initiates an influence attempt on this subordinate (in terms of demanding some strenuous productive effort) and
3. has reason to suspect that the subordinate would like to resist this influence attempt, then;
4. if this individual has a high degree of surveillance over the subordinate, and
5. he perceives compliance on the part of the subordinate,
6. he can actually have relatively little information about the loyalty, reliability, or trustworthiness of the subordinate, and
7. he will locate causality for the compliance external to this subordinate.

This inference of external causality, if made, should have some consequences for the individuals' future behavior. If he enters a new situation where his own goal is the same but where something in the situation limits his freedom to apply his power continually and comprehensively, he will:

1. trust his subordinate less than he would had he perceived the compliance as stemming from some cause lying within the subordinate himself; and
2. make greater efforts to keep him under surveillance (had he made this alternative location of causality) (p. 202).

The results reported by Strickland are consistent with this general chain of reasoning. The supervisor ascribed the performance of the more monitored worker to the external theat of punishment (proposition 7 on Strickland's list), verbalized less trust of him, and monitored him more on the subsequent task.

In a later investigation, Kruglanski (1970) generally replicated Strickland's findings when the supervisor had the power either to reward or to punish the subordinate. Kruglanski therefore contends that Strickland's findings concerning trust cannot be explained on the basis of anticipated hostility from the monitored subordinate.

In sum, power over another, even if not used, results in attributions for successful outcomes to that power source. Attributions of confidence and trust to another person apparently are not made unless there has been an opportunity to exhibit positive performance under nonpower conditions. Yet in school settings the power to reward and punish via grading is always in the teacher's possession. No wonder, then, that students are often considered untrustworthy or undependable. The power situation inherent in the student-teacher relationship may foster this attributional error. Inducing achievement behavior through external rewards may also function to reduce trust, and even result in the student ascribing his motivation to external, rather than achievement-related, motivations (see the prior discussion of overly sufficient justification).

Achievement Training Programs

Evidence has been presented that a subgroup of individuals labeled as low in resultant achievement motivation do not develop mediating cognitive structures that embody the efficacy of effort. Further, they learn that failure is an indication of a lack of ability. How might achievement striving be induced among individuals with this attributional pattern? Perhaps investigators attempting to enhance achievement motivation have already provided some answers to this question. For example, in the change program advocated by McClelland and Winter (1969) the participants learn to take self-responsibility for their actions. They are taught the value of intermediate risks and are required to formulate plans for reaching their goals, to keep records of their achievement progress, and so on. McClelland and Winter state, "A continuing theme throughout the course is that the participants can initiate and control change" (p. 150). Thus, it appears that the participants in this program are learning that effort (internal causation) mediates between the task stimuli and final achievement outcome. In a similar manner, de Charms has attempted to enhance school performance by giving "Origin" training.

Training Programs and Social Class. The cognitive systems pertinent to achievement motivation may be unequally represented in various racial and social class groupings. In discussing the disparities in academic motivation between racial groups, Katz (1967) states:

I think the crux of the matter is the differential capability of children from different social backgrounds for vigorous and sustained effort on tasks that are not consistently interesting and attractive [p. 140].

Katz suggests that Negroes may not develop structures that represent the efficacy of effort. He states, "A major handicap of many Negro pupils was an inability to sustain academic effort . . . which resulted from inadequate early reinforcement of such effort" (p. 163). Thus, attributional change procedures seem especially appropriate in early education programs.

Successful programs resulting in increments in the academic performance of Negro school children might be explained in terms of attributional change. For example, Coleman et al. (1966) report that the school performance of Negro children increases as a function of the proportion of whites in their classes. The report states:

It appears that children from advantaged groups assume that the environment will respond if they are able to affect it; children from disadvantaged groups do not make this assumption, but in many cases assume that nothing they will do can affect the environment—it will give benefits or with-hold them but not as a consequence of their own action [p. 321].

Perhaps in the predominantly white classrooms the Negro children become exposed to the attributional patterns of the whites, and come to accept self-attributions for success and failure. That is, they learn that they are responsible for achievement outcomes. Coleman et al. report that Negro children who respond that hard work is more responsible for success than good luck perform higher on a test of verbal ability than those who pre-dominantly ascribe outcomes to luck.

The intent of the above discussion is to suggest that causal structures be directly examined and manipulated in achievement change programs. No such program is offered here, although the goals of such program fol-low directly from the prior discussion: The perception of causality for success and failure should be altered so that success is ascribed to high effort and failure to low effort rather than to lack of ability.

SUMMARY

An attributional model of achievement motivation has been formulated in which the perceived causes of success and failure are identified as *ability, effort, task difficulty,* and *luck.* These elements are comprised within two causal dimensions: *locus of control* (internal or external) and *stability* (stable or variable). These dimensions influence, respectively, affective reactions to success and failure and changes in the probability of success following achievement outcomes.

Individuals differing in level in achievement needs differ in their dis-positions to allocate causation to these attributional factors. Persons high in achievement needs ascribe success to high ability and high effort, and ascribe failure to a lack of effort. Persons low in achievement needs, on the other hand, relatively attribute success to external factors and failure to a lack of ability. The causal dispositions, in turn, mediate between achievement tasks and the final achievement-related responses of approach behavior, intensity of performance, persistence of action, and risk-pref-erence. Atkinson's model of achievement motivation is reexamined with the use of attributional language.

In addition, resistance to extinction, morality, and educational processes are examined from an attributional viewpoint. The discussion of morality includes a comparison of the theories of individual and societal development of Piaget and Karl Marx, and compares and contrasts achievement and moral systems.

Attribution theory is not conceived as a panacea for the solution of all problems in the study of motivation. Nor is it held to be the only possible cognitive approach to motivation. Rather, it is a reasonable direction toward the formulation of a theory of motivation in which thoughts are systematically related to action. The general goal of a theory of motivation, which guided the attributional formulations in this chapter, is eloquently stated by Bruner (1970):

Psychology has always been bedeviled by separation in its theories of action on the one hand and sensing-knowing on the other. Tolman was accused by Guthrie of leaving his organism locked in thought, and Hull surely could be accused of letting his organism remain as perceptually innocent as the day he was born, save for a little afferent neural interaction. There is a structure in action and a structure in knowing (whether we are speaking of perception or imaging or thought). Any conscientious contemporary theorist recognizes some deep relationship between the two forms of structure—that action must be affected by the nature of perceptual organization and, in turn, that perception must be programmed by the requirements of action [p. 83].

The specification of the relationship between the "structure in action and structure in knowing" is the goal of a cognitive model of motivation.

VII

Review and Reinterpretation: The Cognitive Argument

The most systematic analysis of motivation, from both a theoretical and an empirical point of view, has been provided by drive theory. Although the hold this conception had upon psychology from 1940 to 1960 has now weakened, drive theory remains the most influential of the motivational conceptions. We will now reexamine some of the empirical foundations of the Hull-Spence approach, bringing to bear the more recent theoretical and empirical contributions outlined in prior chapters. It is argued that a mechanistic psychology is no longer adequate to account for the very data it generated (see Heckhausen and Weiner, 1972). Then some difficult issues cognitive theorists must face are outlined.

DEPRIVATION AND TISSUE INJURY STATES

The Mechanistic Analysis

The vast majority of research conducted by drive theorists has involved food or water deprivation or aversive stimulation, and has examined the effects of these drive operations upon a variety of dependent variables, such as the amount of consummatory activity, speed of learning, resistance to extinction, and so forth. The general finding in this area is that drive level is positively related to the dependent variable being assessed, although decreasing performance is observed when deprivation or stimulation is so intense that it interferes with organismic functioning. The early experiments conducted by Perin (1942) and Williams (1938), discussed in Chapter II, are typical of many deprivation studies. Groups varied according to the number of reinforced responses they received during learning. Different groups of animals were then deprived of food for either 3 or 22 hours. Reward was withheld during the test phase, and resistance to extinction of the instrumental response was assessed. The data, shown in Figure 2:4, reveal that at all levels of prior reinforcement, animals under 22 hours of deprivation display greater resistance to extinction than animals deprived for 3 hours.

Very similar data are reported when the strength of an aversive stimulus is the independent drive manipulation. For example, experiments conducted by Spence and other investigators, reported in Chapter II, demonstrate that the probability of a conditioned blink response to a puff of air to the eye is positively related to the strength of the aversive air puff. The greater the level of drive, in this instance operationally defined as the strength of a UCS, the more likely the activation of the blink response (see Figures 2:7 and 2:8).

The findings reviewed above logically follow from the Hull-Spence conception of behavior. Drive theory specifies that behavior is in part a function of the level of drive multiplying habit strength. Hence, the index of performance (resistance to extinction, probability of the response) should be augmented as the antecedent drive operation increases in magnitude. Drive is conceived as acting upon stimulus-response bonds, activating potential behavioral responses. The organism literally is driven from its resting state through a mechanical sequence of motor acts leading to the goal.

The Cognitive Analysis of Drive States

According to cognitive psychology, the stimuli accompanying a drive state provide the organism with information about its well-being. These internal stimuli are not rigidly connected with certain responses, as association theory specifies, nor do they necessarily increase the arousal or activation level of the organism, as drive theory specifies. Rather, appropriate action is taken on the basis of certain beliefs or knowledge. For example, if a deprived organism does not "know" about his hunger he will not initiate food-seeking behavior. There is a vast amount of data indicating that need states are not necessarily drive states. That is, deprivation or potential tissue injury may not have psychological consequences. Certain vitamin deficiencies and a lack of proper air can prove fatal, yet these conditions may not motivate appropriate instrumental behaviors. This fact often has been cited as embarrassing for drive theory, but it has not been pointed out that such data are very consistent with a cognitive conception of motivation.

One implication of the cognitive position is that if hungry organisms are "misinformed" about their internal state, they may act "as if" they are not hungry, and vice versa. One manner such misinformation perhaps has been conveyed to infrahumans is by direct electrical stimulation of brain centers. In humans, however, other methods have been employed, with the result that the individual inaccurately gauges his true deprivation state. For example, consider the experiments conducted by Brehm (1962), generated by the dissonance theory. Recall that dissonance has been aroused in "insufficient justification" paradigms. Individuals perform certain behaviors, such as telling a lie or agreeing to undergo continued food or water deprivation, when there is insufficient justification (little external reward) for such actions. According to Festinger's (1957a) theory of cognitive dissonance, the cognition of the act coupled with the cognition of the small reward for the action create dissonance. Dissonance is a drive state theoretically instigating behaviors that reduce the aroused dissonance. One manner in which the dissonance may be reduced is to perceive the unpleasant behavior as less aversive than it really "is."

It seems unlikely that the theory of cognitive dissonance and the research paradigm of insufficient justification would challenge the empirical base of drive theory, for dissonance is conceived as a drive state. One expects that the experiments generated by this cognitive conception of motivation merely would fall beyond the boundary conditions of mechanistic conceptions of motivation, as is true of most experiments growing from Lewinian field theory and Atkinson's theory of achievement motivation. That is, the dissonance research would not be amenable to interpretation from the Hull-Spence framework, but also would not lead one to question the drive theory explanation of behaviors instigated by food or water deprivation. But the research studies of Brehm do call into question the Hullian conception of drive. In these experiments, subjects are given insufficient justification to undergo continued food or water deprivation. These subjects rate themselves as less hungry and consume a lesser amount of water after agreeing to undergo continued deprivation than do subjects given sufficient justification for their action (see Figures 5:5 and 5:6). Apparently, subjects in the insufficient justification condition reduce their dissonance by "misjudging" their level of hunger or thirst.

It thus appears that hunger is a cognitive state. One's perception of his hunger and the degree of consumption based upon that perception may be influenced by a multiplicity of factors. Cues from the viscera provide one source of evidence concerning one's degree of hunger, while other sources of information are available that may validate or contradict the information provided by a parched throat or hunger cramps. Further, these other information sources may be weighted more heavily in the personal judgment of hunger or thirst than the more peripheral bodily cues. This is one explanation of the data reported by Brehm—the dissonance-generated information is more influential in determining the psychological hunger level than the actual amount of deprivation.[1]

In sum, it appears that the stimuli accompanying a drive state do not goad the organism into activity, acting directly upon the motor apparatus. Rather, deprivation stimuli are a source of information that is taken into account when making a decision to pursue a goal.

The experimental results of Grinker (1967), reported on pp. 304–5, lead to a similar conclusion. Grinker's experimental subjects were given high or low justification to continue in an aversive eyeblink experiment. These subjects subsequently were less likely to display the conditioned eyeblink response than control subjects not given the dissonance induction. Further, subjects in the high dissonance condition were less likely to respond with the conditioned blink than subjects in a low dissonance condition (see Figure 5:7). Apparently, subjects in the high dissonance condition conclude that the air puff is not very aversive. Thus, the subjective aversiveness and the contingent overt behavior are not invariably a direct function of the strength of a puff of air to the eye. The perception of the magnitude of pain may be veridical or nonveridical, and both "true" or "false" knowledge provide equal bases for action. In most instances the perceived aversiveness is judged only or primarily from the objective aversiveness of the stimulus. Thus, behavior may be predicted from the antecedent drive operation. But, as Grinker has demonstrated, this need not be the case.

Therefore, it is incorrect to conceive of a stimulus as acting directly upon an arousal mechanism without considering the intervening interpretation made by the organism. A mechanistic conception of behavior is not adequate to account for motivated behavior in the very deprivation and tissue injury situations that drive theory has most actively investigated.

---

[1] Still another possible explanation of the Brehm data, suggested by the writings of Bem (1967) and Kelley (1967), is that the organism infers his attitude (hunger) from his behavior. That is, the individual thinks, "I am volunteering to forgo food for little reward. Therefore, I must not be hungry." For this explanation to be plausible, the individual must not perceive the strong induced force from the experimenter to participate in the deprivation experiment, and thus can reach "false" causal inferences.

LEARNED DRIVES

The Mechanistic Analysis of Fear

Drive theorists realized that the vast majority of behaviors observed among humans, and much of infrahuman behavior, are instigated when organisms are neither hungry nor thirsty. Thus, these theorists had to broaden the base of the drive conception and postulate energizing conditions other than those resulting from immediate tissue damage. Mowrer (1939) and Miller (1948) provided the theoretical rationale and research paradigm to demonstrate the existence of immediate sources of drive other than food or water deprivation or aversive stimulation. By pairing distinctive cues with the onset of shock, these investigators demonstrated that these distinctive stimuli acquire the motivational properties of the shock itself. That is, they motivate and direct behavior, and their offset is reinforcing. It was contended that cues paired contiguously with aversive stimulation arouse fear or anxiety and that fear is a learned drive. More generally, Hull postulated that any stimulus could acquire drive properties if it were paired with the rapid onset and offset of a primary drive. Secondary drives, however, have been essentially limited to cues paired with shock or other aversive stimulation, such as a loud noise, bright light, and the like.

The emotion of fear is thus conceived as automatically and involuntarily aroused in the presence of cues previously paired with an aversive state. Fear is conceptualized as a drive, providing the motor for behavior. The behavior, in turn, results in the offset of the fear reaction. This analysis of fear not only extended Hullian theory, but also was employed to explain neurotic patterns of behavior (Dollard & Miller, 1950) and the great bulk of human activity (Brown, 1961). Thus, the stimulus-response conception of anxiety as a drive state apparently provided a powerful set of psychological principles with extensive behavioral implications.

The Cognitive Conception of Fear and Emotion

Cognitive psychologists contend that the stimuli or cues associated with pain indicate to the organism that danger is impending. Purposive behavior is undertaken to avoid an anticipated unpleasant event. The cues do not initiate an associative chain of reactions, nor do they necessarily result in continued arousal of the organism. Rather, the cues convey information; they are evaluated and appraised. Emotional expression and action are a result of the meaning imposed upon the environment.

The investigations conducted by Lazarus (1966) and his colleagues, discussed in Chapter V, demonstrate the effects of cognitive processes on emotional reactivity. In the research paradigm employed by Lazarus, subjects view a stress-inducing film. Some of the subjects watch this film while receiving defensive orientations of denial or intellectualization. These defenses generally are conceived as ego processes or higher mental functions that aid the organism in coping with its environment. The data from the Lazarus experiments indicate that subjects receiving defensive orientations do exhibit less emotionality toward the contents of the film than subjects in whom coping behavior is not facilitated (see Figures 5:1 and 5:2).

The research of Schachter and Singer (1962) and Valins (1966) also provides convincing evidence concerning the role of cognitive processes in determining emotional reactions and contingent behaviors. Recall that Valins and his associates give subjects objectively incorrect information pertinent to their liking of nude pictures or their fear of snakes. This misinformation systematically influences the subjects' overt actions toward these objects. For example, subjects who "incorrectly" cognize that they are not afraid of snakes will subsequently pick up and hold these animals.

In sum, the cues associated with an emotion-provoking event are a source of information influencing behavior. As in the case of hunger or thirst, in most instances the subjective effects of the behavior-inducing stimuli are in one-to-one correspondence with their objective properties. Thus, behavior may be predicted from antecedent operations such as hours of deprivation, strength of the shock, or size of a snake; cognitive processes apparently need not be inferred. But the relationship between objective antecedents and subjective meaning may be experimentally severed, altered, or masked to reveal that cognitions are the effective behavioral determinants. For example, the individual may be induced to feel that he is not hungry, despite a long period of deprivation; to think that a shock is not painful, despite its magnitude; or to experience that a film does not arouse fear, despite the stressful events it is portraying. In all instances, it is the thought processes that control behavior.

INDIVIDUAL DIFFERENCES IN EMOTIONAL REACTIVITY

The Mechanistic Analysis of Verbal Learning

Spence, Taylor, and their co-workers extended the Hull-Spence conception to incorporate individual differences in the strength of drive. The initial investigations in this area were suggested by the findings in the study of aversive conditioning. As indicated, it was demonstrated that as the strength of a UCS (puff of air to the eye) increases, the probability of a conditioned eyeblink response also increases (see Figures 2:7 and 2:8). Guided by these data, Spence and Taylor reasoned that if individuals differed in their emotional reactivity toward a UCS, some individuals would behave "as if" that UCS were stronger than others. The emotionally reactive (high drive) individuals should be more likely to display the conditioned eyelid response than individuals low in emotional reactivity (drive).

The Manifest Anxiety Scale was developed as a measure of emotional reactivity, and theoretically orders individuals according to their drive strength. It was then demonstrated that individuals scoring high on this self-report inventory do condition faster in the aversive eyeblink paradigm than individuals scoring low in drive (see Figure 2:8). This finding provided construct validity for the scale, as well as additional evidence for the Drive $\times$ Habit conception of motivation.

The above analysis subsequently was amplified to include human instrumental learning situations. It was reasoned that the conceptual analysis of the instrumental learning of a task labeled as "easy" is in some ways similar to the analysis of the learning of an eyeblink response in an aversive conditioning paradigm. In both the easy task and the aversive conditioning situations there is an initially highly dominant response to the presented stimulus. Further, this response is "correct" in that it results in the avoidance of the aversive stimulation (the air puff) or in the attainment of positive reinforcement (the confirmed right answer). Hence, individuals high in drive were expected to perform better on easy instrumental learning tasks, as well as in the conditioned eyeblink situation, than persons low in drive.

To test this hypothesis, subjects were given a paired-associates task to learn in which the correct responses were synonyms of the stimuli to which they were paired. Thus, the responses were dominant associates to the stimuli prior to the onset of the learning task. The learning data substantiated the prediction of drive theory: subjects high in drive performed better at this task than subjects low in drive (see Figure 2:9).

On difficult tasks, however, drive theorists hypothesized that subjects high in drive are hampered by their anxiety level, for incorrect responses are activated that compete with the correct response. Thus, it was predicted that at difficult tasks, subjects low in drive would perform better than the high drive subjects. As Figure 2:10 indicates, this prediction also was substantiated.

In sum, an interaction was expected between task difficulty and level of drive. High drive (high score on the Manifest Anxiety Scale) was hypothesized to lead to superior performance at easy tasks, but to inferior performance at difficult tasks. The confirmation of these hypotheses seemed to demonstrate that the mechanistic drive conception could uniquely and accurately predict speed of learning in disparate verbal-learning situations. These data have been cited extensively in the psychological literature.

The Cognitive Analysis of Verbal Learning

As a subject participates in a psychological experiment, many different thoughts might enter his mind. What is the experimenter trying to prove? What am I learning about myself from this experience? In addition, if the experiment includes an achievement-related activity, the subject is likely to be concerned with the quality of his performance. He might wonder, Am I doing well or poorly? How well have others performed at this task? What are my chances of getting this problem correct on the next try?

The possibility that subjects are evaluating their performance during an experiment is of special interest in the present context, for self-evaluative processes might account for the observed interaction between task difficulty and level of drive (anxiety). Perhaps an individual learning a task rapidly perceives that he is succeeding; that is, performing well relative to his own standards and/or relative to others in his social comparison group. On the other hand, an individual learning a task slowly may interpret his performance as a failure. He may infer that others are learning more rapidly than he, that his performance is not at a personally acceptable level, and so on.

It has been shown that subjective reactions to perceived success and failure mediate between response feedback and subsequent task performance, and that the motivational consequences of these reactions are, in part, determined by individual differences in level of anxiety. Investigations of achievement motivation have demonstrated that the performance of highly anxious individuals is inhibited by failure but facilitated by success experiences. Conversely, subjects low in anxiety are motivated by failure, but tend to "relax" following success. If it were assumed that performance at a difficult task results in a subjective failure experience because of the relatively slow rate of learning, while performance at an easy task produces subjective success because of the speed of mastery, then the results reported by Spence and Taylor are consistent with the data in the more cognitive achievement literature. That is, highly anxious subjects perform better given success experiences (easy task) and worse given failure experiences (difficult task) than subjects low in anxiety.

To test the hypothesis that individual differences in reactions to success and failure are the determinants of the interaction observed by Spence, Taylor, and their colleagues, Weiner (1966b), and Weiner and Schneider

(1971) experimentally severed the inherent relationships between failure-difficult task and success-easy task. Their subjects were given false social norms indicating that they were succeeding at a difficult verbal learning task or failing at an easy verbal learning task. Now the cognitive position led to the hypotheses that subjects high in anxiety would perform better at the difficult (successful) task and worse at the easy (failed) task than subjects low in anxiety. These predictions were directly contradictory to those derived from the drive theoretical analysis.

The data substantiated the hypotheses from the cognitive conception, while contradicting drive theory (see Table 2:3). The subjective evaluation of one's performance, interacting with individual differences in anxiety, were the essential determinants of speed of learning in this situation. A mechanistic conception therefore cannot account for the empirical results in the verbal learning investigations; performance is not merely determined by drive level activating mechanistic associative bonds. Rather, social comparison and self-evaluative processes mediate between the perception of the task stimulus and the behavioral response.

As in the investigations of hunger, thirst, aversive stimulation, and learned fear, a new experimental paradigm was needed to demonstrate the effects of mediating cognitions on performance. By separating the antecedent task stimuli operation (task difficulty) from the subjective effects of those stimuli (success and failure), it was demonstrated that the stimulus effects are mediated by interpretive (evaluative) thought processes.

RESISTANCE TO EXTINCTION

The Mechanistic Analysis of Extinction

Resistance to extinction, which was discussed when the deprivation experiments of Perin and Williams were examined, has been one of the most widely investigated dependent variables within experimental psychology. This may be because of the unusual, reliable, and extensive finding that partial reinforcement increases the resistance to extinction.

There have been a variety of theoretical attempts to account for experimental extinction and the partial reinforcement effect (PRE). The explanation most clearly related to the neobehaviorism of Hull and Spence was advanced by Amsel (1958, 1967). Amsel contends that the nonattainment of an anticipated reward produces frustration. That is, when an instrumental response repeatedly has been followed by a reward, and then the reward is withheld, frustration is produced. Frustration is conceptualized as a drive state that energizes behavior. In addition, the aversive frustration reaction generates distinctive stimuli, or frustration-produced cues, that can become the basis for new learning. In a straight-runway situation, the paradigm often used by Amsel and his associates, it is assumed that the cues in the alleyway are similar to those in the goal box. The frustration experienced at the goal when the reward is withheld is assumed to generalize back through the alleyway, and frustration-produced cues are presumed to be evoked when the animal is placed at the start of the runway.

Therefore, the animal at the start of the runway following an extinction trial is conceptualized as in an approach-avoidance conflict situation. The cues in the alleyway evoke approach behavior because they previously had been followed by reward, and avoidance behavior because the cues were followed by frustration when the reward was not attained. Amsel contends that when the avoidance tendency exceeds that of the approach due to the continued nonreinforcement, extinction is displayed.

Amsel employs this frustration analysis of extinction to explain the PRE. In a partial reinforcement schedule, the responding organism is repeatedly both rewarded and not rewarded in the identical stimulus situation. Amsel states that this sequence of positive and negative reinforcement results in the anticipatory frustration-produced cues evoking approach as well as avoidance behavior. The conditioning of the frustration cues to reward is believed to retard extinction when the reward is permanently withheld. That is, the animals learn to persist in the face of cues signaling nonreward because these cues also are associated with positive reinforcement. In sum, Amsel (1967) accounts for extinction and the PRE by "stressing the role of hypothetically classically conditioned responses and their assumed motivational and associative effects" (p. 4).

The Cognitive Analysis of Extinction

There have been many cognitive interpretations of experimental extinction and the PRE. Three theoretical approaches to extinction were introduced in Chapter VI: dissonance theory, social learning theory, and attribution theory. All three theories call attention to the role of higher mental processes in determining the persistence of behavior.

Cognitive Dissonance.   The prior discussion of the experiments conducted by Brehm (1962) and Grinker (1967) suggest that when actions are performed for insufficient justification, dissonance is aroused. During partial reinforcement or extinction, the animal engages in some action, but reward does not necessarily follow. Hence, these reward-withholding manipulations theoretically arouse dissonance, and the data generated in these situations are amenable to interpretation from the dissonance viewpoint.

According to Festinger (1957a), when dissonance is aroused the organism is motivated to reconstruct his cognitions so they attain a more balanced state. Lawrence and Festinger (1962), guided by the demonstration experiment of Aronson and Mills (1959), suggest that one manner in which cognitive consonance might be attained is to perceive greater rewards in the situation than there really are. For example, the physical situation might be perceived as interesting, thus satisfying curiosity motivation; the occasional reward might be perceived as especially tasteful, or of great magnitude, and so forth. If this were true, then the motivation to engage in the instrumental action would be augmented. One consequence of such an increment in motivation would be to retard extinction.

Lawrence and Festinger claim that a variety of experimental manipulations employed by psychologists arouse dissonance, such as partial reinforcement, delaying the reward, and requiring an effortful response. Further, they have summarized data and have demonstrated that these manipulations increase resistance to extinction (see Table 5:3).

Social Learning Theory.   According to Rotter (1954), the tendency to engage in an action is determined by the expectancy of reinforcement and the value of that reinforcer. The expectancy of the goal event is a function of two factors: a specific expectancy, based upon the prior reinforcement history in that specific stimulus situation, and a generalized expectancy, which is determined by previous behavioral outcomes across a variety of relevant situations.

The generalized expectancy of reinforcement, in turn, is in part determined by the perception of a situation as internally or externally controlled. It is argued by Rotter that when reinforcements are not perceived as contingent upon one's own behavior, then one cannot infer the likelihood of future reinforcement from the prior outcomes. For example, a reinforcement gained in a situation perceived as chance determined may not increase the subsequent expectancy of further reinforcement. When five dollars is found on the street, he states, the finder does not believe that another five dollars will be found at the same spot on another occasion. On the other hand, when outcomes are perceived as skill or internally determined, future consequences can be inferred on the basis of prior reinforcement history.

Social learning theory and the concept of locus of control were used by Phares (1957) to elucidate resistance to extinction. In Phares' investigation, subjects in one experimental condition were informed that the outcome of the task they were attempting was decided by skill. Subjects in a second condition were informed that a correct response (reinforcement) was entirely a matter of chance. Following an identical schedule of partial reinforcement, extinction procedures were initiated. It was found that subjects in the chance instruction condition took longer to extinguish (inferred from the amount of money bet) than subjects who were told that the task was skill-determined. Thus, resistance to extinction is a function of the perception of the causes of an outcome.

Rotter and his colleagues then extended this finding, examining the interaction of locus of control with reinforcement schedule in influencing resistance to extinction. They report that when reinforcement is perceived as skill-determined, continuous or 100 percent reward results in greater resistance to extinction than partial reward. This finding is in opposition to the empirical generalization in the animal literature that partial reinforcement most retards extinction. On the other hand, Rotter and his co-workers report that when a task is perceived as chance-determined, resistance to extinction is greater given a 50 percent than 100 percent schedule of reinforcements (see Table 5:4 and Figure 5:14). In spite of some serious theoretical and methodological shortcomings of these experiments, the evidence again demonstrates that the relationships between reward schedules and resistance to extinction are in part a function of mediating thought processes concerning the assignment of responsibility for the reinforcer.

Attribution Theory. My colleagues and I have argued that in achievement-related contexts, success and failure are attributed to four causal factors: ability, effort, task difficulty, and luck. When evaluating an achievement-related outcome, the person assesses his (or another's) level of ability, the effort expended, the luck experienced, and the difficulty of the task. Relative weights are then assigned to these factors as the perceived "reasons" for the prior success and failure.

Two of the four causal factors listed above, ability and task difficulty, are conceptualized as relatively stable. That is, they remain comparatively invariant over time. On the other hand, the remaining two causal factors, effort and luck, are relatively variable. They may change from moment to moment (see Table 6:1).

Weiner et al. (1971) argue that the perceived stability of the causal factors in part determines the changes in the expectancy of success following success or failure. Outcomes attributed to stable factors are believed to be more likely to recur in the future than outcomes ascribed to unstable factors (see Figure 6:8). Thus, for example, if one believes that success was caused by high ability or by the ease of the task, then on subsequent occasions success should be expected again when attempting the task. In a similar manner, failure ascribed to low ability or to the difficulty of the task should promote the belief that failure will again be encountered on subsequent attempts at the task. Conversely, if failure is ascribed to the variable causal determinants of behavior, that is, luck or effort, then success might be expected on subsequent occasions. Luck may change, and effort can be increased if there is an intent to succeed.

Attributions of the outcome to ability and task difficulty theoretically have similar effects on the expectancy of success, although one is considered internal and the other external in locus of control. Ability is a property of the person while task difficulty is a property of the environment. Similarly, ascriptions of achievement outcomes to effort and luck may have similar effects on the expectancy of future success, although they also are properties of the person and of the environment, respectively. Thus, the stability of the attributional dimension, rather than its locus of control, theoretically determines future expectancies of success and failure.

The hypothesized relationships between the stability of the causal dimension and the expectancy of success have been examined by Meyer (1970). Meyer had subjects estimate their expectancy of success on five trials at an achievement-related task. On all trials failure was induced. In addition, following each failure the subjects attributed the prior outcome to the causal factors of ability, effort, task difficulty, and luck. The data, shown in Figures 6:10 and 6:11, reveal that factor stability is related to expectancy shifts. When prior failure is attributed to lack of ability or to task difficulty, expectancies drop to a greater extent than when failure is believed to be caused by a lack of effort or bad luck.

Weiner et al. extended this analysis to the study of extinction. They reasoned that ascription of nonattainment of a goal to bad luck or to a lack of effort retards extinction. Thus, partial reinforcement—which is an antecedent cue making one think that the outcome is due to luck—is presumed to (and does) retard extinction. Similarly, the requirement of an effortful response (Lawrence & Festinger, 1962), which is a cue leading one to infer that effort is an important causal determinant, also retards extinction. On the other hand, it is contended that attributions of the attainment of a goal to low ability or to a hard task hasten extinction. Experimentation by Weiner et al. offers some support for these hypotheses (see Figure 6:16).

Weiner et al. also employ this causal analysis to explain the differential persistence of behavior (which may be considered a measure of resistance to extinction) exhibited by individuals classified as high or low in achievement motivation. Persons high in achievement motivation frequently persist in the face of failure. This behavior apparently is mediated by a general tendency to ascribe failure to a lack of effort, which presumably is modifiable. Hence, following failure, individuals high in achievement needs keep trying and work harder. Conversely, individuals low in achievement needs tend to quit the activity in progress when experiencing failure. This behavior apparently is mediated by a general tendency to ascribe failure to a lack of ability, which presumably is fixed. Hence, following failure they may give up and become disengaged from the task. In sum, differential reactions to frustration exhibited by individuals high or low in achievement needs appear to be due to the disparate psychological interpretations of the reasons for the failure.

In sum, there is ample evidence indicating that attributions of causality mediate between task outcomes and future behavioral expectancies. Schedules of reinforcement are related to resistance to extinction because they systematically influence the thought processes evoked by the reinforcement patterns.

ISSUES FOR A COGNITIVE PSYCHOLOGY OF MOTIVATION

It has been contended that a mechanistic psychology of motivation is no longer viable. The empirical foundation upon which drive theory was built is strongly in question. Recent investigations of hunger, thirst, pain, fear, anxiety, and resistance to extinction all indicate that cognitive processes mediate between stimulus onset and the final behavioral response. The empirical evidence leads to the inescapable conclusion that thought influences action. In addition, a vast amount of data in the motivational literature, such as the experiments reviewed in Chapters III and IV, fall beyond the boundaries of a mechanistic theory. The Hull-Spence conception of behavior simply is unable to account for the richness and complexity of human action. A cognitive psychology of motivation is the alternative toward which psychologists must turn. Indeed, the trend toward cognition certainly has been evident in recent years.

A multitude of problems must now be faced by a cognitive psychology in general, and the cognitive study of motivation in particular. Some of the issues in question are now briefly outlined. The list is far from complete, including only a small subset of problems and obstacles that require a great deal of thought before some resolution is attained.

Science versus Ethnoscience

The motivational models postulated by Hull, Lewin, and Atkinson supposedly contain the *true* determinants of action. For example, speed of running down an alleyway is postulated to be determined by drive level and the habit strength of the running response, interacting in a multiplicative manner; performance at an achievement-related activity is postulated to be a function of the strength of achievement and anxiety personality dispositions multiplying the perceived probabilities of success and failure.

But the cognitive psychology of motivation proposed by Heider, this writer, and others outlines what individuals *perceive* as the determinants of action. The naive psychology of behavior may or may not be isomorphic with the actual determinants of performance. For example, one may perceive that the outcome at a task is determined only by effort expenditure. He believes that if he or another person tries hard success will be attained; if he or another is not diligent, failure is expected to be the outcome. But the true or "real" determinants of outcome may be effort interacting with ability, or even luck. Thus, in this situation, the science of motivation might specify that performance is a function of ability and effort, although the enthoscience of motivation states that performance is a function of only effort.

It is evident that the science of motivation and the ethnoscience of motivation overlap. But their interrelationships remain to be clarified. For example, it might be contended that thoughts about motivation completely determine actual performance. But this is not likely. Nor is it reasonable to assume that the naive person is conversant with the complete laws of behavior, including the mathematical relationships between the components in a motivational model. Yet if action is determined by thoughts, then naive science must in some way influence what the true science will be. For this reason free will and determinism are not mutually exclusive.

Levels of Consciousness and a New Methodology

Early in the history of psychology, the psychoanalytic movement, with its concern with dynamics and conflict, presented one alternative to the static approach of the structuralists. In addition, psychoanalytic theorists argued that the introspective method advocated by the structuralists was inadequate. The important determinants of behavior, they reasoned, are unconscious and unavailable to the conscious mind given a simple introspective approach. Freud and others, therefore, developed novel methodological techniques, such as free association, dream analysis (the "royal road" to the unconscious), and projective instruments to discover these unconscious thoughts and ideas.

The cognitivists of today, like the structuralists of yesterday, face identical methodological problems. A cognitive psychology of motivation generally requires that cognitions be treated as observables; the cognitions should be available for examination and introspection is accepted as a viable methodology. But if the determinants of behavior are unconscious, then a naive analysis of action could not possibly be complete, for the "common man" does not have access to the real causes of action. In addition, even if the causes of behavior are not unconscious, they may be difficult or impossible to communicate accurately.

Lewin apparently did not feel that this was a critical problem. Although he was a phenomenologist, he contended that the life space need not be conscious. But the life space then has to be inferred from the behavior of the individual, resulting in a post-hoc analysis of action. Further, if feelings as well as thoughts may be unconscious, then the study of the experience of the subject becomes very difficult indeed.

Of course, one can manipulate cognitions and not be overly concerned with the consciousness or unconsciousness of these thoughts. For example, Lazarus does not discuss the consciousness of the coping mechanisms of denial or intellectualization. His approach stresses the *consequences* of *inferred* processes.

But what obviously is needed is a new methodology that allows one to reliably and validly infer the thought processes of oneself and others. Projective techniques, free association, dream analysis, unguided introspection, and other techniques already evolved may be able to provide the foundation for the development of such a methodology.

The development of this methodology is needed not only to provide access to *unconscious* thoughts. The investigation of *preconscious* ideas also requires new research techniques. Theoretically, these preconscious ideas are available to the person without overcoming repressive barriers. Yet the very act of making these ideas conscious might alter their behavioral consequences. In achievement-related contexts, for example, behavior is in part determined by a subjective expectancy of success. To discover this *subjective* probability level, the methodology most frequently used is merely to ask the subject what are his chances of success. But ascertaining the expectancy in this manner may make the probability a salient component of the action, and perhaps alter its influence on the action. In addition, the very act of asking may affect the subjective expectancy. What is needed is a method in which the expectancy becomes known by the investigator, but remains "unknown" or not necessarily verbalized by the subject. The expectancy would then remain in the preconscious of the subject, but be in the consciousness of the experimenter.

Problems also exist in the tapping of conscious thoughts. This is a delicate task, for biases may be introduced, content neglected, interference with the normal flow of behavior injected, and so on. In sum, a methodology adequate for a cognitive psychology must be built.

The Body-Mind Problem

The body-mind distinction often attributed to Descartes remains a fundamental problem for psychologists. Presenting the complexities of this issue is beyond both the scope of this book and the capabilities of this writer.

But if a mind-body dualism is held, and it is believed that both the body and the mind are responsible for action, then the cognitive motivational theorist must ask how does the mind influence, act upon, and interact with bodily processes. What is the mode of the relationship between thought and action? What mechanisms mediate this interaction? If this relationship is not specified, then the acting organism, like Tolman's rat, may end up "buried in thought." This is one problem the mechanists do not have to face.

A Cognitive Psychology of Infrahumans

There is general agreement that the attainment of knowledge does not presuppose the ability to verbalize. Psychotics, mutes, and infrahumans may not verbalize, yet higher-order structures do develop. Inasmuch as the concepts of "cognition" and "knowledge" are interchangeable in many ways, it is reasonable to presume that lower organisms also have cognitions. In infrahumans, however, cognitions are not directly assessible via introspective reports. But they may be inferred from behavior in an acceptable scientific manner, providing that such inferences are not reached in a repeatedly post-hoc manner. The inferences must be consistent with other empirical facts and fit within a useful conceptual framework. For example, Maier, Seligman, and Solomon (1969) report that learning is retarded in an instrumental avoidance situation because of the prior learning in a classical aversive conditioning paradigm, although the stimulus situations in which the two learning experiences take place appear to have no common cues. They then ask what are the general principles of the two learning situations the animals are extracting. Given the experimenters' conclusion that the general principle in this instance concerns the locus of control, it would be profitable to examine the extant empirical and conceptual thoughts in the control area that might lead one to expect speed of learning to be retarded in the second learning situation. In sum, a logical chain of reasoning permits the reasonable inference that cognitive processes are operative in this situation. Superstitious behavior, the partial reinforcement effect, and other phenomena discussed earlier in this chapter and in Chapter V are amenable to similar cognitive analyses.

Of course, the cognitive structures of humans are more complex than those of infrahumans, and suppositions concerning the cognitions of animals must be made with care. Morgan's Canon (1896) states, "In no case is an animal activity to be interpreted as an outcome of the exercise of a higher psychical faculty, if it can be fairly interpreted as the outcome of an exercise which stands lower on the psychological scale" (p. 59). This is not an unreasonable warning, for it reminds one to exercise caution when using mental processes as psychological constructs. But it is justifiable to employ higher mental faculties to explain behavior that is interpretable with mechanistic principles, *if* such an explanation has greater generality, is more consistent with the related empirical findings, and so forth, than the mechanistic interpretation. Morgan's Canon should be considered a guiding statement, rather than an invariant law.

Quantitative Exactness

The Hull-Spence conceptions of motivation are especially impressive in that the terms in the drive models are anchored to manipulable antecedents, the components in the theories are treated quantitatively, and exact predictions are derived mathematically from stated relationships between the theoretical concepts. Some of these virtues are found in Lewinian field theory and in Atkinson's theory of achievement motivation, but to a lesser extent.

The cognitive conceptions of motivation outlined in Chapters V and VI have not reached the high level of theory formation that characterize drive theory. Perhaps the lack of mathematical precision is advantageous at this early stage of development, for premature formalization can stifle new ideas and conceptual growth. But in the future, more formal cognitive models are the goals toward which motivational psychologists must strive.

References

Abelson, R. P., Aronson, E., McGuire, W. J., Newcomb, T. M., Rosenberg, M. J., & Tannenbaum, P. H. (Eds.) *Theories of cognitive consistency: A sourcebook*. Chicago: Rand McNally, 1968.

Ach, N. *Uber den Willensakt und das Temperament*. Leipzig: Quelle und Meyer, 1910.

Adler, D. L., and Kounin, J. S. Some factors operating at the moment of resumption of interrupted tasks. *Journal of Psychology,* 1939, **7,** 255–267.

Allport, F. H. *Theories of perception and the concept of structure*. New York: Wiley, 1955.

American Psychological Association, American Educational Research Association and Council on Measurement Used in Education (Joint Committee). Technical Recommendations for psychological tests and diagnostic techniques. *Psychological Bulletin,* 1954, **51,** 201–238.

Amsel, A. The role of frustrative nonreward in noncontinuous reward situations. *Psychological Bulletin,* 1958, **55,** 102–119.

Amsel, A. Partial reinforcement. In K. W. Spence & J. A. Taylor (Eds.), *The psychology of learning and motivation*. Vol. 1. New York: Academic Press, 1967. Pp. 1–65.

Amsel, A., & Maltzman, I. The effect upon generalized strength of emotionality as inferred from the level of consummatory response. *Journal of Experimental Psychology,* 1950, **40,** 563–569.

Amsel, A., & Roussel, J. Motivational properties of frustration: I. Effect on a running response of the addition of frustration to the motivational complex. *Journal of Experimental Psychology,* 1952, **43,** 363–368.

Amsel, A., & Ward, J. S. Motivational properties of frustration: II. Frustration drive stimulus and frustration reduction in selective learning. *Journal of Experimental Psychology,* 1954, **48,** 37–47.

Amsel, A., & Ward, J. S. Frustration and persistence: Resistance to discrimination following prior experience with the discriminanda. *Psychological Monographs,* 1965, **79** (4, Whole No. 597).

Arkoff, A. Resolution of approach-approach and avoidance-avoidance conflicts. *Journal of Abnormal and Social Psychology,* 1957, **55,** 402–404.

Aronson, E., & Carlsmith, J. M. Effects of severity of threat on the deviation of forbidden behavior. *Journal of Abnormal and Social Psychology,* 1963, **66,** 584–588.

Aronson, E., & Mills, J. The effect of severity of initiation on liking for a group. *Journal of Abnormal and Social Psychology,* 1959, **59,** 177–181.

Atkinson, J. W. The achievement motive and recall of interrupted and completed tasks. *Journal of Experimental Psychology,* 1953, **46,** 381–390.

Atkinson, J. W. Explorations using imaginative thought to assess the strength of human motives. In M. R. Jones (Ed.), *Nebraska symposium on motivation.* Vol. 2. Lincoln: University of Nebraska Press, 1954. Pp. 56–112.

Atkinson, J. W. Motivational determinants of risk-taking behavior. *Psychological Review,* 1957, **64,** 359–372.

Atkinson, J. W. Thematic apperceptive measurement of motives within a context of motivation. In J. W. Atkinson (Ed.), *Motives in fantasy, action, and society.* Princeton, N.J.: Van Nostrand, 1958. Pp. 596–616. (a)

Atkinson, J. W. Towards experimental analysis of human motivation in terms of motives, expectancies, and incentives. In J. W. Atkinson (Ed.), *Motives in fantasy, action, and society.* Princeton, N.J.: Van Nostrand, 1958. Pp. 288–305. (b)

Atkinson, J. W. Personality dynamics. *Annual Review of Psychology.* Palo Alto, Calif.: Annual Reviews, Inc., 1960. Pp. 255–290.

Atkinson, J. W. The final diminution of drive. *Contemporary Psychology,* 1961, **6,** 91–93.

Atkinson, J. W. *An introduction to motivation.* Princeton, N.J.: Van Nostrand, 1964.

Atkinson, J. W. Change of activity: A new focus for the theory of motivation. In T. Mischel (Ed.), *Human action.* New York: Academic Press, 1969. Pp. 105–133.

Atkinson, J. W., & Birch, D. *A dynamic theory of action.* New York: Wiley, 1970.

Atkinson, J. W., & Cartwright, D. Some neglected variables in contemporary conceptions of decision and performance. *Psychological Reports,* 1964, **14,** 575–590.

Atkinson, J. W., Earl, R. W., & Litwin, G. H. The achieving motive, goal setting, and probability preferences. *Journal of Abnormal and Social Psychology,* 1960, **60,** 27–36.

Atkinson, J. W., & Feather, N. T. (Eds.) *A theory of achievement motivation.* New York: Wiley, 1966.

Atkinson, J. W., & Litwin, G. H. Achievement motive and test anxiety conceived as a motive to approach success and to avoid failure. *Journal of Abnormal and Social Psychology,* 1960, **60,** 52–63.

Atkinson, J. W., & McClelland, D. C. The projective expression of needs: II. The effect of different intensities of the hunger drive on thematic apperception. *Journal of Experimental Psychology,* 1948, **33,** 643–658.

Atkinson, J. W., & O'Connor, P. *Effects of ability grouping in schools related to individual differences in achievement-related motivation.* Final report, Office of Education Cooperative Research Program, Project 1283, 1963. Available in microfilm from Photoduplication Center, Library of Congress, Washington, D.C.

Baldwin, A. L. A cognitive theory of socialization. In D. A. Goslin (Ed.), *Handbook of socialization theory and research.* Chicago: Rand McNally, 1969. Pp. 325–346.

Barefoot, J. C., & Straub, R. B. Opportunity for information search and the effect of false heart feedback. *Journal of Personality and Social Psychology,* 1971, **17,** 154–157.

Barker, R. G. Ecology and motivation. In M. R. Jones (Ed.), *Nebraska symposium on motivation.* Vol. 8. Lincoln: University of Nebraska Press, 1960. Pp. 1–49.

Barker, R. G. (Ed.) *Stream of behavior.* New York: Appleton-Century-Crofts, 1963.

Barker, R. G. Explorations in ecological psychology. *American Psychologist,* 1965, **20,** 1–13.

Barker, R. G., Dembo, T., & Lewin, K. Frustration and regression. In R. G. Barker, J. S. Kounin, & H. F. Wright (Eds.), *Child Behavior and Development.* New York: McGraw-Hill, 1943. Pp. 441–458.

Barker, R. G., Dembo, T., & Lewin, K. Frustration and regression: An experiment with young children. *University of Iowa Studies in Child Welfare,* 1941, **18,** No. 1.

Barker, R. G., Dembo, T., Lewin, K., & Wright, M. E. Experimental studies in frustration in young children. In T. M. Newcomb, & E. L. Hartley (Eds.), *Readings in social psychology*. New York: Holt, 1947. Pp. 283–290.

Barker, R. G., & Gump, P. V. (Eds.) *Big school, small school: High school size and student behavior*. Stanford, Calif.: Stanford University Press, 1964.

Barker, R. G., & Wright, H. F. *Midwest and its children*. New York: Harper & Row, 1955.

Battle, E., & Rotter, J. B. Children's feelings of personal control as related to social class and ethnic group. *Journal of Personality*, 1963, **31,** 482–490.

Beach, F. The descent of instinct. *Psychological Review*, 1955, **62,** 401–410.

Beckman, L. J. Effects of students' performance on teachers' and observers' attributions of causality. *Journal of Educational Psychology,* 1970, **61,** 76–82.

Bem, D. J. Self-perception: An alternative interpretation of cognitive dissonance phenomena. *Psychological Review,* 1967, **74,** 183–200.

Berlyne, D. E. *Conflict, arousal and curiosity*. New York: McGraw-Hill, 1961.

Berlyne, D. Behavior theory as personality theory. In E. F. Borgatta, & W. W. Lambert (Eds.), *Handbook of personality theory and research*. Chicago: Rand McNally, 1968. Pp. 629–690.

Bernard, L. L. *Instinct: A study of social psychology*. New York: Holt, 1924.

Bindra, D. Neuropsychological interpretation of the effects of drive and incentive-motivation on general activity and instrumental behavior. *Psychological Review,* 1968, **75,** 1–22.

Bindra, D. The interrelated mechanisms of reinforcement and motivation, and the nature of their influences on response. In W. J. Arnold & D. Levine (Eds.), *Nebraska symposium on motivation*. Vol. 17. Lincoln: University of Nebraska Press, 1969, Pp. 1–38.

Bindra, D., Patterson, A. L., & Strzelecki, J. On the relation between anxiety and conditioning. *Canadian Journal of Psychology,* 1955, **9,** 1–6.

Birch, D., Burnstein, E., & Clark, R. A. Response strength as a function of food deprivation under a controlled maintenance schedule. *Journal of Comparative and Physiological Psychology,* 1958, **51,** 350–354.

Birney, R. C. Research on the achievement motive. In E. F. Borgatta & W. W. Lambert (Eds.), *Handbook of personality theory and research*. Chicago: Rand McNally, 1968. Pp. 857–889.

Bitterman, M. E. Thorndike and the problem of animal intelligence. *American Psychologist,* 1969, **24,** 444–453.

Black, R. W. On the combination of drive and incentive motivation. *Psychological Review,* 1965, **72,** 310–317.

Blodgett, H. C. The effect of the introduction of reward upon maze performance of rats. Berkeley: *University of California Publication in Psychology,* 1929, **4,** No. 8, 113–134.

Blum, G. S. *A model of the mind.* New York: Wiley, 1961.

Bolles, R. C. *Theory of motivation.* New York: Harper & Row, 1967.

Boring, E. G. *A history of experimental psychology.* (2nd ed.) New York: Appleton-Century-Crofts, 1950.

Braun, H. W., Wedekind, C. E., & Smudski, J. E. The effect of an irrelevant drive on maze learning in the rat. *Journal of Experimental Psychology,* 1957, **54,** 148–152.

Brehm, J. W. Post-decision changes in the desirability of alternatives. *Journal of Abnormal and Social Psychology,* 1956, **52,** 384–389.

Brehm, J. W. Motivational effects of cognitive dissonance. In M. R. Jones (Ed.), *Nebraska symposium on motivation.* Vol. 10. Lincoln: University of Nebraska Press, 1962. Pp. 51–77.

Brehm, J. W., & Cohen, A. R. *Explorations in cognitive dissonance.* New York: Wiley, 1962.

Brown, J. S. Gradients of approach and avoidance responses and their relation to level of motivation. *Journal of Comparative and Physiological Psychology,* 1948, **41,** 450–465.

Brown, J. S. Principles of intrapersonal conflict. *Conflict Resolution,* 1957, **1,** 135–154.

Brown, J. S. *The motivation of behavior.* New York: McGraw-Hill, 1961.

Brown, J. S., Anderson, D. C., & Brown, C. S. Conflict as a function of food-deprivation during approach training, avoidance training, and conflict tests. *Journal of Experimental Psychology,* 1966, **72,** 390–400.

Brown, J. S., & Belloni, M. Performances as a function of deprivation time following periodic feeding in an isolated environment. *Journal of Comparative and Physiological Psychology,* 1963, **56,** 105–110.

Brown, J. S., & Farber, I. E. Emotions conceptualized as intervening variables—with suggestions toward a theory of frustration. *Psychological Bulletin,* 1951, **48,** 465–495.

Bruner, J. Going beyond the information given. In *Colorado symposium on cognition.* London: Oxford University Press, 1957. Pp. 41–67.

Bruner, J. S. Constructive cognitions. *Contemporary Psychology,* 1970, **15,** 81–83.

Brunswik, E. Organismic achievement and environmental probability. *Psychological Review,* 1943, **50,** 255–272.

Brunswik, E. *Perception and the representative design of psychological experiments.* Berkeley: University of California Press, 1956.

Bugelski, B. R. Extinction with and without sub-goal reinforcement. *Journal of Comparative Psychology,* 1938, **26,** 121–133.

Butterfield, E. C. The interruption of tasks: Methodological, factual and theoretical issues. *Psychological Bulletin,* 1964, **62,** 309–322.

Butterfield, E. C., & Zigler, E. The effect of success and failure on the discrimination learning of normal and retarded children. *Journal of Abnormal and Social Psychology,* 1965, **70,** 25–31.

Byrne, D. *An Introduction to personality: A research approach.* Englewood Cliffs, N.J.: Prentice-Hall, 1966.

Campbell, B. A., & Sheffield, F. D. Relation of random activity and food deprivation. *Journal of Comparative and Physiological Psychology,* 1953, **46,** 320–322.

Cannon, W. B., & Washburn, A. L. An explanation of hunger. *American Journal of Physiology,* 1912, **29,** 441–454.

Carlson, A. J. A study of the mechanisms of the hunger contractions of the empty stomach by experiment on dogs. *American Journal of Physiology,* 1913, **32,** 369–388.

Carmichael, L. (Ed.) *Manual of Child Psychology.* New York: Wiley, 1946.

Caron, A. J., & Wallach, M. A. Recall of interrupted tasks under stress: A phenomenon of memory or learning? *Journal of Abnormal and Social Psychology,* 1957, **55,** 372–381.

Cartwright, D. Lewinian theory as a contemporary systematic framework. In S. Koch (Ed.), *Psychology: A study of a science.* Vol. 2. New York: McGraw-Hill, 1959. Pp. 7–91.

Child, J. L., & Whiting, J. W. Effects of goal attainment: Relaxation versus renewed striving. *Journal of Abnormal and Social Psychology,* 1950, **45,** 667–681.

Clark, R. A. The projective measurement of experimental induced levels of sexual motivation. *Journal of Experimental Psychology,* 1952, **44,** 391–399.

Cofer, C. N., & Appley, M. H. *Motivation: Theory and research.* New York: Wiley, 1964.

Coleman, J. S., et al. *Equality of educational opportunity.* U.S. Department of Health, Education, and Welfare. Washington, D.C.: U.S. Government Printing Office, 1966.

Conger, J. J. The effects of alcohol on conflict behavior in the albino rat. *Quarterly Journal of Study of Alcohol,* 1951, **12,** 1–29.

Cook, R. E. *Relation of achievement motivation and attribution to self-reinforcement.* Unpublished doctoral dissertation, University of California, Los Angeles, 1970.

Cotton, J. W. Running time as a function of amount of food deprivation. *Journal of Experimental Psychology,* 1953, **46,** 188–198.

Cottrell, N. B., & Wack, D. L. Energizing effects of cognitive dissonance upon dominant and subordinate responses. *Journal of Personality and Social Psychology,* 1967, **6,** 132–138.

Cowles, J. T. Food tokens as incentives for learning by chimpanzees. *Comparative Psychology Monograph,* 1937, **14** (Serial No. 71).

Crandall, V. C. Sex differences in expectancy of intellectual and academic reinforcement. In C. P. Smith (Ed.), *Achievement-related motives in children.* New York: Russell Sage, 1969. Pp. 11–45.

Crandall, V. C., Katkovsky, W., & Crandall, V. J. Children's beliefs in their own control of reinforcement in intellectual-academic achievement situations. *Child Development,* 1965, **36,** 91–109.

Crandall, V. J., Katkovsky, W., & Preston, A. Motivational and ability determinants of young children's intellectual achievement behaviors. *Child Development,* 1962, **33,** 643–661.

Crespi, L. P. Quantitive variation of incentive and performance in the white rat. *American Journal of Psychology,* 1942, **55,** 467–517.

Cronbach, L. J., & Meehl, P. E. Construct validity in psychological tests. *Psychological Bulletin,* 1955, **52,** 281–302.

Darwin, C. *The descent of man and selection in relation to sex.* New York: Appleton, 1896.

Davison, G. C., & Valins, S. Maintenance of self-attributed and drug-attributed behavior change. *Journal of Personality and Social Psychology,* 1969, **1,** 25–33.

de Charms, R. *Personal causation.* New York: Academic Press, 1968.

de Charms, R., & Moeller, G. H. Values expressed in American children's readers: 1800–1950. *Journal of Abnormal and Social Psychology,* 1962, **64,** 136–142.

Deese, J., & Carpenter, J. A. Drive level and reinforcement. *Journal of Experimental Psychology,* 1951, **42,** 236–238.

Dollard, J., Doob, L. W., Miller, N. E., Mowrer, O. H., & Sears, R. R. *Frustration and aggression.* New Haven, Conn.: Yale University Press, 1939.

Dollard, J., & Miller, N. E. *Personality and psychotherapy.* New York: McGraw-Hill, 1950.

Dulany, D. E. Awareness, rules, and proposition of control: A confrontation with S-R theory. In T. R. Dixon & D. L. Horton (Eds.), *Verbal learning and general behavior theory*. Englewood Cliffs, N.J.: Prentice-Hall, 1968. Pp. 340–387.

Dunlap, W. Are there any instincts? *Journal of Abnormal Psychology,* 1919, **14,** 35–50.

Escalona, S. K. The effect of success and failure upon the level of aspiration and behavior in manic-depressive psychoses. University of Iowa *Studies in Child Welfare,* 1940, **16,** 199–302.

Estes, W. K. Stimulus-response theory of drive. In M. R. Jones (Ed.), *Nebraska symposium on motivation.* Vol. 6. Lincoln: University of Nebraska Press, 1958. Pp. 35–69.

Fajans, S. Die Bedeutung der Enfernung für die Starke eines Aufforder-ungs-schararakter beim Saugling und Kleinkind. *Psychologische Forschung,* 1933, **17,** 215–267.

Feather, N. T. The relationship of persistence at a task to expectation of success and achievement-related motives. *Journal of Abnormal and Social Psychology,* 1961, **63,** 552–561.

Feather, N. T. The relationship of expectation of success to reported probability, task structure, and achievement-related motivation. *Journal of Abnormal and Social Psychology,* 1963, **66,** 231–238. (a)

Feather, N. T. Persistence at a difficult task with alternative task of intermediate difficulty. *Journal of Abnormal and Social Psychology,* 1963, **66,** 604–609. (b)

Feather, N. T. Effects of prior success and failure on expectations of success and subsequent performance. *Journal of Personality and Social Psychology,* 1966, **3,** 287–298.

Feather, N. T., & Saville, M. R. Effects of amount of prior success and failure on expectations of success and subsequent task performance. *Journal of Personality and Social Psychology,* 1967, **5,** No. 20, 226–232.

Feldman, S. (Ed.) *Cognitive consistency.* New York: Academic Press, 1966.

Feshbach, S., & Singer, R. D. *Television and aggression.* San Francisco: Jossey-Bass, 1970.

Festinger, L. Wish, expectation, and group standards as factors influencing level of aspiration. *Journal of Abnormal and Social Psychology,* 1942, **37,** 184–200. (a)

Festinger, L. A theoretical interpretation of shifts in level of aspiration. *Psychological Review,* 1942, **49,** 235–250. (b)

Festinger, L. A theory of social comparison processes. *Human Relations,* 1954, **7,** 117–140.

Festinger, L. *A theory of cognitive dissonance.* Evanston, Ill.: Row, Peterson, 1957. (a)

Festinger, L. The relation between behavior and cognition. In *Colorado symposium on cognition*. London: Oxford University Press, 1957. Pp. 127–150. (b)

Festinger, L. The motivating effects of cognitive dissonance. In G. Lindzey (Ed.), *Assessment of human motives*. New York: Rinehart, 1958. Pp. 65–86.

Festinger, L. The psychology of insufficient rewards. *American Psychologist*, 1961, **16**, 1–11.

Festinger, L. *Conflict, decision, and dissonance*. Stanford, Calif.: Stanford University Press, 1964.

Festinger, L., & Carlsmith, J. M. Cognitive consequences of forced compliance. *Journal of Abnormal and Social Psychology*, 1959, **58**, 203–210.

Festinger, L., Riecken, H. W., & Schachter, S. *When prophecy fails*. Minneapolis: University of Minnesota Press, 1956.

Fontaine, G. Some situational determinants of causal attribution. Unpublished doctoral dissertation, University of Western Australia, Nedlands, Australia, 1972.

Frank, J. D. Individual differences in certain aspects of the level of aspiration. *American Journal of Psychology*, 1935, **47**, 119–128.

French, E. G. Motivation as a variable in work-partner selection. *Journal of Abnormal and Social Psychology*, 1956, **53**, 96–99.

French, E. G., & Thomas, F. The relation of achievement motivation to problem-solving effectiveness. *Journal of Abnormal and Social Psychology*, 1958, **56**, 45–48.

Freud, S. (1915) Instincts and their vicissitudes. *Collected papers*. Vol. 4. London: Hogarth Press and the Institute of Psycho-Analysis, 1948, Pp. 60–83.

Frieze, I., & Weiner, B. Cue utilization and attributional judgments for success and failure. *Journal of Personality*, 1971, **39**, 591–606.

Gardner, R. W., Holzman, P. S., Klein, G. S., Linton, H., & Spence, D. P. Cognitive control. *Psychological Issues*, 1959, **1**, No. 4.

Glixman, A. F. Recall of completed and incompleted activities under varying degrees of stress. *Journal of Experimental Psychology*, 1949, **39**, 281–295.

Goffman, E. *Asylums*. Garden City, N.Y.: Doubleday, 1961.

Goldberg, L. Grades as motivants. *Psychology in the School*, 1965, **2**, 17–24.

Green, D. R. Volunteering and the recall of interrupted tasks. *Journal of Abnormal and Social Psychology*, 1963, **66**, 397–401.

Grice, G. R., & Davis, J. D. Effects of irrelevant thirst motivation on a response learned with food reward. *Journal of Experimental Psychology,* 1957, **53,** 347–352.

Grinker, J. *The control of classical conditioning by cognitive manipulation.* Unpublished doctoral dissertation, New York University, 1967.

Gurin, P., Gurin, G., Lao, R. C., & Beattie, M. Internal-external control in the motivational dynamics of Negro youth. *Journal of Social Issues,* 1969, **25,** 29–53.

Hall, C. S., & Lindzey, G. *Theories of personality.* New York: Wiley, 1957.

Haner, C. F., & Brown, J. S. Clarification of the instigation to action concept in the frustration-aggression hypothesis. *Journal of Abnormal and Social Psychology,* 1955, **51,** 204–206.

Hartmann, H., Kris, E., & Loewenstein, R. M. Comments on the formation of psychic structure. In *The psychoanalytic study of the child.* Vol. 2. New York: International Universities Press, 1946. Pp. 11–38.

Hebb, D. O. *The Organization of Behavior.* New York: Wiley, 1949.

Heckhausen, H. *The Anatomy of Achievement Motivation.* New York: Academic Press, 1967.

Heckhausen, H. Achievement motive research: Current problems and some contributions toward a central theory of motivation. In D. Levine (Ed.), *Nebraska symposium on motivation.* Vol. 16. Lincoln: University of Nebraska Press, 1968. Pp. 103–167.

Heckhausen, H. Change in attractiveness of task after failure: Cognitive dissonance theory vs. achievement motivation theory. *Proceedings of the international conference on psychology of human learning.* Vol. 1. Prague, 1970. Pp. 195–203.

Heckhausen, H., & Weiner, B. The emergence of a cognitive psychology of motivation. In P. Dodwell (Ed.), *New horizons in psychology:* II. London: Penguin Books, 1972 (in press).

Heider, F. Attitudes and cognitive organization. *Journal of Psychology,* 1946, **21,** 107–112.

Heider, F. Trends in cognitive theory. In *Colorado symposium on cognition.* London: Oxford University Press, 1957. Pp. 201–210.

Heider, F. *The psychology of interpersonal relations.* New York: Wiley, 1958.

Heider, F. The Gestalt theory of motivation. In M. R. Jones (Ed.), *Nebraska symposium on motivation.* Vol. 8. Lincoln: University of Nebraska Press, 1960. Pp. 145–172.

Heider, F., & Simmel, M. An experimental study of apparent behavior. *American Journal of Psychology,* 1944, **57,** 243–259.

Henle, M. The influence of valence on substitution. *Journal of Psychology,* 1944, **17,** 11–19.

Hilgard, E. R. *Theories of learning.* New York: Appleton-Century-Crofts, 1956.

Hilgard, E. R., & Bower, G. H. *Theories of learning.* (3rd ed.) New York: Meredith, 1966.

Holden, K. B., & Rotter, J. B. A nonverbal measure of extinction in skill and chance situations. *Journal of Experimental Psychology,* 1962, **63,** 519–520.

Holt, E. B. *Animal drive and the learning process, and essay toward radical empiricism.* Vol. I. New York: Holt, 1931.

Holzman, P. S., & Gardner, R. W. Leveling and repression. *Journal of Abnormal and Social Psychology,* 1959, **59,** 151–155.

Holzman, P. S., & Gardner, R. W. Leveling-sharpening and memory organization. *Journal of Abnormal and Social Psychology,* 1960, **61,** 176–180.

Hoppe, F. Untersuchungen zur Handlungs—und affekt—psychologie. IX. Erfolg und Misserfolg. *Psychologische Forschungen,* 1930, **14,** 1–63.

Horner, T. *The motive to avoid success.* Unpublished doctoral dissertation, University of Michigan, 1966.

Hull, C. L. *Principles of behavior.* New York: Appleton-Century-Crofts, 1943.

Hull, C. L. *Essentials of behavior.* New Haven, Conn.: Yale University Press, 1951.

Hull, C. L. *A behavioral system.* New Haven, Conn.: Yale University Press, 1952.

Hume, D. (1739) *A treatise of human nature.* London: Clarendon Press, 1888.

Hunt, J. McV. *Intelligence and experience.* New York: Ronald Press, 1961.

Hutt, M. L. A clinical study of "consecutive" and "adaptive" testing with the revised Stanford-Binet. *Journal of Consulting Psychology,* 1947, **11,** 93–103.

Isaacson, R. L. Relation between an achievement, test anxiety, and curricular choices. *Journal of Abnormal and Social Psychology,* 1964, **68,** 447–452.

James, W. *Principles of psychology.* New York: Holt, 1890.

James, W., & Rotter, J. B. Partial and 100% reinforcement under chance and skill conditions. *Journal of Experimental Psychology,* 1958, **55,** 397–403.

Jecker, J. D. The cognitive effects of conflict and dissonance. In L. Festinger (Ed.), *Conflict, decision, and dissonance.* Stanford, Calif.: University of Stanford Press, 1964. Pp. 21–30.

Jenkins, H. M., & Ward, W. C. Judgment of contingency between responses and outcome. *Psychological Monographs,* 1965, **79** (1, Whole 594).

Johnson, T. J., Feigenbaum, R., & Weiby, M. Some determinants and consequences of the teacher's perception of causation. *Journal of Educational Psychology,* 1964, **55,** 237–246.

Jones, E. E., & Davis, K. E. From acts to dispositions: The attribution process in person perception. In L. Berkowitz (Ed.), *Advances in experimental social psychology.* Vol. 2. New York: Academic Press, 1965. Pp. 219–266.

Jones, E. E., Davis, K. E., & Gergen, K. J. Role playing variations and their informational value for person perception. *Journal of Abnormal and Social Psychology,* 1961, **63,** 302–310.

Jones, E. E., & Goethals, G. R. *Order effects in impression formation: Attribution context and the nature of the entity.* New York: General Learning Press, 1971.

Jones, E. E., Kanouse, D., Kelley, H. H., Nisbett, R. E., Valins, S., & Weiner, B. (Eds.) *Attribution: Perceiving the Causes of Behavior.* New York: General Learning Press, 1972.

Jones, E. E., & Nisbett, R. E. *The actor and the observer: Divergent perceptions of the causes of behavior.* New York: General Learning Press, 1971.

Jones, E. E., Rock, L., Shaver, K. G., Goethals, G. R., & Ward, L. M. Pattern of performance and ability attribution: An unexpected primacy effect. *Journal of Personality and Social Psychology,* 1968, **10,** 317–340.

Jordan, N. Behavioral forces that are a function of attitudes and cognitive organization. *Human Relations,* 1953, **6,** 273–287.

Kagan, J., Moss, H. A., & Sigel, I. E. Psychological significance of styles of conceptualization. *Monographs of the Society for Research in Child Development,* 1963, **28** (86, Whole No. 2), 73–112.

Kant, I. (1781). *The critique of pure reason.* In R. M. Hutchins (Ed.), *Great books of the western world.* Vol. 42. Chicago: Encyclopedia Britannica, 1952. Pp. 1–250.

Karabenick, S. Valence of success and failure as a function of achievement motives and locus of control. *Journal of Personality and Social Psychology,* 1972, **21,** 101–110.

Karsten, A. Psychische Sattigung. *Psychologische Forschung,* 1927, **10,** 142–254.

Katchmar, L. T., Ross, S., & Andrews, T. G. Effects of stress and anxiety on performance of a complex verbal-coding task. *Journal of Experimental Psychology,* 1958, **55,** 559–563.

Katz, I. The socialization of academic motivation in minority group children. In D. Levine (Ed.), *Nebraska symposium on motivation*. Vol. 15. Lincoln: University of Nebraska Press, 1967. Pp. 133–191.

Kelley, H. H. Attribution theory in social psychology. In D. Levine (Ed.), *Nebraska symposium on motivation*. Vol. 15. Lincoln: University of Nebraska Press, 1967. Pp. 192–237.

Kelley, H. H. Moral evaluation. *American Psychologist*, 1971, **26**, 293–300.

Kendler, H. H. Drive interaction: I. Learning as a function of the simultaneous presence of the hunger and thirst drives. *Journal of Experimental Psychology*, 1945, **35**, 96–109.

Kestenbaum, J., & Weiner, B. Achievement performance related to achievement motivation and test anxiety. *Journal of Clinical and Consulting Psychology*, 1970, **34**, No. 3, 343–344.

Kiesler, C. A., & Sakumura, J. A. A test of a model for commitment. *Journal of Personality and Social Psychology*, 1966, **3**, 349–353.

Kimble, G. A. *Hilgard and Marquis' conditioning and learning*. New York: Appleton-Century-Crofts, 1961.

Kimble, G. A., & Posnick, G. M. Anxiety? *Journal of Personality and Social Psychology*, 1967, **7**, 108–109.

King, R. A. *The effects of training and motivation on the components of a learned instrumental response*. Unpublished doctoral dissertation, Duke University, 1959.

Klein, G. S. Need and Regulation. In M. R. Jones (Ed.), *Nebraska symposium on motivation*. Vol. 2. Lincoln: University of Nebraska Press, 1954. Pp. 224–274.

Klein, G. S. Preemptory ideation: Structure and force in motivated ideas. In R. Jessor & S. Feshbach (Eds.), *Cognition, personality, and clinical psychology*. San Francisco: Jossey-Bass, 1968. Pp. 1–61.

Koch, S. Psychology and emerging conceptions of knowledge as unitary. In T. W. Wann (Ed.), *Behaviorism and phenomenology*. Chicago: University of Chicago Press, 1964. Pp. 1–41.

Koffka, K. *The growth of the mind*. London: Kegan Paul, Trench, Trubner, 1924.

Kohlberg, L. The development of children's orientations toward a moral order: Sequence in the development of moral thought. *Vita Humana*, 1963, **6**, 11–33.

Köhler, W. *The mentality of apes*. New York: Harcourt and Brace, 1925.

Kolb, D. Achievement motivation training for underachieved high-school boys. *Journal of Personality and Social Psychology*, 1965, **2**, 783–792.

Kounin, J. S. Field theory in psychology: Kurt Lewin. In J. W. Wepman & R. W. Heine (Eds.), *Concepts in personality*. Chicago: Aldine, 1963. Pp. 142–161.

Kruglanski, A. Attributing trustworthiness in supervisor-worker relations. *Journal of Experimental Social Psychology,* 1970, **6,** 233–247.

Kukla, A. *Cognitive determinants of achieving behavior.* Unpublished doctoral thesis, University of California, Los Angeles, 1970.

Kukla, A. Cognitive determinants of achieving behavior. *Journal of Personality and Social Psychology,* 1972, **21,** 166–174.

Kuo, Z. Y. A psychology without heredity. *Psychological Review,* 1924, **31,** 427–451.

Kuperman, A. *Relations between differential constraints, affect, and the origin-pawn variable.* Unpublished doctoral dissertation, Washington University, 1967.

Lanzetta, J. T., & Hannah, T. E. Reinforcing behavior of "naive" trainers. *Journal of Personality and Social Psychology,* 1969, **11,** 245–252.

Lao, R. C. Internal-external control and competent and innovative behavior among Negro college students. *Journal of Personality and Social Psychology,* 1970, **14,** 263–270.

Lashley, K. S. Experimental analysis of instinctual behavior. *Psychological Review,* 1938, **45,** 445–471.

Lawrence, D. H., & Festinger, L. *Deterrents and reinforcement.* Stanford, Calif.: Stanford University Press, 1962.

Lawson, R. *Frustration: The development of a scientific concept.* New York: Macmillan, 1965.

Lawson, R., & Marx, M. H. Frustration: Theory and experiment. *Genetic Psychology Monographs,* 1958, **57,** 393–464.

Lazarus, R. S. *Psychological stress and the coping process.* New York: McGraw-Hill, 1966.

Lazarus, R. S. Emotions and adaptation: Conceptual and empirical relations. In W. J. Arnold (Ed.), *Nebraska symposium on motivation.* Vol. 16. Lincoln: University of Nebraska Press, 1968. Pp. 175–270.

Lazarus, R. S., & Alfert, E. The short-circuiting of threat by experimentally altering cognitive appraisal. *Journal of Abnormal and Social Psychology,* 1964, **69,** 195–205.

Lazarus, R. S., & Eriksen, C. W. Effects of failure stress upon skilled performance. *Journal of Experimental Psychology,* 1952, **43,** 100–105.

Lazarus, R. S., & Opton, E. M., Jr. The study of psychological stress: A summary of theoretical formulations and experimental findings. In C. D. Spielberger (Ed.), *Anxiety and behavior.* New York: Academic Press, 1966. Pp. 225–262.

Lazarus, R. S., Opton, E. M, Jr., Nomikos, M. S., & Rankin, N. D. The principle of short-circuiting of threat: Further evidence. *Journal of Personality,* 1965, **33,** 622–635.

Leeper, R. W. *Lewin's topological vector psychology.* Eugene: University of Oregon Press, 1943.

Lefcourt, H. M. Internal versus external control of reinforcement: A review. *Psychological Bulletin,* 1966, **65,** 206–220.

Lewin, K. *A dynamic theory of personality.* New York: McGraw-Hill, 1935.

Lewin, K. *Principles of topological psychology.* New York: McGraw-Hill, 1936.

Lewin, K. *The conceptual representation and the measurement of psychological forces.* Durham, N.C.: Duke University Press, 1938.

Lewin, K. *Resolving social conflicts.* New York: Harper, 1948.

Lewin, K. *Field theory in social science.* New York: Harper, 1951.

Lewin, K., Dembo, T., Festinger, L., & Sears, P. S. Level of aspiration. In J. McV. Hunt (Ed.), *Personality and the behavioral disorders.* Vol. I. New York: Ronald Press, 1944. Pp. 333–378.

Lissner, K. Die Entspannung von Bedurfnissen durch Ersatzhandlungen. *Psychologische Forschung,* 1933, **18,** 218–250.

Litwin, G. H. (1958) Motives and expectancies as determinants of preference for degrees of risk. In J. W. Atkinson & N. T. Feather (Eds.), *A theory of achievement motivation.* New York: Wiley, 1966. Pp. 103–115.

Liverant, S., & Scodel, A. Internal and external control as determinants of decision-making under conditions of risk. *Psychological Reports,* 1960, **7,** 59–67.

Loess, H. B. *The effect of variation of motivational level and changes in motivational·level on performance in learning.* Unpublished doctoral dissertation, State University of Iowa, 1952.

Lowell, E. L. The effect of need for achievement of learning and speed of performance. *Journal of Psychology,* 1952, **33,** 31–40.

Lucas, J. D. The interactive effects of anxiety failure and interserial duplication. *American Journal of Psychology,* 1952, **65,** 59–66.

MacLeod, R. B., Phenomenology: A challenge to experimental psychology. In T. W. Wann (Ed.), *Behaviorism and phenomenology.* Chicago: University of Chicago Press, 1964. Pp. 47–73.

Mahler, W. Ersatzhandlungen verschiedener realitatsgrade. *Psychologische Forschung,* 1933, **18,** 27–89.

Mahone, C. H. Fear of failure of unrealistic vocational aspiration. *Journal of Abnormal and Social Psychology,* 1960, **60,** 253–261.

Maier, N. R. F. *Frustration.* New York: McGraw-Hill, 1949.

Maier, S. F., Seligman, M. E. P., & Solomon, R. L. Pavlovian fear conditioning and learned helplessness: Effects of escape and avoidance behavior of (a) the CS-UGS contingency and (b) the independence of voluntary responding. In B. A. Campbell & R. M. Church (Eds.), *Pun-*

ishment and aversive behavior. New York: Appleton-Century-Crofts, 1969. Pp. 299–342.

Mandler, G., & Sarason, S. A study of anxiety and learning. *Journal of Abnormal and Social Psychology,* 1952, **47,** 166–173.

Marrow, A. J. Goal tensions and recall: I. *Journal of General Psychology,* 1938, **19,** 3–35.

Marx, K. (1875) The critique of the Gotha Program. In K. Marx and F. Engels, *Basic writings on politics and philosophy.* Garden City, N.Y.: Anchor Books, 1959. Pp. 112–132.

Marx, M. H. Motivation. In C. W. Harris (Ed.), *Encyclopedia of Educational Research.* (3rd ed.) New York: Macmillan, 1960. Pp. 888–900.

Marzocco, F. N. *Frustration effect as a function of drive level, habit strength and distribution of trials during extinction.* Unpublished doctoral dissertation, State University of Iowa, 1951.

Maslow, A. H. *Motivation and personality.* New York: Harper, 1954.

McClelland, D. C. *Personality.* New York: Holt, Rinehart & Winston, 1951.

McClelland, D. C. Some social consequences of achievement motivation. In M. R. Jones (Ed.), *Nebraska symposium on motivation.* Vol. 3. Lincoln: University of Nebraska Press, 1955. Pp. 41–65.

McClelland, D. C. Personality: An integrative view. In J. L. McCary (Ed.), *Psychology of personality.* New York: Grove Press, 1956. Pp. 321–366.

McClelland, D. C. Methods of measuring human motivation. In J. W. Atkinson (Ed.), *Motives in fantasy, action, and society.* Princeton, N.J.: Van Nostrand, 1958. Pp. 7–42.

McClelland, D. C. *The achieving society.* Princeton, N.J.: Van Nostrand, 1961.

McClelland, D. C. Business drive and national achievement. *Harvard Business Review,* 1962, **40,** 99–112.

McClelland, D. C. Toward a theory of motive acquisition. *American Psychologist,* 1965, **20,** No. 5, 321–333.

McClelland, D. C. Longitudinal trends in the relation of thought to action. *Journal of Consulting Psychology,* 1966, **30,** 479–483.

McClelland, D. C. *Assessing human motivation.* New York: General Learning Press, 1971.

McClelland, D. C., & Atkinson, J. W. The projective expression of needs: I. The effect of different intensities of hunger drive on perception. *Journal of Psychology,* 1948, **25,** 205–222.

McClelland, D. C., Atkinson, J. W., Clark, R. W., & Lowell, E. L. *The achievement motive.* New York: Appleton-Century-Crofts, 1953.

McClelland, D. C., Clark, R. A., Roby, T. B., & Atkinson, J. W. The projective expression of needs: IV. The effect of the need for achievement on thematic apperception. *Journal of Experimental Psychology,* 1949, **39,** 242–255.

McClelland, D. C., & Winter, D. G. *Motivating economic achievement.* New York: The Free Press, 1969.

McDougall, W. *Outline of psychology.* New York: Scribner, 1923.

McGuire, W. J. The current status of cognitive consistency theories. In S. Feldman (Ed.), *Cognitive consistency.* New York: Academic Press, 1966.

McKeachie, W. J., Motivation, teaching methods, and college learning. In M. R. Jones (Ed.), *Nebraska symposium on motivation.* Vol. 9. Lincoln: University of Nebraska Press, 1961. Pp. 111–142.

McMahon, I. *Sex differences in causal attribution for success and failure.* Unpublished doctoral dissertation, City University of New York, 1971.

Mehrabian, A. Measures of achieving tendency. *Educational and Psychological Measurement,* 1969, **29,** 445–451.

Meryman, J. J. *Magnitude of startle response as a function of hunger and fear.* Unpublished master's thesis, State University of Iowa, 1952.

Meyer, W. V. *Selbstverantwortlichkeit und Leistungsmotivation.* Unpublished doctoral dissertation, Ruhr Universität, Bochum, Germany, 1970.

Michotte, A. (1946) *The perception of causality.* New York: Basic Books, 1963.

Miller, G. A. *Psychology: The science of mental life.* New York: Harper & Row, 1962.

Miller, N. E. Experimental studies of conflict. In J. McV. Hunt (Ed.), *Personality and the behavioral disorders.* Vol. 1. New York: Ronald Press, 1944. Pp. 431–465.

Miller, N. E. Studies of fear as an acquirable drive: I. Fear as motivation and fear-reduction as reinforcement in the learning of new responses. *Journal of Experimental Psychology,* 1948, **38,** 89–101.

Miller, N. E. Learnable drives and rewards. In S. S. Stevens (Ed.), *Handbook of experimental psychology.* New York, Wiley, 1951. Pp. 435–472.

Miller, N. E. Liberalization of basic S-R concepts: Extensions to conflict behavior, motivation, and social learning. In S. Koch (Ed.), *Psychology: A study of a science.* Vol. 2. New York: McGraw-Hill, 1959. Pp. 196–292.

Miller, N. E. Some reflections on the law of effect produce a new alternative to drive reduction. In M. R. Jones (Ed.), *Nebraska symposium on motivation.* Vol. 11. Lincoln: University of Nebraska Press, 1963. Pp. 65–112.

Mischel, W. Delay of gratification, need for achievement, and aquiescence in another culture. *Journal of Abnormal and Social Psychology,* 1961, **62,** 543–552.

Mischel, W. *Personality and assessment.* New York: Wiley, 1968.

Morgan, C. L. *An introduction to comparative psychology.* London: Walter Scott, 1896.

Morgan, J. J. B. The overcoming of distraction and other resistances. *Archives of Psychology,* 1916, **35,** 1–84.

Morris, J. L. Propensity for risk taking as a determinant of vocational choice: An extension of the theory of achievement motivation. *Journal of Personality and Social Psychology,* 1966, **3,** 328–335.

Moss, F. A. Study of animal drives. *Journal of Experimental Psychology,* 1924, **7,** 165–185.

Moulton, R. W. Effects of success and failure on level of aspiration as related to achievement motives. *Journal of Personality and Social Psychology,* 1965, **1,** 399–406.

Mowrer, O. H. A stimulus-response analysis of anxiety and its role as a reinforcing agent. *Psychological Review,* 1939, **46,** 553–566.

Mowrer, O. H. *Learning theory and behavior.* New York: Wiley, 1960.

Mowrer, O. H., & Viek, P. An experimental analogue of fear from a sense of helplessness. *Journal of Abnormal and Social Psychology,* 1948, **43,** 193–200.

Murray, E. J. A case study in a behavioral analysis of psychotherapy. *Journal of Abnormal and Social Psychology,* 1954, **49,** 305–310.

Murray, E. J., & Berkun, M. M. Displacement as a function of conflict. *Journal of Abnormal and Social Psychology,* 1955, **51,** 47–56.

Murray, H. A. *Explorations in personality.* New York: Oxford University Press, 1938.

Murray, H. A. *Thematic Apperception Test Manual.* Cambridge: Harvard University Press, 1943.

Murray, H. A. Preparations for the scaffold of a comprehensive system. In S. Koch (Ed.), *Psychology: A study of a science.* Vol. 3. New York: McGraw-Hill, 1959. Pp. 7–54.

Neisser, U. *Cognitive psychology.* New York: Appleton-Century-Crofts, 1966.

Newman, J. R. *Stimulus generalization of an instrumental response as a function of drive strength.* Unpublished doctoral dissertation, University of Illinois, 1955.

Nisbett, R. E., & Schachter, S. Cognitive manipulation of pain. *Journal of Experimental Social Psychology,* 1966, **2,** 227–236.

Nisbett, R. E., & Valins, S. Perceiving the causes of one's own behavior. New York: General Learning Press, 1971.

Office of Strategic Services Assessment Staff. *Assessment of men.* New York: Rinehart, 1948.

Osgood, C. E. *Method and theory in experimental psychology.* New York: Oxford University Press, 1953.

Ovsiankina, M. Die Wiederaufnahme unterbrochener Handlungen. *Psychologische Forschung,* 1928, **11,** 302–379.

Pavlov, I. P. *Conditioned reflexes.* London: Oxford University Press, 1927.

Peak, H. Psychological structure and psychological activity. *Psychological Review,* 1958, **65,** 325–347.

Pepitone, A. Motivational effects in social perception. *Human Relations,* 1950, **1,** 57–76.

Perin, C. T. Behavior potentiality as a joint function of the amount of training and the degree of hunger at the time of extinction. *Journal of Experimental Psychology,* 1942, **30,** 93–113.

Phares, E. J. Expectancy changes in skill and chance situations. *Journal of Abnormal and Social Psychology,* 1957, **54,** 339–342.

Piaget, J. *The moral judgment of the child.* New York: Harcourt, Brace, 1932.

Postman, L. J. Comments on papers by Professors Brown and Harlow. In M. R. Jones (Ed.), *Nebraska symposium on motivation.* Lincoln: University of Nebraska Press, 1953. Pp. 55–58.

Postman, L. Rewards and punishments in human learning. In L. Postman (Ed.), *Psychology in the making.* New York: Knopf, 1962. Pp. 331–401.

Pribram, K. H. A review of theory in physiological psychology. *Annual review of psychology.* Palo Alto, Calif.: Annual Reviews, Inc., 1960.

Ramond, C. K. Performance in selective learning as a function of hunger. *Journal of Experimental Psychology,* 1954, **48,** 265–270.

Rapaport, D. The structure of psychoanalytic theory. In S. Koch (Ed.), *Psychology: A study of a science.* Vol. 3. New York: McGraw-Hill, 1959. Pp. 55–183.

Rapaport, D. On the psychoanalytic theory of motivation. In M. R. Jones, (Ed.), *Nebraska symposium on motivation.* Vol. 8. Lincoln: University of Nebraska Press, 1960. Pp. 173–247.

Raynor, J. O. Future orientation and motivation of immediate activity: An elaboration of the theory of achievement motivation. *Psychological Review,* 1969, **76,** 606–610.

Raynor, J. O. Relationships between achievement-related motives, future orientation, and academic performance. *Journal of Personality and Social Psychology,* 1970, **15,** 28–33.

Richter, C. P. Animal behavior and internal drives. *Quarterly Review of Biology,* 1927, **2,** 307–343.

Roback, A. A. *The history of American psychology.* New York: Library Publishers, 1952.

Rogers, C. R. Toward a science of the person. In T. W. Wann (Ed.), *Behaviorism and phenomenology.* Chicago: University of Chicago Press, 1964. Pp. 109–133.

Rosen, B., & D'Andrade, R. C. T. The psychosocial origins of achievement motivation. *Sociometry,* 1959, **22,** 185–218.

Rosenstein, A. J. *The specificity of the achievement motive and the motivating effects of picture cues.* Unpublished doctoral dissertation, University of Michigan, 1952.

Rosenthal, R., & Jacobson, L. F. Teacher expectations for the disadvantaged. *Scientific American,* 1968, **218,** 19–23.

Rosenzweig, S. An experimental study of "repression" with special reference to need-persistive and ego-defensive reactions to frustration. *Journal of Experimental Psychology,* 1943, **32,** 64–74.

Ross, L., Rodin, J., & Zimbardo, P. G. Toward an attribution therapy: The reduction of fear through induced cognitive-emotional misattribution. *Journal of Personality and Social Psychology,* 1969, **12,** 279–288.

Rotter, J. B. *Social learning and clinical psychology.* Englewood Cliffs, N.J.: Prentice-Hall, 1954.

Rotter, J. B. Generalized expectancies for internal versus external control of reinforcement. *Psychological Monographs,* 1966, **80,** (1, Whole No. 609), 1–28.

Rotter, J. B., Liverant, S., & Crowne, D. P. The growth and extinction of expectancies in chance controlled and skilled tasks. *Journal of Psychology,* 1961, **52,** 161–177.

Rotter, J. B., Seeman, M., & Liverant, S. Internal versus external control of reinforcement: A major variable in behavior theory. In N. F. Washburne (Ed.), *Decisions, values, and groups.* Vol. 2. London: Pergamon Press, 1962. Pp. 473–516.

Sarason, I. G. The effects of anxiety and two kinds of failure and serial learning. *Journal of Personality,* 1957, **25,** 383–392.

Sarason, S. B., Davidson, K. S., Lighthall, F. F., Waite, R. R., & Ruebush, B. K. *Anxiety in elementary school children: A report of research.* New York: Wiley, 1960.

Sarason, S. B., Hill, K., & Zimbardo, P. A longitudinal study of the relation of test anxiety to performance on intelligence and achievement tests. *Monographs of the Society for Research in Child Development,* 1964, **29** (7, Whole No. 98).

Schachter, S. The interaction of cognitive and physiological determinants of emotional state. In L. Berkowitz (Ed.), *Advances in experimental social psychology.* Vol. I. New York: Academic Press, 1964. Pp. 49–80.

Schachter, S., & Latané, B. Crime, cognition, and the autonomic nervous system. In D. Levine (Ed.), *Nebraska symposium on motivation.* Vol. 12. Lincoln: University of Nebraska Press, 1964. Pp. 221–272.

Schachter, S., & Singer, J. E. Cognitive, social, and physiological determinants of emotional state. *Psychological Review,* 1962, **69,** 379–399.

Schachter, S., & Wheeler, L. Epinephrine, chlorpromazine, and amusement. *Journal of Abnormal and Social Psychology,* 1962, **65,** 121–128.

Schmitt, D. R. The invocation of moral obligation. *Sociometry,* 1964, **27,** 299–310.

Schoenfeld, W. N. An experimental approach to anxiety, escape, and avoidance behavior. In P. M. Hoch and J. Zubin (Eds.), *Anxiety.* New York: Grune and Stratton, 1950. Pp. 70–99.

Sears, R. R. *Success and failure: A study of motility.* New York: McGraw-Hill, 1942.

Seeman, M. Alienation and social learning in a reformatory. *American Journal of Sociology,* 1963, **69,** 270–284.

Seeman, M., & Evans, J. Alienation and learning in a hospital setting. *American Sociological Review,* 1962, **27,** 772–782.

Sheerer, M. Cognitive theory. In G. Lindzey (Ed.), *Handbook of social psychology.* Vol. I. Cambridge, Mass.: Addison Wesley, 1954. Pp. 91–142.

Shipley, T. E., & Veroff, J. A projective measure of need affiliation *Journal of Experimental Psychology,* 1952, **43,** 349–356.

Siegel, P. S. Drive shift, a conceptual and experimental analysis. *Journal of Comparative and Physiological Psychology,* 1943, **35,** 139–148.

Singer, J. L. *Daydreaming: An introduction to the experimental study of inner experience.* New York: Random House, 1966.

Smith, C. P. (Ed.) *Achievement-related motives in children.* New York: Russell Sage, 1969.

Solomon, R. L. Punishment. *American Psychologist,* 1964, **19,** 239–253.

Spence, K. W. *Behavior theory and conditioning.* New Haven, Conn.: Yale University Press, 1956.

Spence, K. W. The empirical basis and theoretical structure of psychology. *Philosophy of Science,* 1957, **24,** 97–108.

Spence, K. W. A theory of emotionality based drive (D) and its relation to performance in simple learning situations. *American Psychologist,* 1958, **13,** 131–141. (a)

Spence, K. W. Behavior theory and selective learning. In M. R. Jones (Ed.), *Nebraska symposium on motivation.* Vol. 6. Lincoln: University of Nebraska Press, 1958. Pp. 73–107. (b)

Spence, K. W. Anxiety (drive) level and performance in eyelid conditioning. *Psychological Bulletin,* 1964, **61,** 129–139.

Spence, K. W., Farber, I. E., & McFann, H. H. The relation of anxiety (drive) level to performance in competitional and non-competitional paired-associates learning. *Journal of Experimental Psychology,* 1956, **52,** 296–305.

Spence, K. W., & Taylor, J. A. Anxiety and strength of the US as determiners of the amount of eyelid conditioning. *Journal of Experimental Psychology,* 1951, **42,** 183–188.

Spence, K. W., Taylor, J. A., & Ketchel, R. Anxiety (drive) level and degree of competition in paired-associates learning. *Journal of Experimental Psychology,* 1956, **52,** 303–310.

Spielberger, C. D. The effects of manifest anxiety on the academic achievement of college students. *Mental Hygiene,* 1962, **46,** 420–426.

Spielberger, C. D., & Katzenmeyer, W. C. Manifest anxiety, intelligence, and college grades. *Journal of Consulting Psychology,* 1959, **23,** 278.

Stevenson, H. W., & Zigler, E. Discrimination learning and rigidity in normal and feebleminded individuals. *Journal of Personality,* 1957, **25,** 699–711.

Storms, M. D., & Nisbett, R. E. Insomnia and the attribution process. *Journal of Personality and Social Psychology,* 1970, **16,** 319–328.

Strickland, L. H. Surveillance and trust. *Journal of Personality,* 1958, **26,** 200–215.

Strodtbeck, F. L., McDonald, M. R., & Rosen, B. Evaluations of occupations: A reflection of Jewish and Italian mobility differences. *American Sociological Review,* 1957, **22,** 546–553.

Strong, S. R. Causal attributions in counseling and psychotherapy. *Journal of Counseling Psychology,* 1970, **17,** 388–399.

Taylor, J. A. A personality scale of manifest anxiety. *Journal of Abnormal and Social Psychology,* 1953, **48,** 285–290.

Taylor, J. A. & Chapman, J. P. Anxiety and the learning of paired-associates. *American Journal of Psychology,* 1955, **68,** 671.

Thorndike, E. L. *Animal intelligence.* New York: Macmillan, 1911.

Tolman, E. C. *Purposive behavior in animals and men.* New York: Appleton-Century, 1932.

Tolman, E. C. Principles of performance. *Psychological Review,* 1955, **62,** 315–326.

Tolman, E. C., & Honzig, C. H. Introduction and renewal of reward, and maze performance in rats. Berkeley: *University of California Publication in Psychology,* 1930, **4** (19), 267.

Underwood, B. J. Degree of learning and the measurement of forgetting. *Journal of Verbal Learning and Verbal Behavior,* 1964, **3,** 112–129.

Valins, S. Cognitive effects of false heart-rate feedback. *Journal of Personality and Social Psychology,* 1966, **4,** 400–408.

Valins, S. Emotionality and information concerning internal reactions. *Journal of Personality and Social Psychology,* 1967, **6,** 458–463.

Valins, S. Persistent effects of information about internal reactions: Ineffectiveness of debriefing. In R. H. London and R. E. Nisbett (Eds.), *The cognitive alteration of feeling states.* Chicago: Aldine, 1972 (in press).

Valins, S., & Nisbett, R. E. *Some implications of the attribution processes for the development and treatment of emotional disorders.* New York: General Learning Press, 1971.

Valins, S., & Ray, A. A. Effects of cognitive desensitization on avoidance behavior. *Journal of Personality and Social Psychology,* 1967, **7,** 345–350.

Van de Geer, J. P., & Jaspers, J. M. F. Cognitive functions. *Annual Review of Psychology,* 1966, **17,** 145–176.

Verplanck, W. S., & Hayes, J. R. Eating and drinking as a function of maintenance schedule. *Journal of Comparative and Physiological Psychology,* 1953, **46,** 327–333.

Veroff, J. Development and validation of a projective measure of power motivation. *Journal of Abnormal and Social Psychology,* 1957, **54,** 1–8.

Walker, E. L. The one ring. In J. Trapp (Ed.), *Reinforcement and behavior.* New York: Academic Press, 1969. Pp. 47–62.

Walker, E. L., & Atkinson, J. W. The expression of fear-related motivation in thematic apperception as a function of proximity to an atomic explosion. In J. W. Atkinson (Ed.), *Motives in fantasy, action, and society.* New York: Van Nostrand, 1958. Pp. 143–159.

Warden, C. J. *Animal motivation.* New York: Columbia University Press, 1931.

Watson, D. Relationship between locus of control and anxiety. *Journal of Personality and Social Psychology,* 1967, **6,** 91–93.

Watson, J. B. Psychology as the behaviorist views it. *Psychological Review,* 1913, **20,** 158–177.

Watson, J. B. *Behaviorism.* New York: People's Institute, 1924.

Watson, J. B., & McDougall, W. *The battle of behaviorism.* New York: Norton, 1929.

Webb, W. B. The motivational aspect of an irrelevant drive in the behavior of the white rat. *Journal of Experimental Psychology,* 1949, **39,** 1–14.

Weber, M. (1904) *The protestant ethic and the spirit of capitalism.* New York: Scribner's Sons, 1958.

Weiner, B. The effects of unsatisfied achievement motivation on persistence and subsequent performance. *Journal of Personality,* 1965, **33,** 428–442. (a)

Weiner, B. Need achievement and the resumption of incompleted tasks. *Journal of Personality and Social Psychology,* 1965, **1,** 165–168. (b)

Weiner, B. The effects of motivation on the availability and retrieval of memory traces. *Psychological Bulletin,* 1966, **65,** 24–37. (a)

Weiner, B. The role of success and failure in the learning of easy and complex tasks. *Journal of Personality and Social Psychology,* 1966, **3,** 339–344. (b)

Weiner, B. Implications of the current theory of achievement motivation for research and performance in the classroom. *Psychology in the School,* 1967, **4,** No. 2, 164–171.

Weiner, B. New conceptions in the study of achievement motivation. In B. A. Maher (Ed.), *Progress in experimental personality research.* Vol. 5. New York: Academic Press, 1970. Pp. 67–109.

Weiner, B., Frieze, I., Kukla, A., Reed, L., Rest, S., & Rosenbaum, R. M. *Perceiving the causes of success and failure.* New York: General Learning Press, 1971.

Weiner, B., Heckhausen, H., Meyer, W. U., & Cook, R. E. Causal ascriptions and achievement motivation: A conceptual analysis of effort and reanalysis of locus of control. *Journal of Personality and Social Psychology,* 1972, **21,** 239–248.

Weiner, B., & Kukla, A. An attributional analysis of achievement motivation. *Journal of Personality and Social Psychology,* 1970, **15,** 1–20.

Weiner, B., & Potepan, P. A. Personality correlates and affective reactions towards exams of succeeding and failing college students. *Journal of Educational Psychology,* 1970, **61,** 144–151.

Weiner, B., & Rosenbaum, R. M. Determinants of choice between achievement and nonachievement-related activities. *Journal of Experimental Research of Personality,* 1965, **1,** 114–121.

Weiner, B., & Schneider, K. Drive versus cognitive theory: A reply to Boor and Harmon. *Journal of Personality and Social Psychology,* 1971, **18,** 258–62.

Wertheimer, M. Experimentelle Studien uber das Sohen von Bewegungen. *Zeitschrift Psychology,* 1912, **61,** 161–275.

White, R. W. Motivation reconsidered: The concept of competence. *Psychological Review,* 1959, **66,** 297–333.

Whitehead, A. N., & Russell, B. *Principia mathematica.* Cambridge, Mass.: Cambridge University Press, 1925.

Wicker, A. M. Undermanning, performances, and students' subjective experiences in behavioral settings of large and small high schools. *Journal of Personality and Social Psychology,* 1968, **10,** 255–261.

Williams, S. B. Resistance to extinction as a function of the number of reinforcements. *Journal of Experimental Psychology,* 1938, **23,** 506–522.

Winterbottom, M. R. *The relation of childhood training in independence to achievement motivation.* Unpublished doctoral dissertation, University of Michigan, 1953.

Witkin, H. A., Dyk, R. B., Faterson, H. F., Goodenough, D. R., & Karp, S. A. *Psychological differentiation.* New York: Wiley, 1962.

Woodworth, R. S. *Dynamic psychology.* New York: Columbia University Press, 1918.

Wright, J. H. Test for a learned drive based on the hunger drive. *Journal of Experimental Psychology,* 1965, **70,** 580–584.

Yates, A. B. *Frustration and conflict.* London: Methuen, 1962.

Zajonc, R. B. Cognitive theories in social psychology. In G. Lindzey and E. Aronson (Eds.), *Handbook of Social Psychology.* Vol. 1. (2nd ed.) Reading, Mass.: Addison Wesley, 1968. Pp. 320–411.

Zeigarnik, B. Uber das Behalten von erledigten und unerledigten Handlungen. *Psychologische Forschung,* 1927, **9,** 1–85.

Zeller, A. F. An experimental analogue of repression: III. The effect of induced failure and success on memory measured by recall. *Journal of Experimental Psychology,* 1951, **65,** 59–66.

Zigler, E. Rigidity in the feebleminded. In E. P. Trapp and P. Himmelstein (Eds.), *Readings in the exceptional child.* New York: Appleton-Century-Crofts, 1962. Pp. 144–162.

Zimbardo, P. G. *The cognitive control of motivation.* Glenview, Ill.: Scott, Foresman, 1969.

Zubin, J., Eron, L. D., & Schumer, F. *An experimental approach to projective techniques.* New York: Wiley, 1965.

Author Index

Subject Index